GREEK TEMPLES, THEATRES AND SHRINES

Paestum. Temple of Hera I, so-called Basilica. View of cella, and north and east colonnades

GREEK TEMPLES THEATRES AND SHRINES

TEXTS BY HELMUT BERVE

AND GOTTFRIED GRUBEN

PHOTOGRAPHS BY MAX HIRMER

HARRY N. ABRAMS, INC. *Publishers*

NEW YORK

LIBRARY OF CONGRESS CATALOGUE NO. 62-19131

ALL RIGHTS RESERVED. NO PART OF THE CONTENTS OF THIS BOOK MAY BE
REPRODUCED WITHOUT THE WRITTEN PERMISSION OF THE PUBLISHERS
HARRY N. ABRAMS INC., NEW YORK

COLOR AND MONOCHROME PLATES PRINTED IN WEST GERMANY

TEXT PRINTED IN ENGLAND

BOUND IN HOLLAND

CONTENTS

THE ARCHITECTURE OF THE TEMPLES, THEATRES AND SHRINES

BY GOTTFRIED GRUBEN

FOREWORD

THE AIM of this book is twofold. Not only does it set out to show the monuments which still stand within the large territory covered by ancient Hellas, as expressions of a living art, but it also intends to reveal the actual purpose of these buildings and to reconstruct in our mind's eye what today are only ruins.

Even if the temples and shrines of ancient Hellas were today still standing unharmed and in their original state, they would be no more to us than examples of architecture and art. One is only able to grasp their essential meaning if one has first come to an understanding, through the study of Greek culture and religion, of the beliefs which were the reason for their having been built; of the ceremonies which took place in them and of the mythology which had permeated them since ancient times and justified their existence. To reveal all this for us once more is the aim of the first part of this book.

I should like to thank Professor Dr Helmut Berve for writing this section with great clarity and that wide knowledge gained by his ever-inquiring mind.

The further task of this book is to present the architecture itself in its formal and historical aspects. Certainly whoever roams through Hellenic regions today—whether in Greece itself or in South Italy and Sicily or in the area of Hellenic settlements on the west coast of Asia Minor—will be everywhere enchanted by the magic of the ruins and by the landscape which spreads out magnificently around them. But beyond these purely romantic impressions the second part of the book sets out, for the sake of the Graecophil and the historian alike, to reconstruct the buildings as they were—magnificent, self-contained creations, independent of their whole environment, the manifestations of the highest art of building which, from before the earliest period of Hellenic life, were already clearly and prophetically conceived, during the centuries in which the flowering of Hellenic culture found its fullest expression.

As well as giving a picture of each building in its entirety and final form, this part of the book shows the development of Greek architecture as a whole, gives the history of each individual temple and shrine, and discusses the forms of mythology and religion of their time. The discrepancy between the wish of the contractor, who was governed by the demands of his cult and who insisted that the remains of an older holy building be incorporated in the new, and, on the other hand, the creative urge of the artist, who did not want to be limited in any way and who, in making use of these limitations, still achieved supremacy, is often apparent.

Dr Gottfried Gruben is to be thanked for dealing with the architecture and history of the monuments of the whole of Hellas. With a scrupulous exactness he describes the architecture, and with the strength gained by his deep involvement with the Hellenic spirit coupled with his extensive knowledge he lifts the most factual picture of the particular into the sphere of the generally significant.

The picture section is not restricted to the purely architectural aspects; sculpture too, in as far as it is closely related to architecture, is also represented. The central section of the Parthenon frieze on the eastern section of the cella, representing the Panatheniac procession which has never before been shown complete, is also illustrated—reconstructed from the fragments in London, Paris and Athens.

The colour pictures which appear in the first part of the book attempt to give a living picture of the monuments and their environment in all seasons. Whoever knows fleetingly these sites in Greece, Italy, Sicily and Asia Minor may find that some of the pictures are alien to him, but he must bear in mind that Hellas is not always under a blue sky, has not always the magic of early spring. Hellas too can have clouds and storms and knows the hot summer with its shimmering air and the autumn skies over the sun-scorched countryside. And the magic of early dawn, as well as that of the almost over-brilliant light which permeates everything just before sunset, should also come to mind, as should the world of colour of the afternoon hours.

I should like to thank the following, who helped me to obtain the photographs in this book: In Greece: The Director General of Greek Antiquities at the Greek Ministry of Culture, Dr Joannes Papadimitriu and his predecessor, Professor Spyridon Marinatos, and also the Directors of the National Museum and the Acropolis Museum in Athens, Professor Christos Karusos and Dr Jannis Miliadis. In Italy: Dottore Pellegrino C. Sestieri, Soprintendente alle Antichità in Salerno; Professor Luigi Bernabò Brea, Soprintendente alle Antichità in Syracuse; Dottore Pietro Griffo, Soprintendente alle Antichità in Agrigento; and especially Signora Iole Marconi Bovio, Soprintendente alle Antichità in Palermo who so kindly allowed me to take photographs of the Hera Temple (E) of Selinus which had been reconstructed under her supervision, before her own work on it had been published. In Turkey: the General Director of the Department of Foreign Relations of the Ministry of Education, Ankara, Mr Ferid Saner, for permission to photograph Pergamum, Sardis, Ephesus, Priene and Miletus-Didyma.

I should also like to thank Mr D. E. L. Haynes for permission to photograph in the British Museum, Department of Greek and Roman Antiquities, and also for obtaining the two pictures of the cella frieze from Bassae; Professor Friedrich Krauss of the Institut für Bauforschung und Baugeschichte, Technische Hochschule, Munich, for so graciously loaning the drawings of the foundations of the Temple of Paestum which he has specially prepared for his forthcoming publication; and Mr Gert Kaster for the execution of the many new drawings for this book.

The majority of the photographs were taken with the assistance of Mrs Julia Petzi-Asen, and many of them with the aid of my son, Albert Hirmer. I should like to thank both of them here, and in particular the former, who helped me with technical problems.

MAX HIRMER

THE HISTORY OF THE TEMPLES, THEATRES AND SHRINES
by Helmut Berve

Anyone visiting those Mediterranean countries that over two thousand years ago were settled by the Greeks will, in a good many places, come across ruins or at least traces of Hellenic temples and sanctuaries. These are regarded by the modern tourist as monuments worth looking at, and their scenic position delights him just as their formal beauty and technical perfection arouse his admiration. Many visitors have, however, only vague notions of the history and religious functions of these places. Yet nothing less than knowledge of them will, beyond their aesthetic effect, induce these stone witnesses of a distant past to speak, and tell about one of the most wonderful phenomena in mankind's spiritual life: Greek religion. It is in this light that Greek temples and sanctuaries, particularly those displayed here in the plates, will be interpreted on the following pages. True, this means limiting ourselves to a selection of famous cult centres still impressive today; but even if it were possible to present a survey of all the known sanctuaries, it would only embrace a fraction of those that once existed in the Hellenic world. For the Greeks considered everything to be full of gods, as Thales, the earliest of the philosophers, attested; and wherever they sensed an active deity, whose favour they needed and whose wrath was to be feared, they dedicated the site to him and to his adoration. The presence of gods or demigods might be felt on towering mountain heights or on a headland overlooking the storm-lashed sea; in mysterious woodland thickets, ravines, and caves, the solemn stillness of a grove, or the middle of a sunny, fertile field. From ancient graves heroes buried in the distant past wrought good or ill, while the defence of forts and cities, the activities of street and market, the deliberations of governing bodies and decisions of public assemblies could none of them do without the proximity of guardian and guiding deities. And for these a dwelling had to be prepared.

As a result, countryside and settlement abounded in sacred precincts, each of which, as the property of a god, represented so to speak a piece cut off (temenos) from the land of the community, and was therefore often surrounded by a wall. A sacrificial altar or an offering table formed the earliest and on many cult sites also the only equipment, even when the gods had long been conceived in human form and been given bodily presence in many places by means of an image. If, however, a god lived as it were physically at a certain spot, he required a dwelling suited to his high dignity. For the first temples, built during the eighth century B.C., and also for all later ones, whether surrounded by an ambulatory or developed architecturally in some other way, the ancient megaron (great hall), with its rectangular enclosed space and its open porch supported in front by columns, continued to provide the model. Indeed, it was not unusual for a place of worship in this form to arise on the actual foundations of an old megaron. The new building was the abode of the deity present in the cult image, not the room where believers met for the collective observance of rites; nor was it in general a place of sacrifice. On the contrary, the altar usually stood before the entrance to the temple, in which one only set foot to pray in the god's presence or place bloodless offerings on a table. Larger and durable gifts were set up around the temple, or else housed in special treasuries, which, as divine property, themselves took the form of little temples. In addition to these sacred treasures and monies, for which in the larger temples a room set behind the naos could also serve as a depository, there were others of a profane order, placed in the god's protection by communities or individuals. For it was considered a grave sacrilege, which the deity would certainly punish, to remove objects or people by force from a holy precinct. There, since earliest times, the persecuted and the condemned had been able to find refuge.

The rites observed in Greek sanctuaries were many and varied, corresponding to the diversity of human desires and the differences between the gods themselves. Sacrifice was, of course, universal, whether the deity received bloodless gifts such as farm produce or a cake, or whether some specially chosen animal was slaughtered before him, and part of the flesh burned in accordance with a prescribed ritual. There was one ritual when the sacrifice was intended for the powers of the underworld and death, but quite another when it concerned the gods of light. In the first case, people were not allowed to eat of the oblatory flesh, since they would otherwise have been dedicating themselves to death, whereas when offerings were made to the celestial gods, the sacrificial feast played an important role. This applied even in the private sphere, where every slaughter was connected with a sacrifice, but how much more so on the occasion of public banquets! For these, a hundred head of cattle (hecatomb) were sometimes killed, and their flesh served to those taking part in the celebration. However, the offering was not just a gift accompanying petitions or thanksgivings. From the beast's entrails or the way the sacrificial smoke rose, the favour or displeasure of the gods could be discerned. To this extent, the offering could be associated with the delivery of oracles, which, admittedly in a different manner, occurred at many holy places. Anyone who approached a divinity in his sanctuary to make an offering or to take part in some ritual had to be clean in the religious sense, which meant, above all, physically clean as well as free from blood-guilt and innocent of sacrilege. Likewise, it was customary for ablutions and, if necessary, expiation to precede dealings with a god. The demand for moral purity and genuine piety was already being made at an early date by Apollo at Delphi, but it did not penetrate more strongly until the deeper awareness of ethics shown in Greek religion during classical times.

Besides sacrifices, the gods received in their sanctuaries an abundance of thank-offerings from private persons, associations, and the state, in return for the favours that they had bestowed. Figurines and large statues of the deity worshipped, bronze tripods and cauldrons, weapons taken from the enemy, and monuments that had been donated out of a tithe of the crop, a trading profit, or the spoils of war all accumulated in the sacred precincts, together with statues of men and youths, women and girls, by means of which the male members of the community offered up themselves. They appeared not in naturalistic portraits but so to speak idealized as figures of the greatest beauty, vitality and strength, intended to delight the gods. The same notion underlay the contests without which virtually no major festival occurred at the famous sanctuaries from the archaic period onwards. True, these celebrations fulfilled the agonistic urge peculiar to the Greeks and evinced by them in every sphere of life; but the contest was only able to become one of the highest forms of worship because no more splendid gift to the immortals was known than that of human beings, dedicating to them their bodies and their greatest possible physical or mental achievements. The fact that collective hymn singing and magnificent processions, in which the cult image and sacred gear were frequently carried, also formed an essential part of the celebrations was not something specially characteristic of Greek festivals. On the contrary, devoted to life on earth and also taking part in it, the Hellenic gods no doubt thoroughly enjoyed the festive gathering as such, with its sacrificial banquets and gay activities that often continued long into the night.

A few words must also be said about the significance and role of priests in Greek religion. In the sense of an institution qualified through special ordination to mediate between humanity and the gods, or one absolutely necessary for this communication, a clergy was broadly speaking unknown, and so no specific preparation for priesthood was required. Any head of a household could make sacrifices, and in so far as special knowledge of the rites to be observed was necessary for public celebration, this was often passed on from generation to generation within particular families. For state religion was at one time attended to by the most eminent families, or else it actually sprang from the cult of a single family, which thenceforth had the right to appoint the priests of the god in question from among its own members. The seer, too, not infrequently came from a family in which the art of interpreting omens was handed down from one generation to the next. It is true, however, that most priests of the public cult were chosen for a year or even for life by lot, so that up to a point the deity himself selected his own servants. Purity in the sense of freedom from bodily defects, and—for priestesses at least—also chastity, were both prerequisites for the tenure of holy office. Many priests, specially those who during the delivery of oracles and performance of mysteries stood in closest contact with the deity, were distinguished by an appropriate title; all, however, stood out from the multitude on account of their long robe, long hair, sceptre-like staff, and, during religious observances, their magnificent attire and fillet or garland. The fact that in many communities priestly offices were saleable and found buyers reveals the prestige of priesthood, which made it sought after; but at the same time it shows particularly clearly how little we can here talk of a clergy or a priestly vocation in our sense of the terms. His official duties, which included, besides carrying out sacrifices and other rites or celebrations, custody of the temple and all the god's possessions, left the priest time for other activities, at least in the smaller sanctuaries. Hence, he no more received a salary than did the holders of other honorary offices, obtaining instead a share of the sacrificial flesh and the hide of the slaughtered animal, as well as fees in natural produce or money. At the bigger shrines these revenues were indeed so rich that they alone sufficed to tempt people into assuming or buying priestly office.

The larger sanctuaries—about the history and religious life of which something will be said on the following pages, whereas the entire sphere of private religious practice must remain beyond our scope—were generally under the control of the communities that had founded them, or in the territory of which they lay, just as public religion with its many sacred festivals was, for the Greeks, a part of the political system. The majority of the priests was appointed from the citizenry, and it was they who determined the religious laws—those, say, requiring the payment of dues to a particular sanctuary. Not only at Athens did one of the highest government officials supervise state religion. Public authorities or specially constituted commissions were also made responsible for the performance of the major celebrations and for awarding prizes at the athletic contests. Despite this close interweaving of state and religion, it will be easier to give a complete picture by classifying the temples and sanctuaries now to be considered not politically, but according to their position in Greek religious life as a whole, and to the range of their influence. Therefore, the first sacred places discussed will be those recognized as important for all Greeks, then those that formed the religious focus of a region and often also of its wider sphere of influence, and finally the urban sanctuaries, which were by nature very closely bound up with the city state and its life. With this last group are to be associated the theatres, although there were some outside the cities as well. Even then, however, the celebrations for which they were built originated in an urban sanctuary: that of Dionysus at Athens.

I

PAN-HELLENIC SANCTUARIES

The fact that Pindar's songs of victory were already in antiquity grouped as Olympian, Pythian, Nemean, and Isthmian odes, shows that the public games held during the great celebrations at Olympia, Delphi, and Nemea, and on the isthmus of Corinth, surpassed all others in importance and fame. The expression 'national festivals', which is used to designate these four celebrations, may not be wholly apt in so far as 'national', with its political implications, can mislead one as to the state of affairs in Greece. Nevertheless, it is undeniable that the Hellenes, who assembled in vast numbers from far and near for these festivals, there became conscious as on few other occasions, in their collective veneration of a great deity, that they belonged together and were spiritually one. Significantly, all four celebrations, after having already long existed as local entertainments which attracted the inhabitants of neighbouring regions, acquired both their new status and their pan-Hellenic character almost simultaneously during the first decades after 600 B.C. This was the period when, before the full development and definition of the city states, an aristocracy with common purpose covered and bound together the entire Greek world with a network of family connexions and personal ties. As meeting-places of the nobility and sites of the most famous contests between men of equal social status, the pan-Hellenic sanctuaries exerted a unifying influence. Just like the passionate demand to participate in the 'national' contests that accompanied the rise of the commoners, this consolidating effect also spread to the non-aristocratic classes, though without harming the political independence of the states that had meanwhile become firmly established.

O Olympia, mother of the gold-wreathed games, lady of truth, the shrine where skilled diviners seek, with burnt offerings, to know the pleasure of the high King, Zeus of the shining thunderbolt, and to read his purpose concerning men who yearn for glory and for rest from toil and weariness.

PINDAR

To the visitor from the north, the spacious, level, tree-covered landscape on the lower course of the Alpheus seems almost like home. What otherwise mostly determines the appearance of Greece—bare, steeply rising mountains, narrow valleys, bays biting deep into the countryside—is absent in the north-west of the Peloponnese: only on the eastern horizon do the mountains bordering Arcadia gleam, and even the wide Ionian sea, the coast of which is ill-supplied with harbours, seems to lie far off, its shimmering surface barely visible from the heights that rim the valley. Nor does Elis rank historically among the parts of Hellas enlivened by vast contrasts; rather has it led a little troubled, withdrawn life on the edge of great events. Perhaps this is the very reason why a sacred place could develop there at which Greeks from the geographically and politically fragmented motherland, and from the daughter-cities in south Italy and Sicily across the Ionian sea, assembled to worship jointly, and where they became conscious, over and beyond all differences and boundaries, of their unity. Likewise, the founder state's relatively loose-knit form, which was peculiar to the Eleans and the north-western Greeks generally, offered more favourable conditions for this development than did the precisely demarcated polis of the Ionians and Dorians. Round about the passage from the second to the first millennium B.C., these 'Eleans', as they were thenceforth called after their new area of settlement, had immigrated from the north, though the southern part of the region long continued to be controlled by the early Greek rulers of Pisa, a place not far from Olympia. Disputes with the Pisatae about the site on the Alpheus, and about who should preside over the contests held there since early times, occurred repeatedly down to the beginning of the sixth century. It is possible, indeed probable, that it was the new immigrants who first dedicated the spot to Zeus, and called it Olympia after the Thessalian mountain.

The earliest celebrations held there concerned not the sky god but the hero Pelops, from whom the entire peninsula gained the name Peloponnesus. Pelops is said to have beaten Oenomaus, king of Pisa, in a chariot-race and thereby to have won the hand of his opponent's daughter Hippodamia. Funeral games and sacrifices were offered to the hero near where the Cladeus stream flows into the Alpheus, at an unwalled burial-ground without buildings on it, which, like some neighbouring houses, dates from the

II   Olympia. View of Mount Cronus, the Altis, and the Alpheus valley, from the high ground
to the north-west, above Druwa

second millennium. According to the legend, Heracles marked out the Altis, the sacred grove planted all around with trees, for his father Zeus. In any case, from the start of the first millennium at the latest, Zeus was lord of the precinct, in the middle of which sacrifices were made beneath the open sky on an altar site that grew steadily higher owing to the superimposed layers of ash. Just as the wooded hill beyond the north edge of the Altis was allotted to Zeus's father Cronus, so too did his wife Hera find her way into the sanctuary, perhaps from Argolis, where she had long been deeply revered. By the eighth century, she appears to have acquired a temple at the foot of Mount Cronus, and on its site, at the beginning of the sixth century, was raised the elongated Doric building, of which the remains are still visible today. The cult image inside it showed Hera enthroned, with Zeus standing beside her. Zeus himself, the father of the gods, for centuries possessed neither temple nor cult image at Olympia, though costly statues of him were set up in the neighbourhood of the altar by rich and powerful worshippers before 600 B.C.

Olympia would never have achieved its unique importance in the Greek world and the fame that has lasted for thousands of years if nothing more than sacrifices to the supreme god had occurred there, or questions been put to his oracle, which was managed by the seer family of the Iamidae, and was at an early date overshadowed by Delphi. It was the contests transferred from Pelops to Zeus that made the unlikely site by the Alpheus into a social and religious focal point for all Greeks west of the Aegean, through the attraction they exerted on the inhabitants of the entire mother-country and of the colonies across the Adriatic. Numerous as were the sites and celebrations at which sporting contests were presented for the gods, nowhere was the Greek awareness of the body, the aesthetic and ethical value of physical training, the enhancement of the individual through the matching of strength and agility, more splendidly apparent than at Olympia. According to an ancient tradition, the reliability of which is admittedly not beyond question, the Olympic games were founded in 776 B.C. as a festival taking place once every four years. At all events, this is the date that later headed the roll of victors (Olympionicae), which refers to the foot-race through the stadium (210 yards) as the earliest and, at first, the only contest. It also shows that, during the first fifty years, the competitors came in the main only from Elis itself and from the neighbouring regions of Achaea and Messenia. The range soon increased, however. Besides Spartans, who during the seventh century provided a considerable portion of the winners, there appeared also Athenians and men from the cities on the isthmus, as well as Greeks from Sicily and South Italy. Round about 600, Olympia had already achieved pan-Hellenic importance, and a notable contribution to this development may have been made by the fact that the festival, and especially the contests, had meanwhile come to be presented in a manner without parallel at any other sanctuary. The first thing added to the single course was a double one, for which the stadium had to be covered in both directions, and then came a long-distance race that involved completing a course of twenty-five lengths of the stadium. New kinds

16

of sport were also introduced: the pentathlum, which comprised running, jumping, spear-throwing, discus-throwing, and wrestling; plain boxing; and the pancratium, in which entrants had both to wrestle and box. Four-in-hand chariot-races—two-horse chariots were not admitted until much later—are said to have been introduced during the seventh century too, though they may have been held earlier in honour of Pelops, according to ancient custom. While participation in all these contests, which towards the end of the archaic period were further augmented by a foot-race in full armour, was reserved for men, youths of between seventeen and twenty are said to have gained the opportunity to compete in running, wrestling, and boxing before 600. Yet despite all these extensions of the games, the oldest contest—the foot-race through the stadium— continued to be held in the greatest honour. Whoever won it was considered the Olympic victor *tout court*, after whom the four-year interval between two celebrations, known as an Olympiad, was named. Since the fragmented Greek world lacked a uniform calendar, the list of these victors later provided the historians of antiquity with a useful means of establishing events chronologically. For practical purposes, however, cities never reckoned in Olympiads, but by the names of their annual magistrates.

The place where most of the contests occurred was the stadium, a race-track flanked by earth banks, which in the fifth century still did not lie entirely outside the Altis. Instead, it stretched to near the altar of Zeus, so that the runners dashed towards the spot where sacrifices were offered to the god for whom these athletic feats were being performed. A hippodrome to the south of the stadium was used for chariot-racing, but all trace of it disappeared when the Alpheus changed its course during the Middle Ages. No care was taken for the comfort of the spectators; they sat on the earth banks bordering the arena, and only the chief officials had special places prepared for them. Nor did those who participated in the celebration find special buildings to accommodate them. The crowd numbered many thousands during the sixth and fifth centuries, the heyday of the games, and in the summer warmth it camped all around under the open sky, while high-ranking lords were accommodated in tents that they had brought with them. Unpampered as he was at this period, the Greek expected nothing else; moreover, his devoutness prepared him for any privation, so long as he could attend the great, beneficial act of public worship constituted by the games. Every free Greek was admitted, providing he had not sullied himself with blood-guilt or sacrilege, but non-Greeks, slaves, and women, except for the priestesses of Demeter, were forbidden to take part on pain of severe punishment. It was an Elean governing body, the college of the hellanodicae, that kept an eye on the observance of these regulations, and, supported by a staff of lesser officials, managed the entire celebration. Freshly appointed for each occasion, the members of the college started making the necessary preparations ten whole months before the festival began, first in Elis itself, then at Olympia, to which they proceeded in a solemn procession accompanied by the offering of sacrifices.

Anyone wanting to take part in the actual contests arrived some time before the date of the festival, which, according to the variations of the calendar, sometimes occurred in August, sometimes in September. He continued the training begun at home, and if he was still unknown, he did so under the surveillance of the hellanodicae, who excluded the insufficiently qualified aspirants. As the moment of the games drew nearer, messengers went out from Olympia into the entire Greek world, to proclaim the truce of the god for the weeks of the outward journey, the festival itself, and the return home. All feuds and wars were to remain at a standstill throughout this period, so that everyone could come unhindered, and participate in the great pan-Hellenic celebration. Still more than concern about being debarred from future games for having disregarded the command, it was clearly religious awe, the fear of incurring the Olympic god's anger, that, as long as faith remained intact, caused hostilities really to be suspended in a Greece at other times so full of conflicts. Even when in 480 the Persians were advancing from the north, Sparta's allies considered it more important to celebrate the games undisturbed than to send out their levies to meet the enemy. Just as all Greeks were admitted to the festival but all barbarians excluded, it was in this universal recognition of the truce of the god that Olympia revealed itself as a stronghold of Greek unity.

The celebration itself, for which traders, festival delegations and the vast multitude of spectators now arrived, continued for several days and, after its rearrangement in 468, probably for over a week. Something is known about the way it started during this later period. The first day was not devoted to the actual games. Instead, sacrifices were made at the tomb of Pelops and at various altars within the Altis; then, before the altar of Zeus Horkios, the preserver of vows, the hellanodicae swore a solemn oath that they would perform their duties as umpires impartially, and those entering for the contests, that they would behave fairly. One last trial took place, after which the final qualifiers had their names listed and their places for the particular events assigned to them by lot. The competitive spirit, which dominated the whole celebration, even determined the choice of heralds and trumpeters, who competed for the honour of being allowed to announce the victor. On the second day, the games themselves began. At sunrise, the hellanodicae entered the stadium with the heralds and trumpeters. They were followed by the contestants, who, from the middle of the fifth century, were completely naked and anointed with oil, though earlier they had worn a loin-cloth. How the individual events were spread out on this and the following days cannot now be said for certain. It is possible that the youths came first, their running, wrestling, and boxing perhaps counting as a sort of prelude to all the various men's contests. The latter evidently began with the oldest and most famous event: the simple race along the stadium. In groups of four, composed by drawing lots, the runners took up their starting positions behind a cord stretched crosswise, and on separate stone slabs, of which there were twenty at each end of the course. Though the distance of 210 yards to be covered was not all that long, the entrants had to run through soft sand. In the first heat, what mattered was for the three fellow-runners of each group to fight it out among themselves, after which the winners continued to compete in groups until one of them finally proved himself the best. The same thing happened with the double course, whereas the long-distance race was naturally held only once for all entrants. For the wrestling, which occurred on one of the subsequent days, groups had again to be made up, with the winner from each pair fighting another winner, so that here too the ultimate victor received the prize. The aim was to throw one's opponent three times and, when necessary, continue to fight him lying on the ground, until he acknowledged defeat by stretching out his hand. If the number of wrestlers was uneven, the same man was allowed one 'bye' only, so that he had at most one bout fewer to fight than those who continually found partners through drawing lots. However, wrestling played an important role not just as one of the main individual contests, but also within the framework of the pentathlum. For this, competitors began with a long jump, holding jumping-weights in their hands, ran the length of the stadium, threw a four-pound discus, and hurled a light, thin spear with a long point. Only those who had done well in these four types of contest were admitted to the last one: the wrestling tournament. This was decisive for the whole pentathlum, inasmuch as final victory in it could not be awarded to anyone who had failed to show himself superior to everyone else at wrestling.

Hands and arms were bound round with leather straps for the boxing. The contestants used both arms to hit out and defend themselves, though it was not the final knockout that counted for most, but tiring one's opponent by skilfully warding off his attacks without giving or receiving punches. Besides boxing as a separate contest, there was also the pancratium, for which both wrestling and boxing were required—under exceptionally tough conditions, moreover. For while on other occasions as well, certain forms of attack were permitted that modern sport does not allow, in this particular contest, which a Greek writer called the most terrible of all, one even had the right to throttle one's antagonist. Few dared to enter the lists and it actually happened that, when some famous and notorious fighter appeared, nobody else came forward, with the result that he won a 'dustless' victory. It was regarded as the most honourable kind, since the absence of any rivals had shown that this man was indisputably the best pancratiast among the Greeks. Finally, the gymnastic events were concluded by the foot-race in full armour covering two lengths of the stadium. As with the similarly tiring long-distance run, all the competitors began at the same time.

Undoubtedly the chariot-racing offered the most brilliant spectacle, particularly the four-in-hand race with two-wheelers built like the old war-chariots. In comparison with this, the riding-race, one of the old events, and the two-horse chariot-race or race with four colts harnessed to each chariot, both introduced round about 400, were unimportant. The scene of action was the horseshoe shaped hippodrome, of which the outer circuit measured a good 1,600 yards, while the inner one was about 1,250 yards long. At the end of the central axis opposite the semicircular curve stood a round construction like an altar—probably an old tomb—and before it was the winning-post, round which the chariots had to steer. Near the lower end of the hippodrome there rose a similar post, which the chariots also doubled, since the entire circuit of the course had to be completed twelve times. The starting-stalls were so arranged that, at the start, none of the chariots had an advantage over the others. There, on an altar, sat a bronze eagle, while further forward an imitation dolphin was suspended. When the dolphin sank, and, at the same time, the eagle was hoisted into the air, the race began. Thereupon the barrier ropes fell, and the chariots stormed off all together—about forty of them or even more in the heyday of the games. There were two things of which the drivers had to take special care: not to exhaust their horses prematurely while covering the total course of about eight and a half miles; and to round the posts each time as closely as possible, a feat requiring the greatest skill, and one that often led to bitter, highly dangerous struggles with other teams. Naturally, the final spurt during the last circuit was just as exciting, for whoever then first crossed the line between the winning-post at the start and the seat of the hellanodicae had won. Yet it was not the charioteer who was proclaimed victor, and received the triumphal wreath, but the owner of the team, though the owner's glory certainly increased if he himself had mounted the chariot and driven the horses. It was thus really a contest between proprietors of racing stables, which meant the rich and distinguished noblemen who since early times had enthusiastically gone in for training horses. In the gymnastic games, on the other hand, wealth and station played no part, and only the personal performance of the competitor counted.

With the horse-racing, the games came to an end. On the following, final day of the celebrations as a whole, first the great, solemn sacrifice at the high altar of Zeus was made, then the most eminent among the hellanodicae undertook the coronation of the winners. Holding palm branches and with fillets about their heads, they stepped up to him one by one. To the sound of trumpets, the herald loudly proclaimed not only the name of the man himself, but also those of his father and his homeland, while the hellanodices placed on his brow the wreath that bound him to the deity. This crown consisted of a branch bent into a ring, which a youth, whose parents had still to be alive, had cut with a sickle from the olive-tree by the altar of the nymphs. The thousands of spectators all around accompanied the act with shouts of applause, a hail of flowers, and songs of rejoicing. To him who received the simple prize, however, this moment brought the fulfilment of all his endeavours: the finest and the best that life had to offer had been awarded him. And his father, whose name had been called out too, felt as he did: blessed in the highest degree and exalted to the skies. When it was granted to the Rhodian Diagoras to look on as both his sons received the wreath of the supreme god, the crowd was so affected by this superhuman good fortune that the cry rang out: 'Die, Diagoras,

III   Olympia. Temple of Hera seen from the north-west

for you cannot climb up into heaven!' The victor's native city likewise considered itself honoured above all other Greeks through him, and it was a bitter moment for his homeland if he renounced it to be proclaimed citizen of some foreign state that had courted his favour. Only in the chariot-races where the owner of the best team was singled out for honour, was it possible to forgo the prize and have someone else who had not taken part in the games proclaimed the winner. The father of the famous Miltiades did so in favour of the tyrant Pisistratus, but this was certainly a rare exception. On the other hand, it often happened that a contest ended in a draw, so that the prize could not be awarded to anyone. In such a case, as also when nobody had entered for an event, or an unfortunate accident had prevented victory, the garlands that had been provided were dedicated to the god.

Various victory celebrations were connected with the distribution of prizes. Thank-offerings were made at the many altars in the sacred precinct, from which the festival delegations marched in a stately procession with show-pieces intended to attest the glory and splendour of their city. As regards the winners themselves, the Elean authorities arranged a splendid meal for them in their administrative building. Already on the day of their success, the Olympionicae had celebrated the great event among their friends and fellow-citizens; but now at the end of the festival, the rich ones—particularly the chariot-race winners—acted as host to whole legions of participants. Tyrants from the Greek cities of South Italy and Sicily even entertained the entire crowd, as also did Alcibiades, when in 416 he gained the wreath with one of his teams, two others coming second and third. Besides this, the festival delegations and other wealthy men invited a more or less large number to the banquet. Everywhere men raised their voices in happy concert, singing hymns to the gods and old familiar songs of victory in honour of the Olympionicae. The 'lovely light of the fair-faced moon shone into the evening. And, at the merry feast, the whole grove rang with the airs of the songs of praise' (Pindar).

Honours almost greater than those that he had received at the sanctuary itself awaited the champion on his home-coming. With his fellow citizens swarming round him, he entered his native city on a chariot drawn by four white horses—though not through one of the gateways! Instead, a piece of the wall was torn down, as he had acquired superhuman status through his victory. He seemed the equal of a hero and near to the gods; after his death, Theagenes of Thasos, who won the boxing, and then at the next games the pancratium, and who is said to have gained 1,400 wreaths in all at many different festival sites, really did receive religious veneration. In the city itself, the victor was not just entertained magnificently by the authorities at his home-coming; for the whole of his life, the man who had brought such great glory to his state had to be fed at public expense in the prytaneum. Yet other privileges were bestowed on him, while it was the custom that he for his part should dedicate the wreath he had won to the chief god of the state. If he was rich enough, he commissioned a festal song, which a choir rehearsed by the composer performed at a public celebration or a gathering of his compeers. During the great period of the games, especially the first half of the fifth century, extremely famous writers—Simonides, Pindar, Bacchylides—saw that their path to glory lay in, and applied their greatest skill to, extolling distinguished Olympionicae in spirited songs invoking their mythical archetypes; and not only the champions themselves, but also their families and native cities. Just what Olympia was at that time is nowhere more directly and grippingly discernible than in Pindar's powerful Olympian odes, which have immortalized the favoured victors and pious spirit of the great pan-Hellenic religious celebration.

With the elaboration and increase in number of the games, and with the growing stream of visitors from far and near, the site on the Alpheus won a fame outshining that of every other sanctuary of Zeus. Countless offerings filled the Altis, for Olympic winners were allowed to have a bronze statue with a simple inscription set up there, through which they so to speak dedicated themselves to the god. Nevertheless, the image was no more a portrait than the majority of sculptured figures at that period, since a real likeness would have seemed arrogant and profane; instead, it represented the ideal model of the champion. Likewise, the chariot-race winners did not themselves appear on the little votive pictures that they were allowed to offer, but simply their team. Statues or statuettes of Zeus had been presented by grateful worshippers since earliest times. Besides these, however, images of the god were to be seen in the sacred precinct that had been erected as a penance by those who had broken the rules of the games, contrary to their solemn oath. These monuments stood in the north of the grove before the treasury terrace. The mass of gifts—namely those that, apart from the statues set up in the open, were offered to Zeus—had already become so great by shortly after 600, that separate states housed their presents, and those of their individual citizens, in their own special temple-like buildings. It was mainly rich South Italian and Sicilian colonies that did this, just as they played a particularly active part in the games; but distant cities in the south and east—Cyrene and Byzantium—also felt an urge to do so. It is surprising that, out of the twelve treasuries lined up along the terrace, only two came from states in the mother-country: Megara and Sicyon; the absence of the Greek communities of Asia Minor, on the other hand, accords with their more limited participation in the contests. Even though Olympia was open to all Greeks and attracted Athenians as well as western Ionians, at bottom it remained imbued with the spirit of the north-western Greeks and the related Dorians. It is no mere chance that there was no building in the Ionic order in the Altis until the one put up by Philip II of Macedonia.

Back in archaic times, trophies from victorious wars—especially shields and helmets—were already being delivered as thank-offerings to Zeus and exhibited on the stadium walls. After defeating the Etruscans at sea in 474, Hieron, the tyrant of Syracuse, dedicated an enemy helmet; round about 420, the Messenians and Naupactians even had a tall pillar constructed out of the booty they had taken from their foes, and on it was poised a goddess of victory by Paeonius. All the same, it is worth noting that at Olympia, whose oracle—significantly—was not in the habit of giving judgements on internal Greek conflicts, this seems to have been the only great monument glorifying a victory of Greek over Greek, in marked contrast to the Delphic sanctuary, which was richly stocked with such memorials. The Altis also differed from Delphi in that, corresponding to the exclusion of all non-Greeks from the games, no barbarian votive monuments could be set up there. Thus it was only statues and altars presented by Greeks that the grove of Olympia contained—though it certainly harboured them in teeming, bewildering abundance. Without any orderly arrangement, they crowded round the high altar, and, from the middle of the fifth century onwards, round the temple of Zeus.

For whereas up to then the god had only been worshipped under the open sky, during the sixties of that century a mighty Doric temple was built for him in the middle of the Altis, the huge remains of which still dominate the site today. It was a creation of the Eleans, who not long before had bound together the whole extensive region in a unified state, and in 468 had remodelled the festival of the games, increasing its magnificence. Libon, the architect, came from Elis too. Even if the noble venture had no direct connexion with the successful resistance to the Persians, it was none the less sustained by the growing power, the exultation, and the sense of unity strengthened by the existence of a danger threatening all that most of the Greeks had experienced. It was no accident that precisely then a temple without its equal in the motherland was raised to the highest of the Greek gods at the unifying pan-Hellenic sanctuary. Great deeds from the mythical past—some concerning Elis in particular, others Hellas as a whole—were displayed by its sculptural decoration, with a dramatic tension that was full of the deepest human passion, and that became all the more strongly effective through its restraint. The ancient legend of the chariot-race between Oenomaus and Pelops, native to Olympia, formed the subject of the group on the east pediment, in the middle of which stood Zeus himself. On the west pediment, however, one saw the struggle of the Lapiths led by Pirithous against the half-animal centaurs, which mirrored the war between the Greeks and the inhuman barbarians. There, radiantly beautiful and in truly divine majesty, Zeus's son Apollo appeared above the bitter conflict, directing the Lapiths' action to its victorious conclusion. The guardian of correct behaviour and of law, he was at once the protector and embodiment of the virile youth that presented itself at Olympia for the contests. Nor could Heracles have been left out, the battling hero who feared no toil, who undertook the most arduous tasks, and who successfully cleansed the Augean stables right there in Elis itself. Above all, however, the son of Zeus and hero to all the Greeks was regarded as the founder of the Olympic games. His twelve labours were represented on metopes over the entrances to the pronaos and opisthodomus of the temple.

Decades passed before the edifice that was so magnificently adorned on the outside received what, when all is said and done, it had been erected for: the great cult statue of Zeus. Not until after the end of his activity in Athens, during the twenties, when Hellas was rent by the fratricidal Peloponnesian war, did Phidias create it out of gold and ivory in a specially constructed workshop beyond the western edge of the Altis. Already overpowering because of its colossal dimensions, which threatened to burst open the whole building, it showed the father of the gods sitting on a richly decorated throne, a sceptre in his left hand, the goddess of victory on his right. The image possessed a sublimity that continued to fill with awe not only devout visitors right down to the close of antiquity; but, for the pious, the god of heaven was physically present at his greatest sanctuary in this miraculous creation.

Yet at that very period, the religious emotion of the competitors, as well as of the participants in the festival generally, began to decline; the devotional character of the celebrations was in danger. Olympia threatened to become a place where the vain display of gymnastic achievements, or even of wealth, took precedence over the dedication of these exploits and pious gifts to the god. Nowhere else could one show off before such a large public, which had flocked together from all parts of the Greek world. Not only professional athletes, who were gradually driving out the amateur contestants, took advantage of this, but also men of intellectual accomplishment. When Herodotus read out part of his history at Olympia, or when sophists spreading the light of learning— such as Prodicus, Gorgias, and the Elean Hippias—actually paraded their rhetorical virtuosity there, it had but little to do with the cult of Zeus, which recognized no contests in the arts. At most, it was relevant in so far as the idea of Greek unity, which since early times had been active at Olympia, also underlay the historian's work, and was consciously publicized at the festival by Gorgias as well as other rhetoricians. People not infrequently used the occasion of the pan-Hellenic celebrations for political conferences and were in the habit of drawing up the documents of treaties between states at them. Olympia was also the accepted spot for political demonstrations intended to attract the attention of Hellas as a whole. There, in 476, the assembled Greeks gave a rapturous ovation to Themistocles, the victor of Salamis; there Alcibiades could draw thousands under his spell through the number of his chariot-teams and his princely expenditure; there, in 388, the general hatred felt for tyrants vented itself in the destruction of Dionysius's pavilion; and it was at the Olympic stadium that, in 324, Alexander had an ambassador proclaim a decree enjoining all Greek states to readmit their exiles.

During the fourth century, the religious aspect of the great festival in the grove of Zeus continued to grow more superficial. The architectural development in the Altis made this all the more unmistakable, in that, apart from a shrine for Hera, the new buildings were neither temples nor treasuries, but stoas along the eastern and southern margins of the site, in the shade of which the visitors could stroll. They also included a spacious edifice to accommodate distinguished guests (Leonideum), bathing installations, and others besides. In Hellenistic times, they were joined by a palaestra and a gymnasium, which, like the last-named buildings, stood outside the wall enclosing the sacred precinct. Formerly, such places would not have been needed, and people would have done their training anywhere in the area. When Philip of Macedonia had a tholos constructed in the Altis for himself and his family, after his victory at Chaeronea in 338, he was virtually abusing the holy site for political and dynastic purposes. True, offerings were lacking neither in quantity nor in splendour even during the fourth century and after: the Hermes by Praxiteles, rediscovered in the temple of Hera, is the most distinguished witness to that. Nevertheless, for all their beauty and high artistic quality, they—like the games—suffered more and more from the loss of deep religious feeling, of pure devotion and adherence to the deity. A further decline, this time in Olympia's significance as a pan-Hellenic centre, was inevitable once the hand of Rome had stretched out over Greece. Political expediency, coloured by mythological associations, dictated that the Romans were not included with the barbarians, and were allowed to take part in the festivals. The setting in which these occurred now became more brilliant than ever; splendid buildings arose on the edge of the Altis. Yet it made no difference if, in imperial times, one entered the sacred precinct through magnificent propylaea, and proceeded from it along an arcaded passage into the stadium, which by shortly after 400 had been pushed right outside the grove; or if, under the great philhellene Hadrian, the Maecenas Herodes Atticus supplied visitors with water by means of an impressive fountain installation near the treasury terrace, and the festival itself enjoyed a beautiful though weakly second blooming: the dedicated spirit that once filled competitors and spectators alike, the deepest meaning of the celebration, could no longer be evoked. The games had long since become sensational sporting events, disputed by professional athletes, at which the god to whom they belonged was honoured and worshipped more as a matter of form than through genuine piety. To oblige Nero, even the hallowed four-year cycle could be broken, and, to satisfy his vain artistic pretensions, musical contests could be added to the festival programme, contrary to ancient custom.

Nevertheless, the force of the tradition and the power of fascination that Olympia radiated remained effective till the triumph of Christianity, which saw this sanctuary as a bastion of heathen religion. Even after part of the Altis had been turned into a fortress built with stones from the buildings and monuments during the war-ravaged third century, the games were still celebrated for more than another hundred years. The last festival took place in A.D. 393, after which Theodosius I banned them. Under the emperor's grandson of the same name, the great temple was burned down in A.D. 426, Phidias's huge statue of the god being taken off to Byzantium; and it was not long before a Christian church grew up near the former Altis built out of old dressed stones. The human work of destruction was carried on during the sixth century by earthquakes and, in the course of time, by the flooding of the Alpheus, which buried the remains of the sanctuary under sand and gravel. Olympia was first rediscovered by an Englishman,

Richard Chandler. Then, in 1875, German excavations began to bring it back to light, and the work still continues today.

The great festival of Zeus at Olympia was observed for more than a thousand years. Even in its declining days, it remained covered with the lustre of the sixth and fifth centuries B.C., when, unconstrained by the mania for records, men saw the free testing of physical abilities and the competitive display of the highest virile qualities as the finest way of serving their god; and when, regardless of all differences and political conflicts, they came together at this site under the auspices of the pan-Hellenic Zeus. Something of what was then a blessed reality has been revived in the modern Olympic games, which, like the high value at present set on sport in general, make us better and more deeply aware than earlier generations of what Olympia and its sacred games meant to the Greek people in their striving for bodily and spiritual harmony; or, at any rate, they allow us an inkling of it, even if they lack the old religious content.

Delphi

*On her sacred tripod sits the Delphian priestess, chanting
to the Greeks the oracles charged to her by Apollo.* EURIPIDES

Olympia: the site of the most famous games in the ancient world; Delphi: the location of the most celebrated oracle. At the former: Zeus, the mighty god of the heavens; at the latter: Apollo, his radiant son. Apollo had no more been resident in primitive times in the place where he was later most highly honoured than had his father. Not until the migratory movements at the time of the passage from the second to the first millennium B.C. was he brought from the north, or from Dorian Crete, to the spot originally known as Pytho. There, the shining rock faces of Mount Parnassus rise up steeply into the sky, where eagles wheel; below, the deeply incised valley of the Pleistus stretches away, opening out towards the west into the plain of Cirrha, which is covered with olive-trees. Beyond it gleams the gulf of Corinth, while the high mountains of the northern Peloponnese stand out against the southern horizon. The grandeur of this landscape, among the most solemn and imposing in Greece, makes one sense the closeness of the divine, and it had been called upon to serve religious ends long before Apollo arrived. It is true that the remains of human habitation from the second millennium show no traces of religious buildings; but the collective memory of the Greeks themselves attests that, even then, the earth mother Gea was worshipped there, at the ravine from which the Castalian fountain gushes. The story goes that in the depths of this gorge dwelled the dragon

Python, whose foggy breath sometimes penetrated into the valley. It is possible, even probable, that oracles were already being sought from Gea; and she was also identified with Themis, who showed mankind the natural order of all existence. When Apollo became lord of the site, after having—according to the legend—slain the dragon, it was he who gave divine responses to those who came for consultation. This took place through the casting of lots as well as through the utterances of his priestess. The second way of delivering oracles could hardly have been established by Dionysus, the god of ecstasy, who at an early date found a place at Delphi. To the Greeks, Dionysus was not an oracular god; the raptures that he provoked had nothing in common with the psychic condition of the woman who, in a trance, pronounced what Apollo dictated to her. Moreover, it is significant that in the winter months, when Apollo was known to be far away among the Hyperboreans and Dionysus was regarded as master of the sanctuary, the delivery of oracles ceased.

The spot that had once belonged to Gea, who was still remembered, and that was now dedicated to 'Pythian' Apollo, lay not at the entrance to the sinister Castalian gorge, but on the neighbouring mountain slope to the west. There, probably as early as the eighth century, a wooden temple with bronze-covered walls arose on a stone base. In 548, a fire destroyed it, and not until decades later was it replaced by a large, magnificent stone building with richly decorated pediments. Behind the naos, the new temple includes a small room set at a lower level; this, the adytum, was the actual seat of the oracle. The offerings that have been discovered and literary evidence prove that already in the seventh century, if not even earlier, its fame had spread far beyond the borders of Phocis, the mountainous region in which Delphi lay. People first came to consult it from the various provinces of the mother-country, then, before long, from South Italy and Sicily, from the Aegean islands and the Greek cities of Asia Minor, and even on behalf of the kings of Lydia; for, unlike the one at Olympia, barbarians were not excluded from the sanctuary at Pytho. The visitors reached it along arduous mountain paths, or else they travelled by sea to the harbour of Cirrha, from which they then toiled up to the god. This journey was not without danger, since the inhabitants of Cirrha quite often robbed the pilgrims. Likewise, the temple and its growing treasures could lure them into making raids. An alliance of the central and northern Greek tribes, which had already banded together on behalf of a Demeter sanctuary at Anthela near the Thermopylae pass, put an end to this trouble. During the so-called First Sacred War, in which Athens and the Sicyonian tyrant Clisthenes also took part, they destroyed Cirrha round about 590 under the leadership of the Thessalians. Delphi became a state on its own, outside the Phocian tribal league and led by members of local aristocratic families, which provided the priests and high religious officials as well. Thenceforth, these families together with the Phocians were supposed to watch over its autonomy, which was of great importance for the independent delivery of oracles. A council of 'neighbours' (amphictyons), made up of

IV Delphi. View of the bay of Itea (ancient Cirrha), the gulf of Corinth, and the mountains
of the northern Peloponnese, shortly after sunrise

delegates, met alternately at the old centre of Anthela and at Pytho; it had charge of the sacred property and its management, as well as of the direction of Pythian Apollo's great festival, which was combined with games. The old celebration was reorganized for the first time in 582, and from then on it occurred during the late summer of every fourth year.

Like Olympia, Delphi flourished most vigorously during the sixth and fifth centuries. It is above all to this period that the following account of the nature and significance of the Pythian oracle refers. Of the two ways in which it was delivered lots could be used in two instances. Firstly, when Apollo was asked to declare which of various proposals was the one that had divine approval—which, for example, of several rival chieftains should command a joint military action, or which among a number of mythical heroes under consideration should be honoured as the tribe's progenitor; secondly, when a question was put requiring a decision between two possibilities. That most queries were of the latter kind is shown by the stereotyped interrogatory formula: 'Is it more beneficial and better to do this or that?' The response, which was evoked by Pythian Apollo's priestess, called the 'Pythia', came in the second case from the picking up of one of two rods, in the first from shaking a dish holding lots, so that one of them jumped out. People did not regard the result as accidental. It was the god who had produced it through the agency of his servant; his wisdom had settled the matter. As an oracle by lot cost less than one uttered by Pythia, but above all because the majority of questions, asked in a moment of indecision or dilemma, permitted response by lot, this form of delivery was always more popular. None the less, Delphi would certainly never have been able to exert the world-wide influence that continued for centuries if no spoken oracles had been given. Interest rightly concentrated on them in antiquity, as it has in modern times; it is they that primarily reveal the Delphic spirit.

Anyone who came to Pytho in order to request advice from the god, either on his own behalf or his employer's, remained there for some time and acquainted the priests with what he wanted, before formulating the question and submitting it in writing. Then, busy with sacrifices and ritual observances, he waited until the day arrived when oracles would be delivered. Originally, this occurred only once a year on Apollo's birthday, Bysios 9, then from time to time on the ninth of those months when the god was present; later still, it became more frequent, so that the number of priestesses uttering oracles had to be raised from one to three. A privilege bestowed on special patrons of the sanctuary allowed them to question the deity outside the prescribed dates as well. If the sacrifices had proceeded favourably—if not, the man concerned was sent away—and the fees had been paid, the consultants washed ritually, and then entered the temple in groups, in an order established by lot. Once inside, they proceeded to the adytum, nothing of which, unfortunately, has survived. It was divided in two by a wall that did not reach up to the ceiling, with the result that the consultants in one part could hear, though not see, what was going on in the other. Here, in a niche between two golden eagles, was the venerable omphalos stone, held to be the navel of the earth; while in the centre stood the golden tripod covered with a slab on which the Pythia sat, after she had climbed down into the adytum accompanied by a priest (prophetes). The idea that fumes rising up out of the earth put her into a trance, as was later supposed on the strength of philosophical-cum-physical theories and is still widely believed today, was long ago proved impossible by geological investigation. If one is determined at all cost to assume some material stimulus, then no better suggestion comes to mind than the chewing of laurel leaves, by which the Pythia so to speak received into herself the god, whose sacred tree the laurel was; for drinking from the little Cassotis fountain, which bubbled up in the sanctuary, cannot have caused any strong psychic agitation. Were special excitants really necessary, however? Could not the very awareness of now becoming Apollo's voice have produced spiritual exaltation, visionary rapture? It certainly was not the case that the priestess, without being really conscious, simply uttered sounds from which the prophetes standing beside her was able to compose sentences and even stanzas. Like the god-inspired poets, the Pythia herself spoke or sang the replies in verses, and the consultants in the next room heard her voice. Nevertheless, the prophetes, who had put the questions, now announced the responses in ceremonial form, and the enquirers also received a written version of them.

Just as, according to Greek belief, the muses inspired a poet's words, so did Apollo speak through the mouth of his priestess; and since he was the god of wisdom, he filled her with his divine knowledge, so that she had the power to discern the true facts of the case and, accordingly, to give the right advice. It is characteristic that, during the period of Delphi's greatness, the Pythia was an elderly, experienced unmarried woman, chosen from the most high-ranking Delphic families, which looked after the sanctuary. She probably took part in the priests' deliberations over the questions that had been submitted, or at least she would have been informed of their outcome. Yet when, stirred by her high calling and conscious of now becoming the god's instrument, she mounted her tripod, it was Apollo's wisdom that she pronounced. From him who had already guided the opinion of the priests in council, she received the poetical diction that compassed the full range of man's experience, instead of constricting it with sober words; it was consciously obscure, full of riddles, and—examined superficially—quite often misleading. 'The lord whose oracle is at Delphi', said Heraclitus, 'neither states nor conceals, but indicates.' Every holy sign required interpretation, however, including the sayings of the oracle: they needed to be thought over carefully, and probed as to their meaning. Consequently, interpreters (exegetes) skilled in this art were to be found everywhere, and all consultants ought to have known that they should not be satisfied with the apparent meaning of a pronouncement. This applied in particular to oracles predicting the future, which admittedly were requested and given only very seldom; the obvious question regarding the date of one's own death was hardly ever put, let alone answered. Though it is true that now and then occurrences could be clearly foretold, such as the destruction of Athens by the Persians invading Greece, in most cases the course of events depended so much on incalculable factors that the utterance confined itself to what was bound to happen. The oracle delivered to the Lydian king Croesus: 'If you cross the Halys, you will reduce a mighty power' said no more than that a war with the king of Persia would lead to the downfall of one of the two empires; yet Croesus, who did not ponder the words more deeply, could regard it as a promise of victory. It is understandable that such replies caused the god to be chided for ambiguity, a reproach that his epithet 'Loxias'—interpreted as 'the Devious'—was thought to sanction.

What Pythian Apollo, and through him his priests, possessed was understanding of the pattern of life, within the frame of which the future too could be indicated; and as he was the god of knowledge, but also the healing god, he knew what would promote the welfare of humanity in its diverse troubles. Advising, not foretelling, was the real sphere of his effective action. Thus, kings or states put questions before a campaign, and were counselled, say, to gain this or that ally; thus, men confronted with a grave decision requested instructions, while those visited by ill-fortune asked for advice on what to do in the case of a bad harvest, childlessness, disease, or whatever else afflicted them. Apollo, for his part, had the power to discern the root cause of the present distress; and, as the healing god, he provided the diagnosis, and showed the way to overcome the ailment. Here, it was a question of appeasing through sacrifice a hero who, angry at not having up to then had his share of veneration, was sending out plague and deadly cattle-pest from his grave; there, victory could only be gained if one transferred a hero's remains from enemy territory to one's own city, and thereby obtained the help of their mighty owner. Often unexpiated blood-guilt, of which later generations were unaware, lay heavy upon a family, and brought ruin. Apollo not only knew about it, but was also acquainted with the rites of absolution; indeed, this formed his special province, because as well as the god of wisdom, he was the god of purity. Add that in countless cases where doubts arose as to the right mode of worship the Greeks appealed to him, the knowing god, for a decision, and we have some idea of the Delphic oracle's immense importance to the practical exercise of religion among the entire Hellenic people.

Yet Apollo had knowledge not just of the religious, but also of the physical causes of a misfortune, and named the means of redressing it. Lingering famine was often enough occasioned in Greece by overpopulation, and constant discord within a community frequently stemmed from the same thing too. At such times, the god recommended that part of the inhabitants should emigrate, that a colony should be founded on distant shores. By the eighth century, his directives had evidently already proved so reliable that, without them, one hardly dared to establish another daughter-city. Besides being authorized in his venture by Delphi, the leader of the expedition also learned there which

V   Delphi. Theatre and Temple of Apollo, with the rock face of the Phaedriades in the background

religious or civil institutions were to be taken with them from the homeland; and, thanks to the exceptional knowledge of geography built up at Pytho on the basis of reports from existent colonies, if possible even the most favourable spot for the projected settlement. The Delphic priests were no more concerned than the mother-cities with extending Greek power; what mattered was to re-establish settled conditions at home, and to give the surplus population the possibility of leading a healthy political life somewhere else.

For the god acquainted with the inner pattern of all existence was also the god of due proportion and correct human ordinances. Hence, he warned the Greeks as individuals not to get above themselves, but to keep within bounds. 'Nothing in excess!' and the famous 'Know yourself!' meaning: 'Recognize the limits set on you as a human being!' were what those who entered the pronaos of Apollo's temple read from inscriptions there. In archaic times, when the Greek communities were achieving stable political form, many of them submitted their draft constitutions and laws to Pythian Apollo for him to sanction, and then regarded them as his commandments. Even in the sphere of international relations, which among the Greeks were to an exceptional extent left to arbitrary action, the influence of the god who established form and proportion could have its effect. When, after the razing of Cirrha, the amphictyons (mentioned at the beginning of this section) swore a solemn oath thenceforward not to destroy any cities in wars against each other, nor to cut off their water-supply—in short, to avoid total war, as we would say—a certain standard of international law was set for the greater part of Hellas, and the Delphic god saw that it was maintained. His concern for the correct ordering of things is no less apparent, however, in what it is customary to call the politics of the oracle. Delphi made a point of never taking sides in disputes between Greek states, unless the independence of its own community was threatened by one party and defended by the other; instead, it gave cities and tribes the advice that at any given time was most beneficial to them, as it did to individuals. It is not surprising that this led to the appearance of a conservative spirit, Pythian Apollo being after all a god of static forms and not of dynamic, subversive forces. Outside the political sphere too, he always stood up for preserving the *status quo*, as when, for example, he rejected the Cnidians' plan to cut a channel across their peninsula, on the grounds that if Zeus had wanted to make Cnidus an island, he would have done so. With respect to the states, this attitude revealed itself in efforts to maintain the existing communities and in a preference for aristocratic or oligarchic systems of government, since they offered a better guarantee of the stability of Greece's political structure than did democracies. For in these the far greater number of fully enfranchised citizens sought to increase their own living space at the expense of other states. It was not due to chance that oligarchic Sparta had particularly close relations with the sanctuary at Pytho.

Awareness of the formative influence exerted by Delphi on the religious, moral, and political life of the Hellenes, which can hardly be overrated, might lead one to miss the weaknesses that were present in it, as in any other human institution. Failure to make every effort to prevent internal Greek wars was certainly not among them, since bellicose wrangles were for the Pythian god, as for his worshippers, unchangeable realities of life. Perhaps it was more a question of Delphi's attitude towards the tyrants. Even at a period when—not without the oracle's influence—the idea of a constitutional state subject to the rule of law was being developed, lawless autocrats were still neither condemned nor sent away, if they recommended themselves with costly presents. At other times too, magnificent gifts or other material benefits had their effect. Not only were they able to obtain for the donor the privilege of consulting the oracle outside the appointed times of access, but they could also induce the Pythia to take a special interest in one's affairs, seeing that, possibly on behalf of the Attic family of the Alcmaeonidae, she kept enjoining the Spartans to drive out the tyrant Hippias. Indeed, cases are even known of the priestess being influenced in a sordid fashion or actually bribed. They remained isolated, however, and, in an age of unbroken faith, can hardly have shaken the oracle's authority. Still less was this impaired by Delphi's conduct during the Persian war, which modern critics were the first to brand as defeatism or betrayal of the pan-Hellenic cause. The god could not think differently from the Greeks themselves—that is, in terms of small states, not of the nations conceived by modern politics. Then as always, he recommended to the individual communities, in so far as they consulted him, what was best for them as things stood; and, by virtue of his knowledge, he foretold what would unquestionably come to pass, so that people could make ready for it. The Hellenes, who expected nothing else, thanked him after the victory with offerings unequalled in splendour and profusion by those presented to any other sanctuary on that occasion. Even in the misery of the Persian wars and during the following decades, Delphi lost none of its religious authority, and remained the holy centre that it had been since the seventh century.

Already early on, the gifts had piled up in the god's precinct, which was surrounded by a wall. As at Olympia, individual cities put up their own treasuries along the processional way that wound through the sanctuary to the temple. Corinth and Sicyon took the lead; Cnidus and Clazomenae followed in about 550, Siphnos in 525, and round about 500 came Potidaea on the Chalcidice peninsula and Athens with the building re-erected in recent times. Even distant Massalia (Marseilles) and an Etruscan city required a treasury. For whereas Olympia's effect remained limited to the mother-country and the Sicilian or South Italian states, Pythian influence spread to the Aegean islands and the colonies along the coast of Asia Minor, as well as far into the west; and Delphi also admitted non-Greeks. The Lydian kings, especially Croesus, consulted the god, rendering their thanks to him with costly presents. Works of art of high quality were housed in the treasuries, which themselves displayed rich sculptural decoration, as did that of the Siphnians with its magnificent frieze, or that of the Athenians with its metopes representing the exploits of Heracles and Theseus. Close by arose monuments of varying size, all of which were overtopped by a huge marble sphinx on a tall column, presented by Naxos round about 560. In most instances, the occasion for a splendid gift was probably a pronouncement by the oracle that had turned out to be beneficial, as may even have been the case with the bronze bull that the inhabitants of Corcyra (Corfu) set up in gratitude for a particularly fruitful catch. Most often, however, people dedicated a bronze, or even a gold, tripod to the gods, but especially to Delphic Apollo, as it was the object characteristic of him and his priestess. Gelon and his brother Hieron, rulers of eastern Sicily, presented a gold one. A third brother, Polyzalus, who won the chariot-race, gave a bronze quadriga, on which the famous charioteer stood firmly erect. For at the Pythian games too, the victors were allowed to place statues in the sanctuary as thank-offerings and monuments to the glory they had acquired. Such were also the gifts that the god even received from the spoils of victorious wars when his oracle had made no, or only a slight, contribution to the success. Thus, after the battle of Marathon, the Athenians set up bronze sculptures near their treasury, and, ten years later, they built a stoa to receive part of the booty from the battle of Salamis. For the decisive victory at Plataea, the Greeks who shared in it thanked Apollo with a large gold tripod resting on a column of bronze serpents. To dedicate the best, or even a tithe, of the plunder from a war was almost considered a religious duty. It is true, however, that, from the end of the fifth century, the desire to raise an impressive monument to one's own achievement in the much-visited holy place took precedence over gratitude to the god. After the fall of Athens in 404, the conqueror Lysander arrogantly had statues showing himself with his admirals set up beside images of the gods in a building near the main gateway. In the incessant wars waged by Greek states against each other, the victorious side loved to proclaim proudly to all the world, through a monument at Delphi, that they had over-come their enemy; yet they could not prevent the latter, if they succeeded in avenging the defeat, from erecting a no less imposing monument directly opposite their own. The site of Apollo's oracle presents a picture of the Hellenic people's religious unity just as of their political disunity. Even today, the splendour and the tragedy of Greek history are apparent to everyone who, between its stone witnesses, ascends to the temple area.

The temple of the classical period, before which stood a large altar given by Chios, was erected at the end of the sixth century by the Attic family of the Alcmaeonidae on the site of the building burned down in 548. It was paid for with money collected throughout the entire Greek world, and—partly at the family's expense—provided with a marble pronaos and magnificent pediment figures. An earthquake destroyed this edifice in 373, and its replacement could not be completed until about 330. Thus, what can still be seen today of the foundations, structural members, and recently re-erected columns belongs to the period when Greece came under the shadow of Macedonian power. On the other hand, part of the remains in a precinct situated to the east of the large sanctuary is sub-stantially older. Now called Marmaria, this spot was dedicated to Athena Pronaea, the

VI   Delphi. Sacred Precinct, Phaedriades, and Pleistus valley

guardian of temples, who alone among the gods—apart from Apollo—possessed her own temple at Delphi. Indeed, she came by it as early as the sixth century, from which the near-by marble treasury also dates, whereas a splendid round building (tholos), the purpose of which is unknown, did not appear until shortly after 400. Like Apollo's sanctuary, but unlike the Altis of Doric-dominated Olympia, this Athena precinct included edifices of all styles and orders. For Greeks of every stock and region came to Delphi in order to consult the Pythian god, to thank him, or to take part in his festival.

Apollo, the divine master of the lyre and leader of the muses, had certainly been honoured with musical contests at Pytho since early times. He himself was said to have instituted the cithara competition, which at one time occurred every nine years. From 582, however, the festival was celebrated in the late summer of every fourth year, and following Olympia's example, it also began to offer the god gymnastic and horse-racing contests, which were decided on the plain of Cirrha. As for the Olympic games, so too for this great pan-Hellenic celebration, which the amphictyons directed, a universal truce of the god was proclaimed through messengers; and here as well, the winner's prize consisted of a simple wreath, which was cut by a youth from Apollo's sacred tree, the laurel. Likewise, the different types of event, beginning with the foot-race along the stadium, broadly corresponded to those promoted beside the Alpheus, except that the young god took a special delight in the competitions of youths. As Pindar's Pythian odes show, victory in the Delphic chariot-race did not come second in glory to the equivalent success at Olympia. Yet it was neither the horse-racing nor the gymnastic events that gave the Pythian games their lustre and their individual stamp, but the lyre- and lute-playing contests, the rendering of hymns specially written and set for the festival—some of which, their texts furnished with musical notes, still survive from Hellenistic times —and especially the performance in the middle of the programme of the *Pythikos Nomos*, a choral work perhaps accompanied by mime, extolling Apollo's fight with the dragon Python. When, from the fifth century onwards, famous rhetoricians like Gorgias also appeared with exhibition speeches, or when, later, contests between poets and other writers took place, this was much more suitable at the abode of the lord of the muses than in Zeus's sanctuary at Olympia. Where the musical competitions were held during Delphi's great period is no longer known; in any case, the theatre still occasionally used for festival presentations only dates from the second century B.C. Considerably earlier, the gymnastic events appear to have been transferred from the plain of Cirrha to a stadium set high up under the cliffs, and, as reconstructed in Roman times, their new home is well preserved. From the fourth century, a gymnasium with adjacent palaestra near the precinct of Athena served for training.

Anyone who was present at the Pythian games and who saw the enormous number of costly gifts or the many splendid buildings, must have felt very strongly that this was the greatest religious centre in the Greek world. In point of fact, here stood the omphalos, the navel of the earth, here the altar, the 'common hearth' of the Hellenes, from the fire of which the flames were rekindled at local sanctuaries where they had been put out during the Persian war. Yet it was the oracle around which in the last analysis everything revolved, even if no direct link with it existed. When, from the middle of the fifth century, the spirit of enlightenment granted men the recognition and knowledge that had previously seemed to belong to the god alone, Delphi's authority was still only slightly impaired. It is true, however, that in political life, which thenceforth grew increasingly secular, it no longer played a decisive role, except where conservative Sparta was concerned; indeed, it too finally tumbled into the whirlpool of the Peloponnesian war. Under leaders avid for power, the Phocians, who a century earlier had already destroyed the sanctuary's independence for a time, took possession of Delphi in 356, robbed it of all valuable offerings, so that they could gain control over part of Greece by using mercenaries, and profaned the delivery of oracles. Though Phocian dominion was ended after ten years with Philip of Macedonia's help, and Delphi's autonomy formally re-established, the conqueror proceeded to assert his own influence, with the result that Demosthenes could say that the Pythia now only spoke Philip's mind. From then on, there was hardly any trace of important political influence; the prerequisites for this had gone with the passing of classical Hellas.

However, the oracle's dominant position in the sphere of worship and expiatory rites remained unaffected by the decline of its political importance. In accord with the ethical demands of contemporary philosophers, the god now required not only freedom from external pollution, but a pure heart as well; and as always, he named the religious remedy for any trouble due to sins of omission. Thus, in cases of this kind, individual men and states went on just the same requesting his instructions; Hellenistic rulers did so too, and even Rome. When it was believed after the battle of Cannae that the terrible disaster could only be repaired with the aid of gods previously unworshipped, an embassy went to Delphi, and had Apollo specify the deities and rites through the power of which Hannibal could be overcome. Likewise, during the fourth and third centuries, Greek cities and overlords often asked the Pythian god for advice at the founding of a sanctuary, when miraculous visions regarded as omens had been seen, and about everything connected with the veneration of heroes or with rites of expiation; and if some locality or sanctuary was to be guaranteed security against violent trespasses people liked it to be done with the help of a Delphic pronouncement submitting any offender to Apollo's punishment. In the Hellenistic age, however, the belief in and the spiritual link with the Pythian god grew continually weaker among rulers and members of the upper classes. One should not be misled by the fact that the sacred precinct—where, even after it was robbed by the Phocians, 3,000 gifts were still left standing—filled up with new offerings and imposing monuments. Neither the exedra put up by Alexander's general Craterus, in which a sculptural group showed the donor rescuing the king on a lion hunt, nor the splendid monuments and buildings of the Pergamene and Bithnyian kings, nor yet the giant column erected by Aemilius Paulus to record his victory at Pydna in 168 were real pious offerings; instead, like many presents from as early as the fourth century, they were proud memorials of their giver's own fame, which nowhere else in the world could be more effectively proclaimed than there. In this sense, Delphi remained the focus not only of Hellas, but of all the hellenized countries, until severe looting by barbarian hordes and the Roman Sulla in the first century stripped it of its outward splendour. By this time, the oracle's importance even in religious matters had declined so much that many could claim it had completely disappeared.

Such was not the case, however. Throughout all the changes wrought by time, private individuals continued with unshaken faith to seek Apollo's counsel, whether they asked for an oracle by lot or an utterance by the Pythia. The most famous among these private questions, about which information has naturally been preserved in only a very few cases, is that of the Athenian Chaerephon from the end of the fifth century, as to whether anybody was wiser than Socrates. Back came the answer: Nobody! One can hardly explain the remarkable lack of ambiguity in this response, which is undoubtedly genuine, except by reference to the 'Know yourself!' and to the god's oft-repeated warning that man should remain conscious of his limitations. Who could have passed for wiser, in the Delphic sense, than the man who, in order to know, declared that he knew nothing, and who was thus in the highest degree aware of the bounds imposed on humanity? No doubt most of the private queries were much cruder right from the start, and in the late period, when the educated only turned to it on rare occasions, people almost invariably bothered the oracle about quite trivial matters. For Plutarch, himself a priest at Delphi, complained, at the turn from the first to the second century A.D., that nobody now asked anything except: Should I get married? Should I travel by sea? Should I lend money? In so far as states still approached the god, it was at most a question of cattle-breeding, harvest prospects, or the health of the citizens—no longer of worship and rites, let alone political decisions. The Pythia was then a simple girl in whom no intellectual tradition lived on; the well of Delphic wisdom had long since dried up. Even the romantic movement that was so advantageous to the famous sanctuaries at the time of Hadrian, who is actually said to have consulted the god, could not reinvigorate Delphi. Nothing but the continuing spiritual influence of a great past in conjunction with the mystical tendencies of the late imperial age and the common people's faith—or rather superstition—kept the oracle, now without any deep religious import, alive for another 200 years, so that the Fathers of the Church saw themselves obliged to wage impassioned war against this nest of infernal demons. Its end was only brought about by the full triumph of Christianity under Theodosius I.

Together with the oracle, the Pythian games, at which Nero appeared as a singer in A.D. 65, persisted until the outset of late antiquity, though admittedly they too had long

VII   Delphi. Marmaria, Tholos

ago been divested of their solemn religious atmosphere. Besides singers and musicians, acrobats and conjurors were now allowed to show their skill. Likewise, the Delphic community retained a semblance of life, and even the sacred land on the plain of Cirrha as well as the council of amphictyons, revived by Augustus for political reasons, were under the emperor's protection. Apollo's temple, which had suffered severely in the first century B.C. as a result of barbarian raids and Sulla's pillaging, was repaired over a hundred years later. Though Nero, who contributed funds for this, carried off many precious offerings, the sacred precinct, that place of vain self-glorification, did not lack new monuments and buildings even afterwards. As at Olympia, Herodes Atticus gave proof of his patronage, here by furnishing the stadium with marble seats. Nevertheless, when Constantine turned from the old religion to Christianity, the respect felt for what Delphi had still signified even in its degeneration faded away. The serpent column, on which had once rested the golden tripod offered in thanks for victory over the Persians and later melted down by the Phocians, was taken off to Constantinople, where it still stands today in the hippodrome square (at Meidan). With the closure of the oracle in A.D. 393 and the proscription of the heathen cults, the sanctuary was entirely given over to pillaging and devastation. Soon, a monastery came into being on the palaestra near the precinct of Athena, and Delphi, which for more than a thousand years had been the home of Apollo's oracle, became the see of a Christian bishop. On the ruins of the temple, the treasuries and the monuments, however, there arose in later times a village called Kastri, which the French excavators had to demolish in the 1890s before they could uncover the remains, still noble even in their devastation, of the Pythian sanctuary.

THE ISTHMUS AND NEMEA

Since, guided by fortune, he had gained the victor's crown both at the isthmus and in Nemea, he gave the Muses a field to till. PINDAR

The two sanctuaries in the north-east of the Peloponnese—that of Poseidon on the isthmus of Corinth and that of Zeus in the quiet valley of Nemea between Corinth and Argos —could not compete with Olympia and Delphi in fame and importance. Yet for the games that were actually celebrated every other year at both these places, a universal truce of the god was likewise proclaimed. Those participating in the contests arrived from all parts of the mother-country as well as from Sicily and the Aegean islands, and the winners in the Isthmian and Nemean games were extolled by Pindar no less highly than those who triumphed beside the Alpheus or at Pytho. The two lesser festivals also

VIII   Isthmus of Corinth. Temple of Poseidon

developed out of funeral games, and their founding was attributed to demigods or heroes from the distant past. They included gymnastic and horse-racing events, for which the prize took the form of a palm-branch or a wreath of wild celery; musical competitions did not make their appearance until Hellenistic times.

Together with the hero Palaemon, Poseidon, the sea-god and earth-shaker, had since the sixth century possessed a temple in a grove of stone-pines on the sea-girt isthmus, with its many earthquakes, where the festival was celebrated under Corinthian leadership. The Athenians, however, had enjoyed the honorary presidency since early days, as the Attic hero Theseus was said to have established the games. Near the temple lay the stadium, and farther off the hippodrome, though here too no trace of it survives. At both sanctuaries, theatres were only built after the introduction of musical contests.

The Nemean games were held in the broad valley in honour of Zeus, who from time immemorial had been worshipped upon a neighbouring mountain; and on their site, a magnificent temple to the god was erected during the fourth century, with a stoa, a gymnasium, and a palaestra close by. Though they had originally been run by the little town of Cleonae, at that date control over the games had fairly long ago been usurped by Argos, which three generations later transplanted the entire festival to the Argive plain, with the result that Nemea became waste. On the other hand, the isthmus sanctuary, where the Roman Flamininus announced the freedom of the Greeks at the celebration of 196, retained its pan-Hellenic importance even after Corinth had been destroyed in 146. Indeed, when Caesar refounded the city, and it was promoted to capital of the province of Achaea, the Isthmian games enjoyed a new lease of life.

II

REGIONAL SANCTUARIES

Even the four pan-Hellenic holy places were originally the sanctuaries of comparatively small regions. Except at Delphi, which for the oracle's sake acquired a special status, the management of the great festivals held in these holy places was left to neighbouring states, though this did not affect the all-Greek character of the festivities. By contrast, the influence of the other regional sanctuaries was confined to a definite area, and they remained closely dependent on the community to which they belonged politically even if they achieved pan-Hellenic importance, or at least claimed it. Among cult centres of this second type, Eleusis with its mysteries came first for world-wide power of attraction and prestige, as well as the religious value of the ritual.

ELEUSIS

> *Blessed is the man who looked upon them before he passed into the Underworld. He knew about the ending of life; he knew about the God-given new beginning.* PINDAR

To the north of the island of Salamis, beside a bay in the Saronic Gulf, lies the Thriasian plain which is enclosed by mountains and cut off from the plain of Athens by the Aegaleos range. The fertility of the Thriasian soil had already early on led the local population to worship the food-dispensing earth mother Demeter. On the southern slope of the acropolis hill beneath the later telesterium, stretches of wall from the latter half of the second millennium have been found that belonged at least in part to religious buildings of that era. In mature archaic times, the goddess already had a temple on the same spot, and undoubtedly she was by then being honoured with the mysteries the existence of which in the seventh century is attested by a hymn handed down to us as a work of Homer's. Their founding is attributed to Demeter herself. She had borne her brother Zeus a daughter called Persephone; but Hades, the lord of the underworld, abducted the 'Maiden' (Kore) as she was picking flowers in a meadow, and made her his wife—a fact of which his brother Zeus was aware. Though the mother heard from afar her daughter's cry of distress, she did not find her, and only learned what had happened after a long search and enquiry. Thenceforward, she shunned Olympus in bitterness against the sky god, went among men, and came in the guise of an old woman to Eleusis, where she sat down beside the well of Callichorus. Led by the daughters of King Celeus into their father's dwelling, she there enjoyed a friendly reception. Full of grief, she sank down with veiled head upon a hide-covered stool, declined ordinary food and drink, and only sipped a beverage prepared from barley and mint, until a maidservant succeeded in cheering her up with jokes. However, the king and queen entrusted her with the care of their little son Demophon, whom she fondled in her lap, fed with ambrosia, and at night placed in the fire. By this means, he would have become immortal, if his mother had not caught sight of him in the fire and cried out in horror. Thereupon, Demeter made it known that she was a goddess, and announced that, though Demophon would no longer acquire immortality since his mother had broken the spell, he was thenceforth to be honoured by the youths of Eleusis with annual contests. At the same time, she asked for an altar and temple to be raised to her over the well of Callichorus. Then she herself would institute the sacred rites that were to be observed in purity for her propitiation. When thereafter the goddess had vanished in radiant splendour, they built her the altar and the temple, which she made her home, continuing to be angry with the gods and to lament her abducted daughter.

In order to force Zeus to alter his decision, she—the earth mother—finally allowed no more seeds to sprout or fruit to grow, so that men were threatened with famine and the gods with the loss of their offerings. Since all efforts to make her change her mind were in vain, Zeus commanded Hades to release Persephone, and his brother did as he was told. To be sure, he first made his wife eat a pomegranate pip, as a result of which she remained tied to the underworld. Nevertheless, a compromise was found whereby, in every year, Persephone spent on earth the eight months from the time of the first blossoming and only the four months when nature dies at her husband's side in the nether world. Content with this arrangement, Demeter allowed plants to grow as before and, as she had promised, instructed the lords of Eleusis in the rites that thenceforth were to be undertaken at her sanctuary. Indeed, not only did she teach these to Triptolemus—once actually regarded as a daemon, though later as the Eleusinian king's son—but sent him out on a winged chariot, to bring ears of corn and with them corn itself to all mankind.

To begin with, only Eleusinians took part in the ceremonies, which were established during the eighth century at the latest; the exercise of the highest priestly functions was a privilege reserved for local aristocratic families. Like his two female counterparts, the hierophant, who performed the holiest actions and looked after the goddess's treasure, was chosen from a prominent clan: the Eumolpidae. As he had succeeded the king in this office, he still wore the regal fillet at the great celebrations, and could only be addressed by his title. Members of the family of the Keryces discharged the duties of herald (keryx), torch-bearer (daduchus), and altar priest. This remained the case even when Eleusis was annexed to the Athenian state during the seventh century, and when the Eleusinian cult subsequently became part of the Attic public religion, thereby coming under the supervision of the highest Athenian religious officials. In other respects, the close link with Athens, where an 'Eleusineum' appeared as a kind of branch establishment, benefited the holy place not only by widening its sphere of influence. At the time of the tyrant Pisistratus (ruled 560–527), the sacred precinct was enclosed with a wall and given a propylaeum; the well of Callichorus, by which Demeter had sat, acquired an artistic setting, but above all a telesterium (hall of the mysteries) was built over the earliest temple. Around a square space, the walls were lined with flights of steps, from which those taking part in the celebration could watch the proceedings in the hall. A new building designed in the fifth century by Ictinus, the architect of the Parthenon, corresponded to this layout, except that, partly driven into the rock, it was four times as large and provided with galleries on all sides. During the fourth century, it received a magnificent portico, while at the same period, by the processional way, small sites that had long been dedicated to Pluto-Hades, Hecate or Artemis also underwent development. Finally, in Roman times, two imposing propylaea were raised, and a paved forecourt, from which one entered the goddess's precinct through the enclosing wall, was constructed.

According to the Homeric hymn, Demeter had founded two kinds of religious observance: contests in honour of Demophon, at which from the first people's thoughts certainly turned mainly to the goddess; and the 'highly sacred orgies'. Concerning the former, called the Eleusinia, we know that they were organized in the August of every second year as a harvest-thanksgiving, and on a smaller or larger scale by turns. After a procession and a sumptuous offering, gymnastic and horse-racing competitions took place, the winners receiving as their prize barley from the sacred field. The mystery cult, which must be distinguished from this festival, also involved a lesser and a greater celebration, both of which were held annually. However, before anyone was allowed to attend the lesser mysteries, a prerequisite for participating in the great ones, he had to be initiated. This could occur at any time through any of the Eumolpidae or Keryces to whom the would-be initiate applied in person. As at the Olympic games, all free Greeks were

47

admitted who were not tainted with blood-guilt or sacrilege; but at Eleusis, even slaves could attend, though barbarians, who admittedly did not include Romans, could not. With veiled head and almost entirely shrouded body, the person seeking initiation had to sit in an armchair, where he remained in silent meditation. In his left hand he gripped a torch, while his bare feet rested on a ram-skin. Then a winnowing-fan was held above his head—a common purification ritual on other occasions as well; indeed, the whole ceremony served to purify him. By this means, he became a mystes, and as such he from then on had access to the lesser mysteries, which were observed every February at Agrae near Athens. Hardly anything is now known about this celebration except that it resulted once again in purification, and that those who took part probably watched a holy play. Already in antiquity, interest had understandably concentrated on the great mysteries, which occurred during the Attic month of Boedromion (roughly our September). The proclaiming of a universal truce of the god, even for the duration of the lesser festival, was meant to guarantee Greeks from far and near a tranquil visit.

Observance of the great mysteries began with the priests transferring the sacred cult objects from Eleusis to Athens, whose young men formed an escort. On the following day, the Eumolpidae and Keryces assembled for the opening of the celebration in the so-called Painted Stoa beside the agora. The mystae had arrived long ago. They bathed in the sea on the next day, when they also attended the first great sacrifice, which was offered to Demeter and Persephone in the Athenian Eleusineum. After a day of rest, the participants, adorned with myrtle wreaths, formed up on the following morning for the great procession. In front was borne the wooden cult image of Iacchus, a chthonic deity belonging to Athens. He had been admitted into the Eleusinian group like other gods of the nether world such as Zeus-Eubuleus, who was equated with Pluto. Throughout the entire journey along the sacred way, people kept calling out Iacchus's name, and they spontaneously struck up hymns to the god. However, the essential feature of the procession, and its real purpose, was the returning of the sacred objects to Eleusis. Priestesses carried them, with the entire body of the priests following on foot; only from the end of the fifth century were vehicles used. The crowd numbering thousands did not advance in a solemn mood, for they were beckoned on by a promise of joy; and even the thought of death may have heightened the exhilaration of the moment, perhaps also giving rise to boisterous behaviour in accordance with ancient magical practice. At all events, jokes and gibes must have been uttered. While this activity itself prevented the procession from arriving at its destination quickly, there were in addition many other delays at smaller wayside shrines, where sacrifices had to be made or hymns to the deity sung. Darkness had already fallen when the Eleusinian sanctuary was finally reached by the light of torches. There, the image of Iacchus and the hallowed objects were hidden away, but, in a nocturnal celebration, those who had taken part in the procession made ready with singing and dancing for the beatific experience of the ensuing days.

When morning came, the great mysteries opened with offerings to all the gods worshipped at Eleusis; these were taken as the hierophant directed from an enormous cake baked of wheaten and barley flour. Following this, the mystae purified themselves once more, and after preparatory fasting, drank of the concoction that Demeter in her sorrow had not disdained at the home of Celeus. Then the first 4,000 made their way into the darkness of the telesterium and lined the steps along the walls of the room, in the middle of which stood the deity's holiest precinct, the anaktoron, where only the hierophant could set foot. There and in its vicinity were staged the 'performances' that constituted the main item of the entire mystery celebration. If no account has come down to us of what the mystae actually saw, this is almost certainly not only because they were bound by a strict oath of secrecy, but because the essence could not really be described in words. There can be little doubt that the abduction of Persephone, her despairing mother's search, and the Kore's return to the light of day played a part in what was apparently a largely mimed performance; yet it cannot just have been a question of presenting this myth in dramatic form. Certain ritual gestures and actions must have been far more important and affecting, for the crime of profanation that Alcibiades was accused of in 415 consisted not in letting out secrets orally, but in copying. The impact of the solemn proceedings, during which the hierophant revealed the sacred objects and uttered liturgical formulae, was strengthened by lighting effects made possible by an opening in the roof, and by musical accompaniment. Since, even after the telesterium had been enlarged to four times its previous size, there were still far too many mystae for them all to have been admitted at once, the observances had to be repeated on several successive days. Moreover, those who had already taken part in them twice and thereby reached the highest grade of initiate—that of the epoptae or onlookers—had their own special celebration, at which they were shown more than the mystae of inferior rank. There was a good reason for the fact that no further events occurred after the actual mysteries, apart from the presenting of a gift of water to the dead: nothing was to efface the deep impression left by what the participants had been allowed to see in the telesterium.

'Blessed is he who of the people on earth has beheld this! But he who has not been initiated and who does not take part in the holy celebrations will enjoy no such fortune after his death in the musty darkness,' announced the author of the Homeric hymn, and added: 'Thrice blessed is he whom of the people on earth those goddesses favour and love. Forthwith, they send him into the great house as a hearth-mate of Pluto, who bestows wealth on mortals.' Significantly, the second promise which could likewise be made by other gods was not bound up with participation in the mysteries. For no prospect of earthly happiness was held out to the mystae, who simply gained the assurance that some day, after their death, they would obtain a better lot than the uninitiated. Like the bard from the archaic period, later writers—Pindar, Sophocles, Plato, and others —declared this over and over again. What gave rise to the certitude, what was beheld, remains hidden from us. It cannot, or at least cannot only, have been Persephone's temporary return from the underworld, because the mystae did not become convinced by what they saw of some kind of resurrection or of simple survival after death, which did not come into the question, but of the fact that, in the hereafter, they would be favoured above all others. Moreover, this would occur thanks to the solemn celebrations and the mere sight of the divine, not in reward for virtuous conduct or exceptional piety. It is true that those defiled by blood-guilt and sacrilege were excluded from the mysteries, and that the mystae had repeatedly to undergo purification; but not until the end of the fifth century was the demand for ritual purity combined with the idea that the promise of a future existence 'in the sun and sacred light' would only be fulfilled for those who had always, or at least after initiation into the rites, behaved piously in their dealings with familiars and strangers. Nevertheless, even then, and subsequently down to the end of antiquity, the moral influence on the mass of the initiates was probably not unduly strong, particularly as it did not form part of the original aim of the celebrations.

As the sanctuary's elaboration at the time of Pisistratus shows, the Eleusinian mysteries acquired their importance for the religious life of the people of Attica during the sixth century. This happened when, with the gradual disappearance of the light-hearted world of the aristocracy, for whom death was the bitterest of all ills, it ceased to be merely the poor and oppressed who had an unfailing belief in an after-life, and who were filled with the hope of a better existence. Little as the Orphic doctrine of the transmigration of souls had to do with what was at issue in Eleusis, its powerful influence testifies to world-weariness, to a yearning for deliverance, and hence to a mood that responded to the Eleusinian promises. Though these inward needs and anxieties diminished with the coming of the intellectual awakening at the start of the fifth century, the serene security of existence as the Homeric heroes had known it did not return. Greece's greatest era was at the same time her tragic era, haunted by death, and despite all its vital and creative energy, imbued with a profound pessimism, which called in question the meaning and value of human life. Aeschylus, who came from Eleusis, made a character in one of his plays beg for death as a release, and not only in Sophocles is it said that it would have been best not to have been born. No wonder, therefore, that, owing to the joyful expectations the mysteries aroused with regard to the next world, their power of attraction increased still further. External circumstances also contributed to this. Athens, to whose public religion the celebrations at Eleusis belonged, was at that period developing her most dazzling brilliance and greatest strength. Protected and promoted by the Attic state, whose council meeting after the close of the great festival perhaps discussed transgressions that had occurred during its course, and whose laws punished desecrators of the mysteries with death, the sanctuary enjoyed materially too its most flourishing period, and to a large extent it preserved its autonomy. In accordance with instructions from the Delphic god, all Athenian citizens were placed under an obligation to make specific donations to the Eleusinian deities at regular intervals. The many cities belonging to the Attic maritime league, which had to comply with orders from headquarters, and in this case probably did so willingly, were encouraged to follow suit. Indeed, in view of the pan-Hellenic character that the celebration of the mysteries had gradually assumed as a result of the growing influx of participants from the whole Greek colonial area, Athens could call upon all Greeks to contribute—though not without laying claim to the glory of having on her soil and under her protection the place where divine favour was bestowed most liberally on the Greeks.

The collapse of Athenian power in 404 affected Eleusis on the material level, but could not reduce the sanctuary's prestige or the demand for initiation into the mysteries. Even the spirit of enlightenment, which was countered in the Attic state by a sharp reaction against every disrespect shown to the gods and their cult, was not capable of doing this, especially since—as so often—the heightened rationalism was matched by a heightened inclination towards the irrational and mysterious. Moreover, the misery that engulfed countless people when Greece tore herself to pieces during the fourth century could only strengthen the desire one day to share in a life of bliss. Likewise, in the following, war-ravaged period down to the establishment of Rome's dominion over the Hellenic and hellenized world, things were doubtless hardly different, and no better under Roman rule, which brought further distress. Even if no new buildings appeared within the sacred precinct, people continued to pour in for the mysteries, and during the first century B.C. the Romans too felt the attraction. Sulla, Cicero, his friend Atticus, Antony and Augustus all had themselves initiated. Admittedly, one can scarcely avoid the impression that many did so at that time less from real piety than from conventional respect for a great tradition, or because of romantic leanings—when it was not actually a case of sensation-hunting. 'Your Athens', wrote Cicero to Atticus, 'seems to me to have produced and contributed much to human life that is magnificent and divine, but nothing better than those mysteries by means of which we have been educated and refined from a boorish and savage way of life to a civilized state. Initiations, they are called; through them, we have indeed discerned the primordial laws of life, and learned not only how to live with joy, but how to die with better hope.' Fine yet pale, religiously non-committal words, in which one is conscious of nothing more than pious emotion. All the same, the interest taken in the mysteries by educated Romans benefited the sanctuary at least outwardly; after a long interval, round about 40 B.C., it was once more enriched with another stately building: the so-called Lesser Propylaea.

As at other Greek cult centres, the age of Hadrian brought something of a religious second-blooming, and the emperor himself repeatedly took part in the celebrations, reaching the grade of epoptes. The fact that his wife Sabina was honoured as the 'new Demeter', and acquired a hierophant of her own, shows all too plainly the courtly perversion to which the venerable cult was then exposed. Yet it can hardly be doubted that the mystically inclined emperor's wish to participate in the rites came from the heart. The same may surely be assumed in the case of Marcus Aurelius, who also had himself initiated, and who presented the imposing gateway known as the Greater Propylaea; and no doubt of many other people too in this as in the following century. For it was not merely imperial favour that gave the Eleusinian cult a new impetus, but the hopes regarding the next world that determined every aspect of the period's highly assiduous religious life. It was inevitable that the mysteries now entered into rivalry with Christianity, which was gaining ground, and the latter's champions accordingly took the field against them with fanatical zeal. The triumph of the new religion spelt doom for the rites that for a thousand years had brought to countless people solace and the joyous certainty of a blissful life after death. In A.D. 396, the sanctuary itself was laid waste by Alaric, king of the West Goths, so that the imperial edict banning the mysteries was hardly necessary.

SANCTUARIES OF ZEUS AND HERA

We came across the greatest Zeus sanctuary and one of the most venerable temples of Hera at Olympia. Not until later did the god of the heavens receive there a splendid building of his own, in which he was present in effigy; and only later still at Nemea, another pan-Hellenic religious centre dedicated to him. Whereas the womanly Hera was obliged at an early date to seek a home, Zeus's element was the open-air: people felt close to him on mountain heights, or in a grove with its trees stirred by the wind. Many peaks dominating a wide expanse of land or sea bore altars of Zeus, and in looking up at them the surrounding population felt united. With the immigration of the Greeks, many wooded valleys, where already in far-off times a deity was worshipped, became Zeus sanctuaries that not only formed the religious focus of the inhabitants of the particular region but in some cases even achieved pan-Hellenic importance. Thus it was with Olympia and Nemea, as also with the sanctuary at Dodona.

DODONA

Dodona was founded there in the outermost place. Zeus loved it and wished it to be the site of his oracle, dear to mortals. . . . Earthdwellers go there for prophecies of every sort. HESIOD

In a lonely mountain valley of the remote region of Epirus, beneath the lofty Tomarus range, lies the site of Zeus's most famous oracle. The *Iliad* and the *Odyssey* already knew of it. Nevertheless, the building remains that one sees there today belong mainly to Hellenistic times; though a fifth-century temple has been identified, it is not these traces that let one feel the sanctuary's solemn atmosphere, but the landscape, where oak-trees are standing even now. Presumably the sky god and his consort, here called Dione, were brought from the north by Greek immigrants to this spot, which in remote antiquity appears to have been sacred to a fountain deity. Thenceforth, Zeus Naios was lord of Dodona; to him, sacrifices, gifts, and games (Naia) were offered. If at one time people had heard a god's voice in the murmuring spring, now the divine couple spoke through the rustling of a sacred oak that stood above the spring, and priests called hypophetes interpreted the sounds. Oracles were delivered in other ways as well. Two doves were said to have flown from the Egyptian Thebes, one to the oasis of Ammon in the Libyan desert, the other to Dodona; hence, it was believed that in the cooing of the doves that nested amid the oak-tree's foliage, the deity spoke in a language understood by the priestesses, who were thus able to answer the consultants. Likewise, from the way in which a bronze cauldron rang when the wind caused a whip held by a boy to strike against it, the priestesses knew how to reveal precise divine instructions. As regards the questions, which from the end of the fifth century at the latest were submitted in writing, we possess documentary evidence—which is not to be had in the case of Delphi and other oracles— in the form of a quantity of little lead tablets, brought to light during excavations. Here too, as at Pytho, communities or individuals wanted to know which god or hero they should sacrifice to, so that their affairs would prosper. For the most part it was a case of quite trivial concerns: should one remove to this or that house, extend a lease, obtain partners for some enterprise, bathe a child's diseased foot in the holy spring, and so forth. Even the question as to whether the enquirer was the father of the child expected by his own wife is not missing. Rarely do queries crop up regarding political affairs, such as the union of two states; yet since early times, Dodona must have been approached quite often for this kind of decision, although it never had Delphi's importance. At all events it was not just the Epirots, the neighbouring Thessalians, or the Greek colonies along the Ionian sea that used the oracle of the supreme god; for King Croesus of Lydia already sought advice at the distant sanctuary, and both Sparta and Athens were still asking for directives in the fourth century. During the early Hellenistic period, when Epirus enjoyed a sudden advancement under King Pyrrhus, Dodona was still flourishing, but afterwards it declined. Undoubtedly the sanctuary's destruction by the Aetolians in 219 made no small contribution to this, even though new buildings, including a large theatre, were erected later. As with Delphi, it was possible round about the time of Christ to take the view that the oracle had become silent. No new lease of life in the second century A.D. is discernible; only its continuance down to the triumph of Christianity in the post-Constantinian age may be regarded as certain. Over the ruins of this most ancient cult centre too, there soon sprang up a Christian church.

Too short my song to tell of all the splendid things that Argos' sacred stones have seen. PINDAR

Just as Zeus watched over the laws and customs of men, so his wife Hera protected those of women, their running of the home, and especially marriage. On the soil of the mother-country, she was worshipped above all in the northern Peloponnese; from there, colonists travelling westwards from the area of Achaea brought her cult to the shores of South Italy. Her largest and most famous sanctuary in Greece itself was that of Argos, the influence of which radiated both to Olympia and across the Aegean sea to the island of Samos. Since even before the Dorian invasion the goddess had acquired a cult centre on Samos through emigrants from Argolis, she must have had a sanctuary in their homeland by the latter half of the second millennium, though it is true that the building remains from Mycenaean times under the later Heraeum no longer tell us anything about it. Hera, it is said in Homer, was fondest of Argos together with Mycenae and Sparta, the seat of the Atrides, and it is significant that people liked to call the goddess simply 'the woman of Argos'. There were a number of temples belonging to the archaic or classical period, some in the city of Argos, some at other places in the region. Yet all of them were surpassed, in its status of religious centre for Argolis as a whole, by the Heraeum lying on the eastern edge of the plain, and its chief priestess was an eponym, which means that each holder of the office gave her name to the relevant year. In honour of the goddess and to contain her primitive cult image, a building had been constructed at this spot on an artificial mountain terrace as early as the seventh century. After its destruction in 429, a much more magnificent sacred precinct was established somewhat lower down, and it included stoas as well as a telesterium recalling—though admittedly much smaller than —the one at Eleusis. In the middle of the site arose a new temple, for which the most important Argive artist, Polyclitus, created the cult statue out of gold and ivory.

We know nothing about the form of worship or about the rites that took place in the telesterium; only with regard to the great annual festival of the Heraea, which, on account of the giant sacrifice of a hundred head of cattle, was also called the Hekatombaia, has a little information come down to us. In a stately procession, the men, women, and young people of Argos made their way from the city to the sanctuary about nine miles away— those able to bear arms wearing their warrior's finery, the priestess on a car drawn by cows. On one occasion, Herodotus tells us, the draught-animals did not arrive punctually from the field. Therefore the priestess's two sons, Cleobis and Biton, harnessed themselves to the car, and, before the eyes of the admiring members of the procession, they hauled

IX   Argos, Heraeum. Temple of Hera of the late fifth century B.C. seen from the terrace of the earlier Temple of Hera

their mother all the way along the lengthy road to the Heraeum. She, the priestess, then went before the image of the goddess, and implored Hera to give her children the best that could fall to a mortal's lot. After this prayer, the youths made a sacrifice, feasted, lay down to sleep in the sacred precinct—and never rose again. Since they had been carried off by an easy death while still in full possession of the youthful vigour that they had humbly yet proudly proved, the best had in fact been granted them. At Delphi, one can still see the statues of them, bursting with energy, that the Argives dedicated during the sixth century; they are memorials of the Greek belief that whoever died in the prime of life after a glorious deed was loved by the gods.

Once the procession with the hundred cows to be slaughtered in honour of 'cow-eyed' Hera had reached the sanctuary, and the huge sacrifice had been made, contests were held for the goddess. In comparatively early times it would seem that these took the form only of gymnastic games, among which tilting at a shield was a speciality. The warlike character of this sport, as also the parade of men fit for military service, may have pre-served a memory of the fact that Hera had once held sway as a tutelary goddess in the strongholds of the warrior kings. Later, cithara players, flautists, and heralds gathered to compete in their respective arts, and later still, rhetoricians entered the lists with their declamations. For everybody, whether they had won in gymnastic or musical events, the prize consisted of a costly shield supplied by the famous foundries at Argos and a myrtle wreath. Victors and guests of honour banqueted during the evening of every feast-day in a specially provided building with a colonnaded courtyard, while all round the crowd enjoyed themselves eating their share of the meat from the hecatomb. In classical times, there still does not seem to have been a separate enclosure for the contests, since the stadium where the gymnastic games took place during the Roman imperial age was probably only built when the Nemean games were permanently transferred to the Argos area in the third century B.C. At that period, a gymnasium was constructed, no doubt also near the sacred precinct, and in the Roman era it was joined by thermae as well. The celebration of the great Heraea can be traced until the beginning of the third century A.D., though it certainly continued even beyond this down to the triumph of Christianity.

THE HERAEUM OF SAMOS

The Samians built a great temple, the largest of all the temples known to us. HERODOTUS

As we have seen, the cult of Hera had come from Argolis to the island of Samos lying off the coast of Asia Minor by late in the second millennium. Near the shore, about four miles from the town to be built later, the goddess received a sanctuary, the development of which in archaic times can be followed better than that of the other holy places, thanks to excavations carried out during the last decades. By the tenth century, Hera already possessed on this site an altar, which was replaced later by a larger one. A chapel also seems to have been built at that time to house the primitive cult image allegedly found in a lygos tree (*vitex agnus-castus*); and Hera had indeed probably taken over the site of, and succeeded, a pre-Hellenic tree deity. The holy lygos tree stood near her altar, and the columnar form of even later statues of the goddess, such as the celebrated figure in the Louvre, reminds the modern beholder of a tree-trunk. About 800, the first temple for the cult image was erected, a building 100 Samian ft. long (hekatompedos) that not long after acquired a wooden peristyle. A small bath, fed by the little river Imbrasus and once used for cleansing the goddess's statue, shows that certain rites known from later times were being practised by then. During the first half of the seventh century, the sanctuary had already become so important that not only were a new, lighter temple and bigger altar constructed for Hera, but her precinct also gained a long stoa, various other buildings, and a propylaeum, up to which the sacred way led from the town. In the following period, the gifts became increasingly abundant: figures of Hera, sculptural groups, and enormous bronze cauldrons, like the one presented by the Samian Kolaios out of the profits of his trading voyages, which about 600 had taken him as far as the straits of Gibraltar. The Heraeum had grown to be one of the most highly regarded sanctuaries in the eastern Aegean, when shortly before the middle of the sixth century it was decided to reconstruct it entirely, and to erect a temple to the goddess that would be unequalled in size.

Under the direction of the architects Rhoecus and Theodorus, a huge edifice in the Ionic style arose, its aisled naos and deep pronaos surrounded by a double peristyle (dipteros) of 108 columns. Including the pronaos, the cella alone was about 230 ft. long and the whole structure measured over 325 ft., while the columns towered up to a height of 50 ft. This magnificent limestone temple, in the 'nave' of which a great cult statue was displayed, received before its entrance the first of the magnificent Ionic altars: some 100 ft. long and 53 ft. deep. Other buildings also appeared, partly on top of the earlier structures, and included a temple-like edifice that was perhaps intended for the musical contests held during the great festival of the goddess. However, her mighty home had scarcely been covered with a wooden roof when it suffered a disastrous fire. Probably it could have been repaired, yet the ambition of the tyrant Polycrates, who had ruled over Samos since about 538, required an entirely new building. For its foundations, column drums and ashlars from the abandoned temple were used. Although covering only slightly more ground than the latter, the edifice begun by Polycrates—once again of limestone—grew in such a way that it amazed Herodotus three generations later; but, like so many great cathedrals during the Middle Ages, it was never finished. All the same, though still more buildings sprang up afterwards, and Hermes as well as Aphrodite received smaller temples, the general effect of Hera's sanctuary was thenceforth determined by this giant temple. In and around it, the cult of the goddess was carried on in classical times.

Two festivals were celebrated there annually. The larger one, called the Heraea, began with a solemn procession from the city to the sacred precinct. As in Argolis, the men able to bear arms marched wearing their military adornments, and here too gymnastic and musical contests were held in Hera's honour, though unfortunately we have no detailed information about these. The situation is rather better with regard to the other festival, known as the 'Cord Feast' (Tonaia) because its rites included twining lygos branches round the old cult image. It was said that on Samos Zeus had waylaid Hera, who was angrily evading him, and gone to bed with her even before he had made her his lawful wife. At the Tonaia, this event was re-enacted every year, in so far as the cult statue—that is, the goddess herself—had its virginity restored through being cleansed in the bath. Then it was left on its own somewhere or other, and people began hunting for it as if it had really disappeared. After finally tracking it down, they offered it a cake and arrayed it in bridal finery together with the lygos binding. No 'wedding' was celebrated, however, since the union of the two deities had, after all, taken place before their marriage. We do not know what role the priestess, who bore the title Euangelis (bringer of good news), played in the festivals and the cult generally. It appears that a male priest assisted her, but that the administration of the sanctuary and its treasure had for ages been in the hands of a committee of prominent Samians. This may possibly have included Polycrates's father, Aeaces, about whom the inscription on a seated figure dedicated by him tells us that he collected for Hera a tithe of the war booty and the proceeds of trading voyages or piracy.

'The woman of Samos', as people called the mistress of the sanctuary, no doubt after 'the woman of Argos', was regarded by the citizens as the divine personification of their state. On an inscribed stone, Hera and Athena held out a hand to each other above the text of a treaty between Samos and Athens. At various other times as well, Hera— or, more precisely, her cult—was involved in political affairs. Polycrates profited by the fact that the soldiers were far away at the goddess's major festival to make his *coup d'état*. When, after the fall of Athens in 404, the Spartan Lysander forced Samos to surrender too, and brought back the exiled oligarchs, the latter expressed their thanks by setting up an altar to him in the sanctuary, and by honouring him like a god with sacrifices, games, and paeans at the Heraea, which was renamed the Lysandreia. To be sure, Hera came back into her own after this arrogant man's death, and the cult centre lasted for another 300 years in undiminished splendour. During the Hellenistic age, kings and princes bestowed votive gifts upon it; some even assumed the honorary office of director of the great festival and its contests. People also applied themselves at this period to completing and embellishing the temple. The limestone columns were replaced by columns of marble, one of which still stands today; it forms a marker indicating the sanctuary's site, and can be seen from a long way off. All the same, nobody found time to provide these columns with flutes, and likewise much else that was still missing remained unexecuted. Moreover, as a result of pillaging by sundry governors and potentates, the first century of Roman dominion (from 133) brought a decline, which is illustrated by a writer's remark that part of the temple was being used as a storehouse for offerings. With the coming of Augustus, the situation did indeed improve; but neither the building of two smaller marble temples and marble steps leading up to the entrance of the great temple, nor the admittance of the Asclepius cult and emperor worship into the sacred precinct, could cancel the impression that the heyday of the Samian Heraeum had definitely passed. Even before the full triumph of Christianity, it was devastated by the Herulians, and did not rise again. At the end of the sixth century, a Christian basilica sprang up on the ruins of Hera's greatest sanctuary.

SANCTUARIES OF APOLLO

DELOS

> *But at Delos, Phoebus, your heart is most refreshed where long-robed sons of Io assemble with their children and their honourable wives.* HOMERIC HYMN TO APOLLO

When Leto, the Titan's daughter with whom Zeus slept, was awaiting her confinement, she wandered about, harassed by Hera's jealousy. Nowhere would anyone take her in. She gave birth to Artemis on the island of Ortygia, close to Delos, but so great was the fear of Hera's wrath that Delos did not want her to bring the other twin into the world on Delian soil. Then Leto promised that the god to whom she gave life would receive a great temple, that people would flock together from every corner of the earth to attend his sacrifices and festivals, and that in consequence the inhabitants of the barren island would gain an ample living. After this, Delos refused no longer. Except for Hera, all the goddesses came along, including Ilithia who aided women in childbirth, and they were present when Leto, clinging to a palm-tree, bore Apollo. Thenceforth, the little island was sacred to him—indeed, it became one of the Greek world's most famous sanctuaries, round which the other islands settled by Ionians—the Cyclades—seemed to lie in a circle.

Delos was probably a cult centre as early as the second millennium, if not even before. It is true, however, that remains of buildings and a tholos tomb from Mycenaean times, which was regarded as the grave of the Hyperborean maidens whom Leto was supposed to have led to the island, do not reveal whether at that date people worshipped there a pre-Hellenic female deity who later assumed the form of Artemis, or already honoured Apollo and his sister. Nevertheless, the twins were undoubtedly receiving sacrifices and other forms of ritual veneration on Delos from the time of the Dorian invasion onwards. Upon a low terrace above the harbour bay on the western side of the island, which only covers rather more than two square miles, there stood by 800 at the latest an altar of Artemis and probably the first temple of Apollo too. Soon the sanctuary became the religious centre of the Cyclades, the Ionian inhabitants of which banded together in an amphictyony similar to the Delphic league for its protection, for the guardianship of the gods' possessions, and the joint celebration of the festivals. Evidence of this is provided both by the 'Homeric' hymn to Apollo and by the multitude of buildings that, during and after the eighth century, were put up not only on the old cult site, but also in its immediate and more distant environs. Delos's few inhabitants would not have been in a position to do this alone. The nobles of the rich island of Naxos made their mark before others by erecting their oikos and presenting an abundance of gifts including a colossal statue of Apollo. It was probably also the amphictyons who dedicated a temple to Artemis and another to Hera, whom people sought to appease. Her abode stood on the ascent to Mount Cynthus, the island's 368-ft.-high summit, on the slope of which Zeus, the divine twins' father, and his daughter Athena, the protectress, were both worshipped. Leto too obtained a temple during the sixth century—not far in fact from the sacred lake that lies to the north of Apollo's sanctuary, beside which she was said to have given birth to the god. Her swans and geese enlivened its waters, on which a row of marble lions— unique products of seventh-century Greek art—looked down from a terrace beside the processional way leading to the lake. Until not long before 550 Apollo himself had to be content with his early, primitive temple and an 'Altar of Horns' round which the 'crane dance' (geranos) was performed in his honour; but at that period he moved into a new home, a limestone temple containing a cult image over 26 ft. tall, which showed him with the Charites (Graces) on his hand. Soon flanked by treasuries, the building lay near the old precinct, which had been enlarged on account of the ever-increasing number of offerings and growing influx of worshippers and participants in the festivals.

At that time Ionian Athens, which every year sent a delegation to the great festival of Apollo, had already achieved importance for Delos. Not long afterwards, the tyrant Pisistratus purified even the island dedicated to the god of purity by having all tombs removed. It is true that Polycrates of Samos also took an interest in the sanctuary, to which he attached the neighbouring island of Rhenaea; but with its rise to power from about 500, the Attic state gained a controlling influence. This became exclusive when Delos, which in its weakness had yielded to the Persians and thereby saved its holy places, was made the religious focus of the maritime league led by Athens (478/7)—a

X   Delos. One of the lions beside the Processional Way leading to the Sacred Lake

development from the old amphictyonic arrangement. As the meeting-place of delegates from the whole Aegean area the sacred island now enjoyed an increase in fame, and no doubt in commercial prosperity too. The fact, however, had to be admitted that control over the league's money deposited in the temple of Apollo was in the hands of Athenian officials. Even when the treasure was transferred to Athens in 454, the Delians did not escape from the tutelage—indeed, the dominion—of the powerful city. In 425, the Athenians once again purged the island of graves, forbidding anyone thenceforth to die there, and soon afterwards they actually evacuated the Delian population for a short time. In addition, they erected a new dwelling for Apollo, the so-called temple of the Athenians, even though before 454 the amphictyons had already begun building a second temple which was probably intended to house the league's funds, but which remained unfinished right into Hellenistic times. Only for a few years did the downfall of the mighty Attic state afford the Delians a certain independence under Sparta's protection; then they once more came under Athenian control, which, despite their occasional efforts to break free, lasted until 314. While it is true that the island did not become Attic territory during classical times, the sanctuary's relationship to Athens was nevertheless similar to that of Eleusis. In both places, the Athenians claimed the pan-Hellenic glory of the celebrations for themselves.

Among the countless festivals held in honour of the individual gods worshipped on Delos, the great celebrations for Apollo surpassed all others in splendour and importance —even that of Artemis's birthday. There were two in particular: the Apollonia and the Delia. The former took place annually in May; the latter, which was founded by the Athenians in 426, during the February of every fourth year. Processions, abundant sacrifices with associated feasting, gymnastic games for youths and men, and horse-racing were all just as much in evidence at the Apollonia as at the other great Greek festivals of the gods. It obtained its distinctive flavour, however, from the musical performances that on Delos were featured even more prominently than at the home of the Delphic oracle. Besides the above-mentioned crane dance round the Altar of Horns and no doubt other dances as well, the god received the songs of choirs that had come to compete from all the cities of the amphictyony. Athens, which was already sending festival envoys in the sixth century, later alone provided four girls' choirs (Deliads) which competed with each other. So long as the festival embassy existed, no death sentence was allowed to be carried out at home, because this would have impaired Apollo's purity. Hence, Socrates had to wait awhile for his death. Established by the Athenians and regarded by them as one of their own state festivals, the Delia was celebrated even more magnificently than the Apollonia. Not only Apollo was honoured at it, but other gods too, as when, following the example of the Athenian feast of Dionysus, a cult image of this deity was carried along in the procession on a float. Although the festival ships usually tied up in the harbour near the old sanctuary, in 418 the Attic state vessel moored off the neighbouring island of Rhenaea, from which a pontoon-bridge was thrown across to Delos by night, so that the Athenians could cross over it next morning in a solemn procession to the cult sites. Even in the fourth century, as many as a hundred head of cattle were brought to the island from Attica for the Delia, and sacrificed to the god.

After the ending of Attic sea-power in the years following Alexander's death, the Delia was no longer celebrated, and Athens paid out nothing more for the upkeep and embellishment of the sanctuary. Nevertheless, it soon found a new patron, and one who respected the autonomy of its administration, in the diadochos Antigonus, who in 315 revived the old Cycladic amphictyony in a league of the island Greeks (nesiots) under his protectorate. Antigonus's son, Demetrius Poliorcetes, had a long hall-like building put up, which his own son, Antigonus Gonatas, completed round about the middle of the third century. It sheltered an entire warship, as a votive offering and at the same time as the trophy of a naval victory over Ptolemy I, who had temporarily usurped the protectorate. Besides this, the same Antigonus gave the sacred precinct, once again enlarged, a dignified northern boundary in the form of a large stoa. In the same way, the Ptolemies, the Rhodians who followed them about 200 as leaders of the island league, and the Romans during the early period of their encroachment upon Hellas all honoured Delian Apollo with gifts. In the one and a half centuries of Delos's formal independence dating from 314, religious life on the island became outwardly still more opulent. By about the turn from the fourth to the third century, Apollo's son Asclepius received a temple, and not long after an altar, and on Mount Cynthus a temple was raised to Zeus; then, decades later, a new abode was built for Artemis, and her precinct acquired a portico. Furthermore, as a result of the links with the Ptolemies and the importance Delos won at this period as an entrepôt for trade in the eastern Mediterranean, foreign, mainly Egyptian deities—such as Serapis, Isis, and Anubis—also found accommodation. Apollo's sacred island, which for ages had sheltered numerous gods, seemed to become an international pantheon, and one for which there was no shortage of expensive gifts and commercial profits. If in the fourth century the temples already possessed considerable real property, notable capital resources, and a large income from making loans, this wealth now grew still further—not without danger to the island's strictly religious affairs.

After defeating Perseus, the king of Macedonia, at Pydna in 168, the Romans put Delos back under Athenian control, while at the same time giving it the status of a free port. At the expense of Rhodes, oppressed by Rome, and as a beneficiary of Corinth's destruction in 146, the island was from then until the beginning of the first century B.C. a centre for the trade conducted between Italy and the Orient. Admittedly, the Delians themselves did not gain by this mercantile prosperity; they were evacuated *en masse,* and replaced by Attic settlers. Yet even these only formed part of the population. Merchants from all over the ancient world, but especially from Rome and Italy, had long ago established themselves on the little but highly lucrative island, whose slave market became the largest in the East. They liked to band together in associations under the protection of their native gods, with the result that the old Greek cults were in danger of being stifled by the foreign ones. Nor was this all. The island once dedicated to a god, on which a considerable urban settlement had arisen while sacred buildings were hardly being built any more, lost its old character. The cult sites had already been pushed more and more into the background by the markets, when extremely heavy plunder and carnage by the troops of Mithridates, who in earlier years had sent offerings like so many other Hellenistic rulers, put a sudden end to the economic prosperity too. Destruction by pirates and grievous disasters during the Roman civil wars finished Delos off. Neither as a trading-post nor as a cult centre did it rise again, even though festival delegations continued to come from Athens, and Hadrian endeavoured to renew its religious life. Not long after the emperor died, a contemporary found the island uninhabited, and a little later Athens actually wanted to sell it—but could find no buyer. Even before Christianity had triumphed, the sanctuary was dead. Thenceforth, its decaying buildings stood empty, a quarry in later centuries for Venetians, Turks, and the inhabitants of the surrounding islands.

DIDYMA

And today, of all the oracles we know in Greece, undisputedly the most powerful after Delphi is the oracle of the Branchides. CONON

Delos was highly sacred as Apollo's birthplace; Didyma was considered the most important and the greatest among the oracles that the god possessed in Asia Minor—just as he did in the mother-country. The site, which people used also to call Branchidae after the family of hereditary priests who controlled it, is near the coast of Asia Minor south of Miletus, and lies on high ground with a splendid view. It may have been a cult centre even before Greeks established themselves in Miletus after the middle of the second millennium. Sooner or later Apollo became its Lord; in mature archaic times his oracle was already being consulted by all Hellenes east of the Aegean, and shortly it was also attracting non-Greeks from far and near. If the distant pharaoh Necho sent offerings as early as about 600, Croesus (reigned 560/546) was certainly not the first from the neighbouring kingdom of Lydia to render thanks with abundant gifts. The sanctuary's architectural form corresponded to the high reputation that Didyma then enjoyed. A processional way over eleven miles long led up to it from Miletus via the harbour of Panormus, where many of the pilgrims who came by sea liked to disembark. Its final stretch was flanked by over-life-size marble seated figures, lions, and sphinxes, which had been presented by grateful and self-important worshippers. The temple, of which the Pergamum Museum at Berlin preserves architectural fragments that are still impressive, contained Canachus of Sicyon's bronze cult statue of Apollo Philesios, as he was called here because he had loved the young Branchus, the Branchidae's progenitor. In the building's roof-timber and the surrounding grove nested sparrows and other birds, which were protected by the sanctity of the place. A spring said to have welled up through a cleft in the rock provided the water that the priestess (prophetis) drank before announcing the god's responses. In the same way, the Pythia at Delphi drank from the Cassotis fountain, and, like her, the Didyma prophetess was assisted by a male priest (prophetes), who, freshly appointed every year, headed the entire staff of the sanctuary. Apart from this, we know hardly anything about the delivery of the oracles, though it may already have been usual in the sixth century for the prophetes to write out the pronouncements —a practice of which there is evidence in later times. Nor can it really be said whether Didyma exerted any ethical influence, as we have very little knowledge of the answers given during the earlier period. Even the religious observances not directly related to the posing of questions are largely unknown. It is certain, however, that along with lesser celebrations, a great festival was organized annually in Apollo's honour, and that the Milesians, who had Apollo Delphinios as their state god, advanced in a procession along the sacred way to attend it, after which contests—especially a race with torches— took place in the temple precinct. It is also a fact that, on the eve of the Ionian revolt, which was to bring ruin both to the sanctuary and to the city of Miletus, Didyma was exceedingly rich in offerings and other treasure.

The Persians had ruled over the Greeks of Asia Minor since 545, and not only had they respected the Hellenic sanctuaries, but occasionally they had even shown their gratitude to them—including Didyma. When the Ionians, and particularly the Milesians, rebelled in 500, the latter rejected the advice of their famous compatriot Hecataeus to use Didyma's treasures for financing the struggle. Nevertheless, the Persians must, rightly or wrongly, have considered the Branchidae to be implicated, since after the revolt had been crushed (494), their temple was destroyed, just like the city of Miletus. They themselves were taken off to Susa along with the cult image and the god's treasure. Thereafter the oracle's voice is said to have remained silent for 150 years, and only to have become audible again in the days of Alexander, when it confirmed the king's descent from Zeus-Ammon and prophesied his future victory (331). In point of fact, literary references as well as building remains are completely lacking for the intermediate period. From now on, however, we again hear of oracles being delivered, and excavations have proved that during the last third of the fourth century building operations began again. First of all a little temple (naiskos) arose, and it received the old cult image, which Seleucus I had brought back from Susa shortly after 300. Then the king and his son Antiochus promoted the construction of a temple that rivalled the new Artemiseum at

Ephesus and the Heraeum of Samos in size and splendour. This Ionic edifice measured 358 by 167 ft., and its crepidoma of six steps, over which an outside staircase ran at the entrance end, carried a double peristyle of 108 columns, which were more than 64 ft. tall. In the back wall of the pronaos, which contained another twelve columns, a huge window like a gateway opened on to a hall that could not be entered directly. Instead, one approached the 'adytum' beyond it through two corridors at the side, so that one, as it were, went round the hall, which a flight of steps connected with the 'adytum'. This was a mighty court set nearly 15 ft. deeper and enclosed by the high cella walls. In it stood the above-mentioned naiskos; the place where oracles were delivered, as well as the holy fountain, must have been there too, whereas the writing down of the responses seems to have taken place in a 'House of the Prophetes' near the temple. Capitals, column bases, and fragments of the tendril frieze interrupted by Medusa heads still give an idea of the extraordinary magnificence of the temple's details. Round about 50 B.C., the reigning Ptolemy sent thirty-five large elephant's tusks for facing the doors between the hall and the court with ivory.

At that date, the temple at Didyma still remained unfinished—indeed, it never was finished, although work on it was carried out even in the age of imperial Rome. Yet the holy place had enjoyed the favour of the Seleucids and other Hellenistic rulers, many of whom consulted the god. The oracle flourished, and despite pillaging by the Galatians (277) and 200 years later by pirates, great riches again accumulated. A large staff of priests and attendants looked after the cult, and the resumed annual celebrations were joined by a still more brilliant festival, the Great Didymaea, which was held once every four years. Under Roman rule as well, the sanctuary retained its importance, though naturally account had to be taken of the imperial cult and occasionally of the vanity of particular emperors. Thus Caligula wanted to complete the temple, but at the same time to substitute himself for Apollo, and under Marcus Aurelius's degenerate son Commodus, the Great Didymaea really was celebrated as a feast of Commodus. Moreover, Diocletian used a pronouncement by Didymaean Apollo as religious authorization for his great persecution of Christians; and in his romantic endeavours to reanimate the old faith, Julian even took over the office of prophetes, doing away with the places of Christian worship in the sanctuary's environs. A few decades later, when all heathen cults were banned, the oracle fell silent for ever. Inside the colossal temple, the front of which had as early as the third century been disfigured by a defensive wall to keep out the Goths, a Christian basilica made its home. It was surrounded by the mighty cella walls, which only an earthquake in 1453 caused to collapse.

Great delight of men, soother of pain and sorrow, be greeted,
Lord: to you I pray in song. HOMERIC HYMN TO ASCLEPIUS

Apollo begot Asclepius on the Thessalian king's daughter Coronis. He had the mother, who was unfaithful to him during her pregnancy, killed by his sister Artemis, but saved the child, and handed him over for his upbringing to the wise centaur Chiron, who taught him the art of healing. When, however, having become a master in it, Asclepius ventured to restore a dead man to life, he was struck by Zeus's thunderbolt, which caused him to be hallowed and raised to the rank of god. His sons Machaon and Podalirius took part in the expedition against Troy as physicians, and in historical times the physician families of the Asclepiadae still boasted of being his descendants—particularly that of Cos, to which Hippocrates belonged. All the same, Asclepius remained quite unimportant in comparison with his radiant father, the mighty god of healing, till far into the fifth century and only at Tricca in Thessaly was he specially honoured. Not until the arrival of a period when they craved a more spiritual relationship with the gods, and more personal care and attention from them, did people turn to the divine physician, whose cult spread to such an extent from the fourth century onwards that about 200 Asclepius sanctuaries are still known to us. Among them, first place is shared by that of Epidaurus in the north-eastern Peloponnese, the island of Cos off the coast of Asia Minor south of Didyma, and Pergamum on the Anatolian mainland in the same latitude as Lesbos. Like most of the healing god's precincts, they lie outside the cities in healthy, well-watered districts, and they naturally show common features in their layout as well.

In a quiet valley about five miles away from the port of Epidaurus on the Saronic Gulf, homage was at first paid to Apollo, who had taken the place there of the hero Maleates. Even later on, when his son had arrived from Tricca and in the fourth century had acquired a large sanctuary, people continued to remember him and his sister Artemis. The thing that today arouses the visitor's admiration—the finest theatre in the Greek world—is in a sense only a subsidiary building, like the stadium and palaestra. It did not appear until the mid-fourth century, when it was erected for the musical contests that had joined the gymnastic games and horse-racing going back to the Maleates cult. What really mattered most was contained within the wall surrounding the sacred precinct, namely the altar of Asclepius and his temple decorated with pedimental sculptures. In the temple stood the gold-and-ivory cult image of the bearded, kindly looking god. To these must be added the sacred fountain and facilities for ritual washing; the large, partly two-storied stoas in which the sick rested and looked out towards the abode of their divine helper; and finally an exceptionally magnificent rotunda or tholos. Inside and out its wall was surrounded by a ring of columns, while in the middle of the floor there was an opening above the basement, which consisted of concentric circular ambulatories linked in each case by a gap in the wall. What purpose this substructure served still remains a mystery. Were Asclepius's snakes with their healing powers kept there? Did the sick perhaps have to walk round these ambulatories in order to obtain their share of the god's salutary influence? We do not know, any more than we could identify the 'abaton' in which the invalids lay down for their curative sleep. Their number must at an early date already have been very considerable. Both the construction of a hostelry with 160 rooms and the abundance of the offerings that accumulated in the sanctuary bear witness to this. The inflow continued until the triumph of Christianity, to which the Asclepieum of Epidaurus also fell a victim.

Not until the end of the fourth century B.C. was a small Ionic temple with a large altar set before it constructed upon a mountain slope on the island of Cos, at some distance from the city. Previously, which means in the famous Hippocrates's lifetime (about 450/370), Apollo, the god of healing, and his son had only been worshipped in a cypress grove. However, the second century was no longer content with the modest building set on an artificial terrace; higher up the slope another, larger area was levelled off, and to it a broad flight of steps interrupted by a gateway led up from the earlier site. On the new terrace, a marble Doric temple arose in the middle of a broad court, which was planted with cypresses and surrounded on three sides by long stoas for patients to lie in. Here too there stood a sacred fountain, its water conveyed from an enclosed spring nearly 220 yards above. The god was honoured with gymnastic and musical contests at the Great Asclepieia held once every four years, but their site can no longer be identified. Probably already being celebrated in Hippocrates's day, the festival of the 'Receiving of the Staff', which involved discovering a staff of Asclepius afresh every year, was no doubt at one time held in the grove, then later on in the court planted with cypresses. Yet even over and beyond its importance as a place of healing and a festival centre, the Asclepieum of Cos enjoyed a high reputation in the Greek and Roman world. Offerings from princes and private persons as well as stones inscribed with religious and secular laws or plebiscites filled the holy precinct. Since many states recognized its sacrosanctity (asylie) by treaty, and Tiberius later confirmed it, Greeks and Orientals alike deposited their money in this safe spot. Earthquakes that repeatedly visited Cos were unable to do permanent harm to the lustre of the sanctuary, which in Roman times was again enlarged through the addition of various buildings.

The Asclepieum situated not far from the city of Pergamum also goes back to the fourth century, and the god's cult is supposed to have been brought to it from Epidaurus by a man cured there. In the precinct, extended during the following period under the aegis of the Pergamene kings, not only was Asclepius the 'Saviour' (Soter) worshipped, but —as at Epidaurus—also Apollo and Hygieia, the goddess of health. Besides a sacred fountain, the sanctuary also had other wells for ablutions and special rooms for the 'incubation' sleep. Though not neglected during the first three centuries of Roman rule (from 133 B.C.), it was scarcely enriched; but when the mystical tendency in the second century A.D. brought with it an increased desire for miraculous cures, the site was developed most magnificently. Anyone who came to it from the city along the sacred way, which in those days was flanked by arcades, first crossed a court surrounded with colonnades. Then he passed through a magnificent gate building into the spacious square, which was bordered by stoas on all except the entrance side. Here, to the left of the visitor, stood a round temple similar to the Pantheon at Rome, and since the healing god's power seemed to match that of Zeus, it was dedicated to Zeus-Asclepius. Nearby there was a somewhat later rotunda with six large apses, which seems, at any rate on its ground floor, to have served for ablutions and remedial bathing. A long tunnel connected it to the sacred spring, which, with its beautiful architectural setting, stood in the middle of the sanctuary as a whole. Though the rooms for curative sleep situated next to the spring were extended, in other respects the old cult site remained unchanged; instead, a theatre was laid out behind the north stoa, and at the west end a library—a commodity also possessed by the great thermae in Rome during this period.

These three Asclepius sanctuaries differed from each other with regard to their most flourishing period, which for Epidaurus came during the fourth century, for Cos in Hellenistic times, and for Pergamum in the later imperial age, as well as with regard to their treatment. Whereas Epidaurus was entirely devoted to miraculous cures, and to that extent recalls places like Lourdes, it is clear that on Cos, the seat of the famous school for physicians, people got better as a result of medical attention. Yet in this too, the god was active. For just as the poet sang what Apollo or the Muses had taught him, so the physician acquired his skill from Asclepius, who interpreted the symptoms to him and caused him to adopt the right counter-measures. At Pergamum, however, miraculous healing—whether in sleep or by some other method—and medical care were combined; and it was there that Galen, the regenerator of Hippocratic medicine, lived during the period when the sanctuary underwent its imposing elaboration. Not without irony, the rhetorician Aelius Aristides, who was a contemporary of Galen's, tells of how at the god's command he had in an icy north wind to smear himself with mud from the holy spring, run three times round the temple, and then wash at the spring; and of how, covered with mud, he had to lie down in a stoa, while invoking Zeus. Two other patients did not hold out to the end of the cure, while Aristides himself was only restored to health after thirteen years, by reason of having repeated the course many times. If, besides the nature-treatment itself, belief in Asclepius's power, which the Cos physicians also neither could nor would do without, was very important to the success of this type of procedure, it was all the more so in the case of the miraculous cures effected while people slept, such as occurred in the Pergamene incubation rooms, but above all at Epidaurus. Here, ablutions at the holy spring did not assist the therapy but were intended to make the sick ready to receive the divine influence. For whoever wanted to be succoured by Asclepius had to be pure in body and also in soul—in the sense of being genuinely devout. Probably he had already spent quite a long time in the stoas looking out at the helper's abode, before he lay down, and, in his sleep, watched how the god removed the ailment from his body. This certainly did not take place in the stoas, but in some closed room. On waking up, he felt himself to be cured, unless he had only been told in his dream what he must do in order to be sure of getting better. There can be no doubt that in many cases the illness really did disappear, or at least diminish. It was faith that brought the return to health; and to strengthen it, inscribed stone slabs were set up, on which those seeking to be cured could read of the wonders that Asclepius had worked for people who had put their trust in him unquestioningly.

These accounts run something like this: While he was sleeping, Pamphaes saw a face. He dreamed that the god opened its mouth, kept the jaws apart with a wedge, and removed from the mouth the destructive ulcer. Thereupon, Pamphaes was well again. The boy Euphanes, suffering from a stone, went to sleep in the healing room. He dreamed that the god appeared to him, and said: 'What will you give me if I make you fit?' Euphanes replied: 'Ten marbles,' at which the god laughed, and promised to set him free. Next morning, he came out restored to health. Arybbas's wife Andromache, who had come because she wanted children, dreamed in the sanctuary that a handsome boy uncovered her, and the god touched her with his hand. Afterwards, she had a son by Arybbas. A man whose body was paralysed dreamed in the healing room that the god took him by the hand, led him to the sacred hearth, and ordered him to warm himself at the fire. At sunrise he did so, and was cured. Stories of this kind are associated with others that reveal the effect of a shock, as in the case of a dumb girl who regained her speech on being terrified by a snake crawling from a tree. Other descriptions suggest that treatment occurred during sleep, as when, for example, a man who had been wounded below the eye by a spear-point dreamed that the god dripped the juice of a medicinal herb into his eye. It cannot, however, be accepted that major abdominal operations, which some patients are alleged to have seen the god perform, were really undertaken at the period when these tales of cures were recorded. Finally, Asclepius's sacred animals, particularly snakes, are also supposed to have healed people by licking the diseased parts or biting open an abscess.

In return for his aid, the god demanded sacrifices and other gifts. Occasionally in the accounts that the priests set down on stone, Asclepius presses for the due payment to be made, or, if it is withheld, annuls the cure. However, most people who had been

XI   Bassae. Temple of Apollo Epicurius

restored to health no doubt gladly presented their thank-offering, which by preference took the form of a cock. Socrates, indeed, ordered one to be sacrificed to Asclepius for his release from the pain of being alive. In accordance with a very ancient custom known to us from places of Christian pilgrimage, many also gave replicas of the healed limbs or little paintings showing the miraculous deliverance. Anyone who possessed the means expressed his gratitude through expensive offerings. A lively idea of what gifts of this kind were to be seen as early as about 250 in the then still modest Asclepieum of Cos is given by the writer Herodas, who was born on the island, in a conversation that he makes two simple women hold. They have come with a little votive picture, and now naïvely but realistically pass judgement on the works of art that they look at, including a painting by Apelles. Even during the subsequent ages of more shallow religious feeling, it was not only among the lower classes that the desire to seek a cure at one of the divine helper's sanctuaries remained active. Enlarged with new installations, Asclepius's cult centres were better able to retain their importance than many great sites dedicated to other gods. For the deity who personally, or through his servants the physicians, freed people from bodily torment was indispensable. The leaning towards mysticism in the second century A.D. caused Epidaurus to enjoy a second peak of prosperity, while to the sanctuary at Pergamum it brought its actual prime. Long after this, however, credulous people still went on seeking the aid of Asclepius at these places, as also at Cos, and continued until the Christians' Saviour and his wonder-working assistants supplanted the old healer.

LOCAL SANCTUARIES

Everything tells the initiated beholder
Of the presence of a god. SCHILLER

Even when their fame and glory spread far and wide, the cult sites hitherto discussed were all primarily the religious focus of a region, an island, or an area otherwise defined by nature. Many other sanctuaries of this type could have been mentioned in their company, such as the Artemisium of Ephesus, the temple of Apollo at Thermum in Aetolia, or the temple of Hera Lacinia on Cape Colonne south of Croton in South Italy. However, most of the innumerable holy places outside the cities had only local importance; they were confined in themselves and in their influence to a spot where a deity's power could be directly experienced. Who could possibly name all the caves, jutting cliffs, trees, and springs beside which a god or hero was worshipped? Here we shall consider only three sites, the impressive ruins of which still show how the divine revealed itself to the Greeks in nature, inducing them to raise a temple.

XII Aegina. Temple of Aphaea

From the mountains of south-western Arcadia, the winds sweep down to the Ionian sea, and bring fresh, wholesome air to the more low-lying places. Near the hamlet of Bassae (the glens), at a spot where immediately below the topmost summit one first becomes aware of these winds, a small dwelling was built as far back as the seventh century for Apollo the bringer of health. Not long after, his sister Artemis, the mistress of the mountain forests, and for unknown reasons Aphrodite too, received similar abodes. When later on, during the first decade of the Peloponnesian war, an epidemic that visited the town of Phigalia near the sea was clearly driven out by the mountain winds, the inhabitants thanked Apollo the helper (Epicurius) for this by erecting a large temple to him on the ridge near his old precinct. A connoisseur who lived during the imperial age considered that, in the entire Peloponnese, only the temple of Athena at Tegea surpassed it with regard to the beauty of the stones and the way they were put together. The creator of the Bassae temple, distinguished by a novel arrangement of the interior, is said to have been none less than Ictinus, the architect of the Parthenon. With decorated metopes at both ends and a splendid frieze running round inside the naos walls, the magnificent building stood in its far-off mountain solitude, a witness to a small town's sense of sacrifice and the sublime artistic ability devoted even to fashioning a sanctuary of only local importance.

AEGINA

Since remote times, an altar of Zeus had stood on the towering mountain heights of Aegina, an island that early on became a sea-power and grew rich as a trading centre. To all who dwelled near the Saronic Gulf and to all seafarers, 'the mountain', as people simply called it, was visible as a sacred central point, with the result that the sky god was worshipped there as 'pan-Hellenic'. Pindar styled Aegina 'the twinkling star of Hellenic Zeus'. On its north coast, however, almost nine miles from the ancient town, lay another sanctuary upon a wooded ridge. There perhaps in a neighbouring cave, people were by the second millennium already worshipping a nature deity, who in Greek times bore the name Aphaea. Being similar to Artemis and the Cretan Dictynna, she was sometimes equated with them, and though a mountain and hunting goddess she also protected the shipping that made an important contribution to Aegina's prosperity. Hence she was well qualified to become the island's patroness, and during the sixth century, Aegina's most flourishing period, she received a temple, which round about 500 was replaced by a more magnificent edifice. Of this, a considerable portion is still standing, and other parts could

XIII   Cape Sunium and Temple of Poseidon

be re-erected. With its altar set before the goddess's dwelling, a building for the cult utensils and the enclosing wall through which a propylaeum leads into the precinct, the site presents a clear picture of a middle-sized sanctuary. Every year, a procession made its way up from the town to celebrate the festival of the goddess. Instead of Aphaea, the renowned pediment sculptures show Athena controlling the fortunes of the warriors in the famous Trojan war celebrated by Homer, as well as in an earlier one; but this must not mislead us into thinking that the old patroness Aphaea was displaced by or merged into Athena. Not until later, and rarely even then, were the scenes represented on a temple's pediments directly related to the god of the sanctuary.

SUNIUM

In former times, the sea around the southern tip of Attica was often whipped up by storms, just as it is today. Here Poseidon seemed to be present in all his might, here frightened sailors prayed to him, and here atop Cape Sunium, in the bay of which vessels sought shelter, the powerful god had to be put in a friendly mood by means of sacrifices and offerings. Colossal stone statues of youths were erected up there even before a temple was built in the sixth century. The latter appears to have been destroyed by the Persians in 480. Its replacement, which was constructed of bright marble during the Periclean age, shone far out to sea over the sacred precinct's walls, just as the view from it extends to the Cyclades and the Peloponnesian coast. Since the time of Lord Byron, who scratched his name on one of the columns that are still standing today, visitors have continued to be ravished by the harmonious combination of imposing scenery and most noble architecture. Nevertheless, with respect to what has moved people in modern times, it should no more be forgotten here than at other Greek cult centres where similar feelings are aroused, that the temple was not raised at this spot on account of the wonderful position, or so beautifully fashioned out of regard for it, but because Poseidon, the lord of the sea, displayed his divine power in the vicinity of the wave-lashed headland. Where the religious inducement existed, temples almost as beautiful were also built for gods in unimpressive places and inside urban settlements.

76

III

URBAN SANCTUARIES

CITADEL-SANCTUARIES

It is clear that the word 'polis' once designated the fortress-like settlement characteristic of the Greek ruling class in the second millennium. Not until later did the stronghold, around which a town had meanwhile grown up, come to be called an 'acropolis' (topmost city). Within it, as is natural, lay the most ancient sanctuaries, which often dated from Mycenaean times. Not that temples would have been raised there as long ago as that, for such buildings were put up neither by the Mycenaean Greeks nor the Minoan Cretans; but on altars, in house chapels or on hallowed sites, sacrifices had been made and rites observed since early times. After the turmoil of the Dorian invasion, life gradually moved down into the lower town, and this move became complete when in many places at the turn from the eighth to the seventh century the monarchy ceased to exist. Then it was almost only the old gods of the community who remained as residents of the citadel. During an age when wars between Greek and Greek were customarily won or lost in pitched battles out in the open, and hardly ever led to sieges, the walled acropolis at best became important if a member of the local aristocracy proclaimed himself tyrant of the city, invested the citadel with his troops, and established himself there. Such tyrannies were, however, temporary phenomena, and, besides, the autocrat quite often endeavoured to win the favour of the gods who protected the city by adding to or embellishing their sanctuaries. High above the human dwellings, these deities had their home within the citadel, which was capable of developing into the polis's great religious focus to the point where the *enceinte* constructed for defence could seem more like the wall enclosing a sacred precinct. Nowhere is this more clearly and nobly apparent than on the acropolis hill of Athens.

THE ATHENIAN ACROPOLIS

O gleaming, violet-wreathed, oft-sung, glorious Athens, bastion of Hellas, God-favoured city! PINDAR

As early as the latter half of the second millennium, the rock that rises up precipitously on the southern edge of the city of Athens already bore a stately citadel resembling that of Mycenae or Tiryns. It would seem that Athena the 'palace goddess', who gave the place its name, was being worshipped by then, as also, beside a sacred mark in the rocky ground, Poseidon the earth-shaker and, near him, the earth god Erechtheus. At the time when the *Odyssey* was created, Erechtheus, who probably early on came to be identified with Poseidon, already had a 'permanent home', which may have been the old megaron of the 'Mycenaean' citadel or a temple built over this hall. Athena also dwelt there near him. The rivalry between these two gods is revealed by the legend that tells of their contest for possession of Attica. Poseidon-Erechtheus tried to make it his by thrusting his trident into the rock, and causing a saline spring to appear; but Athena planted the olive tree, and thereby won the day. To appease him, people worshipped the vanquished deity literally next door to Athena, in the home mentioned above, and also in the 100-ft.-long temple (Hecatompedon) that was probably built on its site by the Pisistratids (560/ 510), and in any case was surrounded by them with a peristyle. However, just as Athena dominated the sculptural groups in the marble pediments, so she did the citadel in general, where as the virgin goddess (Parthenos) she had already acquired a second, equally big temple, which—the earliest Parthenon—was dedicated to her alone. It was in her honour that the Athenians held the most important festival on the Acropolis— the Panathenaea, which since 566 had been celebrated every fourth year with special pomp as the 'Great Panathenaea'. To her belonged the statues of maidens and other offerings that from the beginning of the sixth century onwards filled the level space around the two temples in ever-increasing numbers. Yet even this was not enough: as the divine embodiment of victory (Nike), the goddess received a third abode, which was constructed on a projection of rock above the way up to the citadel. Thus the mistress of the city (Polias) held sway over her Athens, together with her father Zeus, who also protected the city (Polieus), and who possessed an altar at the highest point of the

78

XIV Athens. Acropolis seen from the Areopagus

Acropolis. Beside them and Poseidon-Erechtheus, Artemis, who had a home in the Attic deme of Brauron, seemed like a stranger. It was a native of that township, the tyrant Pisistratus, who established for Artemis Brauronia a precinct of her own on the Acropolis, the seat of his court, and the goddess retained it permanently.

It appears to have been the glorious victory of Marathon (490) that afforded the occasion both for providing the entrance to the citadel, which since the end of the tyranny (510) once more belonged to the gods alone, with the monumental gateway known as the Propylaea, and for replacing the temple of Athena Parthenos with a huge marble edifice. Work had started on both buildings when the Persians arrived, and razed not only them but the whole citadel to the ground. Makeshift repairs may have been carried out in the following period on a few buildings, particularly the so-called 'old temple' of Athena and that of Erechtheus, containing Athena Polias's cult image. Larger, new ones were not begun, however, until three centuries later, after the entire citadel had been enclosed by Cimon with a wall made of well-jointed ashlars, into which old column drums were inserted as a memorial, and after the level surface of the citadel had been extended by heaping up rubble within this wall. Since old fragments of building and damaged or ruined votive monuments were used for this, the religious obligation not to remove even the wrecked property of a god from its precinct was satisfied as well. The decades between 450 and 430, when Athens was at its most powerful, were those during which, under the aegis of Pericles, the citadel rose again, grander than ever before. In 447, work started under the direction of the architects Ictinus and Callicrates on the wonderful new Parthenon, for which Phidias and his assistants created the unique decoration of the frieze, the metopes adorned with reliefs, and the pediment sculpture. Long before the end of the fifteen years (to 432) that it took to complete the mighty temple, the magnificent Propylaea, designed by Mnesicles, had been begun. On account of its awkward site, the gateway cost even more to build than did the Parthenon, which it equalled both in beauty and technical perfection. The outbreak of the Peloponnesian war (431) and objections raised against encroaching on neighbouring ground regarded as sacrosanct prevented the large flanking buildings provided for in the plan from being raised; but the Propylaea itself, the most solemnly impressive gateway that a sanctuary ever received, was completed.

In these two buildings, Athens at the apogee of its historical course raised a stone monument to what in theory it aimed to be, and for a brief space of time actually was. Strong, pregnant contrasts that had for generations moved the people of Attica blend in natural harmony. The force and gravity of the homeland Greeks, to which the Doric style corresponded, are combined with Ionic grace and ease; the individual structural member accommodates itself as a matter of course to the organic unity of the whole, just as, despite all his individuality, the Attic citizen took his place as a member of his polis, without which he would not have existed. Indeed, in the calculated balance of load and

XV   Athens, Acropolis. Propylaea seen from the east, with Salamis in the background

support, of practical purpose and ideal meaning, fundamental human tensions find their release. All this happened, moreover, under the banner of the deity in whose honour countless Athenians carried out arduous tasks for scant reward. Jointly with slaves, great artists gave of their best, and stonemasons devoted their amazing talent even to dressing stones that would never be seen by human beings, but only by the goddess. However, she, Pallas Athena, grew to be the divine personification of the polis that she guarded and loved, sharing in its power over the island and coastal cities of the Aegean. Since 454 she had in the Parthenon looked after the maritime league's treasure, up to then deposited in Apollo's sanctuary on Delos; and in return for the protection that she provided, she received a fee out of the tributes arriving every year. Beyond that, money from the league's revenues was used to pay for the extremely expensive buildings that were dedicated to her.

The simple cult image in the 'old temple' no longer sufficed for *this* Athena. For the Parthenon, Phidias created out of gold and ivory an overwhelmingly magnificent statue of the goddess, showing her in all her imposing grandeur with a helmet on her head, a shield at her side, and a winged Nike on her hand. Phidias also produced the standing figure, over 23 ft. tall, of Athena the champion (Promachos), which anyone entering through the Propylaea saw before him; in the sun, the golden point of its spear shone out over the sea. The 'old temple' was demolished, however, so as to make room for a new building intended not just to shelter the Polias in her venerable cult image and Poseidon-Erechtheus, but also to enclose the very ancient holy sites that lay within this area. Probably already projected by Pericles but not begun till about 420, the so-called Erechtheum was put up at great expense while the Peloponnesian war was raging, though a west wing that seems to have been planned never came into being. The building as it still stands today contains the cult rooms of Athena and Poseidon-Erechtheus, covers the grave of the former Attic earth god Kekrops with the famous Porch of the Caryatids, and, with its north porch, extends over the mark made by Poseidon's trident, above which a gap was left in the paving and roof because the sign had to be under the open sky. How the olive-tree planted by Athena and the old precinct of Pandrosos, the goddess of the dew, were to have been included on the west, we do not know.

Like the Erechtheum, the grace and delicacy of which contrast wonderfully with the Parthenon's noble dignity, the little temple of Athena Nike on a projecting bastion beside the way up to the citadel is an edifice in the Ionic style. Though the decision to erect it had been made in 449, it was not completed until during the great war. We can only guess at the appearance of other buildings from Periclean or post-Periclean times, such as the Chalcotheca in which bronze offerings were stored. Likewise, nothing but the cuttings in the rocky ground for their plinths bear witness to the many statues, the most famous of which was Phidias's Athena (Lemnia), dedicated by the inhabitants of the island of Lemnos. By no stretch of the imagination can one picture the forest of sculptured

XVI   Athens, Acropolis. Parthenon seen from the north-west

figures and the splendour of the buildings that from the middle of the fifth century onwards surrounded the Athenian when he entered the sacred citadel, or, during the Panathenaea, marched up the steep road to the Propylaea in the procession from the city. Not only did these buildings shine with the radiant white of the marble, but they also glowed with the strong colours of their paintwork. In the frieze round the cella of the Parthenon, Phidias and his assistants represented the Panathenaea with matchless skill as the most beautiful thing that Athena received from her city. To look at this, the goddess's high festival, can still give us the strongest impression of the extravagant devotion that, upon the Acropolis, fell to Athena's lot.

Hekatombaion 28 (end of July) was regarded as the day on which Athena had been born, springing forth fully armed from Zeus's head. This event, which had deeply impressed all the gods, was visible to everyone on the east pediment of the Parthenon. Every year, people celebrated the day with a festival for the management of which a special committee was appointed. After a preliminary nocturnal ceremony, a procession advanced up to the holy places within the citadel. Sacrifices were made, sacrificial feasts held, a war-dance (pyrrhiche) performed, and the fame of the goddess celebrated by competing choirs. With these observances on the Acropolis were associated chariot-races of a special kind, which took place in the stadium lying well to the west. On each of the chariots that hurled along the course, there stood beside the driver a man who, shortly before they reached the post, leaped down and ran back along the stadium. Whoever crossed the starting-line first received the prize for himself and for the charioteer who had shared in his victory. The fact that nothing further has come down to us about the annual festival is understandable enough, since it was entirely overshadowed by the 'Great Panathenaea', which was founded in 566, and occurred every fourth year in celebration of the goddess's birthday.

This, the most brilliant among Athens's many festivals of the gods, took almost a week. The first part, up to the eve of the birthday, was characterized by musical, gymnastic and horse-racing contests. Not only choirs now competed in singing Athena's praise; to honour her, rhapsodes had since the time of Pisistratus vied with each other in reciting the Homeric epics, and, since Pericles, cithara players and flautists had entered the lists as well. On each occasion, the five best choirs or artists enjoyed the distinction of receiving money prizes, while the outright winners got a gold or silver wreath. Yet however much these performances might delight her, the city's protectress was even fonder of the contests in which her people showed their healthy strength and martial ability. During the gymnastic events, which were supervised by ten judges, boys, youths and men competed separately for the prize in running, wrestling, boxing, the pentathlum, and the pancratium. This prize took the form of large and splendid earthen vessels (amphorae) filled with oil from Athena's sacred trees, and the competitor who came first got five times as many as the runner-up. A boy could thus acquire up to fifty jars, youths

84

XVII   Athens, Acropolis. Erechtheum seen from the south-east

about sixty, and men apparently even more, so that the economic value alone of the prizes won was considerable. Many Panathenaic prize amphorae, such as were distributed in hundreds every fourth year, have been preserved. They bear the image of the armed goddess, attacking impetuously, and the words: 'From the contests at Athens'.

There was also a wider variety of horse events at the great festival than at the annual celebrations. Ceremonial and war chariots lined up, horsemen in full armour galloped down the course, and others rode past a shield that they had to pierce with a spear. Here again, amphorae full of oil formed the prize for those who came first and second. The team that won in the war-dance, on the other hand, received a valuable ox, which was intended for sacrificing and then feasting upon. Finally, the group that had proved itself the best in the 'manliness contest' was awarded a shield. For this event, each of the ten *phylae* into which the Attic citizenry was divided chose a team distinguished by the size, strength, and handsomeness of its members. Her protégés' physical beauty and militant bearings were thus offered as a gift to the goddess, who took as much pleasure in it as her father Zeus did in the flower of Greek manhood at Olympia. The Great Panathenaea's quadrennial cycle itself recalls the Olympic games, and the large number and variety of the gymnastic and equestrian contests, as well as the fact that non-Athenians could be admitted, strengthen one's impression that the Attic state wanted, by means of these celebrations, to compete with the high festival held beside the Alpheus. And indeed, like the conscious stressing of the Eleusinian mysteries' pan-Hellenic character, the Panathenaea probably was meant to demonstrate to all Greeks that Athens was the 'Hellas of Hellas'.

When, on the last day of the contests and eve of the goddess's birthday, darkness fell upon the city, the nocturnal celebrations (pannychis) began. Since 420 their climax had been provided by a torch race from the Academy grove outside the walls, through the potters' quarter (Cerameicus), across the agora, and up to the citadel. Once again, the ten *phylae* had selected teams, which during the race passed the torch from hand to hand until it reached the last man. Whichever of these final ten runners was the first to arrive at the altar of Athena Polias before the 'old temple' and light the logs set upon it, gained an elegant water-jug as a prize—though naturally not just he but his team, together with the *phyle* that had chosen it, counted as victor. Then the first light of dawn on the greatest of the feast-days called the people into the Cerameicus to assemble for the stately procession that was to bring the goddess's old cult image a new robe (peplos).

As long ago as the autumn of the previous year, the authorities had decided about designs for the fabric, which had to show Athena and Zeus fighting the giants. Since then, two maidens specially picked for the task had been working away at it. Now that the morning of the great feast-day had arrived, the saffron peplos was fastened like a sail to the spars of a ship set on wheels, which bore witness to the city goddess's command of the sea. The throng of those who that year filled a public office formed up to bring it through the streets of Athens to the Acropolis. They included the nine archons, the goddess's

86

XVIII   Athens, Acropolis. Erechtheum seen from the south-west before sunset

treasurers, the college of the ten strategi, the heads of smaller sections of the conscripted citizens, and many others—all decked out in honour of Athena. A special escort surrounded the ship, while the 100 oxen for the hecatomb were led by the priests and their assistants. As the Parthenon frieze still shows, old men chosen for their good looks marched along in the procession holding olive branches, and it also included girls who carried the utensils of the cult in baskets. They were followed by chariots and young riders on their fiery steeds, among whom the victors in the horse-races had pride of place, just as all the others who had won a prize at the contests on the preceding days were included in the column. However, it was not only Attic citizens who took part; foreigners living in Athens and festival embassies from the cities of the league and other friendly communities also presented the goddess with sacrificial gifts, utensils, or vessels. By honouring her, they also paid their respects to the powerful state. With the people of Attica swarming round it and rejoicing, the procession, which heralds strove to keep in order, thus made its way slowly up to the citadel. There, before the eyes of the gods who appear on the frieze as spectators of the sacred action, Athena's old cult image was clad in the new robe. Then the enormous hecatomb sacrifice took place, after which all the citizens fed on the animals' flesh. With that, the greatest of the feast-days ended. It seems to have been followed on Hekatombaion 29 by a regatta of ships from the separate *phylae*, and this, at which the entrants could hope to win a sum of money and a sacrificial banquet, brought the Great Panathenaea to a close.

One can understand the Athenians clinging doggedly for centuries to the festival that did most to enhance at once the glory of the goddess and that of her city, even when, after the breakdown of Attic power at the end of the Peloponnesian war, the influx of visitors from the Aegean area grew very much smaller, and the difficult financial situation quite often made it necessary to forgo much of the pomp. The Acropolis received no new buildings till right into Roman imperial times, and it hardly needed them. No longer did a rich league treasure lie in the rear section of the Parthenon, and no longer did strong political ambitions actuate the citizens, who in Demosthenes's day could only look across from their meeting-place on the Pnyx with melancholy or romantic rapture at the stone witnesses of bygone grandeur. Despite many outbursts of patriotism, they adapted themselves more and more to the new balance of power, and at the close of the fourth century carried their devotion to the diadochos Antigonus and his son Demetrius to the point of having their portraits woven into Athena's sacred robe, which until then had only shown her and her father Zeus. During the centuries that followed, the city of Athens was exposed to many storms, but the Acropolis remained essentially intact until the local tyrant Lachares despoiled it of offerings shortly after 300. Reverence and admiration for the site, that was not just religiously sanctified but hallowed by a glorious tradition and the noblest creations of art, even restrained the conqueror Sulla from plundering it, although he violated other Greek sanctuaries without hesitation. While

XIX   Rhodes. Acropolis of Lindus

it is true that account had to be taken of the imperial cult by raising an altar to Augustus and Roma before the entrance of the Parthenon, the setting up of new votive monuments and construction of a broad flight of marble steps up to the Propylaea testify to the veneration that Athens and its goddess continued to enjoy even in the first centuries of the Christian era. Not until about 430 was Phidias's much-admired cult image carried off to Constantinople by Theodosius II. To a great extent, the two temples in the citadel survived intact for more than another thousand years. They were only disfigured by additional structures when the Parthenon was turned by the Christians into a church and by the Turks into a mosque; and when the Erechtheum was likewise first transformed into a church, then later into a harem. A similar fate befell the Propylaea, which served as a palace from the close of the fourteenth century. The fact that in the seventeenth century the Propylaea and the Parthenon contained a powder-magazine proved fatal: lightning blew up the Propylaea magazine (1645), and artillery fire by the Venetians that of the Parthenon (1687), causing the central part of the temple to collapse. During the same period, the small Nike temple was demolished as well, and only in recent times has it been reconstructed out of its original stones. The Erechtheum is the best preserved of the buildings, though admittedly its interior walls are all gone. All the same, even in the ruins that we now behold upon the Acropolis, there still lives the spirit of Athens's great age, when a community of devout citizens offered their gods not only sacrifices and feasts but works of an unrivalled artistic and technical perfection.

OTHER CITADEL-SANCTUARIES

O mighty Zeus and you, Guardian Gods of our City!
AESCHYLUS

On countless citadel hills above Greek cities, deities—particularly Zeus and Athena— were worshipped as divine protectors of the polis. At Acragas (Agrigento) in Sicily, the cathedral situated at the highest point has to all appearances taken the place of a temple dedicated to Zeus Polieus.

He was also worshipped on the island of Rhodes, from which the Greek colonists had come to Acragas. Three independent communities had at one time existed on the island, but in 408 they united to form a single state with newly founded Rhodes as its capital. They still retained their own citadels and citadel-sanctuaries, however. Thus it is not just the heights above the city of Rhodes that display the foundations and column drums of temples of Zeus Polieus and Athena Polias from Hellenistic times; similar cult sites are also present on the acropolis of each of the three older settlements: Lindus, Camirus,

XX   Acragas (Agrigento). Southern city wall and temples. Left Temple D, right Temple F, extreme left Temple A

and Ialysus. Indeed, the rock of Lindus, towering up above the open sea and harbour bay, provides the most impressive example of an urban citadel-sanctuary, after the Athenian Acropolis. As elsewhere, Athena had taken the place there of a local deity, Lindia, to whom a temple constructed in the sixth century may still have belonged. Although the new building put up for Athena Lindia after a fire about 330 received a gold-and-ivory cult image—probably after the example of the Parthenon—this was not so big as one would have expected in view of the high reputation enjoyed by the mistress of Lindus far beyond the island itself. A temple chronicle written in accordance with statements by local historians enumerates the most important of the offerings that since early times worshippers from far and near had, or were alleged to have, presented, and it also tells of the miracles performed by the goddess for her city. Like Rhodes as a whole, Lindus experienced its most flourishing period during the early Hellenistic age. About the turn of the third and the second century, the approach to the upper terrace of the acropolis, where the temple stood, was provided with a flight of steps that began in the middle section of a stoa lying at right angles to it. At the top of the steps, one entered the colonnaded forecourt of the temple through magnificent propylaea.

The top of the hill of Pergamum, the lower parts of which were covered by the settlement in pre-Roman times, appears less as the citadel of a polis, though it was once this too, than as the residence of a prince. Shortly before 280, Philetaerus seized possession of the stronghold. Thereafter, it remained for one and a half centuries the residence of the Attalid dynasty founded by him, for, like many Greek tyrants in earlier days, these kings made their home on the acropolis beside the city's gods, taking special care, of course, of their sanctuaries. Philetaerus himself built a temple for Athena the protectress, and the next ruler but one, Attalus I (reigned 241/197), worshipped her as the bringer of victory (Nikephoros). To thank her for helping him to defeat the Galatians in a great battle near the sources of the Caicus, he dedicated to her monuments of this glorious deed as well as a special festival called the Nikephoria. His son Eumenes II (reigned 197/159), under whom the Pergamene monarchy reached the height of its power and splendour in close connexion with Rome, had two-storied stoas built along three sides of the sacred precinct, on the edge of which the temple dominated the steep rocky slope. In this way, a spacious court was created, with Attalus's victory monuments as its focus. It is true that the whole scheme was still devoted to Athena; but the central position of the monuments, the replicas of captured arms along the upper-story balustrades, the almost museum-like arrangements of important works of art from earlier times in the stoas, and the adding of a library all gave the ensemble too much the character of a grandiose display of Hellenistic sovereign power for it still to express gratefully pious veneration of the goddess. The same spirit is revealed in the reorganization of the Nikephoria festival and raising of the famous altar of Zeus, which Eumenes took in hand after his own successful feats of arms in 182. Occurring every other year, was festival the celebrated with musical

XXI   Pergamum. Looking back towards the Theatre and the small Ionic temple from the
ancient road leading to the temple of Demeter

contests that were supposed to match in style and prestige those at Delphi, and gymnastic contests and horse-races meant to equal those at Olympia. The king sunned himself in its splendour, and the many festival embassies that attended it undoubtedly paid homage just as much to him as to the goddess. Even the mighty altar of Zeus, built in the manner of the big early Ionic altars with a broad flight of steps and a court enclosed by porticoes and containing the actual place of sacrifice, was at the same time a monument to the glory of sovereigns. Its eloquent frieze extolled the Pergamene kings' victories over the Galatians in terms of the combat between the gods and giants, and Eumenes likewise had sculptured groups telling directly or through mythology of the famous battles against the Galatians set up on long bases in the porticoes. None the less, both the Greek city deities, the disposing Zeus and his militant daughter, had their special sites close together in the princely citadel of Pergamum, and their association became still more intimate when, under Eumenes's brother and successor Attalus II (reigned 159/139), Zeus joined Athena in her temple. During the long era of Roman rule, which in 133 B.C. replaced that of the Attalids, only one single new and splendid temple was constructed in the acropolis, which now belonged to the gods alone. This was the temple of the emperor Trajan, crowning the top of the hill. Yet it was the altar of Zeus that made the greatest impression on the people of this period too. The adherents of Greek religion saw it as the most imposing of the places where sacrifices were made to the sky god, the cultured as a work of art of the highest order—indeed, as one of the wonders of the world; but to the many Christians in Asia Minor it was 'Satan's seat', as it is called near the beginning of the Revelation of St. John.

Not always did the earliest, walled settlement, and later the citadel, stand upon a commanding hill. Syracuse, together with the associated island of Ortygia off the mainland, provides the example of a low-lying citadel protected by the sea, from which tyrants like Dionysius and Hieron II could govern the city that had long ago moved on to the coastal plain and the hills bordering it to the north. Here again, the principal sanctuary was dedicated to Athena the protectress—and, indeed, had been so since early times. A new temple erected for her during the fifth century was transformed after over 1,000 years into a Christian cathedral, and today the Baroque edifice still clothes the upright columns, which not long ago it was possible to uncover in part and make visible again. As already mentioned, Zeus Polieus held court on the highest part of the acropolis at Acragas, while Athena was probably worshipped somewhat lower down in a temple that was also later turned into a church. Though no traces have been found of a cult site dedicated to Zeus the protector of cities on Ortygia's low-lying plateau, not only Athena had possessed a temple there since far-off times, but also Apollo the divine leader of colonizing expeditions, to whom Syracuse as well certainly owed its foundation.

Finally, we may include among the citadel-sanctuaries the group of temples on the hill forming the original site of the city of Selinus. This spot, well to the west along the

94

XXII   Selinus, Acropolis. Temple C seen from the north-west

south Sicilian coast and hence in the immediate neighbourhood of the region controlled by Carthage, was settled by people from Megara Hyblaea, a Greek colony in the eastern part of the island. They built a wall round the hill rising above two natural harbours, with the result that a fortified town grew up, but it soon proved to be too small. The residential areas were therefore shifted more and more to the plateau adjoining the site on the north, while the original town took on the character of an acropolis, a third of which came to be covered with sanctuaries. No less than four temples were raised during the fifth century on the part of the hill near the sea, enclosed together in pairs in a walled precinct, which one entered through a propylaeum. As we unfortunately have no idea at all which gods these temples belonged to—Heracles, who appears on the city's coins, Athena, Apollo, and also Demeter and Persephone would seem to be the most likely candidates—the individual buildings have been designated by letters. The oldest of them is the now partly re-erected temple C occupying the highest part of the hill; like its neighbour, the somewhat later temple D, it dates from the sixth century. Besides the remarkable narrow, elongated cella encircled by a rather wide ambulatory, the features distinguishing it and a series of other Sicilian and South Italian temples are the unusually deep entrance portico, the seclusion of the vestibule or pronaos, which one entered through a large door, and the fact that after the naos—which contained a place for sacrifice but not, as elsewhere, a cult image—there followed a third room called the adytum, which did harbour the god's statue. On the other hand, it had no rear room opening out at the back (opisthodomus). If the temples of the mother-country were houses for the cult image standing in the central space, and accordingly showed partiality for a symmetrical layout, here what might be described as a processional movement can be traced through the entire building from the broad flight of steps before the entrance and right to the end of the adytum. Not until one had walked through every section of the temple did one reach the closed room, probably only to be entered by the priests, in which the god dwelt. It was pointed out long ago that this type of plan recalls the structure of Oriental temples, where a stepped succession of halls or courts directs an advance towards the holy of holies, from which the common herd is excluded. Likewise, it has been noted that in buildings such as Temple C at Selinus the deity was removed from human proximity into mysterious, mystical solitude, an arrangement presupposing a relationship between man and god different from that normally found in Greece, where something similar only occurred in connexion with oracle sites and halls of the mysteries. No doubt one tends naturally to think of influence from Phoenician Carthage in Sicily's case, and also of the continuing effect of the native population's religious ideas as regards both Sicily and South Italy; but the fact that those who settled on the fertile soil of the island and South Italy were to an exceptional extent worshippers of Demeter in association with her daughter Persephone, whom Hades abducted, deserves to be emphasized just as much. The cult of these two goddesses, which was by nature bound up with mystical

XXIII   Corinth. Temple of Apollo seen from the south-west

notions and corresponding rites, may have contributed to the religious attitude as a whole, so that other deities as well seemed more mysterious and inaccessible than they appeared in the Greek mother-country.

Temples C and D were even joined in early Hellenistic times by a third, though it was admittedly very small, and to the south of them beyond a cross-road lay a second precinct containing temples A and O, which were erected during the fifth century. In both precincts, the gods' dwellings stood amid altars, treasuries, and other sacred buildings, which were certainly accompanied by a great many votive monuments. When the Carthaginians destroyed Selinus in 409, they spared the sacred area on the hill, which with regard to the number of its stately temples could not easily be rivalled. Whereas the city never fully recovered from the terrible blow, and, after the evacuation of the inhabitants in the first Punic war, only a village settlement was to be found on the northern part of the acropolis hill, the temples remained standing for another 1,000 years. They did not collapse until the early Middle Ages, when they became victims of an earthquake.

Town Sanctuaries

But the laurelled inhabitants of the land are always anxious to venerate the Gods of the hearth with sacrifices of oxen.
AESCHYLUS

As well as on top of the citadel hill, many cult sites also existed upon its slopes, whether because a deity had appeared since remote antiquity to be powerful there, or because in later times, when the city lay on the plain, people liked to settle new gods near the acropolis. Thus the Athenians worshipped Apollo and Pan in caves on the northern slope of their citadel rock, and some private person gave Asclepius a precinct on the south face in 420. Further to the east, at the foot of the hill, a temple had been built for Dionysus as early as the sixth century. To take a second example, we find the same thing happening at Pergamum, where an artificial terrace on the ascent to the acropolis bore sanctuaries of Demeter and Hera. Also half-way up the hill, but on the north side, a small temple of Dionysus stood at the end of a colonnade running along below the theatre.

Within the lower city, it was above all the market-place that, as the centre of public life, called for a temple to be built in its vicinity—just as during the Christian Middle Ages.

Only recently has the uncovering of the entire agora (market-place) at Athens made it clearly apparent to what extent the so-called Theseum dominated the site from its high position. A flight of steps led up to it. In actual fact, this temple, the best preserved of

XXIV   Pergamum. Temple of Demeter

those dating from Greek antiquity, was not dedicated to the hero Theseus but to Hephaestus, and also to Athena as the protectress of crafts. She already exercises this function in Homer, and her link with the god of technical skill is ancient too. Situated between the artisans' quarters, especially that of the metal-workers, and the agora, which about the middle of the fifth century had already become an imposing 'civic centre', the temple was also erected during this period, and its cult image came from the masterly hand of Alcamenes. It was important in two ways. The craftsmen saw it as the place where their deity lived, but for the Athenians collectively it was something more than this, namely an abode of gods that overlooked the public buildings spread out at the foot of the hill. Hence it was political considerations that determined the subject-matter of some of its pictorial decoration glorifying the deeds of the 'national hero' Theseus. The temple cannot, of course, match the Parthenon, its approximate contemporary, either in its political importance or artistically; compared with the noble building in the citadel, the home of the guardian of crafts is characterized by a certain staidness.

As long ago as the mature archaic period, a temple of Apollo stood overlooking the agora at Corinth in a position similar to that of the so-called Theseum, while Aphrodite possessed a large, far-famed temple on the mighty rock of Acrocorinth. About 540, the former was replaced by a heavy Doric building, which survived the city's destruction by the Romans in 146. Indeed, some of its stocky columns, made out of a single piece of stone, are still standing today. We do not know why it was Apollo rather than, say, Poseidon, the lord of the isthmus and begetter of Corinth's armorial beast Pegasus, who received a dwelling above the early Greek agora, of which only remains of fountain-houses under the Roman installations now exist.

At another place, in distant South Italy, a sanctuary of the powerful sea god is also conspicuously absent. Only twenty years ago, it was regarded as certain that the main temple at Poseidonia (Paestum) was dedicated to this deity, who lent his name to the Greek colony, and whose bearded head appears on its coins. Hence, the largest and most beautiful of the three famous ruins was unhesitatingly called the temple of Poseidon or Neptune, until recent excavations established conclusively that neither this building of about 450 nor the 'Basilica' put up a century earlier belonged to Poseidon, and that both, on the contrary, are to be regarded as temples of Hera. Moreover, as the so-called temple of Ceres, which not long before 500 replaced a small building from earlier times, can confidently be assigned to Athena, and as no imposing sanctuary of the sea god is expected to be found in the less explored parts of the city area, we are faced with the strange fact that the city of Poseidonia contained no Poseidon temple within its walls. Another thing is striking too: it lacked an acropolis. For even though the name of the little hill town of Agropoli a couple of hours away on foot to the south ought to indicate an early Greek citadel, this can hardly have been Poseidonia's stronghold. By means of a surrounding wall, the three temples named above were united inside one large sacred

XXV   Paestum. Temple of Hera I, so-called Basilica, seen from the south-west. Behind it, the
Temple of Hera II, so-called Temple of Poseidon

XXVI   Paestum. Temple of Hera II, so-called Temple of Poseidon, seen from the south-west precinct, in the middle of which lay the agora. On the strength of this, it has been conjectured, probably correctly, that a space dedicated to the chief gods was left open at the centre of the urban settlement as a kind of substitute for the missing acropolis, with the agora thereby to some extent taking over the political role of the 'topmost city'. The fact that the Athena temple lies on a slight rise in the ground, and that the goddess was worshipped as the valiant protectress, also suggests a pseudo-acropolis. If, however, Hera appears at Poseidonia instead of Zeus Polieus, this is quite understandable. For, in the first place, the goddess displayed militant features here, too, during relatively early times, without detriment to her function as a divine midwife, which later came to the fore; in the second, she was deeply revered in the West generally, and particularly by the colonists from the north Peloponnesian region of Achaea, who were also concerned in the founding of Poseidonia. Further north, at the mouth of the Silaris (Sele), the first settlers had already created a sanctuary for her, which was brought to light again some years ago. A treasury from the sixth century with splendid metope sculptures, and a no less beautifully decorated Doric temple built about 500, are evidence of the pious care taken of this site even by later generations. There can be no doubt about it: Hera was the great goddess of the city and its territory. She possessed two temples in the 'citadel precinct' of Poseidonia alone, and, like her dwelling beside the Silaris, they were surrounded by altars, treasuries, and the abodes of lesser deities somehow closely connected with her.

The tendency of the Greek colonists in the West to include temples of different deities within a single sanctuary, or at least to form a sacred zone of sorts, is apparent in Sicily not only at Selinus but also—and especially—at Acragas. Pindar called Acragas the loveliest city of mortal man, and today it still presents itself to the visitor as one of those most richly furnished with temples. Though only founded about 580, the polis set high above the sea had before 500 acquired, besides the already mentioned cult sites on the citadel hill, a number of other sanctuaries. It appears that two of these belonged to the goddesses Demeter and Persephone, who were specially revered on the island, while a temple built towards the end of this period, and now partly re-erected, seems to have been dedicated to Heracles. The earliest of a whole series of temples raised here since the fifth century, Acragas's great period, it stands on a natural ridge to the south of the ancient city stretching down from the acropolis, and overlooks its wall. Except in the case of the Zeus temple, one cannot be sure which deities occupied the individual buildings of this imposing sacred zone; not only is the use of the customary names optional, but in most cases they are certainly incorrect. Nevertheless, it is no doubt permissible to consider the claims of Apollo, Poseidon, Dionysus, and Hephaestus, since they are known to have been worshipped in the city. The fact that six large temples appeared here within the compass of three generations testifies to an unprecedented passion for building, almost even more than to the citizens' piety. 'The people of Acragas revel as if they were

XXVII   Acragas (Agrigento).   Southern city wall and Temple F, so-called Temple of Concord,
seen from Temple D

XXVIII   Acragas (Agrigento). Temple F, so-called Temple of Concord, seen from the south-east

going to die tomorrow, and build as if they were going to live for ever,' Empedocles, who lived at this time, is supposed to have remarked with regard to his native city. His *mot* seems to refer above all to the mighty temple of Zeus, one of the biggest in the Hellenic world. It was begun by the tyrant Theron after the glorious victory over the Carthaginians in 480, and its pedimental sculptures extolled the conquest of the barbarians in terms of the battles fought by the gods against the giants and by the Greeks against the Trojans.

The foundations and giant architectural members now only give us a faint idea of this huge edifice, which was never completely finished. In it the spirit and religious feeling of the Sicilian Greeks were overwhelmingly expressed—indeed, two distinct aspects of this spirit appeared. Firstly, the temple revealed an urge for the extravagant and colossal that is a not uncommon trait of colonist communities. Elsewhere among Greeks of the pre-Hellenistic age, one finds it almost only on the coast of Asia Minor—hence, also in a colonial area and also close to the Oriental world. That a part was played by influences from Carthage, which have already come to mind in connexion with the temples on the acropolis hill at Selinus, can hardly be denied. It even appears within the bounds of possibility that the Phoenicians' Baal, identified by the Greeks with Zeus, and the layout of his holy places had importance for both the plan of the Zeus temple and the god's cult there. True, a rhetorical bent was part of the nature of the Sicilian Greeks, who during the very century when the temple of Zeus arose were developing the art of rhetoric. Both factors probably combined to make the highest god appear in an aura of prodigious omnipotence transcending all human measure. The second aspect of this spirit is revealed in the mysteriousness that, as at Selinus, determined the building's character. Here also the deity dwelt in an adytum, to which probably the priests alone had access, at the end of the narrow 'nave' formed by the naos. Even the open peristyle normally surrounding a temple's cella was missing; instead, the immense outer walls were articulated by half-columns so bulky that there was room for a man to stand in every flute. Giant figures (Atlantes or Telamones) projecting from the walls were supposed to hold up the wooden roof, and the building as a whole, which was about 360 ft. long and 170 ft. wide, must thus in its heavy compactness have had the effect of scaring people rather than of attracting or delighting them.

Not long after the latest of the gods' dwellings, the so-called temple of Concord, had been completed, the Carthaginians in 406 laid waste the city, though not the sacred zone. Acragas no more recovered from this blow than Selinus did from hers. The temples still stood in a proud row on the edge of the city as witnesses of a great past, but further afflictions during the Punic wars, as also the burden of Roman dominion, prevented it from ever again achieving more than the importance of an average country town.

As our last example of a holy place situated within a city, let us take the temple of Athena Alea at Tegea in Arcadia. The goddess, as so often, had absorbed a deity already being worshipped during the second millennium, and assumed the name—here Alea—

XXIX   Acragas (Agrigento). Temple D, so-called Temple of Juno Lacinia, seen from the west
before sunset

as her own surname. Hence the festival regularly celebrated in her honour with contests was called the 'Aleaea'. It did not concern the goddess as the protectress of the town—in this role, Athena had her abode on an acropolis-like hill—but as the mistress of the south Arcadian region, of which the open settlement of Tegea formed the focus. The fact that round about 550 trophies from a victory over the Lacedaemonians, and in 479 a bronze manger out of the booty taken at the battle of Plataea, were offered to the deity, testifies to her sanctuary's importance and reputation, just as does the asylum found there by the Spartan kings on being condemned in their homeland. Yet Athena Alea did not receive an imposing temple until the middle of the fourth century—though when it arrived, it was a splendid Doric edifice of marble, designed by one of the greatest masters of the period, Scopas, and decorated with pedimental sculptures full of the liveliest movement. At that time, the ancient cult site of Tegea became a religious centre for the Arcadian league called into being by Epaminondas. Clearly, it was not the inhabitants of the still modest country town but the member states of the alliance that raised the money for building this temple, which according to the connoisseur Pausanias was one of the most beautiful in the whole of the Peloponnese.

Finally, with the many temples or sacred precincts inside the cities, only a few of which we have been able to mention, are to be associated those lying outside the gates but still counting as urban sanctuaries—unlike the independent Asclepiea of Cos and Pergamum. Zeus as the sky god of Olympus with far-reaching powers would not have tolerated being confined within the narrow limits of an urban settlement. Where it was impossible to build him a temple upon a free-standing hill with a good view at the edge of the town, as in Acragas, the edifice had to be raised beyond the walls in the open country. Thus, the Pisistratids began the erection of a giant temple with double pteromata (dipteros) at Athens on a site to the east of the Acropolis, where according to legend there had been a sanctuary of Olympian Zeus ever since Deucalion's time. In size, it rivalled the new Heraeum begun on Samos by Polycrates at about the same date, but unlike the Samian temple it was to be of the Doric order. If to that extent it corresponded to the spirit of the mother-country, it conflicted with it in its colossal dimensions. Just as the tyranny with its boundless craving for power and glory transgressed the order of the polis, so here in architecture it exceeded the measure that held good for the communities of Hellas, and showed itself akin to the spirit of colonial Greece, which was affected by Oriental influences. It is significant that after the overthrow of the tyranny in 510 work on the enormous structure, which had hardly grown beyond its foundations, was not continued; and that, three centuries later, it was not the Attic state but the philhellenic Seleucid king, Antiochus IV (reigned 175/163), who made a Roman architect responsible for carrying out the job begun by the Pisistratids. Yet even this ruler was unable to get it finished. Another three centuries passed, during which Sulla even carried off some columns to Rome in order to adorn the new Capitoline temple with them, before the

XXX   Athens. Olympieum

XXXI Sardis. Temple of Artemis

emperor Hadrian, a no less enthusiastic philhellene than Antiochus, finished the gigantic and now Corinthian building, putting a wall round the whole precinct with its forest of votive monuments. He attached the area around it to the 'city of Theseus' as the 'city of Hadrian', and had his own statue set up in the naos of the temple beside that of Olympian Zeus. The colossal edifice lay outside the old polis not just spatially but also in conformity with the spirit of its princely creators.

Monarchical might displayed itself on the soil of Asia Minor in the construction of two huge temples for Artemis: the famous Artemisium of Ephesus and the goddess's temple at Sardis. Both clearly owed much to the munificence of King Croesus of Lydia (reigned 560/546), who resided in Sardis, both lay some distance beyond the city walls, and at both sites the mistress of the animals and great fertility goddess of ancient Asia Minor lived on in the guise of the Greek Artemis. However, whereas nothing remains to be seen *in situ* of the Ephesian building, which Herostratus burned down about 356, and only some magnificent examples of its architectural details in the British Museum now bear witness to its splendour, at Sardis two mighty columns of a giant Ionic temple still tower up, and American excavations have also revealed the foundations and many other parts. It is true that the visible remains only date from late antiquity. The first large structure was destroyed during the Ionian revolt (499); a new building put up some decades later seems to have suffered severely in the conflicts immediately after Alexander the Great's death; and when the temple had almost been finished again during the centuries that followed, it fell victim to an earthquake in A.D. 17, so that it had subsequently to be built once more. By then, Sardis had long been an entirely hellenized city. However, the temple raised near the seat of his court by Croesus, who maintained close relations with Delphi and other Greek sanctuaries, had itself been Ionic, and able to bear comparison with Didyma, the Heraeum on Samos and the Ephesian Artemisium.

In South Italy and Sicily, some much smaller temples lying outside the walls of towns were no doubt built by the urban community. The fifteen Doric columns to the north of Metapontum, once a flourishing Achaean daughter-city on the Tarentine gulf, date from late archaic times. They probably belonged to a temple of Hera, whose cult, as we have seen, colonists from the north Peloponnesian region of Achaea were particularly inclined to transplant to their new home. A temple of Olympian Zeus lay on a flat-topped hill south-west of mainland Syracuse; it was a severe sixth-century Doric edifice, and two of its monolithic columns still stand upright. Apart from this, impressive ruins of temples outside the cities are to be found in Sicily, above all at Segesta and Selinus. Inland, Segesta, in the mountainous west of the island, was not a Greek colony but the capital of the Elymi, a tribe hard to place ethnologically. Nevertheless, its members were to some extent hellenized, and here at the foot of the hill that bore their city they were capable of building a purely Greek temple, which overlooked a deeply cut ravine. Begun about 430, it was for unknown reasons never completed, as is shown by the absence of

XXXII   Metapontum. Temple of Hera

XXXIII   Segesta. The Temple

fluting on the columns, apart from anything else. Nor do we know to which deity it was dedicated. In this respect, the situation is better as regards the sacred areas on either side of the acropolis hill of Selinus. The first Greek colonists already appear to have created a cult site for the three goddesses connected with the underworld—Demeter, who was worshipped there as the 'apple carrier' (Malophoros), her daughter Persephone and Hecate—near the burial ground to the west of the settlement, and about 600 it was developed into a sanctuary of a special type. Close by, the Zeus who had to be propitiated through rites of expiation (Milichius) received a small temple. One can understand these gods having their seat outside the city at the place of the dead, and it is permissible to suppose that the same thing happened in other parts of the Greek world as well. Why, however, on a hill to the east of the city area, three more large buildings were raised at about the same time as the 'citadel temples' remains a mystery. It is unlikely that the occupants of the dwellings that early on appeared to the north of the citadel settlement would have wanted to compete with the inhabitants of the old town and build temples of their own, as far as possible even grander than the others. Besides, this would not explain their position outside the settlement. But whatever may have determined the choice of the site and layout of a second, isolated sacred area, in this enterprise too, which paralleled the development of the citadel-sanctuaries, both the passion for building and the piety of the Sicilian Greeks were displayed in the most impressive way.

A mid-sixth-century temple probably dedicated to Athena (F), its seclusion specially emphasized outside by stone screens between the peristyle columns, was joined after only a generation by a gigantic temple (G), in which Apollo was apparently supposed to dwell. Building operations went on for decades. The structure was about as long and wide as the Olympieum at Acragas, and like it showed the taste for the colossal that was characteristic of the Greeks of the colonial area. Hardly had this vast undertaking been nearly completed, than, in the first half of the fifth century, work began on raising a third Hera temple (E), which was also large, though not so enormous. Like nearly all the gods' dwellings at Selinus, it was arranged in the western Greek manner as a series of stages leading up to the adytum, which here even lay somewhat higher than the floor of the naos, concluding the latter like a choir. Just as solemnly impressive in its architecture as in its sculptural decoration, which included an exquisite metope relief showing a chastely majestic Hera unveiling herself to Zeus, it was the noblest of the seven stately temples that the people of Selinus built in the course of a single century. To the mountains of debris left by the temples on the eastern hill when they were brought down by earthquakes during the early Middle Ages, the local population gave the name *i pilieri dei giganti*. It was indeed easier to believe that giants had been at work there, than that the citizens of a middle-sized Greek colony had been capable of fitting together column drums and squared stones of such bulk and weight, and of erecting a building like the temple of Apollo.

Come, O Muse, tread a measure to the sacred choirs; come to charm our song; come to see the waiting crowds, assembled here in their thousands. ARISTOPHANES

The theatres are to be classed with the holy places, because the mimed performance for which they provided the setting was originally a ritual observance in honour of Dionysus, and the spectators took part in it as a religious congregation. Hence, the natural site for a theatre was in the neighbourhood of a temple of this god, and we find this still to have been the case during Hellenistic times on the slope of the citadel hill at Pergamum. Yet even where such a direct link with Dionysus did not exist, as for example at the Asclepieum of Epidaurus, the representations were always dedicated to some deity, and like musical or gymnastic contests they were only held during a god's festival. At the same time, Dionysus was never forgotten; right down to late antiquity, those appearing in any dramatic performance felt that they were serving him.

Dionysus was primarily the god of nature's teeming, fructifying vital power and the frenzy related to it. Whoever surrendered to him forgot about himself, stepped outside himself (that is what the word 'ecstasy' really means), and turned into another being, whether man or beast. Thus, the donning of masks and disguises formed part of his cult from the very beginning. Out of observances of this kind, there grew up from the middle of the sixth century two forms of mimed performances, the one serious, the other comic. At that period, choruses dressed up as half-human horses (satyrs) had long been dancing in the isthmus cities and elsewhere, and singing there in honour of the mighty lord the hymn known as the dithyramb, which recalled his deeds and adventures. The transition to drama, however, was made in Athens at the time of Pisistratus, when Thespis from the deme of Icaria opposed to the chorus a 'respondent' who, accompanied by flutes, spoke in iambic verses, and not only recounted mythical events, but himself personated a mythical figure. Thematically, Dionysus gradually lost his importance, just as the chorus no longer assumed the guise of satyrs, but instead projected themselves into and acted out a myth—even though the performance was still called a 'goat-song' (tragoidia). The common people were not content that the Dionysia should consist almost entirely in the adoption of another form, and after a while, of course, account had to be taken of their desires, by presenting a 'satyr-play' as an extra. Actually, it was a performance by sileni, for these goblins with a horse's tail and ears made up the chorus, and amused the spectators with their crazy antics. By contrast, during the period of the Persian wars and particularly since the appearance of Aeschylus, the spirit and subject of the other pieces grew more serious. In terms of mythical, or even directly experienced historical events of a tragic order, they presented a deeply moving exposition of the great problems of life. From the end of the sixth century onwards, the performance of these dramas and satyr-plays formed part of the Great Dionysia, a public festival held every spring.

The second type of dramatic presentation arose out of the boisterous routs (komoi) customary at many Dionysus festivals, with their banter, coarse jokes, mummery of every kind, and the displaying of the phallus as the symbol of fertility. Celebrations like these found poetical form as 'comedies' roughly about 500 at Athens, whereas in Dorian cities of the mother-country and in Sicily popular farces, burlesques, and travesties were by then fully developed. Soon after 490, the performance of comedies too became a permanent feature of the Great Dionysia at Athens, and since the Periclean age, comedies as well as tragedies and satyr-plays had been offered to the god at yet another of his festivals: the Lenaea, celebrated during the winter.

For presenting the pieces, the first thing required was a dancing place (orchestra). There was one by the agora in Athens at the sanctuary of Lenaeus, and since the time when under Pisistratus the ancient image of Dionysus had been transported from the frontier village of Eleutherae to the city and set up in a temple of its own below the southern slope of the Acropolis, one had existed there as well. Only on the latter site did a theatre construction grow up, as far as we can tell. At first quite primitive, it consisted of nothing but the circular orchestra with the god's altar at the centre, and a wooden structure (scene), which was re-erected for each occasion, lying to the south at a tangent. The performance, essentially a piece of team-work involving the actors and the chorus, took place in the orchestra; indeed, dancing and music played a much bigger part in the presentation than we tend to suppose. Even if at other dancing places stands were put up for the onlookers, here they settled on the bare ground of the hillside right up to the foot of the citadel wall, seats being provided only for priests and officials. However, though the theatre as a structure was thus as simple as could be imagined, it did not lack the suggestion of a décor and certain stage fittings. By painting on the wooden 'scene' one could show whether it was meant to represent, say, a palace or a temple, while the opening up of its wall enabled people to see what was going on, or supposed to be going on, inside. A landscape could be simulated on prism-shaped wooden pillars in front of the 'scene', and by means of a crane gods and divine beings could even be made to float in. Only in the fifth century, however, was a stone 'scene' building created, through the erection of a long wall with a projecting central structure to the south of the orchestra. At the same time, it formed the north wall of a stoa opening on to the Dionysus sanctuary. The crowd continued to settle on the slope of the Acropolis, now provided with terraces, but this

XXXIV Syracuse. Greek Theatre at sunset

natural auditorium was cut off from the 'scene' by retaining-walls on either side of the orchestra, which thrust somewhat into the hill, and room was thus obtained for two wide entrances (paradoi) into the circular space. Now as before, nobody considered the comfort of the thousands who for a whole day squatted rather than sat upon the steep slope. After all, they did not come to be entertained, but to take part in a public religious service.

This, then, was the external setting of the dramatic performances at the festival of the Great Dionysia. It began with the fetching of the ancient cult image from a small sanctuary west of the city, to which it had secretly been taken beforehand. Thus, every year in the evening of this day, the god who had once come from Eleutherae re-entered by torch-light the older of the two temples that he possessed below the Acropolis. Next morning, a general procession led by the archon made its way there, and, like that of the Panathenaea, it demonstrated both the power and the splendour of the Attic state. Dionysus received a great sacrifice, his cult image was set up in the orchestra, and then the contests began between choruses singing dithyrambs and other hymns. Masked parades and boisterous antics, accompanied by broad jokes, continued long into the night. On each of the following three days three tragedies and a satyr-play were performed, and on the fourth usually five comedies. Whether the work of a writer who had submitted either three tragedies and a satyr-play or a comedy should be accepted or not was de-cided at the Great Dionysia by the archon, and at the Lenaea by the highest sacred official, the basileus. If it was accepted, the archon or basileus assigned to its author a wealthy citizen as a choregus, who undertook the equipping of the chorus as an honorary duty. The writer, however, who received a kind of honorarium, had the task of preparing for performance the dancing and singing of the chorus, which for tragedies consisted of twelve to fifteen men, and for comedies of twenty-four. At first, he was also the only actor and later—when the number had been increased to two and finally to three—the leading one (protagonistes), until in the course of time professional acting prevailed. He had to become equally proficient in dancing, singing, and expressive diction, though not in the art of facial expressions and only to a small extent that of gesture. For his features were hidden behind the mask that he changed in accordance with the different roles that he had to take in a play, or in the event of gross changes of appearance, as when Oedipus blinded himself; and his movements were impeded by a long, heavy robe. Likewise, the fitting out of the actors in a comedy with a grotesque mask, a fat belly and backside, and a huge phallus hardly permitted a dramatic art of the kind to which we are accus-tomed. Indeed, regarded generally, the purely male performances would have seemed strange to us in many respects. This applies especially to the exceptional importance of the dancing and singing chorus, shown in the award by a carefully selected committee of a bronze tripod as the prize for winning the drama contest to the choregus, even if the author was also pronounced victor along with him. The decision was based on the offering to Dionysus as a whole, not just on the poetic achievement.

XXXV   Epidaurus. Theatre

Overwhelming evidence of the extraordinary artistic productiveness of Athens and its greatest playwrights, who created about a hundred or more dramas, is provided by the fact that till 386 all tragedies, and till 339 all comedies, were new works, so that only first performances were known. Thus, year by year, the god received spiritual gifts specially prepared for his festival, and everyone who possibly could took part in this great event. Since Pericles, the poorer inhabitants had received compensation for their loss of wages on the days of the performance, though not for an entrance fee, which they no more paid than at other cult celebrations. For the whole proceeding was a state religious ceremony, which all citizens were supposed to be able to attend. The priests, with those of Dionysus in a privileged position, sat near the orchestra, as did also the high civil and military officials appointed for the year, and guests of honour from abroad. Behind them, the ordinary people crowded together on the hillside, and at the performance of tragedies they included the women, whose presence was forbidden during the comedies for understandable reasons. One cannot but admire and be amazed at the intellectual level of this audience, before which the great writers of tragedies examined life's most fundamental problems. The comedy writers could rely upon its exact knowledge of dramas performed on previous occasions, and could therefore allude to particular verses from these works. While the tragedies dealt with the ultimate religious, ethical, and intellectual problems of the individual and the community, in the fifth-century comedies demagogues and generals, poets and philosophers, even the audience of citizens itself were lashed unmercifully with unsurpassable and, for all its coarseness, profound wit and ridicule. It was not only the high poetic value of both the grave and the gay pieces that, for every Athenian, set the performances at the festival of Dionysus among the most important events of public life; attending them, people felt spiritually united and raised above their individual selves, and summoned to judge and ponder. This was only possible in the days of the fifth-century polis, which comprised and moulded every aspect of life. When, during the following period, its unifying power declined and the citizens' private interests came to the fore, the plays produced in honour of Dionysus lost their religious significance and became secularized. The chorus diminished in importance until it finally disappeared altogether. The tragedy turned into a psychological problem play, the comedy grew to be no more than an amusing piece about domestic life. Not till this period, when the performances offered more aesthetic pleasure and entertainment than religious and intellectual exaltation, did Athens obtain a large theatre built of stone.

This structure, which was put up about 330 on the site of the old theatre, corresponded in its essentials to what the ruins below the Acropolis still give us an idea of, despite the many later alterations. It was, above all, the huge semicircle of stepped seats in stone that was completely new. Ascending almost to the base of the citadel wall, it was divided horizontally by a gangway running round half-way up, and vertically by twelve flights of steps, which segmented it into thirteen cunei (wedges). Stone armchairs

XXXVI   Segesta. Theatre

in the bottom row—still partly surviving today in copies from later times—were reserved for the priests and officials. A two-aisled building with three doors leading to the orchestra was set in front of what, until then, had been the 'scene' wall, and the space before this frontage was flanked by two projecting squarish structures with colonnades. Inside them stood statues of famous poets and statesmen. Like its wooden predecessors, the new 'scene' building had only one story, and the same goes for all Greek theatres, in contrast with the Roman. However, this was scarcely the result of a desire to give an unrestricted view of the landscape, as the modern visitor tends to suppose. In the imperial age, after further alterations during Hellenistic times, the enlarged 'scene' received another broad projecting structure, which reduced the hitherto round orchestra to a semicircle. This orchestra had long ago ceased to be the place where the chorus danced, and henceforth it served for every possible kind of entertainment.

Outside the city of Athens, dramas had been presented since far-off times in Attic demes on the occasion of rural festivals of Dionysus. For a long time performances took place under primitive conditions, but finally these places received theatre buildings of their own. What kind of a setting was provided for the early Dorian farces and Sicilian comedies we do not know, but at Syracuse, for example, where Aeschylus put on his *Persians* about 470, it was probably arranged as in Athens at the same date. This applies equally to the Zeus sanctuary of Dium in Macedonia at the end of the fifth century, for the great festival of the god was then adorned with drama contests by King Archelaus, at whose court Euripides spent the last years of his life. Here, as elsewhere, the fame and glory of the Attic celebrations led to the offering of such performances to gods other than Dionysus; and the more the Attic tragedies and comedies freed themselves from their religious and political roots to become plays in our sense of the word, the easier it was for the works of the Attic playwrights to spread throughout the Greek world, though not without here and there stimulating the development of a local school. The theatres in many sanctuaries and cities bear witness to this expansion of the drama. All of them were built later than the structure erected at Athens about 330. The 'classical' theatre of Epidaurus, the noble rounded arc and amazing acoustics of which still arouse our admiration, was already being praised for its harmony and beauty in ancient times, but even it belongs only to the end of the fourth century; and the ruins of the constructions at Syracuse, Pergamum, Delphi, and Segesta date from even later. Though they certainly differ in many details from the stone theatre below the Athenian Acropolis, viewed as a whole they present a very similar picture as they lie embedded in a hillside. Hardly a single city throughout the Greek colonial area was prepared to forgo a theatre at this period, especially as it also served very well for public meetings and state ceremonies. Little or nothing, it is true, remained of the religious observance in honour of Dionysus, even though the companies of strolling players that put on old and new dramatic works at the most varied local festivals still called themselves performers of Dionysus.

THE MONOCHROME PLATES

MONUMENTS IN MODERN GREECE

Attica: Athens, Eleusis and Cape Sunium.
Aegina. Olympia and Delphi. Corinth, Nemea,
Heraeum of Argos, Tegea, Bassae, Epidaurus.
Delos and Samos

MONUMENTS IN MODERN ITALY

South Italy: Paestum and Metapontum.
Sicily: Selinus (Selinunte), Acragas (Agrigento),
Syracuse and Segesta

MONUMENTS IN MODERN TURKEY

Priene (Güllübahçe), Ephesus (Selçuk), Sardis
(Sart), Didyma (Yeni-Hisar) near Miletus
(Balat) and Pergamum (Bergama)

1   Athens. Acropolis seen from the Pnyx

2   Athens. North side of Acropolis seen from the Hephaesteum

3 Athens. South-west side of Acropolis seen from the Monument of Philopappus.
Left: Pinacotheca, Propylaea, and Temple of Athena Nike. Centre: Erechtheum.
Right: Parthenon, Below the Acropolis: Odeum of Herodes Atticus (left), Portico
of Eumenes (centre), and Theatre of Dionysus (right)

4 Athens, Acropolis. Remains of western fortification from Mycenaean period, Parthenon in background

5   Athens, Acropolis. Propylaea seen from the south-west, with Pinacotheca adjoining it

6   Athens, Acropolis. Ionic column of central passage of Propylaea

7   Athens, Acropolis. East front of Propylaea seen from the Parthenon

8 Athens, Acropolis. West front of Parthenon

9 Athens, Acropolis. East front of Parthenon

10 Athens, Acropolis. Parthenon, west pteroma seen from the south-west corner. Right: columns of opisthodomus (west vestibule)

11   Athens, Acropolis. Parthenon, south pteroma seen from its west end

12 Athens, Acropolis. Parthenon. Above: south-west corner of entablature and corona. Below: corner triglyph and mutules

13 Athens, Acropolis. Parthenon, south-east corner of naos with south column of pronaos and south colonnade

14   Athens, Acropolis. Parthenon. View from pronaos through naos and adytum to west doorway. Beyond cella walls,
south and north peristyle

15   Athens, Acropolis. Parthenon. View from north-west into naos.
Right: in foreground base slabs of the gold-and-ivory cult figure of Athena Parthenos. Left: south-east part of pronaos
and peristyle

16 Athens, Acropolis. Parthenon. East frieze of cella with main part of Panathenaic procession. Steward and girls with processional equipment. Athens, Acropolis Museum

17 Parthenon. East frieze of cella with main part of Panathenaic procession, continued.
Above: head of southern procession of girls and steward. Below: Pericles with three high officials and citizens.
London, British Museum (figs. 14-19, 20-23)

18   Parthenon. East frieze of cella with main part of Panathenaic procession, continued.
Above: Hermes, Dionysus, Demeter, and Ares. Below: Hera with Iris and Zeus.
London, British Museum (figs. 24-27, 28-30)

19   Parthenon. East frieze of cella with main part of Panathenaic procession, continued.
Above: priests and attendant with the peplos ready for presentation to Athena. Below: Athena and Hephaestus.
London, British Museum (figs. 31-35) and Athens, Acropolis Museum (figs. 36-37)

20   Parthenon. East frieze of cella with main part of Panathenaic procession, continued.
Above: Poseidon, Apollo, Artemis, and (fragmentary) Aphrodite with Eros. Athens, Acropolis Museum (figs. 38-42).
Below: heroes. London, British Museum (figs. 43-48)

21 Parthenon. East frieze of cella with main part of Panathenaic procession, continued.
Above: head of northern procession of girls and steward. Paris, Louvre (figs. 49-56).
Below: continuation of northern procession of girls with processional equipment. London, British Museum (figs. 57-61)

22   Athens, Acropolis. Erechtheum seen from the west

23   Athens, Acropolis. Erechtheum seen from the south with foundations of old Temple of Athena in foreground

24 Erechtheum. Original of second *kore* on front of caryatid porch. London, British Museum

25   Athens, Acropolis. Erechtheum, caryatid porch

26   Athens, Acropolis. Erechtheum, west side of north porch

27   Athens, Acropolis. Erechtheum, south wall of main building

28   Athens, Acropolis. Erechtheum, north porch seen from the east.
Poseidon's crypt with its sacred sign exposed by gap in paving

29   Athens, Acropolis. Erechtheum, main building with portico seen from the east; north porch projecting on right

30   Athens, Acropolis. Temple of Athena Nike seen from the north wing of Propylaea

31 Athens, Acropolis. Winged Nike undoing sandal, from balustrade round Temple of Athena Nike.
Athens, Acropolis Museum

32 Athens. Hephaesteum seen from the south-west

33   Athens, Hephaesteum. Above: temple from the south. Below: capital of column of south colonnade

34   Athens, Hephaesteum. South pteroma seen from the east

35 Athens, Hephaesteum. Above: east front, looking upwards. Below: part of frieze in west portico with Battle between Lapiths and Centaurs

36   Athens. Olympieum seen from the west

37   Athens. Theatre of Dionysus

38 Eleusis, Telesterium.
Above: view from rock terrace. Below: view from rock steps of tiered seats and remains of columns

39 Eleusis, Telesterium. Above: oblique view of eastern rock steps and Telesterium
Below: Telesterium seen from front, with rock terrace above ruins

40　Sunium. Temple of Poseidon seen from the south-east

41 Sunium. Temple of Poseidon seen from the north-east

42   Aegina. East front of Temple of Aphaea

43　Aegina. Temple of Aphaea seen from the south-east

44 Aegina, Temple of Aphaea. Pallas Athena, from west pediment. *c.* 510 B.C. Munich, Glyptothek

53   Olympia, the Altis. Temple of Zeus seen from the west

54 Olympia, the Altis. Temple of Zeus seen from the south-west

55 Olympia, the Altis. Temple of Zeus, collapsed columns of south colonnade

56 Olympia, the Altis. Treasury terrace. Left: south-east corner of Heraeum

57 Olympia, the Altis. Treasury terrace from the north-east. Treasuries of Metapontum and Selinus in foreground, followed
by five more, the last that of Sicyon

58   Olympia, the Altis. Treasury terrace. Treasuries of Gela (left) and Megara (right), Stadium in background

59   Olympia, the Altis. Palaestra

60 Delphi. View from Theatre of Sacred Precinct (Temenos).
Temple of Apollo in centre, rock face of the Phaedriades and valley of the Pleistus in background

61   Delphi. Temple of Apollo seen from the west

62 Delphi. Altar and south-east corner of Temple of Apollo

63   Delphi, Temple of Apollo. East colonnade and pronaos, with altar beyond

64 Delphi, Sacred Precinct. Above: beginning of Sacred Way with Monuments of Philopoemen and Lysander of Sparta (left), and Argos and Athens (right). Below: Sacred Way with semi-circular Argive Monuments on either side, seen from Monument of the Tarentines

65   Delphi, Sacred Precinct. Above: early capital from Sicyonian Treasury.
Centre: Sacred Way with, on left, Sicyonian and Siphnian Treasuries. Below: Siphnian Treasury

66 Delphi. The Dioscuri and companions stealing cattle. Metope from old Monopteros of Sicyon. *c.*570 B.C. Delphi, Museum

67 Delphi, Siphnian Treasury. Central part of tympanum: Heracles and Apollo disputing the tripod before Athena. Shortly before 525 B.C. Below: corner of corona with anthemion and bead-and-reel ornament. Delphi, Museum

68 Delphi, Siphnian Treasury.
Corner-piece of west frieze between cyma reversa (above) and ovolo (below) mouldings. Delphi, Museum

69 Delphi, Siphnian Treasury. From north frieze: Battle between Gods and Giants. Shortly before 525 B.C. Delphi, Museum

70 Delphi, Siphnian Treasury. One of the two caryatids from façade. Delphi, Museum

71　Delphi. Metope from Athenian Treasury. Heracles and Cycnus. Parian marble. *c.* 505 B.C. Delphi, Museum

72 Delphi, Sacred Precinct. Sacred Way and Athenian Treasury

73 Delphi, Sacred Precinct. Naxian Sphinx from beside the Sacred Way. Naxian marble. Before 550 B.C. Delphi, Museum

74 Delphi, Sacred Precinct. Sacred Way. Above: Athenian Treasury (left), base of pillar of Naxian Sphinx (centre back), Athenian Stoa with polygonal terrace-wall (right). Below: inscriptions on polygonal terrace-wall

75 Delphi, Sacred Precinct. View towards Theatre with Exedra of Alexander the Great's Lion Hunt in front. Site of Lesche of the Cnidians back right, foundations of Temple of Apollo in foreground

76 Delphi, Stadium

77   Delphi, Gymnasium

78 Delphi, Marmaria. General view from the west-north-west. Later (third) Temple of Athena Pronaea in foreground, with Tholos adjoining it and behind this the two Treasuries

79   Delphi. General view over Marmaria from the east. Old Temple of Athena Pronaea in foreground, with the two
Treasuries in front of Tholos

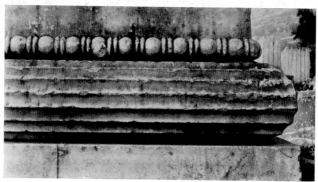

80 Delphi, Marmaria. Above: the two Treasuries (Massalian right), photographed before re-erection of Tholos columns
Centre: wall base of Massalian Treasury. Below left: capital of second Temple of Athena Pronaea. Below right: capital of
third Temple of Athena Pronaea

81   Corinth. West front of Temple of Apollo

82 Nemea, Temple of Zeus. View from the south-west across cella towards two columns of pronaos and one of the east colonnade

83 Nemea, Temple of Zeus. Above: general view from the south-west. Column drums of collapsed south colonnade in foreground. Below: general view from the east

84   Argos, Heraeum. Head of Hera. *c.* 425-400 B.C. Athens, National Museum

85 Argos, Heraeum. Above: view from the south of temple terraces and general layout of temple precinct. Terrace of old Heraeum above, terrace of later Heraeum in centre near tower (cf. colour plate I X), Stoa far right (cf. plate 86). Below: carved stone with two cuckoos

86 Argos, Heraeum. Above: stoa at south-west corner of temple precinct. Below: sima from later Temple of Hera.
Athens, National Museum

87   Tegea, Temple of Athena Alea. Above: part of sima. Tegea, Museum. Below: foundations seen from the west

88   Tegea. Head of one of pediment sculptures by Scopas from Temple of Athena Alea. Athens, National Museum

89   Tegea. Head of one of pediment sculptures by Scopas from Temple of Athena Alea. Athens, National Museum

90   Bassae. Temple of Apollo Epicurius seen from the north-north-east

91   Bassae, Temple of Apollo Epicurius. Opisthodomus seen from the south-west corner of peristyle

92   Bassae, Temple of Apollo Epicurius. East pteroma seen from its north end, with view into pronaos and naos

93　Bassae, Temple of Apollo Epicurius. North portico, pronaos, and naos seen from the east corner of north portico

94 Bassae, Temple of Apollo Epicurius. Naos seen from the pronaos

95   Bassae, Temple of Apollo Epicurius. Naos seen from the south-west corner of adytum

96 Bassae, Temple of Apollo Epicurius. Sculpture from frieze inside cella. Above: Battle between Greeks and Amazons. Below: Battle between Lapiths and Centaurs. London, British Museum

97   Epidaurus, Tholos. Above: sima and frieze. Below: part of coffered ceiling of ambulatory. Epidaurus, Museum

98   Epidaurus, Temple of Asclepius. Aura on horseback by Timotheus, left acroterium of west pediment. *c.* 400-375 B.C.
Athens, National Museum

99 Epidaurus, Temple of Asclepius. Amazon on horseback probably by Timotheus, central figure of west pediment.
c. 400-375 B.C. Athens, National Museum

100 Epidaurus, Theatre. View from the east towards auditorium, orchestra, and west parodos (actors' entrance)

101 Epidaurus, Theatre. North-west part of auditorium and west parodos

102   Delos, Grotto of Apollo. Hellenistic copy of an early Delian shrine, on western slope of Mount Cynthus near Ancient-Way

103 Delos. Apollo. Body of colossal statue, about thirty feet tall, which stood beside the Oikos of the Naxians. *c.* 600 B.C.
Below: its rectangular plinth, on back the inscription: 'I am from the same stone, statue and socle'

104   Delos, Processional Way leading to Sacred Lake. On its terrace nine lions in Naxian marble. Seventh century B.C.
(cf. colour plate X)

105 Delos. View north-westward from Mount Cynthus over Sacred Precinct and, towards right, Sanctuary of Apollo with the three Temples of Apollo and, in front, the curved line of Treasuries. Below: enlarged detail

106 Samos, Heraeum. Bases of prostyle columns seen from the west with echinus in background

107 Samos, Heraeum from the north-east. Echinus with egg-and-tongue ornament to left; line of front colonnade to right

108   Paestum, Temple of Hera I, so-called Basilica. East front from the east-north-east

109   Paestum, Temple of Hera I, so-called Basilica. View from naos of pronaos and east colonnade, with, on left, front column of central row of columns in naos

110 Paestum, Temple of Hera I, so-called Basilica. View from naos of north colonnade; capital from central row of columns
in foreground

111   Paestum, Temple of Hera I, so-called Basilica. The three standing columns of central row in naos, with pronaos and east portico beyond

112   Paestum, Temple of Hera I, so-called Basilica. Antae and columns of pronaos from the south-east, with east colonnade on right

113 Paestum, Temple of Hera I, so-called Basilica. South-west corner

114   Paestum, Temple of Hera I, so-called Basilica.
The four capitals of west and north colonnades with distinctive decoration

115 Paestum, Temple of Hera II, so-called Temple of Poseidon. South-east corner of temple

116   Paestum. Temple of Hera II, so-called Temple of Poseidon, seen from the south-east

117   Paestum, Temple of Hera II, so-called Temple of Poseidon. East front. Large earlier altar in foreground, with small later altar beyond

118   Paestum, Temple of Hera II, so-called Temple of Poseidon. View into naos

119 Paestum, Temple of Hera II, so-called Temple of Poseidon. View of the two double-storied rows of columns in naos

120   Paestum, Temple of Hera II, so-called Temple of Poseidon. South pteroma seen from its east front. Only plinth of
cella wall survives

121 Paestum, Temple of Hera II, so-called Temple of Poseidon. South pteroma seen from the south-west. Only plinth of cella wall survives

122 Paestum, Temple of Athena, so-called Temple of Demeter. View from the south-west

123   Paestum, Temple of Athena, so-called Temple of Demeter. View of calla from the south-east

124 Selinus, Contrada Gaggera. Above: Sanctuary of Demeter Malophoros seen from the north-west. Below: Sanctuary of Zeus Milichius

125 Selinus, Contrada Gaggera. Above: Sanctuary of Demeter Malophoros seen from the west. Below: Propylaeum of
Sanctuary of Demeter Malophoros seen from the east, with Sanctuary itself behind

126   Selinus, Acropolis. View from Temple C of ruins of Temple D

127   Selinus, Acropolis. Part of north colonnade of Temple C seen from the north

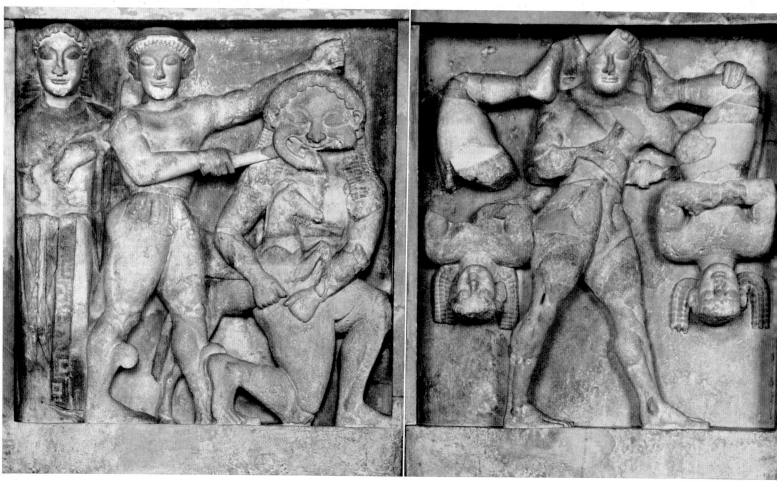

128   Selinus. The three surviving metopes from Temple C on Acropolis. Above: Apollo driving the team of the Sun.
Below left: Perseus beheading Medusa. Below right: Heracles and the Cercopes. 540-530 B.C. Palermo, National Museum

129   Selinus. Frieze including metopes, triglyphs, and horizontal corona from Temple C on Acropolis.
Palermo, National Museum

130   Selinus, city. Temple E, Temple of Hera, seen from the north-east

139 Acragas (Agrigento), Temple A, so-called Temple of Heracles. End of sixth century B.C. Opisthodomus and south colonnade from the north-west

140 Acragas (Agrigento), Temple B, Olympieum. First half of fifth century B.C. Above: head of one of the Atlantes.
Agrigento, Civic Museum. Below: one of the Atlantes, with ruins of the temple beyond it

141   Acragas (Agrigento), Temple B, Olympieum. First half of fifth century B.C. Above: fragments of the temple including capital of half-column. Below: the altar before the temple from the south-west

142 Acragas (Agrigento). Temple F, so-called Temple of Concord, seen from the north-east. *c.* 450-440 B.C.

143 Acragas (Agrigento), Temple F, so-called Temple of Concord. South pteroma seen from its east end

144　Acragas (Agrigento), Temple F, so-called Temple of Concord. Pronaos seen from the south-east corner of the east portico

145   Acragas (Agrigento), Temple F, so-called Temple of Concord. View of cella, altered in Christian times but now free of
later additions

146   Acragas (Agrigento), Temple D, so-called Temple of Juno Lacinia, seen from the east. *c.* 440-425 B.C.

147   Acragas (Agrigento), Temple D, so-called Temple of Juno Lacinia. View from naos through pronaos and east colonnade towards altar

148   Acragas (Agrigento), Temple D, so-called Temple of Juno Lacinia. Pronaos, eastern part of naos, and north colonnade
from the south-east

149   Acragas (Agrigento), Temple D, so-called Temple of Juno Lacinia. View through cella from the east

150 Syracuse, Temple of Zeus (Olympieum). Beginning of sixth century B.C.
Above: the two surviving columns of south colonnade from the south-east. Below: temple ruins from the north-west

151 Syracuse, Temple of Apollo (Apollonium). Beginning of sixth century B.C. Above: view from the south-west of south colonnade and south cella wall. Below: view from the north-west of stylobate of north colonnade and cella

152 Syracuse, Temple of Athena (Athenaeum, now Cathedral). *c.* 480-460 B.C. View of south pteroma, with colonnade
built into south wall of cathedral; south cella wall, now south wall of nave, on left

153 Syracuse. Torso of Nike, probably acroterium from Temple of Athena. Marble. First quarter of fifth century B.C.
Syracuse, National Museum

154   Segesta. Temple seen from the east

155 Segesta. Temple interior seen from the east

156 Priene. Above: view from heights above Priene of ruins of Temple of Athena Polias. Dedicated 334 B.C. Valley of the
Meander in background. Below: various examples of temple's decorative stone-work

157   Priene, Temple of Athena Polias.
Above: pronaos from the east. Below: south supporting-wall and remains of propylaeum of Sanctuary of Athena

158 Priene, Theatre. Above: scene and orchestra seen from the north. Below: auditorium seen from the east

159   Ephesus. Site of former Temple of Artemis

160   Ephesus. Thanatos (?) and Alcestis (?) on cylindrical base of column from new Temple of Artemis by Chirocrates.
From 356 B.C. London, British Museum (No. 1206)

161   Ephesus. Nike (? Muse) on square pedestal of column from new Temple of Artemis by Chirocrates. From 356 B.C.
London, British Museum (No. 1200)

162　Sardis. Temple of Artemis seen from the north-east. After 300 B.C.

163 Sardis. Temple of Artemis seen from the west-north-west. Below: capital

164   Didyma, near Miletus. North-east front of Temple of Apollo. Begun *c.* 300 B.C.

165 Didyma, near Miletus. Temple of Apollo seen from the north. Below: one of the Medusa masks from frieze

166   Didyma, near Miletus. Temple of Apollo seen from the east

167 Didyma, near Miletus, Temple of Apollo. Court seen from the south, with flight of steps leading up to supposed oracle
room (Chresmographium) at far end. Foundations of naiskos in foreground

168 Didyma, near Miletus, Temple of Apollo. View from the south-east of the two standing columns of the north-west double colonnade

169 Didyma, near Miletus, Temple of Apollo. Above: column bases of portico. Below: north wall of vestibule

170   Pergamum. Asclepieum seen from the south-east

171   Pergamum. Theatre seen from the north, with its terrace on right. Altar of small Ionic temple at north (bottom) end of terrace

172   Pergamum, Sanctuary of Demeter. Above: general view over entire Sanctuary area.
Below: base of temple built for Philetaerus and Eumenes I

173 Pergamum, Sanctuary of Demeter. Below: entrance gate built soon after 200 B.C. Behind it, Sanctuary with step seats for mystery ceremonies. Above: supporting-walls and cellar foundations of formerly two-aisled stoa (300 feet long)

174   Pergamum. Above: Sanctuary of Athena. Actual temple near ruin of late antique fortified tower. Below: Palace of
Eumenes II. Site of Altar of Zeus in background near the two large pine-trees

175   Pergamum. *In situ* remains of Altar of Zeus

176   Altar of Zeus at Pergamum. North wing after restoration. Triton and Amphitrite on front; Nereus and Doris with an enemy on stair-case side. Berlin, Pergamum Museum

THE ARCHITECTURE OF THE TEMPLES, THEATRES AND SHRINES

Gottfried Gruben

The measurements in the text are given in feet whereas
for the line illustrations, which are taken from authentic
European sources, the scales in metres have been retained.
For convenience a conversion table is shown below.

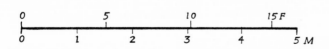

INTRODUCTION

Once upon a time, nearly three thousand years ago, a modest structure was created in Greece out of columns, beams, walls, and a roof, and it was repeated for centuries with only the most trifling changes. People did not even seek to enrich it and to give it a certain variety by adding new forms; on the contrary, they were for ever pruning and simplifying it. Many a hurried but candid sightseer touring Europe may wonder, visiting, say, the temples at Paestum, why such a fuss is made of these moderately large buildings, which can be taken in at a glance. He still beholds in his mind's eye the immense, light-flooded dome, the symphony of form and space of St. Peter's. Or else he is standing before Rheims cathedral, its mass soaring heavenwards and resolved into the stone flames of countless flying-buttresses, points, and figures; he enters the mystic realm of its interior. What comparable charm have these austere ruins to offer him?

Others stand at Paestum and gaze and take away with them a reflected image and a lasting nostalgia. Likewise, many will skim through this book in their usual fashion, while others will, perhaps, feel called upon to seek out these temples and elicit their secrets for themselves. For the latter, the text and illustrations are intended as a pointer but nothing more. How to look and comprehend can scarcely be passed on.

If we, sharing in the inclination of our scientific age for historical accuracy, want to try to understand the past as it saw itself, we must concede that our image patched together from reflections will never tally with the direct view of this creative people. Nevertheless, let us take note of the following basic truth: we are making a mistake if, with our way of looking at nature determined by the romantic movement, we regard temple and landscape as an aesthetic whole. The temple is a completely independent, self-sufficient entity. It rises on a site sacred to a god. Through the planes of its steps it separates itself from the ground, through compact rows of columns its body marks itself off from its surroundings. As an object carrying within it the laws of its own perfection, it remains the same wherever it is built: on a mountain slope, on marshy lowlands, in the narrow confines of a crowded city, in an open grove, on the seashore. A different unity with the landscape does indeed exist: a mythic one. Long before there were any temples, a clairaudient people could at particular spots hear the voice and perceive the actions of a god; and the spirit of these hallowed places may likewise still act upon even our duller senses.

The temple is self-sufficient in another way as well. It pays no regard to neighbouring structures; it does not bother about the spectator. Its builders did not exploit the appeal of perspective intersections and foreshortenings, nor did they try by means of central approaches or optical axes to set it in a planned square and strengthen its impact on the beholder. They only discovered and hesitantly set foot on the new territory of these effects at the end of the classical period. Moreover, the narrow interior of the naos, only dimly lit through the door and its space further restricted by the columns within it, is not an architectonic room in our sense of the term. It is not a room that seizes the eye by means of light and amplitude, through the verve or contrast of its limiting surfaces; an interior that determines the form of the exterior. The naos is clearly not much more than the container required for the cult image, and the few who entered it only did so for the sake of this image. Meetings, sacrifices, and prayers—everything in which the congregation took part—occurred out in the open, around the altar set before the temple.

This means, however, that the temple is deprived of all that the concept 'architecture' signifies to us. What still remains? What, after all these negations, is the temple?

Confronted with the temple at Paestum, Goethe felt that he was in 'a completely alien world', and he 'pictured to himself the severe style of sculpture', in order to become reconciled to it. Greek sculpture is thus the key, its laws being at the same time those of this architecture. It is a sculptural, corporeal architecture built up of solid, tangible parts, of squared stones, columns, and beams that through the secure way in which they stand, support, and bear down constitute an organic whole. In it, it is not the hollows and spaces, but what is substantial, firmly contoured, in fact sculptural that has been given form; and the line that divides it from the two-thousand-year-long tradition of Roman and Western European architecture cannot be too rigidly drawn, especially if we want to distinguish the beginnings of this tradition in Greek architecture.

As with men, whose limbs are kept in due relation to each other by internal laws, the members of the temple grow in fixed proportions as the size of the whole increases. Though the small buildings of the early period have steps and doors of a magnitude determined by a man's stature and the length of his stride, the crepidoma steps of the monumental stone temples dating from the sixth century can no longer be climbed, and the gigantic doors are no longer measured with a human gauge. This growth of the parts along with the whole extends even to the roof tiles, which on the more costly edifices are often carved out of marble, and to the last decorative detail. Here again we meet the self-sufficiency of this architecture, with its dimensions that do not depend on those of the human frame, its structure organized instead according to inherent laws. Yet this very fact makes it all the more fundamentally related to man.

Even when it is only painted, the decoration contributes to the sculptural nature of the temple. The brightly coloured rows of leaves, the restrained key patterns, the exuberant volutes, the delicate yet vivacious friezes of tendrils and blossoms are never just applied from without to enliven dull surfaces. Instead of being decorative trimmings, mere ornaments, they form the joints, the seams, and the crowning feature of the structure. They, so to speak, crystallize out of the building's inner framework, and appear as a mediating 'expression' where the forces of load and support meet or die away. It is significant that we have no suitable word for this type of decoration. In Greek, κόσμος means both inner order and decoration.

Could sculpture itself possibly be absent from an architecture of this kind? At the earliest stage of development, definite places were in fact made available for it. The shallow triangular spaces formed by the pediments at each front of the temple are occupied by celestial beings: by groups of gods, heroes, and daemons. On the rectangular metope panels that encircle a Doric temple below its horizontal corona, the deeds of the heroes and mythical battles are represented. In the long, continuous frieze of the Ionic temple, processions and fights or feasts of the gods run their course. Flying figures or fantastic plant forms crown the top and corners of the pediments.

Just as a sculptural principle inhabits the temple, so the sculpture is characterized by an architectonic element: the lucidity of its construction, the clarity of its articulation, a quality that is more than technical and that has been designated by the word 'tectonic', which people often use without understanding it. Τεκτοσύνη in its primary sense means the carpenter's art, which enables him to join things together correctly. It was precisely this that mattered to the Greeks, whether they were creating an earthen vessel, a statue, or a temple. No blurred transitions were tolerated. The limits and cohesion of the parts present themselves openly and unambiguously to the eye, as does also the inner scaffolding of the whole.

In archaic architecture, a prominent role is at the same time played by the separation of the structural members, each of which on its own account expresses its nature to the full. In the architecture of the classical period, the tectonic quality penetrates manifestly within. The coherence becomes apparent, movement and counter-movement enter into play, the life of the construction at last exists wholly in the union of its parts, a union that like every intellectual synthesis is a harmony of antitheses.

The, economically speaking, quite excessively involved and costly methods employed by the stonemasons cannot be justified on any practical or rational grounds, and they also are only to be explained by relating them to an idea. In the case of the early temples, people strove to make every structural member—shafts, capitals, architraves, and so on—out of a single stone, in order to realize an ideal. (These monolithic shafts could be over 20 ft. long and weigh more than thirty tons, as is shown, for example, by those of the temple of Apollo at Corinth.) Where this was not possible, as in the case of the walls and, with the increasing dimensions, of the columns too, the walls were built up of rectangular stones and the columns of drums with thrusting and bearing surfaces so precisely adjusted that not even a pin could be forced into the extremely fine joints. In this process, amorphous binding agents were always avoided, although lime mortar was very well known and employed for waterworks. (This is why the use of cement in unscrupulous restorations is such an obvious offence against the nature of these buildings.) Metal or wooden clamps and dowels let into the blocks served to hold them together.

Finally, after the setting in position of the stones or drums, the external surfaces of which had until then been left in the rough, undressed condition in which they had arrived from the quarry, all the large parts of 'members' of the structure—steps, walls, shafts, and so on—were evened up, polished, or fluted as a whole—in short, brought to their ultimate form. Thus, one cannot talk of a simple assembling of prefabricated parts, a process like putting together the units of a toy building set; and when collapsed members are re-erected the highly delicate adherence of the forms and surfaces, which depended upon an integrate working procedure, can never be restored.

It hardly needs to be substantiated that the three attributes of the Doric as well as the Ionic Greek temple—its self-sufficiency, its corporeal and sculptural as opposed to spatial and hollow form, and its tectonic construction—are three defining aspects of a single organic whole.

In considering the path followed by this architecture, which basically, of course, had but a single theme—the temple—we shall certainly get to know it as something complex and many-sided, and we shall see that every temple displays, as it were, its own individual countenance. At the same time, however, reference will have to be made again and again —perhaps until the reader tires of it—to the tendency outlined above, which like all that is self-developing had an unconscious beginning, a phase of the purest resplendency, and a period of decline. When this force started to dwindle, there grew up out of the decaying elements a new dynamic architecture of space, with which we are more at home. Greek architecture is more modest, but also more demanding. Its mutations consist in extremely subtle modifications of a by and large permanent formal framework, modifications that we are sometimes not even able to see, but only to measure. One may be quite sure that the Greeks themselves noticed every tiny change of form and proportion. They were men who looked, who used their eyes. As such, the last descendants of this unique people were characterized as late as the fifth century A.D.: 'Those eyes with shining, intense gaze; they are the people with the most beautiful eyes in the world.'

However, one must on no account picture the Greeks as a homogeneous race. They were divided into tribes that had immigrated at different times from different areas, and two of them—the Dorians and the Ionians—constituted the dominant poles of the Greek entity. The Greeks were further diversified in accordance with the region or island that they had settled, and split up into a vast number of small, independent city states, which were mostly hostile to each other and capable of developing their own individual dialect in language as in art. May one here continue to talk of a nation at all? The Greeks were proudly conscious of their unity only *vis-à-vis* foreigners—the barbarians—and it was during the great pan-Hellenic festivals at Olympia and Delphi that they experienced their inmost unity: the so peculiarly real, non-transcendental Greek religion—the source of all things Greek. Thus, the Dorians of the Peloponnese and the Ionians of the islands and the coast of Asia Minor did in fact develop two different architectonic structures, in which the polarities of the two stocks achieved visible form. Already in antiquity, they were strikingly compared to the severe, vigorous body of man and the supple grace of woman; but during the Attic classical period, even these two strains came together in contrapuntal unity as a 'harmony of opposites'.

It would no doubt be a hopeless undertaking to conceive and describe 'the Gothic church' as an entirely distinct phenomenon. Yet does 'the Doric temple', an expression in extremely common use, refer to something that can be very much more precisely defined? In actual fact, it does; and so the inspection of a single temple can reveal the permanent laws of its form more clearly than the comparison of many, which emphasizes rather what is incidental and particular. Here, however, we are dealing with a lot of different temples, and are therefore obliged to consider them from the point of view of their historical development. Nevertheless, by very roundabout ways—a fact that I wish to acknowledge in advance—this approach can only lead us back to that necessity, that internal law, manifest in all its changing variety.

To anticipate again: Greek architecture, but especially the evolution of the Doric temple, differs conspicuously from every comparable phenomenon of art history in its unwavering line of growth. Egyptian architecture is certainly persistent—so much so, however, that it lacks any lively development; and, of course, it serves chiefly the dead and their changeless eternity. Many different currents meet in Oriental architecture. It reacts pliantly and irresolutely to every influence, and is far removed from the imperturbable consistency of Greek building. Developing with unprecedented energy and impetus, the heterogeneous architecture of the Christian era repeatedly changes course in a disjointed fashion. Between Romantic and Renaissance, Gothic and Baroque, the buildings of the past and those of the present, there are indeed transitions, but no common denominator exists.

In the very beginnings of the Doric temple, as in seeds and shoots, every form of the mature tree is anticipated. If ever an entelechy has been achieved in the history of art, it is obviously here. At the same time, the problem of how a formal framework originally roughed out in wood by simple, purely practical carpenter's methods could already then have possessed a latent fitness for monumental expression in stone remains puzzling, and cannot be solved with positive arguments. Goethe's image of the caterpillar, chrysalis and butterfly comes forcibly to mind; for this architecture certainly underwent a

metamorphosis, and a liberating one, moreover. Thus the old wooden construction may be clearly discerned in the stone, just as the caterpillar's body remains perceptible in the form of the butterfly.

The goal, the idea of the 'perfect temple', which appeared indistinctly to the architects of the sixth and fifth centuries, grew continually clearer; certain rules were developed, principally to do with the proportioning of the elements of the structure to each other. Yet there was never any immutable 'canon' in the sense of a precisely defined schema for design, such as Vitruvius, an architectural theorist of the Augustan age, handed down. Hence, the equivocal concept of the 'canon' will, in what follows, be understood not as an exact model but as a general idea.

The prologue to, the preparation for architecture was geometric vase painting, which provided a strict training of hand and eye in the mastery of form. At that period, during the ninth and eighth centuries, the gods were worshipped at altars crudely built up of rough-hewn stones in sanctuaries walled off in the open. Then suddenly during the eighth century— and this was really the beginning of Western monumental art—the Greeks started to produce statues of their gods, and to erect 'houses' for these at first wooden cult images. Thenceforth, sculpture and architecture followed the same path. The first temples were not much more than cult shrines, which revived a type of building that had been inherited from the Mycenaean culture superseded by that of the Dorian immigrants: the megaron. This was a rectangular room with its side walls extending beyond the entrance wall and so forming an open vestibule, at the front of which it was customary to have one or two posts to support the gable. Occasionally this vestibule may have been extended or replaced by a porch consisting of an arrangement of posts roofed over and open on three sides. A stylized, 'geometric' votive model from the *fig. 1* Heraeum at Argos gives an idea of the latter form. Embodied in temples made up of a cella and pronaos *fig. 2* with columns in-antis, and in prostyle temples, both types of plan remained permanent features of Greek architecture. Much was preserved even of the construction of these primitive buildings. The walls were carried up in sun-dried brick over a stone base, and a corresponding wall base of large stone slabs

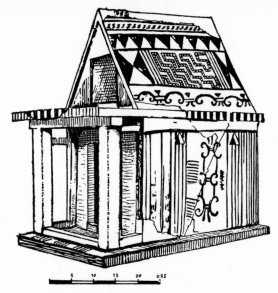

1 Terracotta model from Heraeum, Argos.
G. Oikonomos, 'Eφ. 'Aρχ., 1931

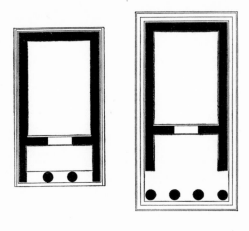

2 Anta temple (Sicyonian treasury, Olympia)
and prostyle temple. Plans (1 : 300). New drawing

standing upright (orthostats) can on every Doric temple be clearly distinguished from the ashlar masonry resting upon it. The narrow ends of the sun-dried brick walls had, like the door opening, to be protected with a facing of planks; the first protection survived in the projecting antae, the second continued as a wooden construction into classical times. Most of the house-like temples were probably covered with the steep ridge roof brought by the Dorians from the north (cf. fig. 1), beside which southern forms—the flat mud roof and slightly inclined hip-roof—seem to have held their ground.

These cult shrines soon had to be enlarged in keeping with the new conception of the gods. For this, remains of palaces raised by the Mycenaean forebears, who lived on heroically transfigured in epics, may have served as models (e.g. at Tiryns and Mycenae, and on the Athenian Acropolis). Indeed, at Thermum, a remote spot in Aetolia, such a chieftain's megaron from late Mycenaean times was not just regarded with wonder as an ancestral relic, but *fig. 3* fitted up as a temple for Apollo (megaron B, 24 ft. by 70 ft. 3 in.). A row of wooden posts must here have propped up the roof ridge, and divided the cella into two naves. Probably still in the eighth century, this temple was surrounded with an oval peristyle of thirty-six wooden columns, on which rested the entablature, likewise of wood, and a roof that now reached out well beyond the walls.

The surrounding colonnade or peristyle, which we meet here for the first time, is hardly likely to have originated at a provincial Apollo sanctuary. This decisive step forward in the development of Doric architecture must have been taken earlier at an art centre, Argos or Corinth, where, admittedly, almost

all traces of the earliest temples were removed by subsequent lively building activity. From the outset, the peristyle must have had an elongated rectangular form, as stands to reason in the case of a building fitted together out of beams. The new system established itself and became prevalent very rapidly. During the second half of the seventh century, partly wooden peristyle temples of the then already defined Doric order were erected in important sanctuaries in areas under the influence of Corinth: in the Heraeum of Argos, at Mycenae, Tegea, Olympia, Thebes and Delphi. At Thermum, too, the old oval *fig. 3* structure was replaced by a rectangular peripteral temple with 5 by 15 columns outside (stylobate 39 ft. 10 in. by 125 ft. 5 in.) and a still narrow, but 100-ft.-long cella divided into two naves by a central row of columns. The form taken by the new building's roof-beams can be ascertained from the clearly organized ground-plan. Like a spine, the architrave above the central supports marked the temple's longer axis, and from it the cross-beams, which were, in part, angled herring-bone fashion, extended over the side walls to the architrave of the peristyle. The saddle-roof must have been correspondingly constructed in two higher, sloping planes. Above the entrance spread a pediment (gable), whereas at the rear the hip-roof of the earlier temple (B) was at first retained. Very soon, however, in response to the developing conception of this form of building, the back also was given a gable, as can be deducted from the roof tiles.

The ground-plan of the Doric peripteral temple of *fig. 8* Hera at Olympia was developed to a state of absolutely transparent simplicity. Central supports which obstructed alike an axial entrance and the placing of the cult image were eliminated. The

309

cella now had two aisles and a nave, and the front accordingly received six columns. Both arrangements thereafter remained binding. With the Heraeum, the actual process of creating the Doric temple was concluded.

The 'idea' of the temple—a rectangular house ringed by columns, the whole covered over by a saddle-roof with a pediment at each of the narrow ends—seems so simple and natural that it is all too easy to lose sight of its many astonishing features. Consider first the extravagant uselessness of this layout: the most modest of cult rooms surrounded even at the back by large open colonnades, which can hardly be accounted for, even superficially, as serving the need for protection against sun and rain, as a kind of encircling porch. Nearer the mark is Vitruvius's typically Roman explanation (III, 8 f.) that the peristyle was introduced to give the temple of the gods *auctoritas*, by which he meant 'dignity', but with a considerable suggestion of the idea of display. In actual fact, the peristyle was a sacred form always reserved for temples, though all its elements could be transferred to other types of building at will. It seems to me that, in the architect's language, the peripteral temple expressed what the statue of the god standing at its centre meant in the language of the sculptor; it was not just the receptacle for, but the most powerful amplification, the most evident enhancement of the cult image. The temple would thus appear to have been a wider embodiment of the deity who was so effectively present, its idea a religious or rather—since gods, life and universe coincided in Greek thought—a cosmic one. Hence, the inexhaustible, physically solid as well as spiritual strength of the temple, which, in image, displayed the ordering of the orders. The notion of the peristyle proved fruitful in a more than formal sense owing to the antithetic relationship between it and the cella: closed, angular core and light, open garland of columns; body and clothing; unchanging centre and rhythmic roundelay. Thenceforth, the perfect bal-

ancing and attuning of these contrasts provided the real theme of Doric architecture.

In order not to neglect the actual form on account of all its 'significance', let us consider what these early wooden temples really looked like. As such a building has nowhere survived in its entirety, we are obliged to piece together a picture of its upper structure from literary sources, fragmentary finds, and deductions from surviving foundations, and by translating back from later stone forms to their wooden prototypes (fig. 4). In the ground-plans of the few known seventh-century temples, we find an exceptionally elongated naos with two naves (Thermum; Sparta, first temple of Artemis), but soon, on the introduction of a tripartite (nave and two aisles) division of the space, it was appropriately widened, and achieved more balanced proportions. The most important change from the old one-fronted 'megaron plan' was the inclusion of a vestibule at the back corresponding to the pronaos with its antae and columns at the entrance end (Thermum, Mycenae, Heraeum). This opisthodomus served no apparent practical purpose, and was not even directly accessible from the naos. Instead, it satisfied the deep urge for all-round development first expressed in the idea of the peristyle. Through their fully symmetrical elaboration, both ends received equal stress, and thereby self-contained, monumental repose took the place of a dominant direction.

To begin with, the peristyle columns stood on separate stone slabs (Thermum C). Later, however, they rested upon a continuous stone step, the stylobate, which raised the building above the ground (Heraeum of Olympia).

On the smooth beam that, in the form of a long horizontal rail, stretched over the wooden columns (architrave) lay the cross-beams of the ceiling. Out of the elementary sequence of beam ends, one of which could be seen from outside above each column and one in the spaces between them, a frieze of simple rhythmic force was now created. Slabs

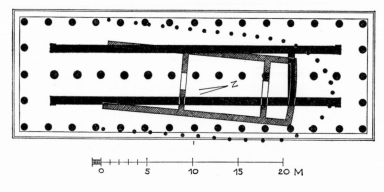

3 Thermum, megaron B and temple of Apollo C. Plan (1 : 400). New drawing after Kawerau

310

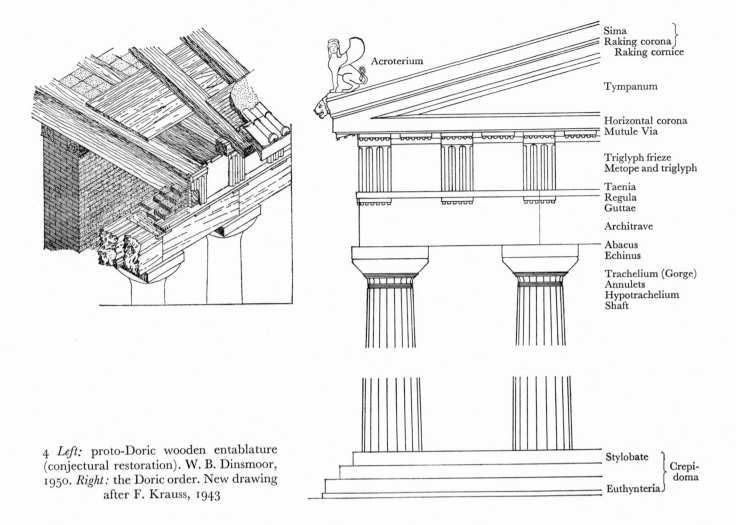

Sima
Raking corona } Raking cornice

Acroterium

Tympanum

Horizontal corona
Mutule Via

Triglyph frieze
Metope and triglyph

Taenia
Regula
Guttae

Architrave

Abacus
Echinus

Trachelium (Gorge)
Annulets
Hypotrachelium
Shaft

Stylobate } Crepidoma
Euthynteria }

4 *Left:* proto-Doric wooden entablature (conjectural restoration). W. B. Dinsmoor, 1950. *Right:* the Doric order. New drawing after F. Krauss, 1943

divided in three by angular grooves (such terracotta triglyphs have survived at Calydon and Thermum) were attached to these beam ends, and between them were inserted panels (metopes), which, as they did not belong to the supporting framework, became fields free for pictorial expression. Painted (Thermum) or sculptured (Mycenae), they wreathed the otherwise so austere building like a picture-book of Greek myths. The triglyph frieze rested on a narrow, jutting fillet, the taenia, across which its rhythm spread to the architrave through a delicately accentuated link. This was the regula, a narrow band lying beneath each triglyph and equal to it in width. A remarkable addition reveals its constructional significance: underneath it extended three to six (the latter was the rule) cylindrical 'drops' (guttae), which at first were undoubtedly wooden pegs or bronze nails.

The frieze was coped with a shallow wooden beam, on which, over each triglyph and metope, lay the plank-shaped rafters. They jutted out over the frieze to support the projecting edge of the roof (the corona, at Thermum a terracotta 'cornice' with coloured decoration on its face and soffit). Under these rafter ends, the mutules, there again appeared the cylindrical 'nail heads' mentioned above, though now set in three parallel rows. The mutules and corona tilted outwards in accordance with the slope of the roof, but on all Doric temples they strangely continued at the ends of the building below the pediments, where neither rafters nor a roof cornice would have served any structural purpose. Here two different forms had clearly been superimposed: the gently sloping Mediterranean hip-roof covered with reeds or mud and the gabled roof introduced by the Dorian immigrants. At Corinth, the latter type was evidently used for the peripteral temple as a balanced terminal to the structure holding it together in monumental unity (see page 342). The fact that it was the encircling cornice of the earlier type of roof that was retained once again demonstrates this architecture's assured handling of form.

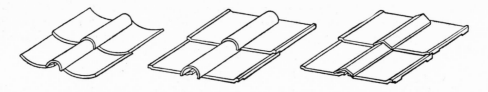

5 Laconian, Sicilian, and Corinthian systems of tiling. W. B. Dinsmoor, 1950, and A. W. Lawrence, 1957

The all-round balance of the effect produced by the four sides of the temple depended on this very arrangement, and the columns straining upwards required a strongly projecting cornice as a counter-weight. With the roof, a new zone had perceptibly begun. The two broadly spreading pediments gave the ends of the temple greater weight *vis-à-vis* the sides, without however disturbing the calm, unifying continuity of the peristyle. A sloping corona bounded each side of the flat, triangular space of the gable (tympanum), which almost seems to have been predestined for large sculptural compositions. Even the roof tiles were included in the articulation of the whole. The earliest form of tiling, which was developed at Corinth, consisted of shallowly concave tiles over the edges of which were inverted cover-tiles semicircular in section, and it long remained indigenous to conservative Laconia ('Laconian roof'). Corinth, however, did not stick to this undulating type of roof, and created a more sharply contoured tile. In Sicily, one often comes across a mixture of both sorts.

fig. 5

The outer edge of the roof was formed by an upward-curving, variously profiled gutter, the sima, which was always painted with rich floral ornament. On the eaves, these simas had to be pierced at regular intervals by water-spouts, which to begin with took the form of trumpet-shaped pipes, then, from the middle of the sixth century, of lions' heads. Often the sima was enriched with antefixes—painted, erect terminations of the lowest cover-tiles, decorated with palmettes or mythic masks. Similar antefixes ran along the ridge. Thus, on the edges of the roof, the building's stern law seemed to be relaxed, its inner life to ramify in contact with the sky through the sprouting of fantastic ornamental forms. In the acroteria that crowned the apex and lower corners of the pediment, this fantasy became quite unrestrained; there, Gorgons, sphinxes, griffins, winged daemons and involved floral compositions stood poised in the open air.

Without design, all the features of the temple's final stone form have entered into this description of its wooden prefiguration, and the transitions were in fact made smoothly. This amazing process of 'petri-

fication' went on for a century, and did not end with each wooden member simply being carved in stone. The earliest stone columns exactly mirrored their delicately articulated models, and for the most part still carried a wooden entablature.

Towards the end of the seventh century, these light constructions of stone were being built all over Greece; but then, in the first half of the sixth century, the weight, solidity, and durability of the new material came to be inwardly understood, and were expressed in heavier structures. Gradually freed, the monumentality immanent in this form of building from the outset broke through—so powerfully, indeed, that following generations had to restrain this excessive energy (Corinth).

This evolution can be clearly illustrated by the column, the most important and expressive part of the temple. In the earliest slender stone columns of the first Athena temple at Delphi (fig. 20), standing widely spaced around the cella like an open wreath, the Doric column stands before us complete, as one of the West's most valid formal creations. Without intermediaries, the shaft rises vertically from the flat stylobate, and, tapering upwards, it strains vigorously towards the entablature. Sixteen to twenty vertical grooves (flutes), separated by sharp edges, have been cut into the shaft, thus enabling the eye to take in the cylindrical volume, and making the energy that strives upwards fully apparent. Between the shaft and entablature intervenes the capital in which the conflict set up by load and support is visibly settled. Like a sensitive organ, this capital indicates the fundamental static and dynamic forces that hold sway in the structure. It consists of two parts: the round echinus curving outwards and upwards over the shaft and amassing the latter's sculptural energy within itself; and the four-cornered slab of the abacus, which forms the direct link with the downward-pressing architrave. In the early period, the echinus was, as it were, crushed to a soft, flatly projecting disk, which moreover did not hide its descent from turned wooden forms. The whole was related to its load in a robustly naïve fashion, and there existed an archaic separation of parts. Shaft and echinus were separated by an incised

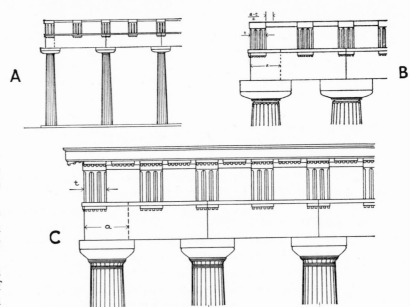

6 The Doric angle conflict
A Wooden structure with architrave and triglyph of equal breadth: no angle conflict
B Stone structure with broader architrave (a) and narrower angle triglyph (t): adjustment through broadening the angle metope by $\frac{a-t}{2}$
C As B, but metopes of uniform breadth and adjustment through contraction of angle interaxial (JE) by $\frac{a-t}{2}$ in relation to normal interaxial (JN). New drawing after F. Krauss, 1943

necking, into which was sometimes countersunk a wreath of sculptured leaves, probably again going back to the Mycenaean heritage. Then, in the course of the sixth century, a loosely uniting flow of lines and forces became more and more clearly defined. The end of the shaft was marked by three narrow grooves, the bottom of the echinus by three delicately applied rings towards which the sharp edges of the fluting stretched upwards.

Around the middle of the sixth century, the newly understood monumentality was expressed by unbelievably heavy, thick-set columns of increased dimensions (Corinth, page 343); the echinus swelled like a tensed muscle beneath the almost insupportable burden of the massive stone architrave. With this extreme intensity of expression, a turning-point had been reached. Henceforth, things were brought into due proportion. Above slimmer columns, the capitals vigorously tautened themselves against the load, resilient energy streamed through the noticeably less constrained members (Delphi, fig. 20, also Aegina, page 350), until finally, in the Attic classical period, the old conflicts of forces and forms were adjusted to a state of harmony, which in its perfection again signified a change.

During the fourth century, the columns that had once been so corporeal began to stiffen and grow cool and elegant. No longer were the now too slender shafts securely planted on the ground, and the echinus hardened into the truncated cone of solid geometry. The Hellenistic age admitted the, so to speak, chilled Doric order into its repertoire of forms as a not specially popular element mainly used for setting off the decorative Ionic order.

The peristyle also has its history—an entangled, complex one, as it was determined on the one hand by the connexion in plan with the cella, and on the other by the form of the columns and divisions of the frieze. Only the main stages of this development can be indicated here, and the first has already been characterized in discussing Thermum and the Heraeum of Olympia: owing to the simplicity of the design, cella and peristyle were to begin with firmly united. This, too, was a 'naïve' arrangement. With the arrival of stone construction, the binding cross-beams were abandoned; the joists of the ambulatory ceiling were no longer related in size to the stone triglyphs, which had grown enormously, and this narrow covering layer was raised to the level of the corona. Ceiling timbers and rafters thus came to be distributed independently of the rhythm of the columns. This meant that the old structural bonds were rent, and, as a result, the cella began to float uncertainly in the peristyle. For a whole century, architects strove to develop new laws based on aesthetic considerations. In so doing, they tried through proportioning to harness together the two ground-plan rectangles of the peristyle and cella. At first this involved great difficulties, because, starting out from such rectangles defined in simple numerical relationships, it was no longer possible to make the distance between the column axes uniform. In this 'interaxial differentiation', the wider spans were always allotted to the fronts of the

313

temple, it being rightly felt that these needed to open up more freely. The broader interaxials also called for thicker columns at the fronts.

However, the discord of the peristyle and cella was not thus to be resolved. On the contrary, the dilemma spread to the subtle system of proportions that applied to every member of the building.

The 'classical simplification' perfected in the temple of Zeus at Olympia depended solely on the fact that the entire ground-plan was built up from an 'internal' basic measurement, the interaxial of 16 Doric feet, by multiplying or dividing it. Hence, the 'external' dimensions, such as those of the peristyle rectangle, were immaterial and derived. An essential framework of axial relations was thus established: the outsides of the walls of the three-interaxial-wide cella were aligned with the axes of the second and fifth front columns; the cella was nine interaxials long, and the fronts of its antae were in the same plane as the bisectors of the second flanking interaxial spaces. However, the fact that these most lucidly deliberate classical connexions matched with such remarkable accuracy the old naïve arrangement, dictated by structural requirements, testifies to the spiritual consistency of this architecture.

Another peculiarity of the Heraeum of Olympia conceals one of the most difficult problems of the Doric peripteral temple: at each of the building's four corners the columns are about 5½ to 9½ in. closer together. This 'angle contraction' issued from a formal conflict between the triglyph frieze and the colonnade. The corner of the frieze was occupied by a corner triglyph, showing a normal triglyph both on the front and on the side of the building. Where triglyph and architrave were equally wide, the corner triglyph came directly over the central axis of the angle column. Hence, when on the earliest wooden temples, as at Thermum, the width of the cross-beams (and accordingly the triglyphs) corresponded to that of the architrave, no conflict arose (fig. 6A). If, however, the triglyphs were made narrower than this stone beam, and the end triglyph still had at all cost to remain above the angle of the architrave, then it became necessary to shift the block away from the axis of the column to the corner by half the difference in breadth between the triglyphs and the architrave. For the latter had, of course, to lie directly over the column axis to achieve stability. Consequently, assuming that one wanted to leave the other triglyphs alone in their normal position, the end metope became broader by precisely the above-mentioned amount (fig. 6B). As was bound to happen, such a conspicuous irregularity soon came to be found disturbing, and there-

fore people in the mother-country usually preferred to reduce the corner interaxial measurement by the amount of the triglyphs' deficit, so that the frieze could be made uniform (fig. 6C). In the Western colonies, however, the architects appear to have devoted themselves to this problem with a curious delight in making experiments. All the possibilities were tried out: widening the corner triglyph (Selinus, temple C), widening the end metope (Paestum, temple of Athena), contracting the corner and following axial measurements ('double angle contraction', Acragas, page 441), and, as the subtlest adjustment, angle contraction by half the deficit and continual broadening of all the metopes (Paestum, temple of Hera II, page 414).

The, by comparison, attractively simple solution of the mother-country—plain angle contraction—contributed to the development of the temple's corporeality, which began around the middle of the sixth century. That is to say it resulted in the corners (which lacked the continuous background of the cella) becoming more solid and compact, and this effect was shortly enhanced by strengthening the angle columns. A virtue had here been made of necessity—indeed, people seem to have regarded this consolidation as the real purpose of contraction. For that reason, the latter was sometimes missing in anta temples (Delphi, Athenian treasury, page 337), which meant accepting a displacement of the triglyphs from the column axes. On the Parthenon, the 'conflict' is quite literally transformed into its very opposite. The contraction, here sought deliberately, goes far beyond what is required to make the columns true up with the triglyphs, and this excess has had, in its turn, to be eliminated in the frieze—now, however, by narrowing the metopes.

The Hellenistic period finally moved away from such formal problems, which lost their significance as the vitality of the form ebbed. Seen in relation to the imposing Hellenistic conception of an architecture based on uniform succession, every divergence had a disturbing effect. Only now did the angle problem become a real conflict, capable of inducing Hellenistic architects to reject the Doric order altogether. One of the greatest, Hermogenes, is said out of sheer vexation over the angle conflict to have allotted the marble lying ready for a Doric temple to an Ionic one instead (Vitruvius IV, 3).

We have indicated the beginnings of the Doric temple, and traced the evolution of its parts. Now all that remains to complete the picture is for us to consider its most perfect manifestation: the temple of Zeus at Olympia.

What raised it so significantly above all earlier ones was its mass—an inward mass, to which its

314

considerable dimensions merely corresponded. It was based on the static energy of the whole, on the robust corporeality and striking simplicity of its members. This is precisely what is meant by the elusive concept of 'monumentality', which has only a remote connexion with size. Even the most enormous Gothic cathedral is less monumental than a Doric temple. The former, a link between earth and heaven, points beyond itself; the latter, a 'cosmos', is complete in itself.

s. 9–13 If the 'canon' has been embodied anywhere at all, it is in the temple of Zeus. As we shall see, a coherent order knit together the ground-plan. Yet over and beyond this, the entire structure was supported by a balance of opposing forces and forms. The great platform of the crepidoma with its rhythmic trinity of steps detached the building from and joined it to the ground. On it stood the vertical walls and columns, the latter canonically numbering 6 by 13. Though themselves rounded, free-standing bodies, these columns were arranged as a whole in the form of a rectangle, in which the rectangular block of the cella, so to speak, faded away. 'The columns are like a mantle into which the light penetrates. They repeat the nucleus in a more richly varied way, and the gradual loosening up of the density outward from within is effected by such an intimate contact between substance and light that the building seems to breathe, and its severe forms never become hard and stiff' (F. Krauss). The two ends of the cella for their part also opened up into an arrangement of columns, over which lay a fully developed entablature. This not only resulted in the primacy of the fronts, but introduced a complementary combination of depth and light into the building's nucleus, which did not remain a mere cuboid block.

The structure was divided into three zones: steps, columns and entablature. Thereby 'a perfect equilibrium was produced by the way in which the forces that strained upward were contained between the supporting horizontal of the steps and the downward-pressing horizontal of the entablature with its cornice' (F. Krauss). The entablature in its turn drew an angular,

precise outline round the mass of the building, which in the dominant zone of the columns was of course opened up, so that the eye could take in from every side its depth and, with this, its all-round corporeality. The grand vertical rhythm beginning in the columns leaped the unadorned beams of the architrave, redoubled and concentrated in the triglyph frieze, which like a beautifully articulated chain extended round the building at the top, came to rest with a further doubling in the mutules under the strongly projecting, shading corona, and found its ultimate echo in the sima with its lions' heads and in the even ribbing of the roof.

Its colourfulness brought the building a final clarification. Only a few basic colours—white, blue, red—were used, and these remained unblended. The structural elements (steps, walls, columns, architrave) stood forth almost pure white, for an extremely fine coat of marble stucco, barely a millimetre thick, covered the porous limestone out of which all Doric temples (except for Attic or Attic-inspired marble buildings) were constructed. The articulation of the frieze was emphasized more strongly and freed from the shadow that the corona cast by a deep blue, and sometimes also black, on the vertical parts (regulae, triglyphs, mutules) and a bright red on the horizontal ones (taenia, soffit of corona). Where they were not sculptured, the metopes remained white, as did also the front of the corona. Pictorial and other enrichment was distinguished by a more lively alternation of colours.

This abode of Zeus was by no means the last Doric peripteral temple in the Peloponnese. Nevertheless, after the middle of the century all buildings were drawn into the predominant current of Attic architecture—indeed, an Athenian architect and one from the Ionian islands designed the most important temples, at Bassae and Tegea. They are included here, however, because the Peloponnesian heritage continued all the same to be active in them, but these mature and late classical temples can only be truly understood when considered in relation to the Attic classical period.

OLYMPIA

THE ALTIS

Plate II, fig. 7

Olympia is more to us than a historical site. It represents the most valid idea that the Greeks formed of themselves, an idea so powerful that, even though scattered and dimmed, its light still shines across the centuries to ours. All that Greeks ever aspired to was fulfilled in the grove of the Altis, in the peaceful, spacious Alpheus valley: piety in the service and under the protection of the sky god and hurler of thunderbolts; competition, the all-pervading leaven of Greek history that very often worked perniciously, but was here kept free from strife and the urge to destroy—the *agones* between free and high-minded opponents; the winning of fame that filled the entire Greek world and was spread by poets like Pindar and Bacchylides; the unity of all Greeks, never achieved in history but here realized every four years, as it were at play; and finally the expression of the characteristic Greek awareness of the beauty and efficiency of the human body—the Καλοκαγαθία, an idea of perfection that completely invests the image of man from its instinctive and physical basis to its spiritual and subjective aspect. It was the true goal of the contest, the object of the glorification, and at the same time it gives us the key to this highly corporeal art and architecture.

Winckelmann believed that through an investigation of this very ground 'a great light would spread over art', and the excavations have fulfilled his prediction. In the temple of Hera the beginnings of the monumental Doric temples have been preserved, in that of Zeus we behold its most perfect development. Since their discovery, the pediment groups and metopes of the latter building have changed our picture of Greek art, and will continue to do so; they form an inexhaustible legacy of the early classical, severe style, which has been called the sublime song of antiquity.

The Altis, the sacred grove of plane-trees and wild olives, was the focus of an extensive area dedicated to the god. As at Delphi, the temenos stood open to all visitors, who had access to it through a number of entrances. The earliest limits, which Heracles himself is supposed to have marked out, were probably no more than a wooden fence or a row of boundary-stones. Not till the fourth century was a wall with several (probably five) gateways put up round the Altis. Following straight lines, it enclosed an area of roughly 220 by 190 yds. The northern side was bounded by the slope of a wooded hill sacred to Cronus, one of the pre-Greek gods over whom Zeus prevailed.

The sanctuary's nucleus, around which the first altars and the Hera temple took their places, was the grave of a hero. It sheltered the remains of Pelops, who with a god's team took part in a chariot-race that was also a life-and-death struggle, and to whose funeral rites the games first belonged. 'Where the Alpheus flows, there he rests, and has a much-frequented tomb' (Pindar, *Ol.* 1, 92). The grave mound was narrowly confined by a special wall with its own propylaeum—a temenos within the temenos. To the east of it extended the stadium, the earliest running track.

North of the tomb, a temple was erected for Zeus's wife about the middle of the seventh century, whereas the Olympian himself continued to be worshipped in the open at an altar consisting of sacrificial ash piled up high. Not until the early fifth century, a period when things were profoundly changed, was a temple built for Zeus.

Meanwhile, a row of treasuries, like a peaceful procession across the slope of Mount Cronus, had been dedicated by Dorian cities, chiefly of Magna Graecia.

These few buildings in the Altis were joined at the beginning of the fourth century by a small peripteral temple for Meter, the mother of the gods—a very ancient goddess who had already long dwelt at Olympia. Philip and his son Alexander recorded their conquest of Greece at the battle of Chaeronea with a further building. The elegant peripteral rotunda was intended for the gold-and-ivory portrait statues of members of the Macedonian ruling house.

The desire awakened in the fourth century to create architectonic spaces now left its mark on the face of the Altis. A long two-naved marble stoa

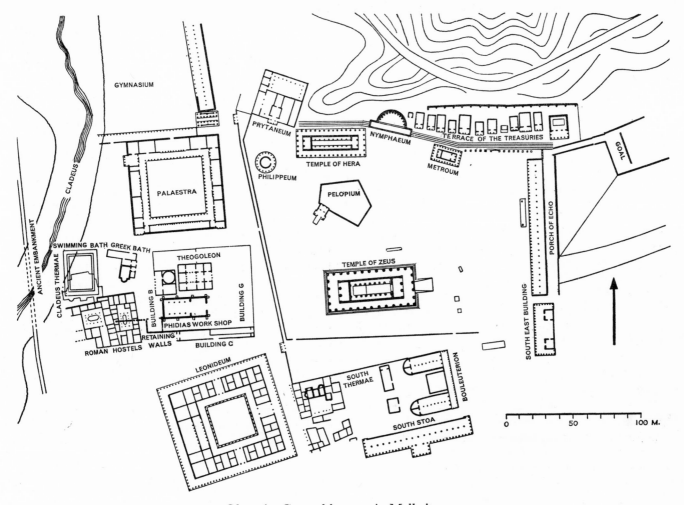

7 Olympia. General layout. A. Mallwitz, 1959

provided it with an imposingly large, eye-catching eastern limit. Outside the temenos, splendid new edifices arose near the prytaneum and bouleuterion, the earlier, more modest administrative buildings. They included another stoa to the south and the Leonideum, an impressive hostel with a spacious colonnaded courtyard within and an endless succession of Ionic columns running round the outside. During Hellenistic times, magnificent sports buildings—a palaestra and a gymnasium—were added.

Its restoration in the imperial age could hardly disguise the sanctuary's decline since the commencement of Roman rule. More pointedly than by all later acts of destruction, the end of Greek Olympia was marked by the last building presented to it: the wealthy Herodes Atticus's theatrical and luxurious fountain, glistening with incrustations of coloured marble and richly garnished with arrogant-looking portrait statues.

THE TEMPLE OF HERA   *Plates III, 47–49, fig. 8*

The discovery of the temple of Hera at the close of the nineteenth century shed the first bright light on the early history of temple buildings. Anyone who today walks through this peripteral structure, which has survived up to the footing of the cella walls, and who can picture these bulky walls of sun-dried brick and the surrounding, lightly-built wooden columns with the coloured wreath of the entablature above them, will here as nowhere else in Greece be able to reflect upon that period when the great goal of the monumental temple was reached.

Beneath the visible structure lie traces of a still earlier one belonging to the middle of the seventh century. The remains of its foundations show it to have been a simple rectangular megaron without peristyle, measuring roughly 33 by 130 ft. The length of the naos was determined by the sacred measure-

317

ment of 100 Doric feet, or 106·96 of ours ('hecatompedon', cf. Samos). A 20-Doric-ft.-deep pronaos with two columns in-antis formed the eastern access. There seems to have been no corresponding opisthodomus at the west end. Inside the naos, four spur walls projected into the room from each of the side walls. This evidently very ancient form of wall pattern originally served to secure walls of sun-dried brick, and in the Heraeum it probably also supported the ceiling beams. However, this technical purpose was permeated by an architectonic one: the spur walls graduated the deep longitudinal space. (We shall meet the same formal element in the classical temple at Bassae.) Moreover, through the placing of a column in the middle of each of the chapel-like bays formed by the spurs, a rhythmic sequence of engaged supports and slim wooden columns came into being, entirely born of this early period's taste for unrestrained contrasts. We know nothing about the upper structure. Above the thick, sun-baked brick walls, one must picture a flat, rustic mud roof.

Barely two generations later—round about 600—a second temple was erected, its naos rising up with an almost unchanged ground-plan from the foundations of the old building. It was characterized by a new spirit, which gave it its inward grandeur. The idea of the peripteral temple, which originated at Corinth and Argos during the seventh century, had penetrated into the remote Doric national sanctuary on the Alpheus, and there produced a building in which rustic devotion to the old style and supreme mastery of the new wondrously blended.

In the naos, everything remained as before, but an important innovation was the joining on to it of an opisthodomus, by which, apart from symmetry, the characteristic corporeality was achieved. For this symmetry entailed the pedimental façades at each

end, a form invented at Corinth, which meant that there was no longer a blank rear end, and that movement in one direction gave way to a calm balance of opposing tensions. This effect was produced above all by the peristyle that now surrounded the cella. The columns stood upon the low stone platform of the stylobate (61 ft. 6⅛ in. by 164 ft. 4⅜ in.), and their arrangement of 6 by 16 (angle columns counted twice) corresponded to the archaically elongated cella. These columns set the excavators a problem: scarcely two of them were alike, their diameter varying considerably (from 3 ft. 3⅜ in. to 4 ft. 2⅜ in.), and their style even more so. We are confronted by a veritable album of capitals, its earliest examples going back to the beginning of the sixth century, its latest to Roman times. A remark of Pausanias's provides the solution: he saw an oak column still standing in the opisthodomus. Sockets in the stylobate prove that at first all the columns were of timber. It is likely that people soon grew ashamed of this back-woodsman's way of building and encouraged visitors to present stone columns, until—centuries later—the peristyle had at last been 'petrified'. Only one of the original wooden columns, admired by visitors as a curiosity, remained in existence down to the imperial age.

The wide intercolumniation leaves no doubt that the entablature was also of wood. It must already have been divided up into the standard triglyph frieze—here certainly still retaining its structural significance—as the contracted intercolumnial spacing at every corner shows (cf. page 314). There is another sign of astonishing 'progressiveness': the cella did not drift uncertainly in the ambulatory, as was usual with sixth-century temples. Instead, the exteriors of its side walls were aligned with the axes of the second and fifth front columns, and in this

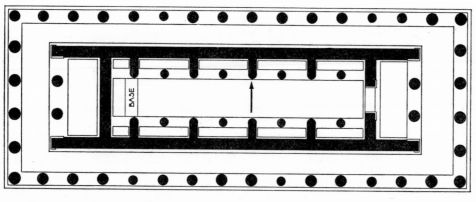

0   5   10   15   20 M.

8 Olympia, Heraeum. Plan (1 : 400). New drawing after *Olympia* II, 1892

318

too the classical solution was anticipated. The subtly graduated widths of the porticoes (east about 17 ft. o¾ in., west about 15 ft. 1⅞ in.) and pteromata (about 13 ft. 1½ in.) also looked forward, and the intercolumniation was correspondingly graded (ends 11 ft. 8⅛ in., sides 10 ft. 8⅜ in.). The remarkable alignment of the internal and external columns did not reappear until the classical temple at Bassae. Perhaps transverse ceiling beams enforced this methodical arrangement. It seems that, on the whole, the old structural bonds of the entablature had not yet been lost in this unsettled phase between wood and stone construction.

Of the cella walls, a stone socle 3 ft. 10½ in. broad and 3 ft. 5 in. high has survived all round; on it rested the walling in sun-dried brick. The large slabs set vertically (orthostats), that formed the outer surface of this socle, became for all times a permanent component of the Doric wall. Like the fronts and inner surfaces of the antae, the door opening was protected by a strong facing of planks, as can still be deduced from grooves and mortises. Both encasements passed over into stone construction: the later antae projections—a short outer and broad inner one—absorbed the wooden form, while the door-facing long continued to be of wood.

At the top, cella and peristyle were bound together by the mighty, sloping sides of the saddle-roof, which now likewise acquired a monumental form. Set in mud, huge concave tiles (about 1 ft. 11¼ in. by 3 ft. 11¼ in.), over the sides of which were inverted narrower cover-tiles semicircular in section, formed an expressive surface articulated by the 'ribs' running across it (the so-called Laconian roof). The lowest cover-tiles bent upwards into round, gaily painted rosettes. Above the pediment, as a last strong accent, towered the enormous, black-and-coloured disk of the acroterium (diam. 7 ft. 7 in.), covered with swirling, forceful geometric patterns. When else has ornament been able to express such uncanny power as at this time in this building? Here the newly created vessel of this great architecture was filled to bursting point with the still untamed energies of the demon-haunted seventh century, energies that only by degrees submitted to static architectonic laws like that of 'load and support'. Instead, 'life and growth' governed this edifice, which at the same time, however, had already hit upon the noblest of forms.

Gradually the venerable building became a sacred museum, the superabundant contents of which are specified for us by Pausanias. Of these riches, only the world-famous Hermes of Praxiteles has been found, protected against robbery and decay by mud from the dissolving walls.

The Heraeum seems to have stood undamaged till, in A.D. 426, Theodosius II ordered the destruction of the heathen temples. It made a strange neighbour for the classical temple of Zeus—the original ancestor beside the descendant which, crowned by sublime beauty, far excelled it.

THE TEMPLE OF ZEUS   *Plates 50–55, figs. 9–13*

Elis's political rise only furnished the outward inducement to build the temple of Zeus, a project paid for with plundered coin. An immeasurable advance in self-awareness had, since the beginning of the fifth century, brought to light previously hidden spiritual realms. In the tragedies of Aeschylus and the hymns of Pindar, the new, solemn knowledge found verbal expression, while on the pediments and metopes at Olympia it gained visible form. For it was during these few decades of the 'severe style' that all was made ready for building the home of the supreme god.

The southern part of the sacred grove had to be cleared to make room for the new structure, put up between 470 and 456. Its foundations rise about 9 ft. 10 in. above the ground. Earth was banked up against them, with the result that today the ruins of the temple, entirely reduced to rubble by earthquakes, still dominate the Altis in a stately manner and, surrounded by their rampart of collapsed columns and fragments of the entablature, give us some notion of their bygone grandeur. With its stylobate measuring 90 ft. 9¾ in. by 210 ft. 4⅜ in. and its 6 by 13 columns, the peripteral temple was in point of fact the biggest in the Peloponnese (except for a temple at Corinth reconstructed from scanty remains). As the most valid embodiment of the Doric canon, it was described in the introduction, and so we can here confine ourselves to details. We know nothing about its architect apart from his name and native city: Libon of Elis. It was built in a porous local shell-limestone, worked with amazing precision, though all the external surfaces were coated in a thin layer of stucco. The top step of the crepidoma was heightened relative to the other two in the proportion 7 : 6 (22 in. : 18⅞ in.), it being intended to give this stylobate its own special emphasis. Unlike that of earlier temples, the ground-plan was not derived roughly from the stylobate and cella measurements, but developed out of a clear basic unit: the interaxial of 16 Doric feet (17 ft. 1½ in.). This determined firstly the length and breadth of the peristyle of 5 by 12 interaxials (80 by 192 Doric ft.), these dimensions being reduced by the angle contraction that the frieze occasioned (16⅞ in.). Owing

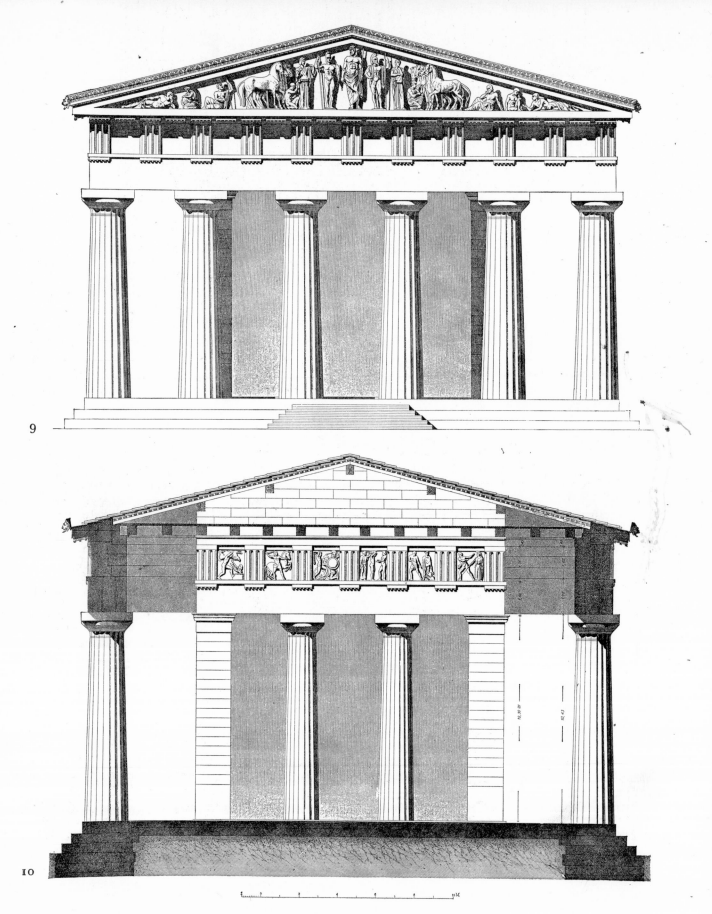

9–10 Olympia, temple of Zeus. *Olympia* II, 1892
9 East elevation. 10 Cross-section with view of pronaos

11–12 Olympia, temple of Zeus. *Olympia* II, 1892
11 Part of side elevation. 12 Cross-section

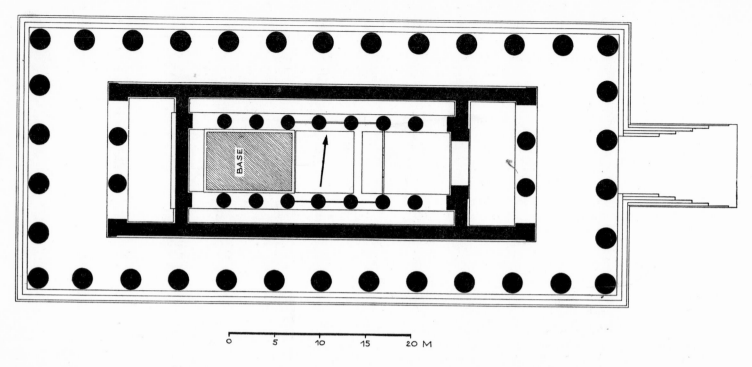

13 Olympia, temple of Zeus. Plan (1 : 400). New drawing after *Olympia* II, 1892

to its canonical encasement, the wholly symmetrically planned cella also had measurements that were exact multiples of the basic unit (3 by 9 interaxials). In the superstructure, this unit extended upwards to the roof in constantly halved multiples: interaxial = 16 Doric ft.; triglyph + metope = 8 Doric ft.; mutule + via = 4 Doric ft.; tile width = 2 Doric ft. Even the heights appear assimilated: the height of the columns (32 ft. 2 in. or a little more) only slightly exceeded two interaxials. Yet this framework of proportions was by no means as rigid as some theorists would claim, and it is after all precisely the anomalies that make us conscious of the life of the building. For it, sculptural forms were created that preserved their freedom and elbow-room even within the most rigorous order.

Compared with, say, the late archaic ones on Aegina, the columns had increased in weight and thickness (height here: $4\frac{3}{8}$ lower diam., Aegina: $5\frac{1}{3}$ lower diam.). At the same time, they tautened their contour to the limit, the entasis being small and the echinus that rose at an angle of forty-five degrees bulging only slightly. This profile was one of calm, restrained power. Strangely enough, the column diameters at the ends were different from those at the sides (ends: 7 ft. 5 in., sides: 7 ft. $3\frac{3}{4}$ in.), and in this the archaic custom of enlarging the end columns and interaxial spacing seems to have survived. The capitals also vary, and reveal a stylistic development

(noted too in the temple's pictorial decoration) following the sequence: east end, west end, sides.

The architectonic means of expression had become exceedingly refined. Thus, the flanking columns leaned inwards about $2\frac{1}{2}$ in. so as to unite the body of the building more firmly. Although those at the ends stood more erect, they shared in this tilt through the pair next to the angle columns, but these had a reduced slant of only about $\frac{5}{8}$ in. The middle interaxial space at the east end was widened by the same amount. How sharp the Greek eye must have been to be able to notice such deviations at all! Even a curvature (see page 377) was probably introduced, but the stylobate has been so displaced by subsidence and earthquakes that it has not yet been possible to detect it.

The interior of the naos was again planned in terms of interaxial units (42 ft. $10\frac{1}{2}$ in. by 94 ft. $3\frac{1}{2}$ in. = $2\frac{1}{2}$ by $5\frac{1}{2}$ interaxials or 40 by 88 Doric ft.). Two double-tiered rows of seven columns divided it into a nave and aisles, the former being twice as broad as the latter (ratio 1 : 2 : 1 = 10 ft. : 20 ft. : 10 ft.). These columns were not aligned with those of the peristyle. The architraves between the tiers of columns supported galleries approached by small wooden staircases at either side of the great entrance door, and obviously installed later.

The temple had been standing for almost thirty years when, around 432, none less than Phidias was appointed to create a statue of Zeus out of gold and ivory. It became the most celebrated work of art of ancient times, one of the seven wonders of the world. What seems intolerable to us—the huge, enthroned image of the god filling the entire height and width of the nave and a third of its length (how could it have avoided bursting open the narrow space?)—did not offend its contemporaries. They saw it as a thing apart, without optical references to its spatial setting. Not until Roman times was it possible to criticize it: 'One gets the impression that the god would break through the temple roof, if he were to rise' (Strabo VIII, 353). Recently Phidias's workshop has been discovered, with clay moulds of drapery parts and extremely delicate floral ornaments of glass, as well as chips of precious stones and remains of pigments. This has enabled a final gleam from the statue to reach us in our day—the statue 'of which it was said among the ancients that whoever had seen it could never be completely unhappy' (G. Hauptmann after Arrian, *Epict.* I, 6).

The outline of the great pedestal measuring 21 ft. 9¾ in. by 32 ft. 7 in. can still be seen in the naos; before it, another third of the nave was paved with dark Eleusinian flagstones, bordered by white marble, and enclosed by painted screens: an inaccessible area at the god's feet. This use of the bluish-black stone in a striking contrast was an Attic invention (Propylaea, Erechtheum), and little suited the air of gravity and reserve that characterized the temple, where a more valuable material was only introduced when the local shell-limestone proved too coarse. The roof, including the large Corinthian tiles as well as the convex simas with their 102 waterspouts in the form of lions' heads, was of Parian marble, like the sculpture of the pediments and the metopes over the pronaos and opisthodomus.

This sculpture is rooted in the same soil as the architecture. Here and there on the twelve metopes with the labours of Heracles, there are still distant echoes of the crude narrative style of archaic representations, but a new note is much stronger: these are moving, symbolic images of events from the life of the long-suffering hero. The mode of composition is downright architectonic. Two or at most three figures, forcefully concentrated round a vertical, diagonal or horizontal axis, are braced across or parallel to each other—so rigorously that, in them, the temple's framework of forces seems to have taken on human form. The pediment groups were 'built' in the same way. No longer did the figures fit unnaturally under the gable slopes. Here it was more as if the shallow triangle of the pediment had been specially created for the composition, which swept outwards in balanced contrasts. At the

centre, grouped round the vertical of the god, was a powerful nucleus from which the movement thrust out, parried by opposing forces directed inwards from the corners—an arrangement reflecting the relationship between cella and peristyle. Finally, the most individual contribution of this first classical temple was the way in which all its parts harmonized to form a single whole, animated by the same breath and cast in the same mould.

THE TREASURIES   *Plates 56–58, figs. 7, 14–17*

On the slope of Mount Cronus, along a terrace raised about 10 ft. above the Altis, there stood twelve little anta 'temples', neatly lined up and all facing south towards the grove. Since there were no altars, they were not cult buildings but treasuries or 'thesauroi'. They had been presented by Dorian cities that competed at Olympia—chiefly by rich colonies thirsting for glory—and in them were installed the most magnificent of their donors' offerings. The arrangement of this row, which guaranteed just treatment to every building, is characteristic of the spirit of fair-play that reigned at Olympia. A vigilant body of priests evidently allotted each donor city its building site, and did not permit the malicious ousting and overtrumping of offerings that turned Delphi into an arena for Greek feuds.

Though a long, stepped terrace wall—a sort of common crepidoma—bound the group together into a whole, a closer look reveals that no system, no architectonic plan underlay it. The horizontal axes, spacing, and height of the buildings varied. The row was completed only gradually during the course of the sixth and fifth centuries, and the closing terrace wall was not constructed until the fourth.

Proceeding from west to east, Pausanias enumerates ten treasuries: I Sicyon, II Syracuse (III already seems to have been destroyed by his day), IV Epidamnus, V Byzantium, VI Sybaris, VII Cyrene (the unusually small building VIII was not a treasury but an altar to Heracles), IX Selinus, X Metapontum, XI Megara and XII Gela. The small altar VII appears to be the oldest building in the row. A little later, towards 560, it was followed by the easternmost treasury XII, that of Sicilian Gela, which was built without a porch as a simple rectangular 'container' around a huge base (28 ft. 4½ in. by 15 ft. 9⅜ in.). The platform carried sculptures, which in the surviving dedicatory inscription are mentioned before the building, and were thus obviously the most important item. This may explain the peculiar ground-plan. As was usual, the roof

56

fig. 7

323

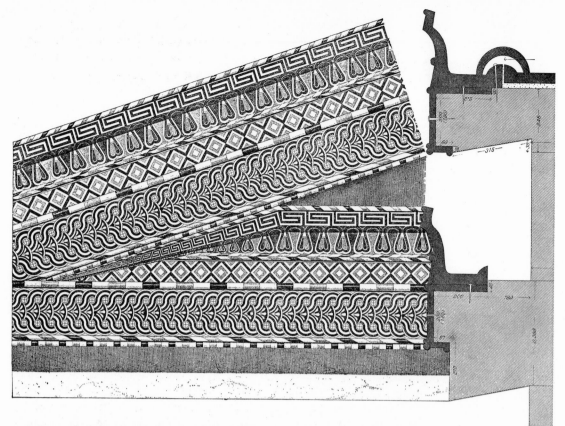

14   Olympia, Geloan treasury. Terracotta revetment of pediment cornices (*above*) and flank cornice (*below*) (1 : 14). *Olympia II*, 1892

gable embellished and stressed the building's narrow east and west ends, but the entrance, and hence the front, lay on the long south side! Here must also have been the bases of the figure groups. In the fifth century, this perverse arrangement of front and entrance was felt to be so disturbing that a porch with 6 by 2 columns was built on to the entrance side. What interests us most is the roof. For from it has survived our most complete ensemble of terracotta cornice revetments as they were brought to their fullest flower in Sicily. Frieze and mutules, those rhythmically organizing elements, are missing. Hence, an almost entirely uninhibited delight in ornament is expressed on these slabs that faced the

fig. 14

raw stone of the corona, as also on the tall sima that, in Sicilian fashion, ran round the flanks and gable ends; and it has covered them with a thick fabric of coloured enrichments (red, black, white). Strange to relate, the sima also appeared over the horizontal corona of the pediment, where in actual fact a gutter has no business to be. In this, the earlier hip-roof lived on, its edge apparently cut off sharply at the corners by the gable cornice placed above it. The technique of nailing on the terracotta revetments likewise recalls construction in wood. All these terracotta members, as also the roof made up of 1,011 tiles, had been prefabricated in Sicily with just the right measurements.

324

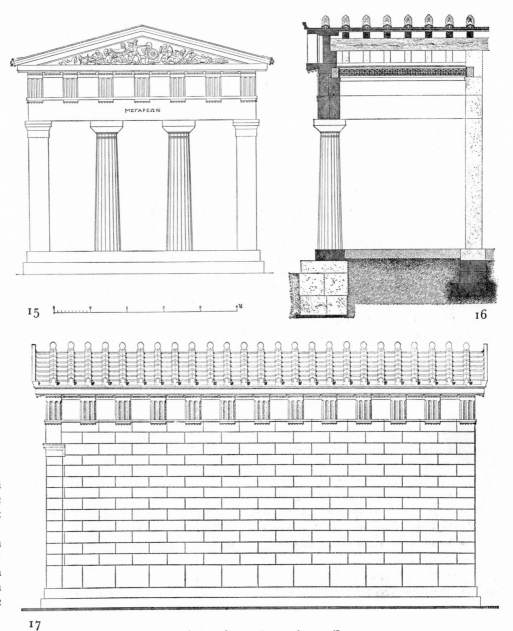

15 ΜΕΓΑΡΕΩΝ

15-16 Olympia, Megarian
treasury. *Olympia* II, 1892
15 Front elevation (1 :
      100)
16 Longitudinal section
through pronaos (1 : 100)
17 Olympia, Sicyonian
treasury. Side elevation
(1 : 100). *Olympia* II, 1892

17

The relatively broad (31 ft. 9⅞ in.) treasury V of Byzantium dates from about the same time, and it, too, should probably be reconstructed as an archaic oikos with continuous walls all round. After the middle of the sixth century, the treasuries definitely took on the form of little anta temples—mostly with two columns in-antis, like those of the South Italian town of Sybaris (VI) and African Cyrene (VII). To the latter have been assigned a terracotta roof with charming enrichment enlivened by Ionic influences, and a 'Sybaritic' girl's head (from an acroterium?) as attractive as it is cheeky. At about the same date were erected the broad treasury X of Italian Metapontum (with three columns in-antis

or a portico in front), and treasury IX of Sicilian Selinus.

Towards the end of the sixth century, a building from the mother-country finally appeared: treasury XI of Megara, filling the last gap in the row on the east. The finds allow us to make a reliable reconstruction of it. Even the south pediment's dramatic battle between gods and giants, which in the unconstrained way it fitted into the triangular space heralded the Agina pediments, has survived. The front displayed the already fully mature Doric order with painstakingly worked details, which again have much in common with the temple of Aphaea. One will have to pardon the thrifty Megarians, with their

figs. 15, 16

325

peasant cunning, for the fact that this care was confined to the façade, that the fluting on the backs of the columns is not complete, that neither triglyphs nor mutules run round the long sides, and that, briefly, they paraded the front while economizing behind in an entirely un-Greek manner.

Treasury II of Syracuse, donated in 480 by Gelon from the proceeds of his victory over Carthage, has recently been reconstructed with the help of various architectural parts which had been used for other building during the imperial era. The simple, clear-cut outlines already herald the advent of the classical style. The small anta temple with its circle of triglyphs was constructed, probably by Peloponnesian artists, of local shell-limestone.

fig. 17

The westernmost building in the row, treasury I, is also the latest. It was presented by Corinth's neighbour Sicyon, an art centre very famous for its sculptors in bronze and its painters. The choiceness of its lucid architectural forms and the harmonious proportions of its structure made the little Doric anta 'temple' (22 ft. 1 in. by 38 ft. 11 in.) worthy of its place near the roughly contemporary Zeus temple, even though the latter so imposingly surpassed it in size. Above two barely projecting steps rose the cella wall, stratified in a precise concordancy of joints. The frieze ran all the way round, as on the

72, 74

Athenian treasury at Delphi (see page 337). In contrast to that building, however, the outer interaxial spaces were here narrower than the middle one (5 ft. 11¼ in.; 6 ft. 5⅝ in.), so that the triglyphs came directly over the centres of the two columns. The gay embellishment of figures and ornament on the archaic treasuries was replaced here by a restrained emphasis of the architectonic structure, clarified in the frieze and cornice by blue and red colouring. Sculptural decoration had been entirely abandoned. Only the gutters and ridge of the marble roof were adorned with simple palmette antefixes.

The treasury's fine-grained limestone was quarried in Sicyon, where its structural members were also fashioned, their place in the building being indicated by Sicyonian letters. When they offered the Zeus of Olympia a pure, an unadulterated masterpiece from their homeland, the Sicyonians did not fight shy of the great labour involved in transporting its parts. This was intended to replace an older treasury, the foundations of which have been preserved under the more recent building.

THE STADIUM   *Plate 58, fig. 7*

The Olympic stadium, where the oldest and most important contest—the foot-race—occurred, remained at all periods a simple, unpretentious affair. The earliest detectable stadium, from the sixth century, was no more than a levelled race-track with markings for the start and finish, situated at the foot of Mount Cronus. It belonged entirely to the sacred precinct—indeed, the goal lay close to the most venerable cult objects: the altar of Zeus and the wild olive-tree from which the victors' wreaths were cut.

Greece determined its most important distance measurement—the 'stadium' of about 627½ English feet—by the length of this course.

In the fifth century, the embankments had to be enlarged. A century later, when the Altis was enclosed all round with walls and a stoa, it became necessary to shift the stadium to the east and cut it off from the Altis. The stone starting and finishing slabs of this layout still exist, and have two parallel grooves for the runners to toe. Twenty starting places for the competitors were separated by posts. A water-channel divided off the 95-ft.-wide course from the terraced embankments, which comfortably seated about 50,000 spectators.

DELPHI

THE SANCTUARY OF APOLLO

Delphi is tied to its unique landscape as no other sanctuary. Here the luminous and the precipitous, inspiration and awe, intermingle. The white rock-faces of the Phaedriades reflect the dazzling sunlight, multiply voices and other sounds, shine through the heady breezes that blow there. Older, crumbling

layers of slate that, in the sanctuary's environs, stand out below the limestone cliffs conduct cool, vigorous spring water; but they also produce dangerous landslides which have descended upon Delphi again and again, in ancient and in modern *fig. 19* times. The youthful god of light has not been able to

326

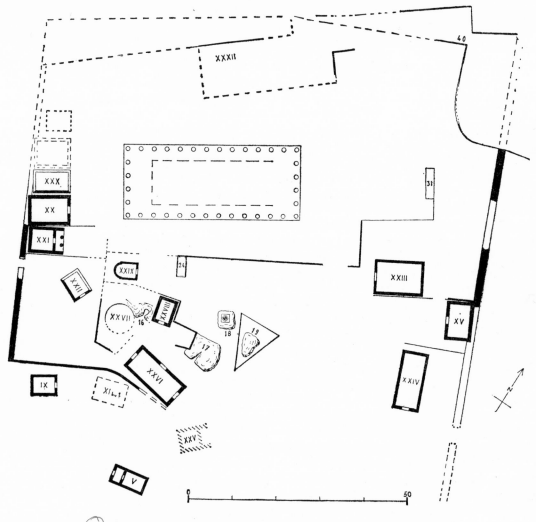

18 Delphi, sanctuary of Apollo, *c.* 550 B.C. (see caption to fig. 19).
P. de la Coste-Messelière, 1936 and 1943

quiet the ousted Gea and the vanquished Python as completely as all that.

The arrangement of the temenos is wholly determined by its position on a steep southern slope. Divided by large terrace walls, it rises stepwise up the mountain-side in three zones, which are again repeatedly terraced. In the lowest area, treasuries and offerings crowd closely round the sacred way, which climbs obliquely upward with a sharp bend, and round its byroads. The buildings are variously orientated in apparent confusion, some towards the way, others towards the slope; or else they have forced themselves into the narrow spaces left over by earlier votive monuments. Bounded on the south by a great wall of polygonal masonry, the central zone is dominated by the god's temple and altar. The sacred way reaches this terrace at its south-east corner, ascending along its eastern flank to the forecourt of the temple. Parallel to the latter's north side, another

strong wall—the so-called Ischegaon—buttresses the upper terrace, and has to take the entire thrust of the noticeably steeper slope. The western part of this upper terrace came to be occupied in the third century by the Delphic theatre, which is reached by an imposing flight of steps from the west end of the temple. A side-road, the final offshoot of the sacred way, leads on to the precincts of Dionysus and Poseidon, which, filled with treasuries and chapels, adjoin the temple area on the east. The road continues to a small temenos with the tomb of Neoptolemus, and finally to the lesche or club-house of the Cnidians. Planted on the highest spot, it contained famous paintings by Polygnotus, to which Pausanias devoted more space in his description than to all the rest of the sanctuary.

The whole of this area belonging to the god, which, as a rectangle of about 142 by 197 yards stretches lengthwise up the slope, was surrounded by the

327

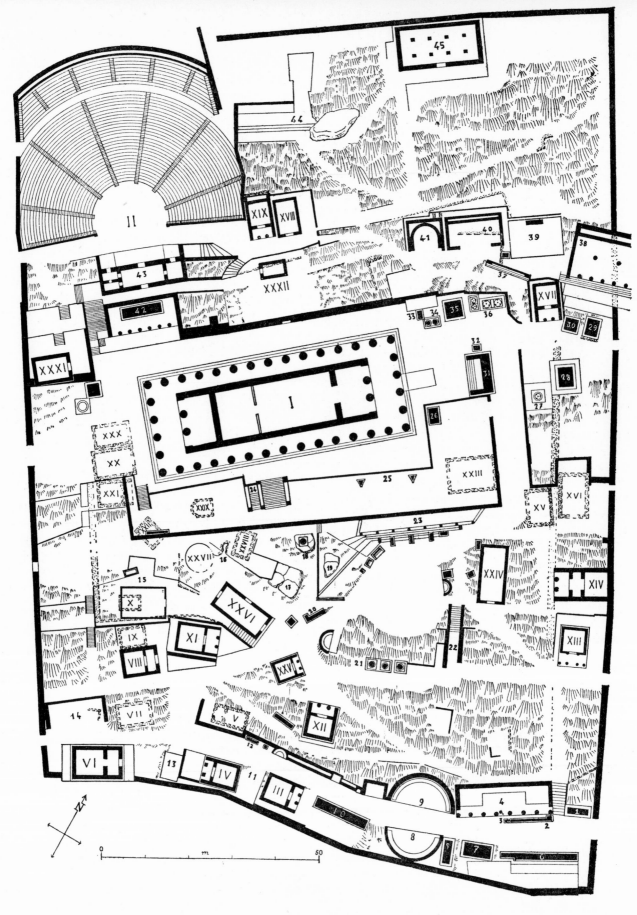

19 Delphi, sanctuary of Apollo, *c.* 150 B.C. P. de la Coste-Messelière, 1936 and 1943

sanctuary wall. Oddly enough, the sacred way led into the temenos through a simple wall opening, which was joined by six others giving access to the byroads. People could come and go freely through all of them. No propylaeum accentuated and barred the entrance, since, after all, everything from the cliffs and the Castalian gorge down to the sacred plain of Cirrha (Crisa) pertained to the god. He had no need of gateways and bolts; the temple guardian, his Olympian sister Athena, had her sanctuary on the other side of the Castalian gorge. Her temple was, so to speak, Delphi's propylaeum.

fig. 18 The sanctuary wall was put up after the middle of the sixth century in the course of a thoroughgoing enlargement of the temenos, and, having been restored after 480, underwent no further changes. Inside it, an earlier boundary is clearly apparent on the site of the older treasuries. Various parts of this earlier wall have been found. They helped to form the first solid enclosure, built at the beginning of the sixth century after Delphi had gained its independence in the First Sacred War. Then, the entrance seems to have been at the north-east corner, flanked by the 'Aeolic treasury' and that of Cnidus. The southern bend in the sacred way obviously belongs to a final extension of the sanctuary.

How differently from the level, spacious Altis of Olympia is this temenos organized on its steep slope! Supremely self-willed, living individuals, the competing treasuries and votive monuments pressed in on the winding way like thirsty animals around a stream. The high temple rose up powerfully and commandingly at the centre, but it did not unify the scene. Not a common reference but diversity prevailed, not a planned architectonic view but animation.

Buildings I: temple of Apollo. II: theatre (second cent. B.C., 5,000 seats) with 43: stage buildings. III to XXXII: treasuries, naiskoi, and administrative buildings, the following nameable: III: treasury of Sicyon; IV: of Siphnos; VI: of Thebes; VIII: of Potidaea (?); XI: of Athens; XII: 'Aeolic treasury'; XIII: of Cyrene; XVII: of Acanthus; XXV: of Cnidus; V, IX (Athens?), XV, XX to XXIII, and XXVIII to XXX: archaic, later destroyed treasuries and naiskoi (cf. fig. 18); XXIV: treasury of Corinth. XIV: prytaneum. XXVI: bouleuterion. *Votive offerings and sites* 1: Corcyrean bull; 2: Arcadian base; 4: Lysander monument; 6: Marathon base; 8: epigoni and 9: kings of Argos; 15: temenos of the Muses (?); 16: temenos of Gaea; 17: 'rock of the Sibyl'; 18: Naxian column; 19: rock of Leto (?); 23: Athenian stoa; 27: tripod from the booty of Plataea (479 B.C.); 31: Apollo altar of Chios (presented *c.* 475 B.C.); 33: equestrian statue of Prusias II of Bithynia; 36: the four god tripods of the Deinomenids of Syracuse from the booty of Himera (480 B.C.); 38: stoa of Attalus II of Pergamum; 40: group of Daochus of Thessaly; 45: Cnidian lesche

Yet one spot was at all times, in awe, left free: a little rocky wilderness amid the universal pomp. Upon a rough boulder beneath the great polygonal wall, the first Sibyl is said to have chanted. This is the realm of the sanctuary's earliest mistress, the earth mother, and here are her mantic fountain Cassotis and the cave of her serpent son. Other conspicuous objects indicate her defeat, such as a rock from which Leto spurred on her son during his fight with Python. The mysterious Naxian sphinx enthroned on an early Ionic column over thirty-three feet tall may have relieved him in his role of guardian. Here as nowhere else, we can picture a primitive open sanctuary of the earliest period—one without a temple, intimately associated with crag, spring, gully, and tree; and in this very Delphi, more vividly than at any other place, we are told legends of the first temples and their growth from the soil of the venerable sites.

73, 74

THE TEMPLE OF APOLLO   *Plates V, 60–63, figs. 20–24*

The peripteral temple that rises in ruins above the polygonal wall is by no means the first on this site. Excavations have led to the detection of two predecessors, but legend distinguishes four: a first of laurel (an arbour or bower?); a second carried off by Apollo to the Hyperboreans; a third erected by Hephaestus and Athena with walls and columns entirely of bronze, which the earth swallowed up; and lastly a fourth, obviously known to Homer, the mythical architects of which—Agamedes and Trophonius—are said to have been helped by Apollo himself (*Hymn to Apollo* 116 ff., 249). Its 'stone threshold' may have been a base of orthostats with a superstructure of wood and sun-dried brick. Was it, as Pausanias believed, identical with a temple burned down in 548, traces of which have been detected? The form of the remains assigned to it (a fragment of a Doric capital, two column drums $38\frac{1}{8}$ and $34\frac{5}{8}$ in. in diam. with 20 flutes, a few orthostats and stylobate slabs, which at first probably bore wooden columns) scarcely indicate a date before about 600. At all events, as the chief temple of the sanctuary, it was a Doric peripteral building.

After the fire in 548, all Hellas contributed to the cost of a bigger and finer home for Apollo. An enormous retaining-wall made room for it to the south by ruthlessly carving up the ancient sanctuary of the earth mother, who had been robbed and displaced quite enough already. This 'jigsaw puzzle for giants' is built of great polygonal stones with curving joints; covered in inscriptions from the second and first centuries, it is also a stone history-

74, below

book for us. The temple, under construction from about 530 to 520, seems in its relationships of volumes and of dimensions to tie up with the Apollo temple at Corinth, and it also has the same archaic elongation of the ground-plan, with 6 by 15 columns (stylobate 71 ft. 1½ in. by 180 ft. 10⅝ in.). It appears to have been based on an earlier design from the decade after the fire; and in point of fact we do hear of a model (παράδειγμα, Herodotus V, 62), which the Athenian nobleman Clisthenes undertook to realize, and surpassed, in that he built the east end in Parian marble instead of poros. (The date 513–505 proposed by the excavators on the grounds of a plausible but not convincing interpretation of what Herodotus states cannot be reconciled with the archaic building forms, which extend up to the roof, as in the tubular water-spouts of the sima.)

The most important remains are the pediment figures carefully hidden in the ground after the collapse of the temple. Their Attic creator, probably none less than Antenor, was disciplined by the Doric building to a simplicity and severity unparalleled during this period so devoted to gracefulness. His composition of the pediments was a first inkling of things to come. In the gigantomachy of the poros pediment at the west end, fallen giants filled the outer gable angles, from which the combatants gradually raised themselves up to the group of gods towering at the centre. On the marble east pediment, Apollo, the master of the temple, solemnly appeared on his four-horse chariot surrounded by the Muses, Delphus, and two sons of Hephaestus: a radiant epiphany. Disconnected heraldic groups of fighting animals, placed either side, still recalled the hitherto prevailing pediment pattern, as did the corner acroteria in the form of Nikes sweeping along with bent knees. Nevertheless, the assurance with which the figures were set in their gable triangle, each pediment completely adjusted to its theme—statuesque manifestation on the east, conflict and movement on the west—pointed ahead to the first classical pediments: those of the temple of Zeus at Olympia. This temple of Apollo stood for only 150 years; in 373 it collapsed owing to a fire or an earthquake.

For the second time, money was collected to pay for a new building, work on which made sluggish progress. During the Second Sacred War, the Phocians stole the building fund, but construction continued after 346 thanks to the payment extracted in

reparation from the beaten enemy. The temple was finally ready round about 320, having been erected over the foundations of its predecessor, with an almost unchanged ground-plan. Here, too, it was the sanctity of the earlier temple and the conservatism of the priests that occasioned such an anachronism,

though this very fact casts a significant light on the continuity of Greek temple construction. At a time when the Parthenon and the temples at Bassae and Tegea, with their broad interior spaces and open, perfectly attuned peristyle, had made their mark on this development, nobody took offence at one of Greece's holiest temples being given a narrow-chested, overlong cella (43 ft. 9⅛ in. by 144 ft. 9¾ in.), which drifted without axial ties in a peristyle that likewise remained full of archaisms. For example, the column diameters and axial spaces were greater at the ends than at the sides.

The foundations, about 16½ ft. high where the ground sloped towards the valley, and the stylobate were built in the blue Parnassian limestone much employed at Delphi, the upper parts in Corinthian poros, use being made of the old column drums. Spintharus, the otherwise unknown architect from Corinth, appears to have died during the course of these slow-moving building operations, as does the Attic sculptor Praxias while working on the pediment groups, now lost without trace.

The details were fashioned in the angular style, like solid geometry, of the later fourth century: the echinus a rectilinear truncated cone, the triglyph cut in a hard, sharp-cornered way, the column stretching out nonchalantly, its sculptural character lost with the entasis. Even the plentiful scattering of Ionic decorative mouldings could not blind one to the building's cool demeanour; as rigor set in, neither the acanthus tendrils with their agitated play of light and shade nor the expressive lions' heads on the simas could bring back any life.

The terribly pillaged ruins of this last temple of Apollo were brought to light by the excavations, and its end columns have in part been re-erected. From the standpoint of architectural history, it is a curiosity: a temple with an archaic plan and late classical details. Nevertheless, as a religious and historical focus of the Hellenistic world, it remains one of the places most worthy of our respect, and we should like to know more about the site of oracle delivery than the sources reveal. Little that is certain has been disclosed by the excavations. The cella's great length bears out the tradition of an adytum, though its exact location is not known. Where did the god speak through the Pythia's mouth? Was Gea's oracle cave transferred to the temple? A hollow in the foundations can be thus interpreted. Did the consultants wait in a western adytum, from which steps led down to the Pythia's tripod? A small, free-standing structure inside the naos has also been considered. The Pythia drank water from the fountain Cassotis, and in point of fact accessible draining-shafts already appear in the foundations of the earlier temple. It is

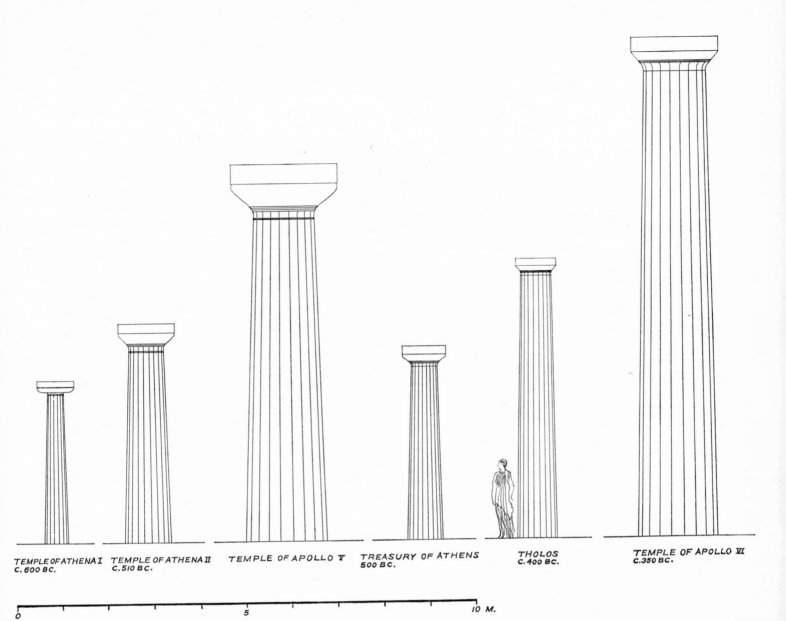

TEMPLE OF ATHENA I
C. 600 BC.

TEMPLE OF ATHENA II
C. 510 BC.

TEMPLE OF APOLLO V

TREASURY OF ATHENS
500 BC.

THOLOS
C. 400 BC.

TEMPLE OF APOLLO VI
C. 350 BC.

0   5   10 M.

20 Delphi. Comparison of Doric columns. New drawing

doubtful if they are connected with the adytum. No trace has survived either of Apollo's cult image or of the sacred monuments in the adytum: the tomb of Dionysus and the omphalos.

Under the Romans, the temple fared no better than Greece as a whole. Sulla despoiled it, Domitian had it repaired, Nero carried off the remaining works of art, Hadrian tried to re-animate it as splendidly as possible. The last pagan on the imperial throne, Julian the Apostate, received the last oracle from the declining sun god: 'Tell the emperor that the place glorified by art lies in ruins, that Phoebus no longer has a home and a mantic laurel; no longer does the spring serve him, the murmuring water is hushed' (Georgius Cedrenus p. 305a).

THE TREASURIES   *Plates 65–72, figs. 25–29*

The Delphic treasuries presented a picture different from the orderly procession of the Doric treasuries at Olympia and from the roundelay performed about the temple group by those on Delos. With the votive monuments, they made up a gaily coloured swarm in lively confusion. They were sumptuous or austere caskets for the most valuable offerings, built in rivalry by the donor cities that thirsted for fame, and speaking in every dialect of Greek architecture: an image of all Hellas in the most confined of spaces.

Only a few of these treasuries are securely named. Thirteen mentioned in the sources (Sicyon, Siphnos, Thebes, Athens, Cnidus, Potidaea, Syracuse, and

331

21

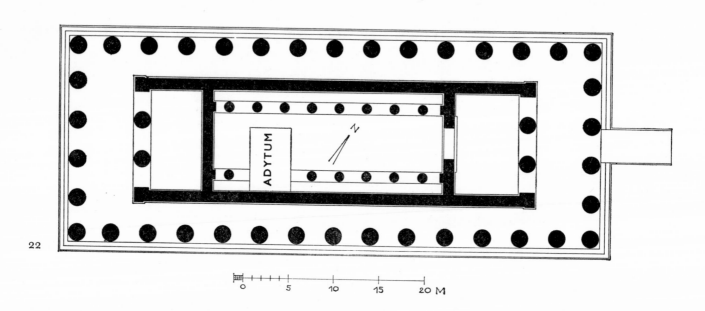

22

0   5   10   15   20 M

21 (*Above*) Delphi, temple of Apollo V, *c.* 525 B.C. East elevation (1 : 167). M. Courby, *Fouilles de Delphes*, 1927
22 (*Below*) Delphi, temple of Apollo VI, fourth cent. B.C. Plan (1 : 400). New drawing after *Fouilles de Delphes*, 1927
23 (*Right, above*) Delphi, temple of Apollo VI. East elevation (1 : 167). M. Courby, *Fouilles de Delphes*, 1927
24 (*Right, below*) Delphi, temple of Apollo VI. South side elevation (1 : 167). New drawing

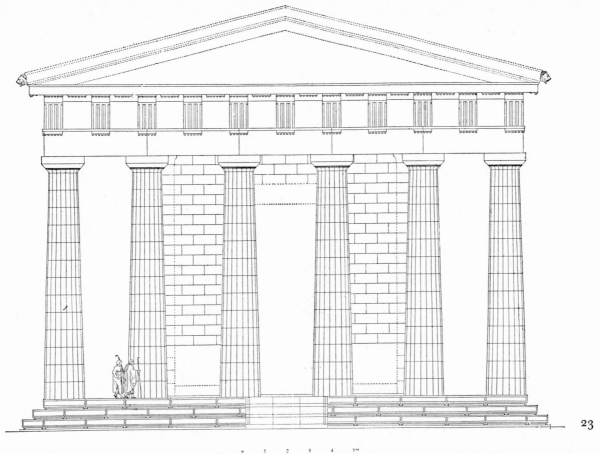

23

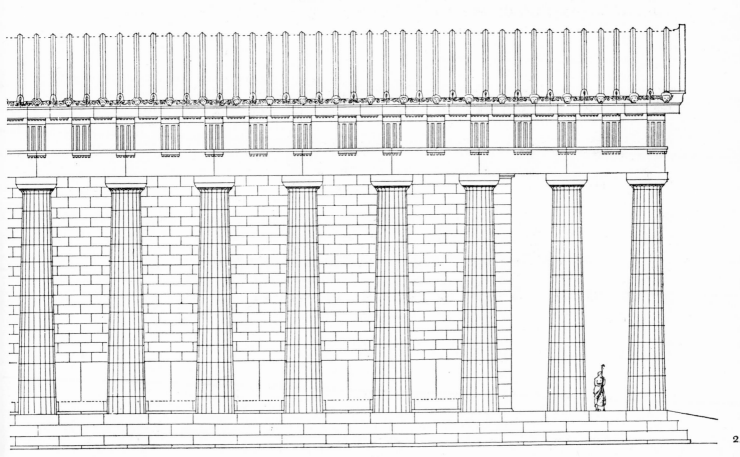

24

Corinth by Pausanias; Acanthus by Plutarch; Clazomenae by Herodotus; Massalia by Appian and Diodorus; Caere and Spina by Strabo) are confronted by the remains of twenty-three excavated in Apollo's sanctuary and two more in the precinct of Athena Pronaea. Here, we shall limit ourselves to the most important.

Ionic Treasuries

figs. 25, 26, 29

In the treasury of *Clazomenae*, as Herodotus (I, 51) mentions, a golden crater given by Croesus was installed after the temple fire. Its position has not been unquestionably established (the base proposed lies outside the earliest enclosure), and the few remains of its upper structure do not justify the obvious dating to the period before the fire of 548; they must have been made one or two decades after. The only slightly later treasury of *Massalia* (now Marseilles), also an Aeolic colony, in the Athena precinct is entirely similar but better preserved, and helps us to fill the gaps between the sparse fragments of the Clazomenian building. It covers an area of 20 ft. 1¾ in. by 27 ft. 10⅝ in., and its height was about 25 ft. 7 in. Hence, both edifices took the form of small anta temples with two columns in front, and both were of Parian marble. The ashlar walls rested on a fluted torus. Remains of a sculptured frieze have been identified as belonging to the Massalian treasury; dentils seem, accordingly, to have been lacking. The corona soffit and the sima were magnificently enriched with lotus-and-palmette bands. The bases of the sharply fluted columns (Clazomenae 18, Massalia 22 flutes) are of Ephesian form, which makes the capitals all the more individual: a crown of slim ascending petals (18 and 22 respectively), their tips curling over, with a square abacus set upon it. This unusual variation of the Ionic capital, with the volutes above the echinus replaced by a simple abacus, obviously later promoted the creation of the Corinthian capital.

figs. 25, 27, 29

The dedicatory inscription of the earliest Ionic treasury (about 560), that of *Cnidus*, has been found. In early Cnidian lettering, it reads: 'Erected in honour of Pythian Apollo from a tithe of the war booty'. To this treasury has been assigned a limestone base of archaically rough polygonal stonework (No. XXV) measuring 16 ft. 10 in. by 21 ft. 7⅞ in., and over it once rose the first marble structure on the mainland. Built of alternating high courses and low, bonding ones (pseudo-isodomic), the walls of this anta 'temple' rested on a torus, like those of the Massalian treasury. As there, the antae were probably crowned by a Lesbian cyma bearing an abacus.

Compared with the three-tiered anta capital of Asia Minor, this is a strikingly simple form, which could have been inspired by the neighbouring Doric buildings; yet it continued to affect the Attic-Ionic style. An innovation with important consequences was the introduction of a frieze in place of dentils.

Continuous sculptured friezes running round the cella walls at the foot or top belong, it is true, to Ionia's earliest stock of forms. There is, however, no precedent in the East for the way in which such a frieze here appeared above the architrave, and in which that primitive Ionic member the dentil course was actually sacrificed to it, so that the entablature should not grow excessively high. The Ionic workmen were evidently trying to produce with their own means something equivalent to the characterful sculptured triglyph frieze of the Doric buildings. Inevitably it was Attica that took up and perfected this ingenious blend of the two frieze structures.

However, the builders' most surprising and imaginative notion was to introduce two figures of girls under the entablature instead of the usual columns in-antis. Stepping forward slightly with their rippling chiton caught up affectedly, these 'caryatids' hardly differ from the standard *kore* of their time; but they also wear a priestly head-dress, the cylindric *kalathos*, in which the form of the column reappears. Upon it, a capital carved with a petal crown, flatter and more widespreading than the Clazomenian type, must have lain, such as has survived over a caryatid head hitherto attributed to the present building but, in fact, belonging to another, somewhat later treasury. From this exact exchange of columns for girls' bodies, one can judge how clearly the Ionians perceived their columns as sculptural, living forms.

In his account of the plundering of the island of *Siphnos* by Samian fugitives in 525 at the latest, Herodotus writes (III, 57): 'The Siphnians' prosperity had at this period reached its peak, and they were in fact the most wealthy of the islanders. For on the island they possessed gold- and silver-mines, thanks to which they established at Delphi with a tithe of the revenue a treasury that in its richness was second to none.' And rich indeed was the building finally accorded to the Siphnians after much scholarly discussion. Securely dated to the years before 525 by the above passage, it constitutes one of the most important fixed points for the history of architecture in the sixth century.

67-70

Above a high substructure of large, squared blocks of limestone (20 ft. 1¾ in. by 28 ft. 0⅝ in.), which compensates for the steep slope at the southern boundary of the temenos, the treasury was built in Parian marble. It opened to the west, where a forecourt was created by means of a wall of polygonal

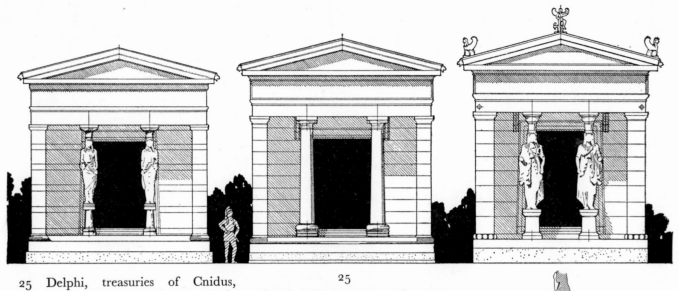

25

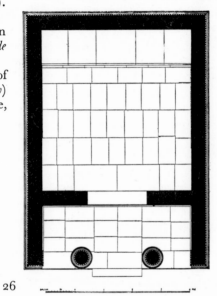

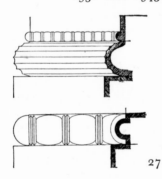

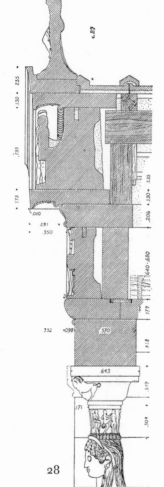

25 Delphi, treasuries of Cnidus, Massalia, and Siphnos (about 1 : 130). W. B. Dinsmoor, *BCH.* 37, 1913

26 Delphi, Massalian treasury. Plan (about 1 : 130). G. Daux, *Fouilles de Delphes*, 1924

27 Delphi. Wall base mouldings of Cnidian (*above*) and Siphnian (*below*) treasuries. P. de la Coste-Messelière, 1936 and 1943

27   26

29 Delphi. Capitals and column bases or caryatid pedestals of Cnidian, Clazomenian, Massalian, and Siphnian treasuries. W. B. Dinsmoor, *BCH.* 37, 1913

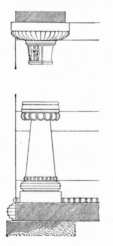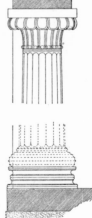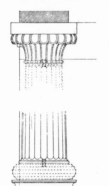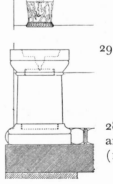

29   28

28 Delphi. Section through entablature and pediment of Siphnian treasury (1 : 33.3). W. B. Dinsmoor, *BCH.* 37, 1913

and curvilinear stones. As the edifice turned its back and side towards the processional way, it has been conjectured that its 'bastion' flanked the pre-classical entrance to the sanctuary. A building with antae (16 ft. 6½ in. by 27 ft. 5½ in., height 22 ft. 1⅜ in.), it can be almost completely reconstructed from the surviving parts. It attempted in every way to surpass its model, the Cnidian treasury. A colossal bead-and-reel (6¾ in. high) formed the wall base. The celebrated frieze (Lullies-Hirmer, *Greek Sculpture*, plates 48-55), among the choicest masterpieces of Ionic art, ran round the whole building, enclosed by an ovolo and a Lesbian cyma. Alternating palmettes and lotus-blooms sprouting up from spiral tendrils overgrew the soffit of the corona and face of the sima, on which they gracefully set off the fierce-looking lions' heads.

The most sonorous decorative harmony came around the door, which was framed by astragals and anthemia. Voluted consoles supported the projecting lintel, which was enriched with rosettes.

These bands of palmettes and lotus-blooms imbued the block-like building with their delicate vegetable life and growth to such an extent, and their movements counteracted the effect of the severe lines of the architecture so strongly, that it is not surprising to find the human form entering into the structure: as with the Cnidian treasury, *korai* supported the entablature. The *kalathoi* on their heads are carved with reliefs showing nymphs and satyrs, and this adornment even encroaches upon the bell-shaped capitals, where we meet the ancient motif of heraldic groups of fighting animals.

In the pediments, the two sculptors active on the treasury tried to press forward to a united composition filling the triangle with free-standing volumes, but they obviously did not yet know their way about this *terra nova* as thoroughly as that. The central group of the stealing of the tripod on the west pediment lacks any convincing connexion with the side figures, which are mere fillers. In the lower part, the figures still adhere closely to their background, and though, in the upper part, they stand free in the air, they remain entirely flat, as if cut out with a fretsaw. The real step forward was taken at Delphi not much later by the Attic master of the Alcmaeonidae temple.

Picture now the whole—ornament, frieze, and figures—bestrewn with colours: mainly red and blue, but also green, ochre, and gold; surrender to the enigmatic gaze of the richly attired *korai*; and do not forget the acroteria: the swiftly flying Nike and the sphinxes keeping watch at the corners. Is not Ionia, with its myths and fantasies, graceful and affected, mirrored in this glittering casket?

Doric Treasuries

The custom of presenting at the big sanctuaries not just splendid offerings but also a building to display them in was begun by Cypselus, under whose government *Corinth* grew to be the most powerful city in Greece. At Delphi, he dedicated the earliest treasury known to us (Herodotus I, 14). Thirsting for fame, other Greek cities eagerly followed his example. Cypselus is reckoned to have ruled from 657 to 628 or, more likely, from 614 to 585, an estimate supported by the building technique. The spacious, elongated 'hall' (about 21 ft. 4 in. by 42 ft. 8 in., i.e., width to height 1 : 2) pointed towards the sanctuary's focus—the altar of Apollo—which its entrance probably faced as well. It appears to have had no antae, the form of the anta temple thus only subsequently being adopted by treasuries. After the fall of the tyrants, the city proclaimed itself donor in a dedicatory inscription that has been recovered.

The first treasury on the classical section of the processional way (No. III) was that of *Sicyon*, a Doric anta temple (20 ft. 9⅝ in. by 27 ft. 9⅞ in., ratio 3 : 4) from the end of the fifth century. It is interesting chiefly for the materials used, the massive base having been pieced together from the remains of two earlier poros buildings. Of the older, the curious rotunda or tholos, we shall be speaking below. From a second poros structure of about 560 were included twelve remarkably broad metopes, works of outstanding quality with forceful representations of mythical events (Argonauts, cattle-raid by the Dioscuri, rape of Europa, etc.), as well as four flattened Doric capitals, two column shafts (8 ft. 2⅜ in. tall), and bits of architrave and cornice. The excavators reconstructed from these a monopteral 'pavilion' of the Sicyonians with 4 by 5 columns (14 ft. 0⅞ in. by 18 ft. 3¼ in.), but other investigators have on good grounds restored a prostyle treasury (of Sicyon or Syracuse?) with a portico of 4 by 2 columns. There were no triglyphs above the intercolumnial spaces, which accounts for the oblong shape of the metopes. Over the triglyphs the mutules had 3 by 5 guttae, but over the metopes 3 by 4. The groping and searching for the valid form was not yet over, the 'canon' not yet established.

With the treasury raised by *Athens*, we are bordering on the end of the archaic period. Presumably, it is a thank-offering to the god for liberation from the tyranny in 507, and Clisthenes himself may have seen to it that the earlier poros treasury of his illustrious city was replaced by an edifice in Parian marble, a very costly material. Pausanias, who mistakenly connected with this building the votive inscription of a later offering from the booty taken at Marathon, has even found stubborn supporters among modern investigators. Nevertheless, there can be no doubt about it: the turning point of the Persian wars, whereafter the entire Greek outlook changed, had not yet been passed. In the by now canonical form of a little temple with two columns in-antis (21 ft. 8⅝ in. by 31 ft. 9½ in.; height 24 ft. 10⅞ in.), the treasury rests upon a limestone base at the bend in the processional way. It has been fully moulded in the cast of temple architecture, even the three steps of the crepidoma being indicated at the front by three narrow ledges. Likewise, the triglyph frieze running round above the end and side walls was doubtless taken over from the peripteral format, as already on the earlier Sicyonian treasury. (A frieze is usual only above the columns.) The fact that the mutules have the normal six guttae makes the five on the regulae recall that mature archaic structure all the more strikingly. Light-heartedly, the builders ignored the problems that so preoccupied the Doric architects: that of the angle conflict. The triglyphs at the front are evenly distributed, and there is no contraction of the outer interaxials. Consequently, not one triglyph is aligned with the axis of the column or anta below it, and the joints of the architrave cut the regulae quite arbitrarily. On the other hand, an orderly system of proportions has now hesitantly infiltrated the structure. For example, the approximate ratio of width to length (2 : 3) is repeated in the relation of triglyph to metope. The slenderness of the columns (height about 5½ lower diams.) is of a different order from that of those on the first temple of Athena or the Sicyonian treasury. Now the columns grow towards their load. They themselves heave and become active, just as each echinus no longer spreads beneath the pressure, but resiliently pushes upwards against its abacus. All have learned how to support, and in doing so are able to submit freely and with ease. Those older, slim columns did not yet understand the heavy burden of stone at all.

The details are carved with incomparable assurance. Painted bands of anthemion ornament bordered the upper edge of the walls. Only the sinkings remain of the magnificent bronze door, which one has to add in one's imagination. In the garland of thirty metope reliefs, the deeds of the Attic hero Theseus confront those of Heracles. Still abiding strictly by the archaic rules, the combatants do not yet turn outwards from their plane into space (as for the first time on the second Aegina pediment). All talent has been addressed to achieving an extreme refinement of detail and to giving a most delicate finish to the surfaces, so that a further advance in this direction seems impossible. Yet one feels the warm breeze of the pre-classical period already wafting here; the ice is ready to break up. The pediment groups (stealing the tripod and killing the dragon?) and acroteria (Nike and Amazons shooting arrows) have been almost completely lost. Everything—architecture and sculpture—is bedewed with Attic grace, which magically transforms and dissolves the Doric severity and firmness.

In 1906, the treasury was re-erected. This has given our imagination a firm purchase, though the problems presented by such an experiment are obvious. Ancient worked stones cannot readily be replaced by substitutes.

THE ATHENIAN STOA   *Plate 74, fig. 30*

For a second highly original dedication, an Ionic stoa built in 478 immediately after the Persian wars, the Athenians knew just how to choose the most excellent site in the sanctuary. The delicate structure with its seven Ionic marble columns between two side walls ending in antae leaned up against the great polygonal wall below the temple of Apollo, and, bordering the round ceremonial 'area', it was the cynosure of every eye. The stoa served here as a kind of open treasury. On its three steps of grey Parnassian stone appears in capital letters: 'The Athenians dedicated this stoa as also the weapons and acroteria, which they captured from the enemy.' These 'acroteria' may have been ships' prows, and the other trophies were exhibited on a three-tiered platform before the rear wall. Whereas Athenian sacred buildings had hitherto always manifested the grave conformity of the Doric style, here the inborn Ionic element was allowed to display all its spontaneous flexibility. Since it was a question of display, the columns were set as far apart as possible. The relationship of column to intercolumniation (1 ft. 3¾ in. : 10 ft. 5⅝ in., or 1 : 8·2) ignores every rule, while the elegant columns themselves (relatively stocky with their height of only 10 ft. 10¼ in. = 8½ lower diams. of 1 ft. 3¾ in.) already heralded the forms of Attic classical architecture. On their bases appears for the first time the classical, Attic tripartite division into torus, linking member (here still an inverted cyma recta profile instead of the later scotia), and torus. Entablature and roof framework were constructed of rough wooden beams. The ensemble would have been little more than a simple open shed, devoid of all monumentality, had it not been ennobled by the peculiar charm of the marble columns and by an unfailing sense of composition, which prevailed here too. Thus, a modest type of archaic building (cf. Argos, page 346 and Samos,

figs. 110, 111

71

30 Delphi, Athenian stoa. Behind it, the polygonal wall and temple of Apollo V. P. Amandry, *Fouilles de Delphes*, 1953

page 450) found its last, highly delicate pre-classical expression; and, in view of the Athenian stoa, one will scarcely be prepared to credit that this very pattern, monumentalized by the classical period, and developed into the mightiest instrument for moulding vast expanses of open space by the Hellenistic age, had within it the power one day to put temple architecture itself in the shade.

CLASSICAL VOTIVE MONUMENTS   *Plate 64, fig. 19*

During classical times there was a change in outlook and values. Instead of treasuries, which seen from the new view-point were mere receptacles for arbitrarily assembled offerings, people now fashioned large, free-standing, interrelated figure groups, which architecture, too, was made to serve. Set upon a monumental, often semicircular base, the composition included the spectator within it. Stoas proportioned to the dimensions of the freely moving groups, and open to their front, enclosed the offerings, which proclaimed the fame of their donors.

64   The series was begun by the ambitious Spartan general Lysander, who, after his naval victory over

Athens in 405, erected a monument to himself in the form of a group composed of thirty-seven bronze statues. It showed him surrounded by his 'admirals' and honoured by the Olympian gods. The Spartans took amiss Lysander's arrogant trespass, but later they had also to put up with a sculptured group of heroes placed by the Arcadians in front of Lysander's monument, in celebration of their victory over Sparta. The two neighbouring semicircular bases (diam. about 42 ft. 8 in.), matching each other across the sacred way, also involved a challenge to Sparta. In the monument on the visitor's right, endowed out of the booty taken from the Lacedaemonians after Leuctra in 371, the kings of Argos were represented; in the one on his left—earlier,   64
it would seem—their successors, the Epigoni.

The pilgrim who had to pass between these groups of national heroes literally found himself at the centre of the ring.

The few treasuries raised after those discussed above (Potidaea about 480; Acanthus about 425?; Syracuse and Sicyon about 413; Thebes about 346) grew noticeably simpler, gave up sculptural decoration, and expressed all that they had to say through the clarity and purity of their proportions, and the crispness and precision of their keen-edged forms.

fig. 31

78, 79

fig. 20

On the other side of the Castalian gorge, at the eastern limit of the town, Athena Pronaea ('before the temple') had her sanctuary. Five buildings all facing south, towards the valley, stood there loosely and arbitrarily grouped upon a terrace about 164 yds. long but only some 44 yds. wide: the older temple close to the eastern entrance through the peribolos, which was bounded by retaining-walls; two treasuries; a rotunda (the 'tholos'); and lastly the later temple, which displaced an unexplained building, the so-called 'priests' dwelling'. This sanctuary, too, grew up by degrees. Beneath the earliest temple a layer was found with offerings from the second millennium. It contained nearly 200 terracotta idols of a goddess with outspread arms—the first mistress of the site. In the eighth or seventh century, this earliest place of sacrifice was surrounded with a winding wall still wholly determined by the natural lie of the land. Roughly jointed but carefully quarried polygonal rubble walling seems, at first, to have much in common with Mycenaean masonry, yet there is a world of difference between those defiantly heaped up cyclopean walls and our, in comparison, more finely jointed wall of small stones that already reveals its constructors' unique gift for fully informing the simplest and most natural elements.

During the second half of the seventh century, Athena received her *first temple*, a peripteral building of which, apart from the remains of polygonal foundations, twelve poros capitals and ten column drums have been preserved in the substructure of the subsequent temple. They constitute the earliest Doric columns surviving *in toto*. The lean shafts (height only 10 ft. 11⅞ in. or 6½ lower diameters; 16 flutes) and very flat, wide-spreading echinuses—as though turned in the lathe—do not tally at all with the heavy, powerful columns that we know from the sixth century, and afford us a glimpse of the lost beginnings of temple architecture. These wide-spaced little columns must have supported a very light entablature, the frieze of which may have been adorned with brightly painted terracotta slabs, like those from Thermum. The projecting rafters bore the corona, likewise gaily decorated with terracotta facings and antefixes. Apollo, who evidently did not have much confidence in the ability of his irreproachable Hyperboreans to create a god's dwelling of this kind, would certainly have had no trouble at all in carrying such an open, breezy little temple through the air to them in the far north.

After the erection of the Alcmaeonid temple, the peribolos round the Athena sanctuary was also expanded, and, at the end of the sixth century, a *second temple* (43 ft. 5⅝ in. by 90 ft. 0¾ in., about 1 : 2), was put up. Cramped by the narrow terrace, it had no opisthodomus, and hence displayed only twelve columns along the sides and six at the ends. The unusual feature of a southern entrance was, perhaps, dictated by the terrain, as the east-facing main altar (surrounded by small ones dedicated to Athena for all her helpful qualities) stood at the side of the temple.

79, figs. 31–34

The Doric canon was almost fully defined: contracted angle interaxials, completely regular frieze, the outside of the cella walls approximately in line with the second and fifth end columns. Nevertheless a few anomalies still betray the archaic uncertainty. Thus, the front interaxials (8 ft. 2 in.) were wider than the lateral ones (7 ft. 11¼ in.), and, instead of the harmonious trinity of steps, we find only two. The capitals belong to a slightly earlier evolutionary stage than those of the Athenian treasury.

80, below, left

As early as the fifth century, the building was damaged by falling rocks. Pausanias saw it in ruins. In 1905, the newly excavated remains fell victim to another landslide, which destroyed twelve of the fifteen columns still standing and shifted the foundations with titanic force. The rebuilding of the Apollo temple during the fourth century was followed by the erection of a *third temple* for his Olympian sister, this time on a site less exposed to danger at the west end of the terrace. Chiselled from a hard, cool material (bluish Parnassian limestone), without sculpture or the splendour of colour, displaying bare walls on three sides instead of the rich garland of a peristyle, and presenting an austere Doric colonnade only at the front, the building might have appeared to us a meagre, impoverished thing compared with its predecessor, until our eyes had grown accustomed to seeing the invisible, and we grasped that here the impression was determined by the relationship of the parts to each other and to the whole. In place of the polyphonic melody of the older structure, there now rang out one single perfectly adjusted chord.

78, 80, below, right

The portico was widened by pushing the side walls outwards. Between the antae stood slim Ionic columns to which corresponded half-columns attached to the walls so that they should not obstruct the space. Already here, and even more strongly in the giving up of the peristyle in favour of a broad cella, the newly awakened urge to mould the interior space proclaimed itself. This structure is in fact one of the first that are to be understood from within, as well as from without, by considering the enclosed space as well as the building as a mass.

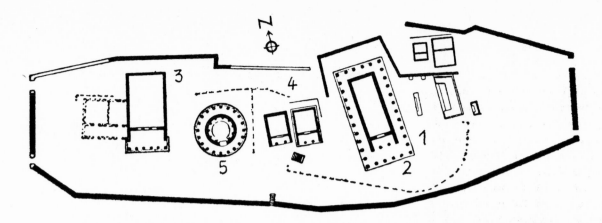

31 Delphi, sanctuary of Athena Pronaea. 1: Altar of Athena; 2: temple of Athena II, *c.* 510 B.C. (beneath it, temple of Athena I, *c.* 600 B.C.; 3: temple of Athena III, fourth cent. B.C.; 4: Massalian treasury (*left*) and Doric treasury (of Athens?) (*right*); 5: large tholos, beginning of fourth cent. B.C. Kirsten-Kraiker, 1957

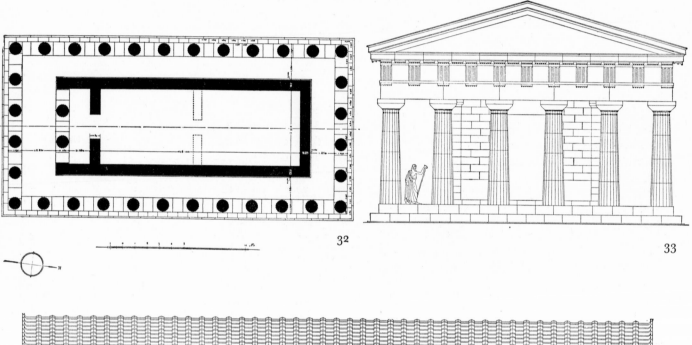

32

33

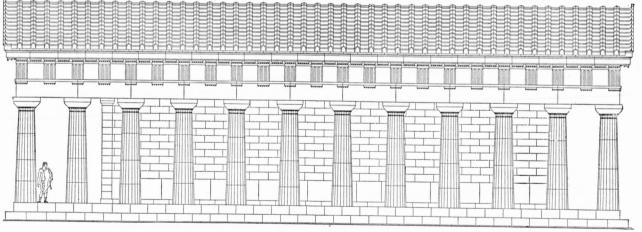

34

32–34 Delphi, temple of Athena II. Plan (1 : 300), south elevation and side elevation (1 : 167, same scale as figs. 23 and 24 of temple of Apollo VI). R. Demangel, *Fouilles de Delphes.* 1924

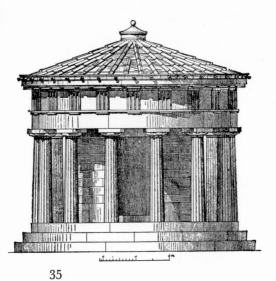

35 Delphi, old tholos. Restoration. H. Pomtow, *Klio* 12, 1912

36–37 Delphi, sanctuary of Athena Pronaea. Large tholos
36 Restoration (columns should be one drum taller, cf. fig. 20). H. Pomtow, *Klio* 12, 1912
37 Section and Corinthian capital from inner columns. A. W. Lawrence, 1957

35

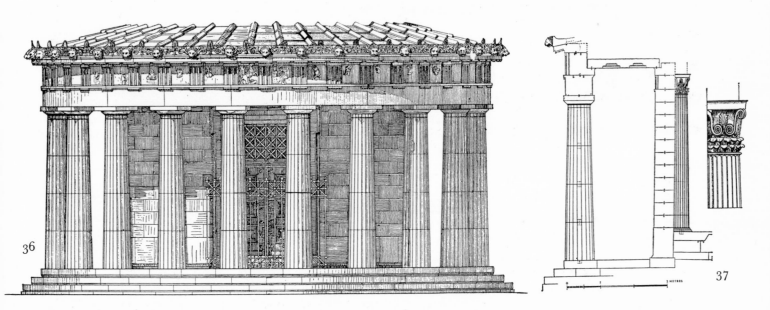

36

37

79, 80,
above

Two treasuries were connected with the earlier temple: a Doric structure and the Massalian one discussed above. The *Doric treasury* so resembled that of the Athenians in material, technique, and style that one might suppose it to have been raised by the same donors to the mistress of their city. Its builders obviously learned a lesson from the edifice, only a few years older, in Apollo's sanctuary: now the outer interaxials were contracted to make allowance for the frieze, and the five guttae on the regulae were replaced by the normal six.

VII, 78, 79
figs. 36, 37

The most surprising and original structure on the terrace was undoubtedly the *tholos* put up at the

beginning of the fourth century. It was a rotunda with its circular cella surrounded by a wreath of twenty Doric columns (diam. of stylobate 44 ft. $3\frac{3}{8}$ in., of cella 28 ft. $2\frac{5}{8}$ in.; total height to sima 27 ft. $3\frac{5}{8}$ in.). Involving as it does all-round 'eye-worthiness' and a manifold but concentrated rich-ness of geometrical relations, the idea of the circular peripteral structure fully accords with the spirit of the late classical period, which embodied it in three of its most sumptuous buildings (after the present one, the tholos at Epidaurus and the Philippeum at Olympia). All the same, it was not new, and here at Delphi parts of a strange tholos from the beginning *fig. 35*

341

of the sixth century were found built into the Sicyonian treasury. This tholos was evidently one of the experiments made in the early years of stone architecture, testing its potentialities—and it looked it. A frieze of 20 triglyphs and metopes ran round it above, but quite unconnected with, the 13 peristyle columns—an absurdity unique in the whole history of Greek building. Twenty is also (by chance?) the basic unit of the later tholos. Each of the 20 columns repeated the ground-plan with the 20 arrises of its fluting. Inside the cella, 10 (less one because of the wide doorway) Corinthian columns corresponded to them, each being on the radius to the mid-point of every second outer intercolumnial space.

fig. 37   Ictinus's influence asserted itself everywhere: the cella floor and bench-like socle of the cella columns (both in dark Eleusinian limestone) formed a noble contrast to the building's Pentelic marble. Corinthian columns had been making their triumphal entry since Bassae, and here they hugged the wall so as not to intrude upon the room's modest width. Bassae likewise provided the model for the lozenge-shaped ceiling coffers. Nevertheless, the tholos's architect Theodorus of Phocaea, who wrote a book about this his masterpiece, was anything but un-original, as is shown by the fresh, inventive line of the profiles (e.g. the Lesbian cyma at the foot of the wall), by the peculiar Corinthian capitals with their sturdy, supporting 'basket' wreathed by two tiers of freely stirring, strongly modelled acanthus leaves, and by the lively acanthus tendrils, palmettes, and

lions' heads on the sima. An understanding of nature that led to a mastery and transformation of natural forms free from the bondage of illusionism underlay everything.

Slender as never before, the columns stretched up effortlessly towards the entablature (height 19 ft. 5½ in. (?) or 6·3 times lower diam. of 2 ft. 10¼ in.; the three standing columns were erected in 1938).

The roof edge was decorated in an unusual manner: behind the outer sima with its straight top border appears a second, smaller sima with a vibrant profile. These ornamental circles, graduated both in depth as well as height, balance the building with an elegance and lightness never before achieved. (Fig. 37 should be imagined without the drum, reconstructed because of the smaller sima.)

Little has survived of the sculptural decoration on the metopes: animated groups of Amazons and centaurs. One example shall serve as evidence of the amazing precision of the stone cutting. The narrow faces of the triglyphs exactly follow (even a practised eye can hardly notice it) the circular form of the architrave.

A carefully calculated system of mathematical proportions now embraced in its strict framework even the smallest detail, down to the sunken riser margins that diminish upwards with the height and width of the steps. It is remarkable that number and geometry did not suppress the building's vitality, that they too served as a means of bringing out as clearly as possible its corporeity already touched with a cool refinement.

CORINTH

Plates XXIII, 81, fig. 38

At Corinth, the Isthmian trading city open to the world, life pulsated more strongly than in any other polis. Corinth formed the gateway of the Peloponnese; together with its powerful daughter-city, Syracuse, it commanded the western seas; and, during its heyday under the important tyrant family of the Cypselids, it also set the fashion in art. Hence, it is here that the sources of early Doric temple architecture are to be sought, and it may be that upon the Isthmus the modest glow of this architecture was fanned into full flame, that here was effected a transition from the wooden to the monumental stone

building. Pindar (*Ol.* XIII, 21) extols the city thus: 'And who set the king of the birds doubly upon the temples of the gods?' Eagle also means gable; but with the invention of the two-pedimented structure, the calm, balanced temple form had been discovered and the decisive step taken towards achieving monumentality, that inward grandeur. Another of Corinth's creations, the monumental temple roof (see page 311), still bears the city's name.

The traces of the earliest structures were obliterated by subsequent building activity on their sites and by disasters. All such events have, however, been

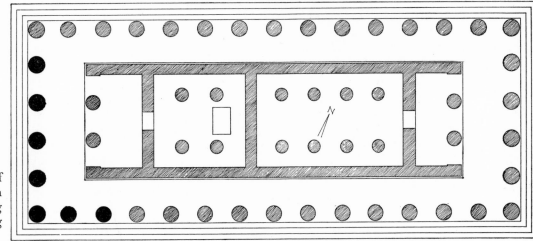

38 Corinth, temple of Apollo, *c.* 540 B.C. Plan (1 : 400). New drawing (columns still standing shown in black)

survived by seven powerful columns of a mature archaic temple above the agora: that of Apollo (about 540). A strange and splendid edifice, it still shows signs of that early conversion into stone, while important innovations bear witness to a skilled architectural sense of form, pointing to the future.

By means of four high steps, the temple's platform raised itself decisively above the rocky ground of the hill, and renounced the building style, simple and close to the earth, of the one- or two-stepped early archaic structures (Thermum, Heraeum of Olympia). Foundation trenches cut into the rock still mark out the ground-plan of the cella, which was symmetrically fronted by a pronaos and an opisthodomus, each with two columns in-antis. The still prevailing longitudinal emphasis was here to some extent determined by the interior space, since the latter was divided into two: the east-facing naos proper, in which two, probably double-storied (cf. Aegina, page 348), rows of 4 columns must have stood, and a nearly square room with 2 by 2 columns opening to the west. Whether this was a second naos for a deity intimately connected with Apollo (as a large base before its rear wall suggests), or a treasury with an offering given special prominence, one's mind automatically turns to the much more freely developed but still formally related ground-plan of the Parthenon. Another yet more astonishing pointer to the future: beneath the west and south colonnades, the earliest instances of curvature have been identified—barely discernible upward bulges of only $\frac{3}{4}$ in. in the stylobate! Likewise, through the approximately canonical 'binding' of the cella into the peristyle, a conflict was resolved that architects elsewhere did not settle till well into the fifth century.

With its narrowing of the side interaxials (12 ft. $3\frac{1}{4}$ in.; ends: 13 ft. $2\frac{5}{8}$ in.), the peristyle of 6 by 15 columns (stylobate 70 ft. 6 in. by 176 ft. $6\frac{7}{8}$ in.) followed an archaic custom. So as to avoid over-conspicuous angle contraction (here by $10\frac{5}{8}$ in.), part of the deficit was made good in the frieze itself by adding 2 in. to the width of both corner metopes.   *fig. 38*

If one submits now to the impact of the columns, one will find it hardly conceivable that such careful refining and ponderation could also have been applied to the proportions of such titanically clumsy creations. Each of the bulky shafts has been carved from a single block of stone nearly 20 ft. long, thereby satisfying the archaic inclination to give every part an independent significance. The capital too constitutes a separate member. Though broad and spreading corpulently, it no longer—as at Delphi—   *fig. 20* lets itself be squashed like a lump of dough by the weight of the entablature. Instead, with the curve of its echinus climbing upward from the start, it begins to resist the pressure. Taken altogether, the heavy, thick-set columns express a newly awakened and hence immoderate feeling for their load, for the weight and permanency of the stone: Atlas with the vault of heaven upon his shoulders. They are in fact the squattest columns in the mother-country (height =4·15 lower diams.), only exceeded on the Apollo temple of the daughter-city Syracuse (3·97 lower diams.). If one recalls the thin, stem-like little columns of the first Pronaea temple at Delphi, it becomes clear that only now was the process of turning the temple to stone completed at a more than material level: in Greece, that is, and as manifestly

343

as possible. No other temple known to us was as permeated with strength, durability, and heaviness as this one.

On the occasion of the barbarous sack and destruction of Corinth in 146 B.C. after the conquest by Mummius, the temple of Apollo was burned out. When the city was refounded, Augustus had it crudely restored, as is still shown by a layer of Roman plaster over the thin Greek stucco on the collapsed columns.

ISTHMIA, THE SANCTUARY OF POSEIDON

Plate VIII, fig. 39

fig. 39

The Isthmus, the narrow bridge of land, repeatedly convulsed by earthquakes, that joins the Peloponnese to the mainland, has from time immemorial belonged to Poseidon. According to the legend, it was Sisyphus, the mythical first king of Corinth, who founded here the sanctuary of the earth-shaker and lord of the seas. Lying near the eastern end of the modern canal (the construction of which was planned by Periander, Demetrius Poliorcetes, Caesar, and Caligula, and begun by Nero), the site has been excavated by Oscar Broneer since 1952.

Modest traces of a temple from the seventh century testify to the age of the cult centre. Measuring about 32 ft. 10 in. by 108 ft. 3 in. (or 128 ft.?), this building had elongated proportions similar to those of the equally old first temple of Apollo at Corinth. Of the superstructure, which must have consisted largely of wood and sun-dried brick, only roof tiles have been preserved—as at Corinth. Around 460, a splendid new building was erected on the same spot. Its ground-plan can be deduced from foundation trenches and remains, and is almost identical with that of the Zeus temple at Olympia, which only surpasses it in size (stylobate, Isthmia: about 77 ft. 9 in. by 177 ft. 10 in.; Olympia: 90 ft. 9¾ in. by 210 ft. 4⅜ in.). It had a peristyle of 6 by 13 columns, symmetrical east and west ends with porticoes 1½ interaxials deep, and pilasters on the east and west walls of the naos corresponding to both naos colonnades. The few shattered members brought to light allow us to surmise that the upper structure was also on the high level of the masterpiece at Olympia: the same taut profiling of the capitals and the same precise yet lively cutting of the flutes on the columns, the lower diameter of which (6 ft. 1¼ in.) stands in the same relation to the interaxial (14 ft. 6¾ in.). A clear, extremely thin layer of stucco coated the fine-grained limestone (poros). Roof covering and pediment sculpture, the fragments of which prove it to have been of the highest quality, were of marble.

The temple had a chequered career. In 394, it went up in flames, but was repaired during the fourth century from the ground upwards, which amounted to creating a new building with an unchanged plan. Even the columns had to be replaced, and a capital from the first stage has survived, remodelled as a corner triglyph, for the second.

To the inner triglyph frieze above the end of the later cella has recently been assigned a beautiful marble metope in the Palazzo dei Conservatori at Rome (torso of a warrior in action). One may therefore assume that the original temple likewise had unadorned metopes above the peristyle and sculptured ones above the pronaos and opisthodomus columns—another resemblance to the Zeus temple. For the games, a stadium running at an angle from the temple was laid out in the fifth century and completed in the fourth. At its north-west end, near the usual starting line, there has survived a unique arrangement for the finish (not the start, as the excavators assert). Sixteen lengths of twine barring the finishing gates for sixteen runners were ingeniously carried to a cavity in the middle of the enclosure, and there each caused a tablet, or the like, to move when a runner arrived (i.e. broke the twine). The judge posted in the hollow could thus determine exactly the order in which the competitors finished.

After the razing of Corinth by Mummius in 146 B.C., the sanctuary declined, Sicyon becoming its patron till Corinth was refounded. The decay continued until, probably under Tiberius, Rome took up the reins, whereupon the appearance of the temenos that spread out freely in the countryside underwent a change. A first rectangular Roman enclosure with its lines parallel to those of the temple was put up in the early imperial age, but it appeared

344

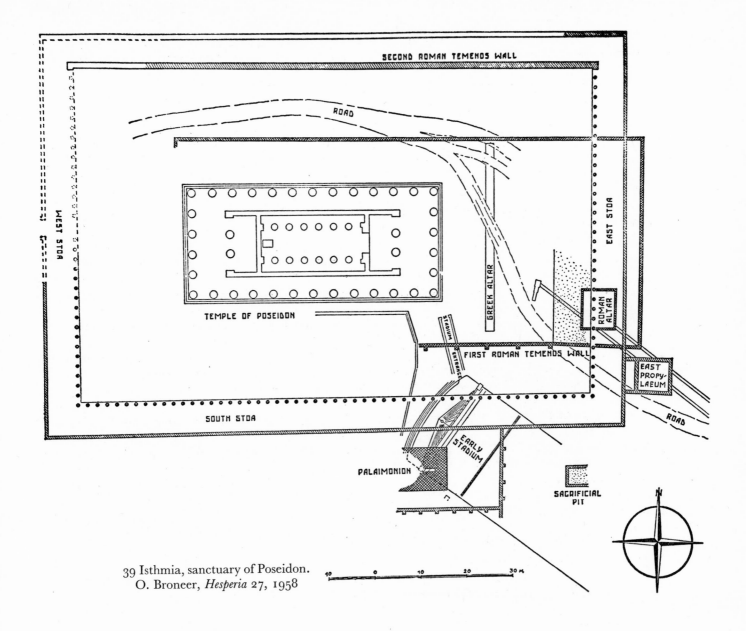

39 Isthmia, sanctuary of Poseidon.
O. Broneer, *Hesperia* 27, 1958

too modest. In the second century A.D., the temple, the cella of which had to submit to being revetted with marble, formed the optical centre of an imposing court bounded by Ionic stoas. How strange and misunderstood the Greek building must have looked amid this setting of stage architecture! Poseidon's temple came to an inglorious end in early Christian times as building material for the gigantic fortified barrier with which Justinian's engineer, Victorianus, secured the isthmus.

fig. 40

The Argive Heraeum was built by Dorus, the ancestor of the Dorians, or so Vitruvius (III, 1) understood. Hence, anyone seeking the roots of Doric temple architecture will make his way to this sanctuary that lies in barren, stony solitude high above the fertile plain of Argos; and there he will stand before the earliest temple remains, which hint at much but, alas, tell little.

The temenos extends up the slope in three terraces. At the very top, the first temple (I) was throned in patriarchal dignity above a wall piled up high out of enormous unworked stones. It was an airy, elongated, gaily coloured wooden structure from the first half of the seventh century. In 423, 'it was burned down because sleep overcame Chryseis, the priestess of Hera, when the lamp before the wreaths set them on fire' (Paus. II, 17, 7). Nothing now remains of this building except a part of the stylobate from the south flank, about $65\frac{1}{2}$ ft. long; in the manner of the earliest temples, it rises only slightly above the terrace paving, and on it traces clearly indicate where four columns stood (lower diam. 2 ft. $7\frac{1}{2}$ in., interval 11 ft. $5\frac{3}{4}$ in.). Judging by this wide intercolumniation (about $4\frac{1}{2}$ lower diams.), the thin shafts must have carried a wooden entablature. Did, however, these supports themselves consist of wood over a stone base, or had they (like the Delphic columns of the first Pronaea temple) already been converted into stone? This problem, like many others set by the Heraeum, has not yet been solved. Even the reconstruction of its ground-plan (peristyle of 6 by 14 columns; a remarkably big cella measuring 27 ft. $10\frac{5}{8}$ in. by 119 ft. $0\frac{1}{8}$ in., the pronaos having two columns in-antis) is hypothetical. None the less, it remains certain that here a peripteral temple was erected which is the earliest known in the Peloponnese.

85, above

As the cyclopean retaining-wall belongs to the geometric period, one may presume that the goddess already had a dwelling in the eighth century—perhaps a little naiskos, of which one can form some notion from the terracotta model (fig. 1).

The actual life and activity of the sanctuary evidently took place on a second terrace, below the temple, and around it were grouped curious buildings for offerings, secret rituals, and banquets.

Two stoas (II, III), both erected at the beginning of the sixth century, stood against the slope. They are the oldest known Doric examples, and with them a new type of structure came into being. Part of the peripteral temple—the pteroma—suddenly turned into an independent building, and began to lead a life of its own. It was a creation that would henceforth be inseparable from Greek communal life. Stoas—far more splendid ones than these of course—were the place for gifts to the gods and statues of men, conversations and leisure, business and politics, in short, for every aspect of Greek affairs. True, the early Argive and Samian (page 450) prototypes were at first set aside for offerings, and thus akin to treasuries; but these freely accessible buildings stood ready to receive the dedications of every donor, invited the beholder into their shade, and hence must soon have become places for all kinds of communication.

During the sixth century, they were joined on the west side of the square by a banqueting-house (VII), in which we again meet for the first time an entirely new architectural form: a rectangular courtyard surrounded by colonnades (here even two-naved), as though a temple peristyle had been turned inwards. Like those of the two stoas, the columns here followed the temple order, with architrave, triglyph frieze, and cornice. To the north side of this interesting building were attached three dining-rooms surrounded by stone couches. There, a noble gathering used once to feast under the goddess's protection in honour of the victors in the games.

About the middle of the fifth century, the square came to be enclosed all round by buildings. On its east side, there arose a four-naved hypostyle hall (IV) recalling the Pisistratid telesterium at Eleusis, while to the south down the slope a further, carefully constructed, stoa (VI) rested upon the third and lowest terrace. The drop to this bottom forecourt of the sanctuary was graduated by strong, stepped retaining-walls, long interpreted as wholly un-Greek monumental stairways.

After the burning of the old temple, work began on a second abode for Hera (V) at the centre of the middle terrace, in spite of the disturbances caused by war. Building took place between 420 and 400, and Pausanias names the otherwise unknown architect as Eupolemus of Argos. Besides the foundations (stylobate 56 ft. 9 in. by 121 ft. $0\frac{3}{4}$ in.), only fragments of the superstructure and rich sculptural decoration (pediment figures and metopes at both ends) have survived. Though this peripteral building largely corresponded to the canon, it infringed it in a few respects, the 6 end columns being accompanied

IX

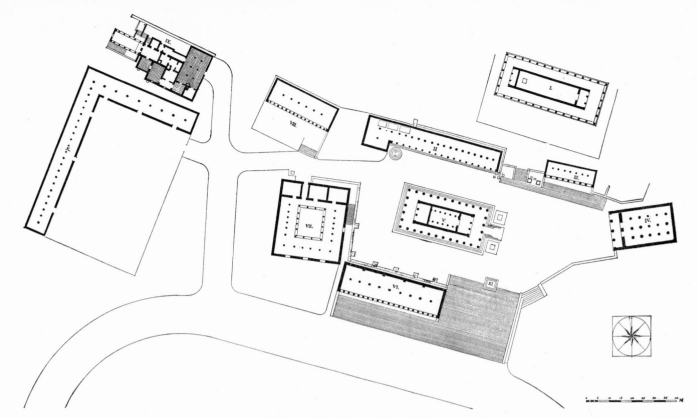

40 Argos, Heraeum. General layout
I: temple of Hera I, before 600 B.C.; II, III, and VIII: archaic Doric stoas before geometric retaining-wall of upper temple terrace; IV: telesterium-like hypostyle hall; V: temple of Hera II, end of fifth cent. B.C.; VI: stoa; VII: archaic 'banqueting-house'; XI: stepped wall. Outside temenos: IX: Roman thermae; X: gymnasium. C. Waldstein, 1902

by only 12 (instead of 13) on each flank. All parts were contained within a frame of ingeniously calculated proportions, derived from simple basic measurements: column diameter = 4 Doric ft., intercolumniation = 6 Doric ft. The same ratio of 2 : 3 also prevailed between the triglyphs and metopes. Like the sculptured ornamentation, the architectonic detail revealed Attic influence. Above the frieze appeared an Ionic ovolo moulding, and the high floral acroteria distinctly echoed those of the Parthenon. In the agitated band of tendrils and palmettes along the sima, Hera's sacred bird, the cuckoo, had made itself at home, a

86, below

harbinger of an incipient naturalism in decoration.

Along with that of Zeus at Olympia, the temple's cult statue was the most celebrated in antiquity. Pausanias (II, 17, 4) describes it thus: 'The cult image of Hera sits upon a throne and, made in gold and ivory, it is remarkably big, a work by Polyclitus. Hera wears a crown on which the Charites and Horae are represented, and in one hand she holds a pomegranate, in the other a sceptre . . . but on the sceptre perches a cuckoo, and they say that Zeus turned himself into this bird when he was wooing Hera in her girlhood, and that she playfully pursued it.'

AEGINA, THE SANCTUARY OF APHAEA

Plates XII, 42–45, figs. 41, 42

Aegina, the mountainous, wooded island between the port of Athens and the coast-line around Epidaurus, was colonized at the end of the second millennium by Dorians, who intermarried with the seafaring native inhabitants to form a breed at once open to all new blood and racially consistent.

It had a unique gift for enriching itself by means of its shipping trade with Ionia and its art industry, while still retaining under all circumstances its Dorian character. Aeginetan sea-power inevitably succumbed to its brutal neighbour, Athens, with the result that one of the choicest schools of Greek

347

sculpture ceased to exist. Its legacy has come down to us in the almost completely preserved pediment groups from the temple of Aphaea.

Along with its mysterious mistress, the sanctuary of Aphaea upon a lonely hilltop was inherited from the natives by the immigrants, who looked after it attentively. A foundation inscription from the early sixth century announces: 'The house and altar for Aphaea were built at the time when [Kl]eoites was priest: the ivory [cult image?] was added, and the enclosure put up.' Previously, therefore, the goddess had been worshipped in an open grove.

Still largely standing, the late archaic peripteral temple rests upon this 'house', dressed stones from which are incorporated in its foundations. The earlier building has been reconstructed as an anta temple with a naos containing a nave and aisles, and an adytum divided into two. Since remains of columns and mature archaic capitals, shallow and spreading broadly, have been found in three graded sizes, two stories of columns separated by an architrave must in the naos have supported the roof—an arrangement not only taken over by the subsequent building, but absorbed into the Doric canon.

The first peribolos obediently followed the winding course dictated by the terrain, just as the small gate-building was placed at the most suitable spot on the hill crest, without any special reference to the temple. This propylaeum was enlarged even before the peripteral temple went up, but retained the unassuming basic form of a roofed gateway. Its ridge was aligned with the peribolos, so that the sloping sides belonged to the two entrance fronts. Strange pairs of octagonal columns supported the probably wooden entablature.

Shortly afterwards, this utilitarian form was altered by temple architecture, which was growing ever more powerfully influential. The pediment now rose up over the entrance side (sanctuary of Demeter near Selinus, fig. 83; propylaea at Sunium and Eleusis), with the result that the propylaeum became a kind of double anta temple. This opened the way for the most magnificent and at the same time most canonical manifestation of the gate-building: the Propylaea of Mnesicles on the Athenian Acropolis.

When work began round about 500 on a peripteral structure, the narrow temenos had first to be enlarged. The temple's monumentality impinged upon its surroundings, the colonnaded building needed open space in which to breathe. Broad terraces were thrown up all round the temple, while its extended precinct was bounded with straight ashlar walls meeting at right angles. Nature had to accommodate itself to the might of the imposing edifice. That, however, this new arrangement was for the benefit of

Aphaea's home and not of its beholders is indicated by the fact that the access remained in its now highly arbitrary position, instead of being shifted into line with the building's long axis.

The temple itself is not only the best preserved in the mother-country from this period, but also the most perfectly developed and progressive of late archaic structures. It was designed by a real master of architecture with a strong sense of form—an Aeginetan whose name has not come down to us. Strangely enough, visitors hardly ever feel the now almost completely re-erected ruins to be small let alone dainty, although in actual fact there is room for four Aphaea temples next to each other on the base of the temple of Zeus at Olympia. One seems unconsciously to gauge the size by means of an inward measure.

Fig. 41 gives a clear idea of the details of the superstructure. The temple was built in the local porous limestone, coated with an extremely thin layer of white stucco. Only the three-stepped crepidoma—as something still belonging to the ground—displayed the natural surface of the stone. The plan of the peristyle is marked out even in the bottom step, as each side-joint lies exactly above the middle of the block below, while the columns *figs. 41,* stand at the centre of every second stylobate block. This 'concordance of joints' was here accurately accomplished for the first time. With 6 by 12 columns (stylobate 45 ft. 2 in. by 94 ft. 6⅝ in., about 1 : 2·1), the ground-plan is remarkably thickset.

Plainly, the architect had gone rather far in his *42, 43* countering of archaic elongation, for during classical times more attenuated proportions in approximately the ratio 3 : 7 (Olympia and Theseum), with 6 by 13 columns, again became the rule. The angle conflict was settled through a simple contraction of the corner interaxials by 8⅝ in. Though there is no curvature, the infinitely delicate proportioning of forms that reaches its climax in the Parthenon has already begun. The columns lean about ¾ in. inwards, and the angle columns are ¾ in. thicker than the rest. On the other hand, there is a faint touch of the archaic in the way, for example, the flank columns are a little closer together than those at the ends (8 ft. 4¾ in. against 8 ft. 7⅛ in.). Likewise, the cella has not yet been tied canonically into the peristyle: extended, the outer faces of the side walls would meet the second and fifth front columns about 7⅞ in. outside their axes. The cella displays the normal symmetrical form of a pronaos and an opisthodomus, each with two columns in-antis, at the front and back of the naos. This balance is not destroyed by a slight deepening of the east portico and pronaos, which nevertheless asserts the primacy

41 Aegina, temple of Aphaea. Sectional view.
A. Furtwängler and E. Fiechter, *Aegina*, 1906

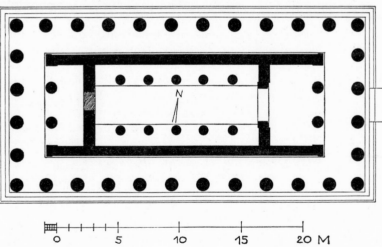

42 Aegina, temple of Aphaea. Plan (1 : 300).
New drawing after A. Furtwängler and E.
Fiechter, *Aegina*, 1906

of the east end. Yet what an oppressive effect this cella, only 20 ft. 11⅛ in. wide in the clear, with its two double-storied rows of five columns, has upon our sense of space! The aisles, 2 ft. 11⅜ in. wide, are no broader than the door of a modern room, and the nave can be crossed in three strides. This arrangement is not justifiable here on technical grounds, since the small space could easily have been roofed

349

over without internal supports. What in fact was being aimed at was an effect of corporeal existence as opposed to one of space. Thus, the columns took their place near the goddess's statue as members of the same class, and the image was not cramped but worthily accompanied by such a sculptural retinue. Instead of being pressed up against the back wall, the figure stood freely between the fourth pair of columns, like the Athena in the Parthenon later on.

As an afterthought, a doorway was pierced through the rear wall of the naos in order to give access to the opisthodomus, the west entrance of which was, at the same time, blocked with a grille. The east portico and pronaos likewise received a grille, probably to protect the island's patroness and her sacred belongings from being insidiously carried off to Athens. There was a good reason for this: Herodotus (V, 83 f.) tells of such an assault on two other cult images, which the Aeginetans themselves stole from the Epidaurians.

The harmonious balance that raises the building above all its archaic forerunners is founded upon a clearly thought out system of proportions, with the Doric foot (here $12\frac{7}{8}$ in.) as its basic unit. Thus, the height of the columns (16 Doric ft.) equals twice the interaxial space (8 Doric ft.) and three times the height of the entablature. The lower diameter of the columns (3 Doric ft.) is related to the intercolumniation (5 Doric ft.) in the ratio 3 : 5, the breadth of the pteromata to that of the cella, and the aisle width to the nave width in the ratio 1 : 3.

Their unusually slender line gives the columns a soaring lightness that reveals Ionic influence (height $=5\frac{1}{3}$ lower diams.; compare Corinth with 4.15 lower diams., Olympia with 4.7). Elsewhere, similarly elegant proportions are to be found only in Attic buildings, such as the but little earlier and formerly closely related Athenian treasury at Delphi (5.44 lower diams.; compare Parthenon with 5.48). In Attica, however, Ionic decorative elements were as early as the sixth century invading the Doric order which the Aeginetan architect strictly and consistently kept free from such impurities. Only at the apex of the pediments did he allow an ornamental form derived from Ionian inventiveness to settle: the central acroterium, a volute 'tree' sprouting coloured palmettes, on either side of which stood a girl in graceful Ionian costume. All the roof decoration—acroteria, sima, and antefixes—and the pediment figures were in Parian marble. The details of the entablature and cornices correspond closely to those, described above, at Olympia (fig. 9), the stylistic difference showing only in subtle divergencies. Compare, for instance, the more tautly upward-thrusting Olympic capitals with the Aeginetan ones,

which have a broader spread. Strange to say, no remains at all have been found of the metopes, for which narrow grooves were provided in the triglyphs. Could they, in the most ancient manner, have been made of wood?

A word now about the colour, here reliably identified. The supporting framework—columns and architrave—were left white, but black or dark blue was used for emphasizing, in particular, the vertical members of the frieze—regulae, triglyphs, and mutules—to make them stand out clearly even in the shadow of the corona. A brilliant red appeared on the horizontal band of the taenia and on the corona soffit. At the edge of the roof—on its leaf-adorned Doric hawksbeak, the sima anthemion, and the palmette antefixes—the colour became most delicately decorative, with a constant interchange of blue and red. The pediments were sprinkled all over with colour—blue and red again, in a strictly stylized alternation—and on them appeared the Aeginetan heroes doing battle before Troy. Shields, helmets, clothes, and hair were variegated, bodies displayed the bright lustre of the Parian marble, while the surface behind was painted blue as a celestial background.

There is something unusual about these pediment groups: they number three. Two, one for the east end and one for the west, belong to the building period round about 500, but the third was produced ten to twenty years later, evidently as a substitute for the original east pediment figures destroyed by lightning. The west pediment displayed, built up in two wings about the central figure of the goddess, a strictly symmetrical composition of warriors who, attacking, falling, kneeling, and lying, were precisely adapted to the gable slope. Yet the movement of the group does not flow, the bodies sculptured in the round with meticulously elaborated muscling still appear silhouette-like and flat, and the smiling wounded soldiers at the corners do not take death seriously. How different is the later east group! One great relationship binds the figures together as a whole, the goddess at the centre unites instead of dividing, the bodies turn freely in space as though released from fetters, and on the faces of the injured appears now the true anguish of death.

Between the dates of these two gable compositions, the thoroughgoing early classical revolution had taken place, a revolution that affected every aspect of Greek consciousness but strangely enough is scarcely perceptible in architecture. There, the route had been so ineluctably prescribed, the inner law was so binding, that even a complete change in mental outlook could alter nothing. It is hard to specify any fundamental difference between the temple of Aphaea and the temple of Zeus at Olympia, although their thematically closely related pediments—the Aphaea west gable and the Apollo gable—speak in such dissimilar languages.

BASSAE, THE TEMPLE OF APOLLO EPICURIUS

Plates XI, 90–96, figs. 43–44

Two hundred years ago, the temple of Apollo Epicurius, since to a large extent re-erected, was discovered high up in the remote mountains of Arcadia, a couple of hours away on foot from the small ancient city of Phigalia. In the opinion of Pausanias (VIII, 41, 8), 'of all the temples in the Peloponnese, it must be judged the best after the one at Tegea [page 354], on account of the beauty of the stone and the precision of its jointing'. We further learn 'that Ictinus . . . was the architect'. The inducement for the dedication is also given: Apollo's succour during a plague in 429—though this assertion turns out to have but little plausibility. Hence, the attribution to Ictinus, who designed the Parthenon and the telesterium at Eleusis, must likewise be regarded with suspicion. How could the illustrious Attic master have been called in for this out-of-the-way provincial temple? May one foist upon this classical architect a building in which archaic and progressive, traditional and original, indigenous and Attic, constitute a whole defying reason and full of tensions?

As we shall see, however, behind this complex structure, which responds to every problem solved by presenting a new one, there is a thinker with a will of his own, an experimenter and innovator who both preserves and changes the forms he has inherited: who else but the master of the Parthenon?

The Apollo temple was dedicated in an old sanctuary. Of its archaic predecessor, nothing remains except tiles and a slight trace of its foundations in the rock.

XI, 90 The new peripteral structure was built in the hard, dull grey limestone of the vicinity. Only the sculptural decoration, interior capitals, roof, and broad coffered ceilings at front and rear were of marble. Measuring 47 ft. 6 in. by 125 ft. 5⅝ in., the *fig. 44* stylobate is of modest size, and, oddly enough, it faces north. Moreover, it contains the first puzzle: its excessive length (6 by 15 instead of the canonical 6 by 13 columns) is an archaic feature, which the extra 2⅜ in. in the axial spacing at the ends further

emphasizes. With this archaic ground-plan, the progressive elevation—columns soaring upwards in their Attic slenderness, capitals forming taut, terse transitions, an exceptionally low and therefore light entablature—is out of harmony. No other temple was erected after the older Parthenon with such a long peristyle, except for that of Apollo at Delphi, which exactly repeated the ground-plan of its archaic forerunner. Now, that very building (page 330, fig. 22) not only displayed the same count of 6 by 15 columns, and the same breadth-to-length ratio of 2 : 5 in the crepidoma, but its external measurements, reduced by a third, were exactly repeated at Bassae. This pious 'quotation' of the most sacred temple of Apollo was naturally dictated to the architect by the priests and donors; but consider what he did with it! *91* By extending both porticoes to make them two interaxials deep—an Ionic-Attic feature already anticipated in the Theseum (page 392) and at Sunium (cf. also page 398)—he turned the length into amplitude, creating light-flooded open spaces at the fronts, which were strongly differentiated by their extremely magnificent marble coffered ceilings from the narrower, limestone-covered pteromata. Also uncommonly deep and roofed with marble, the pronaos brought a further enhancement of the effect. Whoever passed through this sequence of spaces *94, 95,* entered a naos unique in its form. Close to each side *fig. 43* wall stood five tall Ionic half-columns, merging into spurs of masonry that attached them to the wall. Set mid-way between the last pair, a slimmer, free-standing column united the two rows, a device obviously stemming from the basic idea of the Parthenon naos (page 374) with its procession of columns likewise carried round before the rear wall. At Bassae, however, the architect disposed of tradition in an even freer and bolder fashion by substituting for the Doric two-tiered arrangement, with an intervening architrave that ruptured the spatial unity, Ionic columns growing upwards without a break and pressed outwards to the side walls in order to widen the small naos.

351

To the problems and drawbacks of such an experiment belongs the amorphous fusion of wall-projection and column—mutually exclusive elements as regards their structure. Perhaps religious considerations or requirements occasioned the use of this very ancient Peloponnesian form (see Heraeum, fig. 8). At all events, it was a sore point to which the architect paid special attention. He expressly invented a form of Ionic capital identically developed on three sides and tried, with peculiar, broadly flaring bases, to counterbalance the thrust and weight of the spurs.

Still more clearly than by the 'stylobate' that does in fact bend round, and by the corner spurs set logically at an angle of forty-five degrees, the fact that the columns really were intended as a circuit is shown by the Ionic architrave running round on all four sides (i.e. also over the entrance, where it was carried by supports projecting on either side of the doorway). Upon it rested the famous sculptured frieze, topped by a compressed cornice. The whole was nothing else than a fully developed Ionic peristyle turned inwards, and this fact may throw light on the fundamentally new approach to the interior that Ictinus, a pioneer without equal, achieved by applying to the inside all the means at the disposal of the classical period for its almost wholly outward-radiating, corporeal architecture.

It may be necessary to emphasize expressly that the 'beholder' nevertheless played no part, that—despite certain beginnings such as the not really columnar columns—no illusory effects were sought, and that the tension produced by moulded space, the heightening action of light had not yet been discovered. (Incidentally, the naos was lit only through the doorway, the frieze lying entirely in semi-darkness.) Corporeal form was still of central importance.

This interior poses a further problem, which has not yet been definitely solved. Beyond the naos bounded by columns, there lay another room, clearly cut off from it by the axial column and the entablature running across, yet at the same time smoothly and organically joined to it by the two open intercolumnial spaces and constant floor-level. Our only model for such a room set behind and accessible from the naos is the adytum, a forbidden, mysteriously closed cult chamber. One of these may well have been prescribed by the clients with their eyes on Delphi; but their architect had no use for secluded rooms, and therefore made this 'adytum' accord with his own ideas.

However, not only was the adytum freely united with the naos, but it also opened to the east—on to the side of the temple, that is—through a doorway exactly opposite the tenth intercolumnial space

94, 95

counting from the north. Was it then, as has been supposed, a second naos, in which the little archaic Apollo temple lived on? If so, the cult image would at least have looked eastward, even if the lie of the land compelled the temple to face north. In reality, of course, the building could easily have been made to run east-west by means of some terracing, so there can be no question of compulsion. The problem has become even more complicated since it was established that the frieze slabs were shortened as an afterthought. This must have been due to a change of plan that entailed shortening the interior architrave—i.e., the whole naos space—and when the building was already well advanced, moreover. An attempt has recently been made to prove that, in point of fact, a closed adytum was at first provided for, but that then, in connexion with the planning of the east door, it was made to open on to the naos. This would mean that the axial column and encircling entablature were not introduced until the change. In other words, the central idea of the spatial scheme—the surrounding Ionic 'peristyle'—is extracted from the original plan, and explained as the architect's way out of his difficulties, even though he had already realized a wholly similar concept so brilliantly in the Parthenon. Furthermore, deep depressions in the paving (plate 95, foreground) at the site of the projected adytum wall are a sure sign that no foundation—such as would, after all, be required—lies in the ground below.

Even if a hypothesis unconfirmed by the evidence is needed to explain the building, it should at least involve confronting the execution modified by external necessities with a precisely expressed original project. Such a solution, likewise hypothetical on account of the absence of foundations, can here only be touched upon: it is thought that a conflict lies hidden above all in the placing of the columns. The first pair come so close to the projecting, pilaster-like masonry of the doorway that in each case an inaccessible nook has been produced, above which, moreover, the inner angle of the architrave once hung unsupported in the air. Did Ictinus plan this? Following the Ionic custom, the internal columns accord with the external ones, but, contrary to this custom, they are not aligned with them but with the centres of the outer intercolumnial gaps. If one now shifts the internal columns half an interaxial southwards to their proper places, while claiming the entire space to the rear wall for the first scheme, then everything accommodates itself to a clear spatial concept. The first columns stand an intercolumniation away from the door wall; the oblique spurs of the (now sixth) pair at the back project from the south corners of the room, where

43 Bassae, temple of Apollo Epicurius. View of naos and 'adytum'. F. Krischen, 1938

any other form would be quite impossible; and instead of the single free-standing axial support, another column engaged in the wall bears the encircling architrave.

If the architect had his bold, ample, truly classical plan cancelled owing to the stubborn demand for a separate cult chamber, he was still able to get out of the difficulty more successfully than Mnesicles with his reduced Propylaea. He did not give up the full depth of the space, as he knew how to include the sundered part by means of an open arrangement of columns.

The fact that in so doing he used an entirely new type of capital, carved with acanthus leaves and

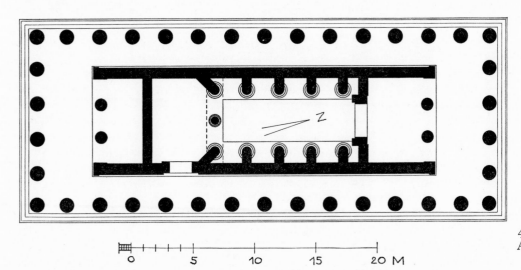

44 Bassae, temple of Apollo Epicurius. Plan (1 : 300). New drawing

353

spirals, for the first time in any building on the specially exposed free-standing axial column, and probably also on its two neighbours, testifies once again to his originality. With this, the 'Corinthian' capital began its triumphant career, soon to put the Doric and Ionic orders in the shade.

Ictinus did not require the building organization, revealed by many Peloponnesian details as a local one, to execute curvature in the hard, recalcitrant stone. All the same, the columns display entasis, and the stonemasons' work is so admirably precise that it was probably possible to do without a coating of stucco. The most important sculptural decoration— the pediment groups—obviously fell victim to one of the usual art robberies perpetrated by the Roman conquerors. Besides the frieze in the British Museum, other fragments have survived of metopes that, as at Olympia, were arrayed above each end of the cella.

In the temple at Bassae, the most tension-ridden, ambiguous, puzzling structure of the classical age, the personality of the creator is apparent for the first time. He was an innovator of genius, who, though himself standing firm and fast in the classical world, prepared the way for the Hellenistic building style through his daring, highly anticipative choice of means. Thus, the Corinthian capital could not but issue in a decorative naturalism; the arrangement of engaged columns ultimately led to façade architecture; and the importance here given to informing space was bound gradually to consume the building's solid corporeality from within.

Like the grand, bold cast of his creations—the Parthenon, the unrealized plan for the Eleusinian telesterium, and his last temple, erected towards the end of the fifth century, at Bassae—this ability to point ahead is something Ictinus shares with Michelangelo the architect.

TEGEA, THE TEMPLE OF ATHENA ALEA

Plates 87–89, figs. 45–49

In 394, the old temple, which with its wooden columns probably dated from the seventh century, was burned down in the sanctuary of Athena Alea near Tegea (see page 106). When, after the long disturbances caused by war, a new building was finally planned, Scopas of Paros, one of the most eminent sculptors of that period, was appointed architect. He had just finished his sculpture for the Mausoleum at Halicarnassus, which later numbered among the wonders of the world. During an age when sculpture and architecture followed the same path, there was nothing unusual in both arts being practised by one person, and so Scopas created a building that was certainly the peer of the pediment groups with which he adorned it. It was the first entirely marble temple in the peninsula. The numerous references to Attic buildings are not so much signs of the master's uncertainty in a new occupation—no other edifice by Scopas has come down to us—as the fashion of the day: richly evocative allusions to unsurpassable works known by all. Thus, the column diameters and intercolumniation, for example, exactly repeated those of the Propylaea (5 ft. 1 in. and 6 ft. 9⅛ in., ratio 3 : 4), while in the ornament, the Erechtheum was 'quoted'. The true model, however, was Ictinus's temple at Bassae, the novelties of which no fourth-century architect could ignore.

With 6 by 14 columns, the peristyle was almost as long as that of Bassae (6 by 15 columns), for Scopas adopted the latter's two-interaxial-deep porticoes, which he too set apart from the narrow pteromata by means of differently constructed marble coffered ceilings. The archaistic widening of the end interaxials by 1¼ in. would also seem to have been borrowed from Bassae, as there was no reason for it here.

The style of the period appeared above all in the even slimmer columns (height = 6·1 lower diams.; Bassae 5·3) and in the lighter entablature (height = ¼ column height; Bassae ⅓). At the same time, we find the most subtle architectonic means being used: all 'level' surfaces had an imperceptible curvature (ends 1⅝ in., sides 2½ in.), while the columns and side walls tilted uniformly inwards, as at Bassae and Olympia. On the other hand, the columns had no swelling (entasis), and even the shallow, truncated-cone echinuses of the squat capitals show how far the mouldable bulk of the building had disappeared. In the feather-light, elongated proportions, the charac-

fig. 45

figs. 46,

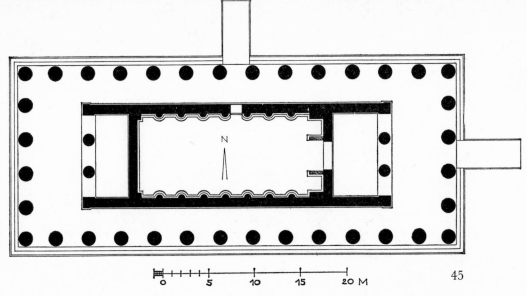

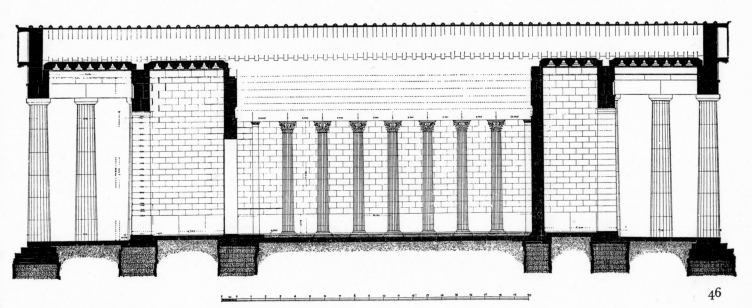

45 Tegea, temple of Athena
Alea. Plan (1 : 400). New
drawing after C. Dugas and
M. Clemmensen, 1924

46–47 Tegea, temple of Athena
Alea. C. Dugas and M. Clemmensen, 1924
46 (*Centre*) Longitudinal section
(1 : 250)
47 (*Below*) Cross-section
through pronaos (1 : 250)

45

46

teristic gravity and concentrated force of the Doric
order had been exchanged for the slender-limbed
elegance that in itself constituted the Ionic heritage.
Thus, the peristyle only outwardly retained its Doric
appearance. Delicate Ionic leaf ornaments penetrated inside it (Ionic ovolo on the ceiling beams,
Lesbian cyma on the wall footing), and concentrated
in the deep porticoes. In the naos, probably the most
astonishing and certainly the most magnificent room
of the fourth century, the Ionic spirit at last ruled
absolutely. Here, it was apparent that a great
architect had been at work, clearly and decisively
transcending his model. The surrounding columns
were now pressed as closely as could be to the walls,
and became half-columns. (In fig. 45, no half-
columns are shown against the rear wall, in accordance with the usual reconstruction. However, as the
meagre finds do not exclude their presence, as, on the
contrary, an encircling architrave demands them for

47

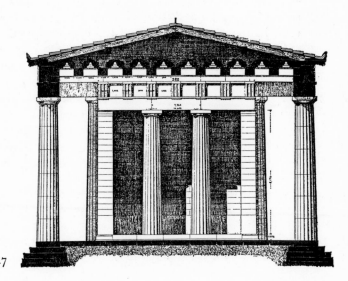

355

48

48–49 Tegea, temple of Athena Alea. C. Dugas and M. Clemmensen, 1924
48 (*Above*) Ornament crowning walls of naos (height 1 ft. 2⅞ in.)
49 (*Below*) Corinthian capital of naos columns (height 2 ft. 5½ in.)

49

formal and technical reasons, and as moreover the building, with its model [Bassae] and younger sister [Nemea] both displaying inner circuits, would otherwise not fit into the picture at all, a restoration with three half-columns projecting from the back wall must be considered.) The problem of the corners was skilfully but a trifle mechanically evaded by placing pilasters in them. That columns and wall really were —against their nature—fused is made clear by the rich profile of the wall base, which, bulging out below each half-column, also formed ·the column bases.

On all these columns with their Ionic fluting sat Corinthian capitals. If one compares them with the stiffer, tectonically constructed Bassae capitals and *fig. 37* the closely related capitals of the tholos at Delphi, one becomes aware of the sculptor's freer, more lively hand. Swelling, fleshy leaves proliferate around and hide the chalice-formed nucleus. From fluted sheaths based on nature (cauliculi), spiral tendrils burst forth with plant-like resilience, and press against the curving abacus. A broad leaf fills the centre. Another sculptor, Polyclitus the younger, treated the same theme at about the same time in the *fig. 54* tholos at Epidaurus (page 360). His taller capital appears more elegant than the massive one of Scopas,

and he has retained the graceful motif of the two thin middle spirals, from which a fleuron blooms. Both designs subsequently merged—the full, dense crown of leaves and cauliculi of Tegea with the elongated proportions and central spirals of Epidaurus—to form a type the structure of which was handed down unaltered through every change of style into Christian times.

The Corinthian columns of the Tegea temple reached nowhere near the ceiling. Allowing for the architrave, there were about 10 ft. to spare, which one can hardly conceive as having been filled by a smooth, oppressively heavy wall. Whether one imagines a pilaster gallery projecting from the naos wall or a succession of little Ionic half-columns, nothing of it has survived. It would have been the earliest hint of that mixing and superimposition of the orders through which the Hellenistic age achieved such tense, attractive contrasts. An arrangement like this could, in any case, have been inspired here by the Doric two-storied interior colonnade.

However that may be, a deep gulf separates the building from the 'canonical' Doric temple. The interior space was excitingly enlarged by the way in which the half-columns not only broke up the walling, its hitherto so firm, inviolable shell, but positively negated it, made it disappear—and this for the first time not with real but with optical means. After all, the Greek eye must have seen the gaps in a colonnade as open space. Though the columns at Tegea were still solid bodies, the cella still retained its closed external form and the rich decoration was still imbued with tectonic significance, a breach had none the less been made in the corporeal classical structure. In the interior with its imaginary expansion, the vivacity and vigour of the temple were revealed, whereas academic coldness and detachment impregnated the extremely conscientiously constructed peristyle.

If one looks at the scant evidence of Scopas's pediment figures—the warriors' heads, for example —one notices something analogous in the passionate gaze directed to imaginary realms, and in the gliding play of light over the otherwise firm, cubic form. Here, too, an interior has been given form, though without that variance with the exterior, with the plastic substance. Does this conflict indicate a crisis in architecture that was not suffered to the same degree by sculpture?

In the almost entirely lost pediment groups, the hunt for the Calydonian boar was represented on the east end, a fight between Achilles and Telephus on the west. As at Olympia and Bassae, the twelve metopes above the pronaos and opisthodomus entrances were also sculptured.

One last feature that the temple shared with Bassae: in the north side wall of the naos, exactly on the building's transverse axis, was set a door. It can scarcely be argued that this architectonically unfruitful, or rather disturbing, motif was taken over from Bassae. Perhaps, after the religious plays of the Eleusinian mysteries had begun to exert a growing influence, other cults also sought to avail themselves of the same idea, and allowed the faithful, hitherto excluded from all proceedings inside the temple, to participate more and more, by displaying rituals to them. At all events, an early Hellenistic temple has survived in neighbouring Lycosura with a similar lateral door, opposite which there is a flight of stepped seats: a small theatre, in fact. Thus, the least forced explanation of the side entrances at Tegea and Bassae is that they, too, were 'exhibition' or 'manifestation' doorways.

NEMEA, THE TEMPLE OF ZEUS

Plates 82, 83, fig. 50

In the sanctuary of Nemean Zeus, a new building was erected towards the end of the fourth century over the remains of an archaic temple. Though embodying a somewhat larger basic measurement, this peripteral temple so exactly repeated the dimensions and proportions of the one at Tegea, and copied its details (e.g. the lions' heads and acanthus *rinceaux* on the sima) so faithfully, that it has been ascribed to the same architect: Scopas. Admittedly, the peristyle of 6 by 12 columns was rather wider and two interaxials shorter than that of Tegea (65 ft. 10⅞ in. by 139 ft. 7⅛ in.; Tegea 62 ft. 11½ in. by 156 ft.). As a comparison of the ground-plans shows, this curtailment was effected by resolutely leaving out the Tegean opisthodomus and by halving the two-interaxial-deep west portico. At the east end, on the other hand, the bold, ample Tegean arrangement was retained for the entrance. A show-front was thus deliberately paraded for the first time, while the rear end shrunk.

With his Tegean design, Scopas gave the evolution of the temple a powerful thrust forward, opening up new dimensions for the interior space. Though these conflicted with the stable Doric order of the exterior, Scopas did not violate this order, as now occurred at Nemea, where the building was no longer to such an extent, as an architectonic organism, bound by its own formal laws. It sought to impress the beholder, in the process of which the east front naturally came to be emphasized, while the back literally went short. The opisthodomus, the balancing of the fronts, and the corporeal 'all-sidedness' of the Doric temple had had their day.

This decline of the old monumentality was accompanied by a stiffening of the forms. The columns stretched out to a pencil slimness not previously attained (height: Olympia 4·7 lower diams., Tegea 6·1, Nemea 6·35), and carried a correspondingly slight entablature (height: Bassae ⅓ column height, Nemea ¼). Attic 'verticalism' here

357

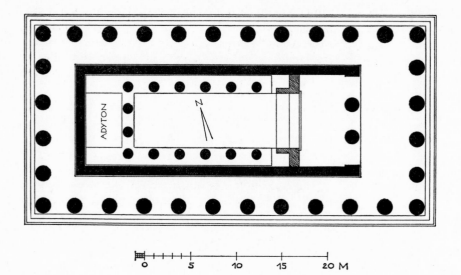

ADYTON

50 Nemea, temple of Zeus.
Plan (1 : 400). New drawing

appeared decidedly overdeveloped into a feeble and anaemic elegance. Little sign was left of the old content, the form, and the precise expression of load and support. The building's refined lifelessness and academic rigidity were re-enforced by details carved in the abstract shapes of solid geometry—the low truncated cone of the capitals or the mutule guttae flattened to shallow discs—and by a rationally adjusted skeleton of proportions.

If one is hoping that the disintegration and stiffening of the Doric exterior were counterbalanced by enrichment and diversification within, the naos will seem a disappointment. Tegea's spatial scheme was not repeated, let alone developed. The timorous architect harked back to the Theseum's arrangement of columns running round close to the walls (now 6 by 4 columns); provided with Corinthian capitals, it had already stood the test elsewhere. Beyond the western columns, the rear part of the cella

was kept separate, on the model of Bassae, and it contains a remarkable, deep cavity—a subterranean adytum?

The temple was built fairly carefully in local limestone coated with stucco, only its sima being of marble. It apparently had no sculptural decoration.

Obviously, Scopas cannot have had anything to do with this work, though it is possible that the builders of the temple at Tegea, deprived, after its completion, of their supereminent chief and his powers of leadership, had to look about for work in another quarter. It is quite plain that the weaknesses for which we feel obliged to criticize the Nemean temple are not to be blamed upon these brave workmen or their unoriginal master, and that it is a question rather of critical signs of the times. The classical period was at an end. In the stiffness, a new departure announced itself, in the atrophy, a new birth: that of the Hellenistic age.

EPIDAURUS, THE SANCTUARY OF ASCLEPIUS

Plates 97–99, figs. 51–54

fig. 51

The appearance of this Asclepius sanctuary was determined in the fourth and third centuries. It was not only owing to the special character of the sacred health resort, but also to the trends of these centuries, that the temple and cult edifices, luxuriously equipped though of modest size, almost disappeared

amid the imposing practical buildings that were arranged all round the precinct. Ample, partly two-storied stoas in which the patients lay down for their curative sleep bounded the square on its north side, and were joined by medicinal springs, a vast palaestra, the theatre extolled as the most beautiful in Greece, a stadium, and—the sanctuary's largest structure—a magnificent two-storied hostel with no less than 160 rooms grouped symmetrically about four colonnaded courtyards. Instead of being enclosed by walls, the broad temenos was only marked out to some extent with boundary-stones. Nevertheless, a stately ceremonial gateway, with six columns on both fronts after the example of the Athenian Propylaea (but now Corinthian and Ionic ones), could not be left out. Even the palaestra had to have its own 'propylaea', the portico of which, also hexastyle, was a third as broad again as the temple front.

Measuring 38 ft. 7 in. by 75 ft. 7⅞ in., the temple of Asclepius, begun around 380, was one of the smallest peripteral buildings in Greece, but it still had room for a splendid gold-and-ivory statue of the god enthroned, a work with which the Parian Thrasymedes emulated the Zeus of Phidias. Hence, the cella was fitted out as a sort of casket, and had

neither interior columns nor an opisthodomus. Pomp and splendour took the place of the absent monumentality. As at Olympia, the flooring was in contrasted black and white marble. We learn from building accounts of a costly wood-and-ivory door with golden nails, also by Thrasymedes.

With 6 by 11 columns, the Doric peristyle surrounding the 'shrine' was very short owing to the lack of an opisthodomus, and, in this, reflected a growing fourth-century tendency to make buildings shorter (cf. Argos and Nemea).

Considerable remains of sculpture have been connected with the pediments, though it is hard to guess the subject of the east gable: an 'Iliupersis'? On the west, mounted Amazons and Greeks dashed against each other. The local sculptor Timotheus, whom we find, shortly after, working on the Mausoleum at Halicarnassus alongside the greatest masters of his day, received 900 drachmas, according to the accounts for 'models'—of these pediment figures?

99

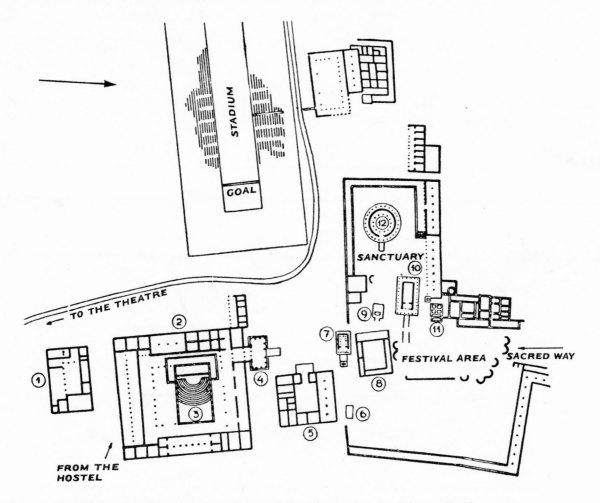

51 Epidaurus, sanctuary of Asclepius. General layout. Kirsten-Kraiker, 1957
1: Greek bath; 2: palaestra with propylaeum (4) and, built inside later, odeum (3); 5: later 'wards' (?); 6: temple of Themis; 7: temple of Artemis; 8: earlier 'wards' for patients; 9: altar of Asclepius; 10: temple of Asclepius; 11: medicinal springs; 12: tholos

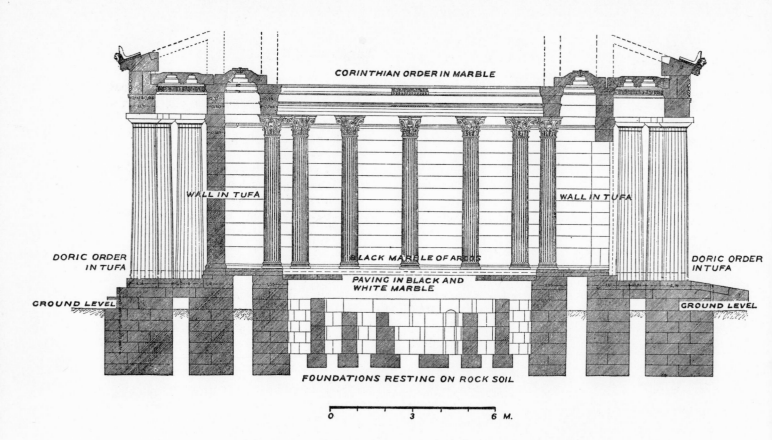

CORINTHIAN ORDER IN MARBLE

WALL IN TUFA

WALL IN TUFA

DORIC ORDER
IN TUFA

DORIC ORDER
IN TUFA

BLACK MARBLE OF ARGOS

PAVING IN BLACK AND
WHITE MARBLE

GROUND LEVEL

GROUND LEVEL

FOUNDATIONS RESTING ON ROCK SOIL

0   3   6 M.

52–53 Epidaurus, tholos. A. Defrasse and H. Lechat, 1895. 52 Section.

He also created personally the acroteria for at least one end. Those that survive come mainly from the west: enchanting horsewomen who, transiently suspended, embody those gentle breezes the *aurai*. *98* The theme that commenced with such expressive force in the winged Gorgons and Victories of archaic buildings here found its most refined, most supple form. In these acroteria, the severe, earth-bound structure at last united with the sky and breezes to form a hovering fantasy.

The jewel of the sanctuary was the tholos, a remarkable rotunda erected with extremely precise workmanship during about 360–320, again according to surviving building accounts. It surpassed its forerunner, the tholos at Delphi (see page 341), by *figs. 36,* about a third in size (diam.: bottom step 71 ft. 1½ in., cella 48 ft. 0¾ in.), and in richness by far more. As at Delphi, a Doric peristyle—now of 26 not 20 columns —encircled the round cella. Inside, a ring of 14 free- standing Corinthian columns, which oddly enough *fig. 52* did not accord with the external one, formed a narrow ambulatory. The architect, as at Tegea, was a sculptor: Polyclitus the younger, probably a nephew of the famous Argive master. This is thought to be perceptible in the devotion, inexhaustible inventiveness and rare ability applied to the carved ornamentation.

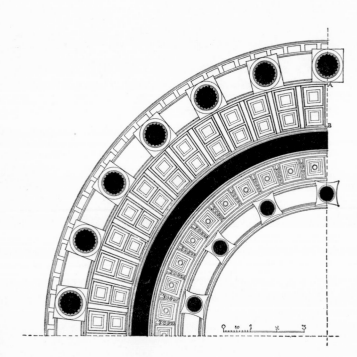

53 Detail of plan with 'reflection' of coffered ceiling

Like the lavishly adorned framing of the door, the anthemion and egg-and-dart at the top of the wall contained deliberate allusions to the Erechtheum. The metopes were for the first time enriched with ornaments instead of sculpture, a large, boldly modelled, brightly painted rosette filling each almost square field. Though the external structure—apart from the marble simas, the ceiling coffers, and the orthostats—was still of ordinary limestone, inside a varied play of different coloured marbles was developed. Not only were the wall base and stylobate emphasized with black marble, but, from the same colour contrasts, a segmental floor pattern—the first of this kind—was created, its black and white lozenges setting up a spiral, wheeling movement. The Corinthian capitals have already been discussed on page 356: an undamaged one was found carefully buried near the tholos—no doubt the model prepared by Polyclitus himself, after which the masons worked. The enrichment of the marble ambulatory ceiling is the most lavish known: meanders, cymas, acanthus motifs, and rosettes united in a real symphony of ornaments. To judge the splendour and profusion, we must add in our imagination the flat or tent-shaped wooden ceiling, gaily coloured and gilded, of the central space, and also the recorded paintings—of Eros and Methe, Pausanias says. In doing so, we may perhaps wonder with slight uneasiness if all this is not excessive.

The frenzy of ornamental forms does, in fact, reveal a questionable late classical tendency. On the Erechtheum, the enrichment gushed and sprouted vivaciously from every joint and articulation of the building; now we perceive the aesthetic aim, the plan. As the path of outward monumentality had come to an end, chosen effects of decoration were made to predominate. This road was, of course, bound to lead to the separation of the ornament from the building's tectonic structure, to pure decoration, that is. Here, however, each ornamental feature still kept to its place, the unity having not yet been destroyed, and we can enjoy without any feeling of uneasiness the sections of the tholos reconstructed in the museum as the last and richest ornamental creation of classical times.

There is a mystery connected with the purpose of the rotunda. Its floor hid an underground 'labyrinth', made up of three circular walls leaving room for three narrow passages. These were linked by three little doorways and barred by three cross-walls. Thus, when one raised the paving slabs that covered the middle circuit and climbed down a narrow spiral staircase into the centre, one had to grope one's way forward with a triple change of direction through the circular passages to the dead end of the outer ring.

54 Epidaurus, tholos. Model Corinthian capital by Polyclitus the younger. New drawing after Defrasse and Lechat

It is not known whether the holy snakes of the healing god dwelt down there, or whether, as the designation 'thymele' in a surviving inscription would seem to imply, chthonic burial rites—secret practices dedicated to the subterranean powers—took place.

THE THEATRE   *Plates XXXV, 100, 101, fig. 55*

'The Epidaurians have within the sanctuary a theatre that, in my opinion, is specially worth seeing. Those of the Romans surpass all others in decoration, and that of the Arcadians at Megalopolis is of unequalled size; but what architect could rival Polyclitus as regards harmony and beauty? For it was Polyclitus who built both this theatre and the round edifice [i.e., tholos]' (Paus. II, 27, 5). These remarks by Pausanias, who otherwise does not waste many words on temples, are enough to seize our attention, as in them the theatre is explicitly rated as an art form. Moreover, it is precisely the harmony of this well-preserved example, embedded in a hollow about 550 yds. south-east of the sanctuary, that still impresses the visitor today.

The descent of the theatre as a form of art from the choral dances performed at the Dionysus festival, which gradually became 'drama', has been indicated in connexion with the Athenian theatre of Dionysus

fig. 54

7, above

7, below

(page 115). As allegories depicting, reconditely and gravely or exuberantly and gaily, the relationship betwen god and man in mutually completing reflections as their theme, tragedy and satyr-play retained their link with the sanctuary and the divine festival. Being thus the holy site of a religious observance, the Greek 'theatre' shares nothing more with ours than its name. In its evolution, a thoroughly Greek process is discernible: the way in which architecture, by creating a structural form exactly suited to the practical requirements of the cult, advanced in a few strides to an eternally valid art form, capable as well of expressing the specific meaning of the drama and the relation of the participants to the characters. An entirely similar process, leading from different postulates to a different form, can be followed in the telesterium at Eleusis (page 401).

The starting-point at Athens was a circular dancing place—the orchestra—in the middle of which stood the altar of Dionysus; the onlookers settled on the slope rising above it. A scene, at first a tent or temporary shed from which the chorus (or the actor gradually developing his performance into drama) could emerge, was enough to begin with. The rectangular dancing space surrounded by seating steps is of earlier, perhaps even pre-Greek, origin. Such a place was recently identified north of the Erechtheum (fig. 66), and it appears to have supplanted a similar but very much older one. There, however, it was a question of another kind of cult performance, which obtained its most canonical

architectonic expression in the telesterium at Eleusis: the congregation sat round and directly participated in a mystery play. From the outset, the theatre was founded on a sharper division between spectators and action, these being, as it were, confronted. Yet when the auditorium was given a monumental form, the principle of the flight of stepped seats could none the less be taken over. In the building of a stone theatre, the mother-country was evidently preceded as early as the fifth century by the rich city of Syracuse. There, three straight flights in a ⌒-shaped arrangement embraced the perform-ance area, whereas in Greece itself the steps plainly fitted round the orchestra as a semicircle from the beginning. This meant that the auditorium or cavea, which always lay in the open, became shell-shaped; and, wherever possible, it was partly cut into a slope and partly, towards its ends, banked up. At its extremities, it was bounded on either side by retaining-walls, the top of which followed the incline of the steps. Opposite this open semi-circle, an at first simple stage building with three doors was put up approximately at a tangent to the orchestra, and represented a royal palace, temple, or whatever the play required. Between stage building (scene) and retaining-walls, approaches (parodoi) were left free on both sides.

This simple primary form was developed to its most perfect state at Epidaurus. The art of propor-tioning learnt in temple construction now came to be applied to the theatre. Of all surviving theatres, the one at Epidaurus displays best the geometrically

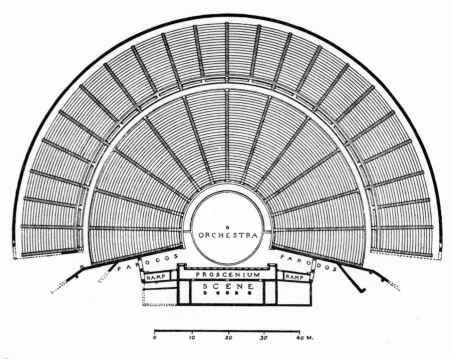

55 Epidaurus, theatre. Plan.
W. Dörpfeld, 1896

determined principles of design referred to by Vitruvius (V, 7), probably after earlier sources. In the basic circle of the orchestra can be inscribed a twenty-sided polygon (according to Vitruvius a dodecagon), from the angles of which radial stairways lead upwards and divide the cavea into equal wedge-shaped blocks (cunei). The cavea includes twelve such cunei, thus extending on either side one cuneus beyond the semicircle. This has not, however, involved keeping rigidly to a circular form, since the arc opens up slightly towards the 'scene', each outermost pair of cunei having been planned with an increased radius, so that a kind of semi-ellipse (more accurately a 'basket-handle' curve) was produced. Above the thirty-four curved rows, a second series cut off from the lower one by a gangway (diazoma) was added later, and this extra twenty rows made room for 14,000 spectators in all. Surrounded by a stone rim, the orchestra constitutes the centre, its diameter (32 ft. o$\frac{5}{8}$ in.) matching that of the Dionysus theatre at Athens (32 ft. 3$\frac{3}{8}$ in.). The stage building received a complex form. Before the actual 'scene' was set a graceful Ionic colonnade (proscenium), its supports (pillars masked by Ionic half-columns) being provided with special grooves to receive painted scenery panels (pinakes). At either end of the stage building, a ceremonial gateway with an Ionic entablature spanned the parodos. The whole ensemble was erected at the beginning of the third century together with the auditorium, as A. von Gerkan has recently established. (This, however, makes Pausanias's statement that Polyclitus built both the tholos and the theatre very doubtful.) The proscenium carried a platform on which—at first, probably only on special occasions—the actors also performed. Nevertheless, ramps that led up to this proscenium show that increasing use was made of the upper 'stage', which must have been afforded a background of its own by a second story of the 'scene' building. With this, the drama, removed from its old focus, became a spectacle. Correspondingly, the seats of honour (proedrie) for priests and privileged guests, hitherto situated in the very bottom row, had to be moved to the first row of the upper series. This change, also detectable in other theatres (Priene, page 475), seems to have taken place in the second century simultaneously with the enlargement of the auditorium. It went hand-in-hand with the secularization of drama. The later comedies were concerned more and more with domestic subjects, though the old, sacred plays of the Attic writers of tragedies, the classic legacy of the great period, did not at the same time lose their power. Indeed, they have retained it right up to the present day, when dramas by Sophocles and Euripides are once again being performed on the same sites, in modern Greek, which has preserved so many of the ancient, deeply significant words.

DELOS

Hail, O heaven-built isle, most lovely scion of the children of bright-haired Leto, O daughter of the sea, thou unmoved marvel of the spacious earth, by mortal men called Delos, but by the blessed gods of Olympus known as the far-seen star of the dark blue earth. . . . PINDAR

Plates X, 102–105, figs. 56, 57

The ruins on Delos, the bleak, barren isle in the middle of the Cyclades which was Apollo's birthplace, and which he chose as his cult centre, reflect an exceedingly eventful history (page 59). Evidence of the most diverse ages and styles is stratified in bewildering abundance.

Mycenaean tombs were the object of religious veneration until well into Greek times. As at other sites (Thermum, Olympia), these numinous relics may have contributed to the sanctity of the place. From the beginning of the first millennium, Ionian immigrants, and foremost the Naxians, built sanctuaries for Apollo and Artemis, the twins born here, for their mother Leto, for Hera, and lastly, on the prominent peak of Mount Cynthus which dominates the island, for Zeus and Athena. Looking round from up there, one understands why this 'rugged, sea-encircled Delos' could not help becoming a holy

363

centre. As in a round dance, the clear contours of the Cyclades ring the Delian isle: Naxos and Paros, Siphnos, Seriphos, Kythnos, Syros, Tenos, and Mykonos. At the same time, one gains a general view across the tangled complex of the excavations. Looking north-west, one sees the harbour, now partly silted up, where the festival embassies once disembarked. Before it can be distinguished the processional avenue flanked by Hellenistic stoas, and before the avenue the extensive square of the agora. The avenue leads rightward to the Doric propylaeum of the temenos of Apollo and Artemis, in the middle of which the foundations of the biggest of the three Apollo temples are clearly discernible. To the north, after the stoa-bounded market-place of an Italian traders' guild, lay the old sanctuary of Leto. From the agora, the narrow, irregular alleys of the Hellenistic residential quarter ascended the slope. A temple of Hera founded as early as the seventh century stood on a small terrace at the top. Near by, a precinct of the Egyptian gods was established during a syncretistic period (the third century?). The small, elegant anta temple (plate 105, front right), with its marble Doric façade masking the plastered side walls, served the cult of Isis. We cannot here go into the immense number of other building remains—those of the theatre, the stadium, the palaestra, the gymnasium, and the many smaller sanctuaries—that lie thickly strewn over this unique little island. Instead, we must confine ourselves to the Apollo precinct.

The earliest cult centre appears to have attached itself to pre-Greek buildings on a terrace right next to the sea. Remains of an altar and a temple in sundried brick (of Artemis?) from the geometric period have been unearthed. During the seventh and sixth centuries, the growing precinct was given a purely island Ionic appearance. A remarkable structure has survived from the first half of the sixth century: the *fig. 56*N so-called oikos of the Naxians, a simple, oblong 'house' with walls of granite ashlar. Before the west end lay an anteroom with the entrance door, its outer wall later being replaced by two columns. There was another door at the east end. Of special interest is a row of eight columns that supported the roof down the long axis of the main room. Their base —tall, simple marble cylinders—reveal the original shape of this member, later so varied. On them rose *fig. 110* up the fluted marble shafts of the slenderest columns known to us anywhere. In addition, fragments have survived of volute capitals already normally formed.

We have met the type of the closed oikos as a treasury at Delphi and Olympia, but it also frequently appeared—and precisely in early archaic times—as a temple. We know nothing certain about the purpose of the Naxian oikos. It may have sheltered dedications or served for ritual meetings, but in any case it was closely connected with the cult and of very ancient, mysterious origin. For beneath its marble paving traces have been found of an entirely similar but narrower building, which, with its two rows of wooden supports let into the floor, dates from the proto-geometric period. A still older, chapel-like structure ('temple Γ') has been *fig. 56* exposed in front of the east end. It seems to belong to the second millennium, and hence to the earlier, Cycladic culture. The immigrating Ionians thus transferred a cult that they had found here to their own gods.

Before the north wall of their oikos, the Naxians raised an enormous offering: a colossal marble *103* statue of Apollo, about 30 ft. tall. Like the row of nine large, uncanny lions, rigid with tension, that *X, 104* guard the processional way by Leto's precinct, it shows how boldly and absolutely the creators of such works achieved a new monumentality towards the end of the seventh century. The contemporary architecture, on the other hand, stood modestly where it was, until the erection of the three Ionic dipteral temples (Samos, Ephesus, Didyma), which were generated by the same spirit.

After the middle of the sixth century, Apollo at last received a more stately dwelling, even if it was still only small. The simple poros temple (A I in fig. 56), probably to be reconstructed as an anta building measuring 33 ft. 2⅛ in. by 51 ft. 6⅛ in., amplified the simple form of the tiny late Cycladic chapel that was perhaps Apollo's first home. Tectaeus and Angelion created a huge, 26-ft.-tall statue of the god in bronze for the almost square naos.

When the Delian league was founded, the sanctuary came wholly under Athenian influence. Soon after 478, the second temple of Apollo was begun, a peripteral structure with 6 by 13 columns (A II). However, scarcely having progressed as far as the crepidoma, work came to a standstill, when in 454 the league's treasure was transferred to Athens and used for the buildings on the Acropolis. None the less, the intended superstructure can be deduced from the exact concordance of the step joints. Probably an Ionic peristyle had been planned, since no provision was made for angle contraction. Following a long pause, the Delians completed the temple in the Doric manner after 303. As there was, in fact, now no angle contraction, the corner metopes had to be greatly widened. Like the earlier one, the peripteral temple faced west towards the old cult site. The space between its two pronaos columns was so broad that three metopes and triglyphs corresponded to it in the frieze above, as on the Propylaea.

Between 425 and 417, at the end of its great century, Athens raised the third temple of Apollo (A III) on Delos. Even though nothing but the foundations remain *in situ*, the temple can be correctly restored from the assembled stones of its upper structure. It displayed all the mastery, the command of form, and also the supreme adaptiveness of those who built the Erechtheum and the temple of Athena Nike. Plainly, the donors sent not only the material—Pentelic marble—but also the workmen from their homeland. Indeed, it is even thought that the architect's handwriting can be recognized: much points to Callicrates, the colleague of Ictinus on the Parthenon and designer of the Nike temple.

The problem was to insert between the old poros temple and the still unfinished peripteral temple a building capable of balancing the latter's hexastyle front. It also involved the creation of an exceptionally spacious naos, in which an already existing group of seven large statues could be accommodated on a semicircular base. The solution, as original as it was obvious, consisted of combining the form of an anta temple with two porticoes (cf. the Nike temple on the Athenian Acropolis) with that of a peripteral one. At either end of a closed naos and its west-facing pronaos were set hexastyle—i.e. 'peripteral'—porticoes. Or vice versa: the cella of a peripteral structure was broadened so unsparingly that its side walls replaced the flanking colonnades. In the Doric articulation exact correspondences existed with the Parthenon (capital dimensions $=\frac{1}{2}$ those of Parthenon pronaos capitals, diam. and intercolumniation $=\frac{3}{7}$ those of Parthenon), though the columns were even more slender (5·7 instead of 5·5 lower diams.).

In place of the four columns that we would expect between the antae of the widened pronaos, we find four slim pillars—precise repetitions of those at the front of the Nike temple. This allowed the pronaos to be unusually light and open, an effect extended to the interior by means of a large window (cf. Propylaea) on either side of the naos doorway.

These pillars returned logically as pilasters at the rear end, where they may in fact have been the first of the great series of walls decoratively

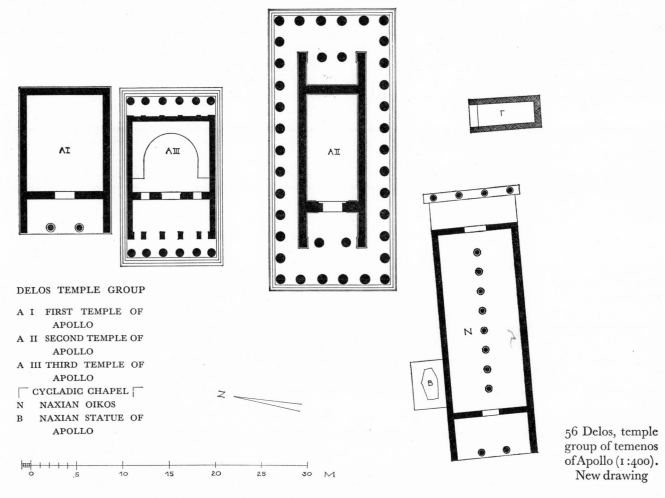

DELOS TEMPLE GROUP

A I   FIRST TEMPLE OF
        APOLLO
A II SECOND TEMPLE OF
        APOLLO
A III THIRD TEMPLE OF
        APOLLO
⌐ CYCLADIC CHAPEL ⌐
N   NAXIAN OIKOS
B   NAXIAN STATUE OF
        APOLLO

56 Delos, temple group of temenos of Apollo (1:400). New drawing

57 Delos, temple of Apollo III, so-called temple of the Athenians. Restored west elevation. F. Courby, *Exploration archéologique de Délos* 12, 1931

articulated with pilasters, a series continuing into our times.

The naos itself was broader than it was long (27 ft. 4⅜ in. by 24 ft. 6⅞ in.; cf. Nike temple). Its wooden coffered ceiling appears to have followed the slopes of the roof, so that gables were formed inside over the cross-walls. Above the perfectly proportioned entablature, and the pediments adorned with groups which are now unfortunately lost, floated the richest acroterium compositions known to us, mythically and symbolically connected with the winds and breezes. Eos, the dawn, lifted up the handsome Cephalus at the west end, while Boreas, the raw north wind, made off with Erechtheus's daughter Orithyia at the east. Here too was an echo of the Parthenon, in whose pediment groups the models could be identified. They were not, of course, timidly copied, but instilled with fresh life in one of the realms newly opened up to the more richly varied art of the century's close: that of light.

'Attica' and 'Athens' are magic words with which a particular spiritual complex is time and again invoked: austere grace, creative prudence, density and freedom of form; and that masterful light, forcing its way distinctly round every shape and tolerating nothing imprecise. Immoderately proud, the Athenians thanked the blue-eyed, sagacious goddess whose name they bore for this intellectual nobility. Plato put his opinion into the mouth of an Egyptian: 'Being a lover of combat and wisdom, the goddess chose a spot that would bring forth a type of person as like her as possible. There she laid the foundations of your state' (*Tim.* 24d). Even in the late imperial age, when Athens had declined to a petty centre of academic education, people were sensible of the goddess's gifts: 'The light also seems brighter to the eyes than usual, because the goddess Athena . . . as it were, removes a vaporous veil from the eyes of those approaching the shore. The view thus arouses a dreamlike happiness, and one feels oneself to be dancing' (Arist., *Panathen.* 97).

To the moderns, the Attic countryside is still the lost home of the mind. Hölderlin beheld it with the soul's eyes: 'Every line of the distance wanders delicately and boldly through space; like steps, the mountains constantly rise up behind each other to the sun. The whole sky is clear.'

Confronted by 'this landscape about which wafted the scent of millennia, this air in which the gold of eternity seemed to be dissolved', Hofmannsthal experienced a profound change upon the Acropolis. Being aware of the unfamiliarity and remoteness of 'impossible antiquity', he was affected all the more bewilderingly, before the Acropolis *korai*, by its proximity. 'Anyone truly capable of appreciating these would have to approach them otherwise than through the eye, as well as more reverently and boldly.' Let us keep this in mind while the image of an obviously incommensurable whole is being outlined below with the aid of photographs, plans, and historical data.

Attica was qualified to mediate between the Dorian and Ionian poles of Greece by its position as a peninsula turned towards the sea and the Ionian East but attached to the Dorian mainland, and by its people, since the resident Ionians certainly did not stand their ground against the immigrant Dorians without interbreeding; and one may count it among the mysterious favours granted to this land that no hybrid came into being, but something distinct and particular that was more than its two elements.

The history of this city always remained bound up with the individual. Here there was no impersonal flow of events determined, say, by the structure of the community, as at Sparta, for example. Athens was what its greatest figures were, and Attic buildings generally bore an individual stamp as well: nowhere else is the question of the architect such a natural and fruitful one. The monumental temple structure made its entrance on the Acropolis under Solon the 'Sage', the statesman and poet who, elected archon in 594, gave the city not only its laws but also the moral concept of 'due proportion', which became much more steadfastly the fundamental law of Attic art than of Attic politics. Under the kingly rather than tyrannical usurper Pisistratus (561–527) and his less temperate sons, the citadel was further adorned with buildings for the gods. Mostly known only from their fragmentary parts, all the sixth-century Doric temples wholly followed the lead of the dominant architecture of Corinth, despite their strongly original pediment sculpture and structural forms. Not until Hippias and Hipparchus, who summoned Ionian poets and sculptors to Athens, set up their court of aesthetes did the Ionic component of Attic architecture break through more freely. When the Solonian Athena temple on the Acropolis and the Pisistratid telesterium at Eleusis were renovated, Ionic elements appear to have entered the structure of the Doric buildings— particularly the slender, graceful Ionic column (page 446), which had already long enjoyed great popularity as a support for offerings. None of these Attic votive columns is like another, and they plainly reveal a characteristic ability not only to invent and vary new forms, but also to embody them in a thoroughly logical way. Typical is the doubly curved 'Lesbian' (instead of convex 'Ionic') profile of the echinus, above which it was usual for a straight intermediate part to effect a smooth transition from the rounded member to the overlapping volutes. On the other hand, the tyrants' attempt to compete with the giant temples of the Ionian East (Olympieum, page 394) outraged the Attic sense of moderation, and had no influence upon further developments.

The democracy re-established in 507 by Clisthenes dedicated two buildings at Delphi: a Doric treasury in which the late archaic hyper-refinement of forms reached its peak, as did the care and precision of the chiselling; and an Ionic stoa that already revealed all the adaptability and constant freshness of Attic architecture. This was only a prelude, however: Attica had been appointed to complete, not to begin.

The Persian wars put Greece, and above all Athens, to the most severe test. As well as by these conflicts, men were affected and changed from within. The simple world of the late sixth century, liberally expended, broke up. Deep down in people's minds the ideas of existence and closeness to the gods united to form a tragic conception of destiny. The expressions and gestures of the sculptor's image of mankind were made grave by the new knowledge embodied and enounced in the tragedies. Sculpture, now conceived outwards from its spiritual centre, began to stir its limbs and turn in space. Its unity was a unity of opposites, movement and counter-movement, axis and counter-axis being harmoniously balanced, and its freedom was a freedom within the law. On the model of counterpoint in music, this principle of composition has gained the name *contraposto*.

During this period of fundamental change, architecture, to begin with, remained entirely in the background. The so-called older Parthenon, the major work of the first half of the century, was left unfinished. Historically speaking, this was due to an oath, allegedly sworn before the battle of Plataea in 479, not to reconstruct sanctuaries razed by the barbarians. Thus, parts of the entablature of the destroyed Pisistratid temple of Athena were built into the north wall of the Acropolis as a memorial visible from afar. Yet does not such a pause at such a time seem more like a long drawing of breath before the apparently unachievable could be achieved? Besides, the Athenians at first had their hands full fortifying the city, extending the harbour, and above all creating the Attic maritime league—or rather empire. After the final peace treaty with the Persians in 449, Pericles started to rebuild the citadel, and for this he had no qualms about falling back on the tributes of the 'confederates' freed from the Persians. Never had such means been made available to artists: the cost of the Propylaea has come down to us as the equivalent of nearly a million pounds.

Rallying round the sculptor Phidias, their pre-eminent chief, and his architect Ictinus, the artists summoned by Pericles seem, for the first and greatest undertaking, the Parthenon, begun in 447, to have united as a group that raised architecture and architectural sculpture to a level unattained before or after. It was a unique operation. To appreciate what was accomplished here, picture the conditions. Though the most mature Doric building, the early classical temple of Zeus at Olympia, had attained a clear, evident unity of plan, and brought the static relations of its parts into perfect equilibrium, there still remained an unresolved archaic residue in the additive fitting together of its members according to

laws. Solely through a complete change of 'structural principle'—from a static additive to a dynamic, synthetic one—could the opposition of the stubborn, unyielding formal material have been broken, and this the Dorians, inwardly bound to the essential fabric of their architecture, were quite unable to effect. There were no two ways about it: a column had to stand and support, an architrave to span and press down. Every part was assigned its limited function, and as regards this structure the Zeus temple was like no matter which archaic temple (Aegina, page 348). All the more momentously different, then, is the Parthenon, which can be called 'Doric' in none but the most superficial sense. Only incidentally do its elements retain their old static functions. The whole edifice is supported by movement and counter-movement, built up of inner oppositions, so that the weight and pressure of its members remain irrelevancies that play no part, while their physical form, caught up in the powerful flow of the structure, stands forth all the more substantially. Only one material, which combines sharpness of form with a gliding, weightless fluidity, was suitable here: translucent, crystalline Pentelic marble. Both the large buildings on the Acropolis, the Parthenon and the Propylaea, were constructed according to the *contraposto* principle developed in the sculpture of the first half of the century, as will be shown in detail.

The Ionic heritage underwent an entirely similar change, though as a formal framework it resisted the inner re-fusion to a dynamic unity far more obstinately. This was because, in the Ionic building, organic life did concentrate in particular components —above all the columns and their capitals, as also the ornamental cyma forms—whereas the severe physical structure, the systematic cohesion of the Doric temple was hardly capable of self-development. The additive quality of members merely put together, exactly what the mature classical period strove to abolish, prevailed more strongly. (On the other hand, Ionic buildings owed to this very defect the freedom and diversity of their ground-plans, which Athens, as we shall see, knew how to make the very most of.) Accordingly, only elements of the Ionic order were included in the two monumental edifices on the Acropolis: the frieze crowning the cella walls of the Parthenon and the columns in the Parthenon west room and Propylaea porch. They confronted the Doric order here as a polar contrast, as something different yet attuned. With a sensitive insight—lacked by the Ionian East itself—into the order's limitations, Athens only erected purely Ionic buildings when gracefulness, not monumental grandeur, was required (Nike temple, Erechtheum).

Significantly, there were no Ionic peripteral temples in Attica. Here, the imponderable but all-powerful means—corrected and interlocking proportions, curvature, extremely delicate modifications of the forms—that were able to renovate the Doric structure so completely did not suffice. A change also occurred in the system and sequence of the members, the staccato dentil course being ousted by a sculptured frieze that surrounded the entire body of the building as a living band. This plainly involved taking a hint from the Ionic treasuries at Delphi, which were made to resemble the neighbouring Doric structures. Thus, the zone of the entablature came to be articulated like that of the Doric temple, except that an evenly flowing frieze now took the place of the rhythmically divided one. In the same way, the bipartite Ionic column base was increased to a rhythmic sequence, charged with energy, of three contrasting profiles, while the capital once full of coarse, florally exuberant life was transformed into clear and elastic tectonic structure (plate 6).

The whole of this thoroughgoing process of change in the Doric just as in the Ionic fabric cannot of course be understood as a 'second blooming of Doricism with assimilated Ionic elements'. Rather was it the specifically Attic achievement of highly talented masters who did not stand between but above the regional manifestations of Greek architecture, and who made free use of the entire formal vocabulary without feeling bound by the archaic limits inherent in it. They then proved able to resolve the two orders and, through a process of spiritual integration, to fuse them into a new one subject to the classical law of harmonious contrasts. Both orders surrendered their restricted validity by entering a higher one.

Another distinctively Attic gift is a logical imagination (if the contradiction will be forgiven) that always seized the essentials, and appears to have been roused by what was adventitious, like the peculiarities of the site or cult. From such factors derived the always individual appearance of Attic buildings, the accidental in the end being absorbed as an essential element in the concept of the edifice. This explains the originality and freshness of every Attic building, and why each task was conceived and accomplished as something unique (Parthenon, Propylaea, Erechtheum, telesterium E, temple of Athena on Delos). That in the process the more pliant, adaptable Ionic order was readily reverted to (Erechtheum) is not surprising. The rigid adherence to type, to which Doric architecture owed its self-consistency, was never found in Attica. This does not mean that Attic buildings were less strongly unified and consistent, but simply that they were individual, through depending upon a personal creative process. The

artist's personality came to the fore; master and work could no longer be separated. Thus, the new conception of the interior that was realized suddenly and without any preparation in the Parthenon and given its clearest expression in the Telesterium design and at Bassae seems to have been the personal achievement of Ictinus—an achievement with immeasurable consequences. The notion of space underlying it can be plainly distinguished from the one current in Magna Graecia. There, people aimed simply at width, and hence wherever possible left out the 'constricting' naos colonnades; in Attica, the interior space was conceived as something to be shaped, as a body, so to speak, everted to its negative—and the most appropriate means of giving it form was precisely colonnading, which, as a peristyle turned inwards, had to express dynamically the amplitude and coherency of the new interiors (Parthenon, Telesterium, Bassae, Tegea).

The concentration of spiritual force and the inward grandeur of the Periclean age—the period of the 'high' or mature classical style—were inevitably followed by a reaction. After the death of Pericles in 429, small-minded politicians cleaving to the old piety came to power. Architecture now had to submit obediently to the petty regulations of the cult. It found an outlet by applying itself to the most subtle diversification of the details, and by introducing the effects of light. A transfiguring glitter and radiance thus enveloped the ornamental 'rich style' buildings, which, with their looser texture, had exchanged the remarkable grandeur and unity of the high classical creations for a delicate animation of the surfaces in light (Erechtheum).

The effect of the buildings raised on the Acropolis was unparalleled. What Athens tried in vain to win during its thirty-year struggle with Sparta—ascendancy over Greece—came to it spontaneously in the architectural sphere through the Periclean edifices. Regional architecture, especially that of the Peloponnese, was stifled by this paramount influence, and even in the most distant provinces, no temple was built after the Parthenon without a reference to it. Ictinus himself designed an immediately famous temple for a small Arcadian sanctuary (Bassae, page 351). It was above all the new conception of space that fascinated people, but the notion of using the two orders in contrast—Ictinus added another variant at Bassae by including the Corinthian capital as well—also became a highly popular piece of common property. The Parian Scopas worked on that amazing Ionic structure, the Mausoleum, and, shortly after, he himself designed a Doric temple with internal columns just as masterfully at Tegea. Hand in hand with the loosening up and expansion of the interior, which reached a climax in the Tegean temple, there now, however, went an increasingly cool, rational adjustment of the proportions and a slight stiffening of the members, which could not be neutralized either by the slim elegance of these members or by the excited mobility of the ornament (Nemea, page 357). It was the announcement of the crisis and of the end of classicism.

Even in Ionia, people forgot their own art and built in the Attic-Ionic style (Nereid monument at Xanthus). In place of architectural dialects, there thus sprang up everywhere a universal tongue, and, like the spreading literary language, it was an Attic one. Thereby were created the prerequisites for the cosmopolitan art of the Hellenistic world. It is true that Athens itself had accomplished the synthesis that formed the basis of this universal Hellenistic style. With its spatial schemes in which the mighty space creations of the future already lay concealed, Athens pointed out the route—but did not take it. It was not just that the city, broken by defeat (404) and quite powerless since Macedonia had won supremacy (338), rested solely on the laurels of its great century; it had also deposited in its classical creations its most essential part, and hence remained so inextricably tied as to be capable of participating only as an outsider and, so to speak, absently in the tumultuous stylistic movements that, centred in the newly founded kingdoms of the East, now came into being. The one important Hellenistic building in Athens, the Olympieum (page 395), was presented by a Syrian diadochos and designed by a Roman architect.

ATHENS, THE ACROPOLIS

Plates XIV, 1–4, figs. 58, 59

Falling away steeply all round and only linked in the west to neighbouring hills, the flat-topped rock that today rises with its incredible crown of beauty above the large, widely spreading city formed the centre of the Attic plain from very ancient times. At first a refuge, it then became the seat of sovereigns and a citadel encompassed by a 'Mycenaean' wall heaped up out of gigantic stones. The growing settlement soon thrust out beyond the level fortified area. When the kings had to yield to an aristocratic régime, their palaces were replaced in the eighth or, at latest, the seventh century by temples of the new, celestial mistress of the city: Pallas Athena.

From 561 to 510 the sceptre was held by the Pisistratids, whose ostentation, dazzling in the tyrannic style, benefited above all their residence, the Acropolis. All archaic structures were razed during the Persian attack in 480. Bits of at least nine temples and treasuries have been preserved in the so-called 'Persian debris' used as a filling at the back of the subsequently extended walls, but the foundations have survived of only one such building: the old temple of Athena. It rose above the remains of the Mycenaean palace between the sites of the Erechtheum and the Parthenon—as, in some measure, their common ancestor. Like the Apollo temple raised at Delphi by the Attic Alcmaeonids (page 330), the peripteral structure, which can be deduced from the parts that have been found, is related to the temple of Apollo at Corinth (page 343). This obviously provided the model not only for the difference between the end and side interaxial spacing (Athens 13 ft. 3 in. and 12 ft. 6¾ in., Corinth 13 ft. 2⅝ in. and 12 ft. 3¼ in.), but also for the angle contraction by about 1 ft. 0¼ in. and the barely perceptible upward curvature of its stylobate. In contrast to the elongated building at Corinth, it had an unusually stumpy peristyle with 6 by 12 columns (69 ft. 10½ in. by 141 ft. 6¾ in.), even though, like the Corinthian one, it was a double temple. Within the actual cella four rooms crowded together: at the east end, an almost square naos containing two rows of three(?) columns, and, at the west, a corresponding, even shorter room into which opened two chambers set side by side. An entirely similar division of space occurred again a century later in the Erechtheum. On the other hand, Ionic elements included in the Doric structure anticipated the Parthenon: above the ends of the cella there seems to have extended a sculptured Ionic frieze (with a procession?), about 3 ft. 11 in. high. Marble imported from Paros was already being used abundantly—not just for roof tiles, simas, raking cornices, and a part of the metopes, but also for the large-scale, forceful pediment groups, the

fig. 66

23

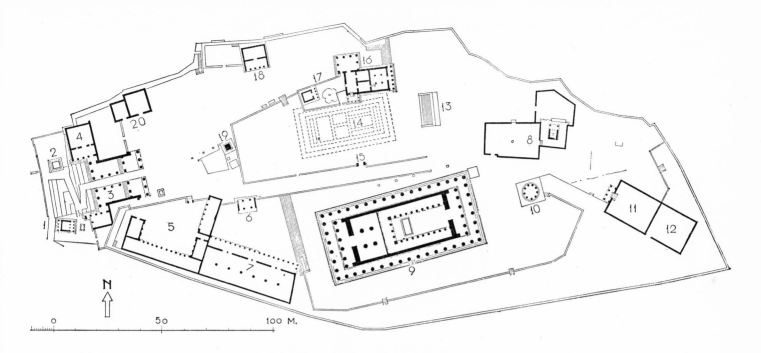

58 Athens, Acropolis. General layout

1: temple of Athena Nike; 2: monument of Agrippa; 3: Propylaea and Pinacotheca (4); 5: precinct of Artemis Brauronia; 7: Chalcotheca with propylaeum (6); 8: precinct of Zeus Polieus; 9: Parthenon; 10: round temple of Roma; 11: heroum of Pandion; 13: altar of Athena; 14: old temple of Athena; 16: Erechtheum; 17: Pandroseum; 18: house of the Arrephoroi; 19: statue of Athena Promachos by Phidias. After G. P. Stevens, *Hesperia* 15, 1946

figures of which here for the first time broke free from the background of the tympanum and distributed themselves significantly within the triangle. On the west pediment, the groups of fighting animals from an earlier citadel temple were repeated, but with the bloodthirsty lions made less ferocious; the gigantomachy of the east pediment (Athena and her falling opponent have survived) initiated the series of ever more freely developed scenes of heroes and gods (Delphi, Aegina, Olympia) that culminated in the great visions of the Parthenon gables.

It may be mentioned in passing that the temple has given rise to complicated discussions among the experts. Was it the 'old temple' of tradition or the 'Hecatompedon' ('hundred-foot-temple')? Do the foundations belong to a still earlier building, to which many architectural fragments and animal groups from the pediment fields bear witness? Was this forerunner, datable to about 570, an anta temple that Pisistratus girt with a peristyle around 520, or was it, already possessing a peristyle, completely rebuilt? Or do these parts belong instead to a hypothetical temple beneath the foundations of the older Parthenon: an 'oldest Parthenon'?

Here we already border on another controversial issue, for below the steps of the Parthenon lies a huge poros substructure (102 ft. $11\frac{7}{8}$ in. by 252 ft. $0\frac{3}{8}$ in.) upon which, evidently after a change of plan, a marble temple with 6 by 16 columns was begun on a somewhat reduced scale (77 ft. $2\frac{3}{8}$ in. by 219 ft. $7\frac{3}{8}$ in.). Work did not progress beyond the lowest wall courses and column drums. Did the new building fall victim in 480/79 to the destructive fury of the Persians, like all the others in the citadel, as is generally supposed on good grounds? If the recently advocated view that the so-called older Parthenon was begun after 479, and given up in favour of Ictinus's design, were to be substantiated, then we should have to change our picture of the Acropolis completely. It would even mean transferring to the days of Cimon the erection of 'Themistocles's' north wall, into which column drums from the temple were built. Moreover, these are only a few of the unsolved problems connected with the citadel buildings, despite their being so well preserved. Indeed, one may say that no other site in Greece has remained so full of riddles for its investigators. This is probably not only due to the fact that the first excavations occurred at a time when the devotion and enthusiasm of the diggers far surpassed their technique (today

fig. 60

371

59 Athens, Acropolis. Restoration. G. P. Stevens, *Hesperia* 15, 1946

it is rather the reverse); it seems to depend more on the buildings themselves—on their singularity, their enigmatic originality.

The colourful, story-book splendour of the archaic centuries vanished when the Persians took the Acropolis. Over the ruins, a new generation rebuilt it more perfectly in scarcely fifty years, giving it the form it still retains today.

When the Attic state stood at the height of its power, control of its destiny was assumed by a man whose every undertaking was grand in conception and in execution. For us, Pericles is quite simply the embodiment of Athens's classical period. His resolve, after the conclusion of peace with the Persians in 448, to rebuild the still devastated citadel came at a mysteriously favourable time. A change in outlook had given the Greek mythical account of man's relationship with the gods a new and profound significance; art had matured to the point of achieving an unlimited command of its means; the state had a marked desire for a symbolic representation of itself, and, to obtain it, made available inexhaustible funds.

Pericles was himself on the building commission, and, from the start, its plans obviously embraced the Acropolis as a whole, with its three main structures: the Parthenon, the Propylaea, and the Erechtheum. Certainly not arbitrary, the spatial relations between them have time and again set people thinking, though it was inevitable that all attempts to distinguish architectonic connexions in the modern sense—optical axes, visual angles, attuned alignments—should fail. The buildings seem instead, like the figures of a sculptural group, to be meaningful in themselves, and to approach each other in free relationships based on inner tension and harmonious diversity. It is thus that they still continue to fill the citadel with their pure triad: the nobility and commanding grandeur of the Parthenon, the severity and solemnity of the Propylaea, and the relaxed charm of the Erechtheum.

A fourth project, concerning the little temple of Athena Nike on the citadel's western salient, had already been agreed upon in 448, but was shelved for the sake of Pericles's great general scheme. When the conservative opposition finally carried it out after all, along with a curtailment of the Propylaea plan, the little temple was disposed so ingeniously before the solemn, weighty background of the Propylaea as the most graceful cabinet-piece of Attic architecture that an Acropolis without its Nike temple is no longer even remotely conceivable.

fig. 59 As territory of the gods, the entire citadel was once separated off by high walls from the city outside. A restored general view makes its former arrange-

ment clear. The temples were joined by a stoa-fringed sanctuary of Artemis and the so-called Chalcotheca to the west of the Parthenon. In the eastern part of the citadel lay a small, open precinct of Zeus and a heroum of Pandion. The only addition in Roman times, a little round temple in the classical idiom, remained modestly unobtrusive.

One must now picture the whole area peopled by images of gods and men, offerings of the most varied kinds, and countless marble stelae recording decrees and settlements—the buildings and statues aglow with carefully harmonized colours—in order to comprehend what it once was, this Acropolis that, notwithstanding all the ravages of time, still passes for the supreme miracle of Western art.

THE PARTHENON   *Plates XVI, 8–21, figs. 60–62*

Ictinus and Callicrates have come down to us as the architects of the Parthenon, begun in 447. The latter seems at that time to have been in special favour, since a year earlier the Nike temple had been commissioned from him, and he was put in charge of the construction of the 'long walls' to Piraeus. Ictinus's masterful hand is known from the design for Eleusis (page 403) and the temple at Bassae (page 351). Here, too, his must have been the leading mind.

To distinguish what is fundamentally new in his conception, one may usefully compare it with the unfinished older Parthenon, which the new edifice superseded. The two works have much in common. Not only did the Parthenon's builders continue the unprecedented venture of erecting a Doric peripteral temple entirely in marble (to which the recently developed quarries on Mount Pentelicum contributed their noble, fine-grained stone), but they employed the old substructure as a base, and, adopting the same column diameter, used the material already prepared for the drums. Moreover, the new ground-plan is closely related to the earlier one.

fig. 60 The old Parthenon project combined a naos containing a nave and two aisles with an approximately square west room, the roof of which would probably also have been supported by four Ionic columns. Instead of the usual two columns in-antis, an independent row of four columns was set before either end of the cella. The antae themselves were reduced to short, pilaster-like wall projections. Together with its strange west room, the older Parthenon evidently inherited this 'prostyle' arrangement of inner porticoes from the old Athena temple, which in its turn seems to have followed Ionic models. It is precisely these elements, deviating so wilfully from the Doric norm—west room and inner porticoes

373

with shortened antae—that characterize the ground-plan of the new structure. Why then was a new building started at all? In what does the much praised novelty of the Parthenon consist?

The first thing that strikes one is the amplification of the peristyle (101 ft. 3¾ in. by 228 ft. 0⅛ in.), which, above all in its width, extends well beyond the substructure of the older Parthenon (stylobate 77 ft. 2⅜ in. by 219 ft. 7⅜ in.). This expansion was not, however, achieved in the usual way through a proportional enlargement of all the parts, but by increasing the number of columns. Instead of six columns at the ends, there are eight, to which, in accordance with a rule developed for hexastyle temples, there corresponds at either side twice this total plus one (i.e. $2 \times 8 + 1 = 17$ columns).

Previously, octastyle fronts had only appeared on Ionic dipteral temples, where they followed necessarily from the doubling of the peristyle, and on two temples in the Western colonies, where a widening of the ambulatory to two interaxials had the same result (Selinus, temple G, page 428; Corcyra). The Parthenon's pteromata, however, are particularly narrow—a natural concomitant of the great enlargement of the cella, which has a five-interaxial spread in place of the older Parthenon's three. Its prostyle inner porticoes with six (instead of four) columns could on their own form the fronts of a peripteral temple.

The naos was designed to contain a colossal gold-and-ivory statue of Athena, on which Phidias himself worked while the building was going up. According to the customary explanation, Phidias asked Ictinus for a naos of such-and-such a width to make room for his cult image. As, however, the harassed architect had to use the column material from the older Parthenon (lower column diam. only 6 ft. 2¾ in.) to achieve such an expansion, the only solution was an octastyle front. This account does justice to neither Phidias nor Ictinus, and least of all to the Parthenon. We shall see that Ictinus here created the first moulded interior space of antiquity, at the same time giving the external form of the peripteral temple its most close-textured expression. The formal principles that link interior and exterior are necessarily of a complex kind making each support and confirm the other, while the means employed have to be purely architectonic.

Standing before the front of the temple, one's attention is first attracted by a corporeal compactness of the colonnade such as one finds in no other Doric temple. This effect is harmoniously countered by the soaring slenderness of the columns, which hold the entablature and the great pediment triangle in suspension almost effortlessly. It is not easy to account for these interpenetrating contrary movements that act directly upon our sense of form—but let us try all the same.

Although the Attic development tended towards light, open porticoes (Theseum, Sunium), here the drawing together of the columns has produced exceptional density (the Parthenon's column diam. is related to the interaxial in the ratio $1 : 2.25$; older Parthenon and Zeus temple at Olympia $1 : 2.32$; Aegina $1 : 2.65$; Corinth $1 : 2.31$; only in Magna Graecia did more compact colonnades appear: temple of Hera II at Paestum $1 : 2.12$). This compactness is re-enforced by exceptionally narrow passageways. Those at the ends fall short of the usual $1\frac{1}{2}$ interaxials (e.g. Olympia), again contrary to the style of the times (cf. Theseum and Sunium), while the pteromata have to be specially narrow anyway, on account of the small interaxial, the outsides of the lateral walls being canonically aligned with the axes of the second end columns. Furthermore, a step has been taken as remarkable as it is complex: instead of the angle contraction (see page 313) by some $11\frac{3}{4}$ in. theoretically required, we find the corner intercolumnial spaces reduced by about twice that amount (2 ft. 2¼ in.). This makes the passageways even narrower, and increases the density and corporeity of the whole. At the same time it concentrates the supporting, bearing forces more intensely at the vulnerable corners of the peristyle, which lack the stabilizing background of the cella wall. An appreciable thickening of the four angle columns (by $1\frac{3}{4}$ in. or $\frac{1}{44}$ lower diam.) heightens the effect. To achieve it, the architects had to face a new problem, the very differences that were originally to be avoided through angle contraction now occurring in reverse within the frieze. They were carefully allowed for by progressively narrowing the metopes.

The impression of soaring lightness that the peristyle gives is due to similar proportioning, the columns being elongated more than ever before (column height $= 5.48$ lower diams.; Olympia 4.7; Aegina 5.32; Corinth 4.15). Correspondingly, the supported members—entablature with cornice—have been kept light and low (height $= 1.73$ lower diams.; Olympia 1.81; Aegina 1.99; Pisistratid temple at Athens about 2.46), the architrave, hitherto always preponderant, being reduced to the height of the triglyph frieze.

One is bound to wonder whether there do not exist in the thickening of the colonnade on the one hand, and in the slimness of the vertical supports and lightness of the horizontal supported members on the other, formally conflicting tendencies that cancel each other out. To find the answer, one must stand

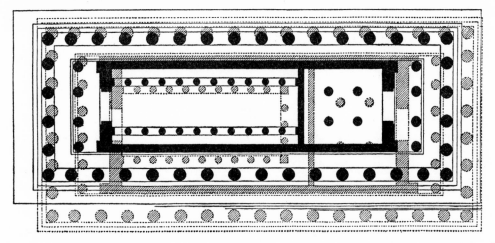

60 Athens, Acropolis. Older Parthenon (black) and Parthenon (hatched). B. H. Hill, *AJA.* 16, 1912

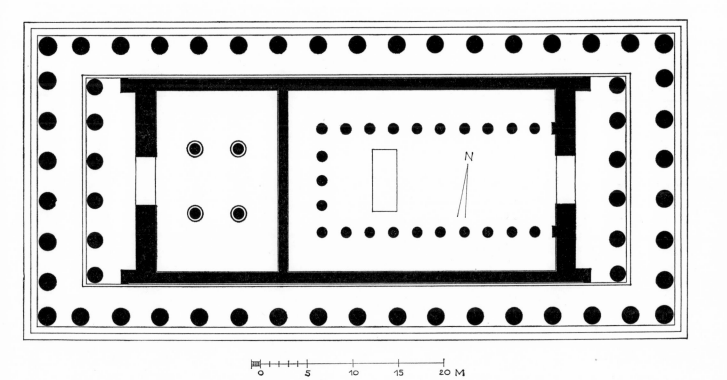

61 Athens, Acropolis. Parthenon. Plan (1 : 400). New drawing

before the temple. There is nothing ragged, nothing discordant about its noble outward form. Apparent impossibilities—floating heaviness, monumental lightness, dynamic calm—belong to its nature, conflicts being blended in such a way that their very tension supports the life that gives meaning to the whole. Let us here recall the related law of classical sculpture known as *contraposto*: movement and counter-movement brace the sculptured body, hip axis swinging in opposition to shoulder axis. Groups of figures are tied together by equally harmonious yet antagonistic bonds, and similar relations determine the spiritual and mythical background of classical art.

Since it was precisely in Phidias's pediment groups that the *contraposto* principle found its deepest embodiment, and since, on the other hand, this sculptural principle has been converted into an architectonic one more discerningly and freely than anywhere else in the building itself, one must presume that here, too, the spiritual influence of Phidias was at work.

fig. 62   On entering the cella from the closely knit porticoes, one is again impressed by a *contraposto* movement, for in opposition to the corporeal density of the exterior has been set the spatial amplitude *14*   within. The latter was achieved not only by widening the cella enormously to five-sevenths of the total breadth (previously only the colossal temples of Ionia and Sicily had had cellas 19½ ft. broad, and the nave's clear width of 34 ft. 9¾ in. remained unsurpassed in the mother-country), but through an attractively simple and ingenious arrangement of the, as usual, two-storied Doric naos colonnades. Instead of extending on either side from one cross-wall to the other in the customary manner, and thereby dividing the space lengthwise into three neutral sections, the columns ran round in a ⊓ before the rear wall. This gave the space the new dimension of amplitude, and made it, at once lucid and taut, encompass the majestic gold-and-ivory statue of Athena Parthenos, which, about 36 ft. tall, could here breathe freely and make its effect from a distance. Again we meet a combination of unlikes: the expansion and contraction of the space, with, as usual, a divine image and not man as its focus.

Another room, equally wide but only 43 ft. 9⅞ in. deep opened to the west. Its coffered wooden ceiling was supported by four columns. Not double-tiered Doric columns but slender Ionic ones were considered suitable for this space as high as it was deep, and, like those inside the Propylaea, they ascended in one unbroken line to the ceiling. We have no information about the original purpose of this room.

However, like the opisthodomus closed with wooden grilles, it was serving in the fourth century at the latest as a depository for all Athena's, and hence Athens', treasure and festival utensils. The name 'Parthenon' at first only designated this west room, and was not applied to the whole temple until later.

We still have to settle how the adjustment of the opposing formal elements was achieved, and, beyond this, what means were used to procure the steady balance of all the parts, the 'harmony' of the whole that people have always felt to be the essence of this temple. If we hear of a theoretical textbook by the most important classical sculptor next to Phidias dealing principally with the harmonious proportioning of the parts and limbs of a statue—the 'canon' of Polyclitus—then such endeavours must have been all the more prominent in architecture, which, because its relationships could only be numerical and dimensional, had been striving, as early as the sixth century, to achieve clear proportions.

During the sixth century, most of the external dimensions of the rectangular temple structure were conceived in round numbers, from which the other measurements were, as far as possible, derived, whereas the early classical architects started out with a definite basic measurement, the interaxial, as their unit, and developed from it a clear, regular ground-plan and elevation, the building's external measurements now becoming derivative quantities (Zeus temple at Olympia); in the design of the Parthenon, however, both principles have been combined with the utmost subtlety. There is also a dominant proportion harmonizing ground-plan, front elevation, and side. First of all, the interaxial was adjusted to the column diameter provided by the older Parthenon in the ratio 4 : 9 (6·27 : 13·22 ft.). This proportion reappears in the outer edges of the stylobate (101·32 : 228·02 ft.), something that could only be achieved thanks to the increased angle contraction and minimal difference between the end and side interaxials (0·2 in.). Without the antae, even the sides of the cella rectangle are related in this 4 : 9 ratio.

Elevation and ground-plan have been linked in the same way, for the temple's width is related to its height (as far as the horizontal corona) as 9 is to 4 (101·32 : 45·01 ft.)! This being so, the length and height of the sides perforce confront each other in the ratio $9^2 : 4^2$—i.e. 81 : 16. All this goes far beyond the simple proportions and mere repetition of a basic relationship that appear elsewhere. Here, after all, a building has for the first time been synthetically comprehended in all its aspects by a single proportion, and attuned by mathematical means to a single chord.

62 Athens, Acropolis. View of naos with the gold-and-ivory statue of
Athena Parthenos by Phidias. C. Praschniker, *OeJh.*, 1952

If the theoretical treatise on the Parthenon composed by Ictinus and a certain Carpion (Callicrates mis-written?), which Vitruvius mentions (VII praef. 12), had come down to us, we should know the real purpose of these relationships that we can only read off from the structure. At the same time, we should probably learn the detailed truth about the much-disputed significance of the so-called 'refinements', which were executed with comparable subtlety on no other building. These slight inflexions of straight lines here embrace the whole building in such a way that literally not one true straight line is to be found. A strong convex swelling of the column (entasis) already appears in archaic structures. It immediately strikes the eye—

say in the 'Basilica' at Paestum—as a sculptural attribute of the column, which, so to speak, expresses the effort of supporting by the tension of its muscles (entasis $2\frac{1}{8}$ in. or $\frac{1}{120}$ column height). The Parthenon's entasis is correspondingly smaller ($\frac{11}{16}$ in. or $\frac{1}{600}$ column height).

Curvature proper, a subtle arching of the long horizontal lines, can also be detected in archaic temples (Corinth; Athens, old temple of Athena). That of the older Parthenon has a rise of $2\frac{3}{8}$ in. In the case of the Parthenon itself, not only is the stylobate curved (rise at sides about $4\frac{3}{8}$ in., ends $2\frac{3}{8}$ in.), but this arching continues in the architrave, the frieze, the corona, and even the pediment! As, however, all the butt-joints are absolutely vertical, there are only a few blocks in the crepidoma and entablature at the centre of the temple's four sides which are given a truly rectangular shape. All the other squared stones and members had to be made trapeziform—and each differently angled too! (To-day, this phenomenon is still incredible to engineers who can judge the precision required in the cutting to achieve it.)

Nor was that enough: nearly all the 'vertical' members and surfaces lean inwards, the columns by about $2\frac{3}{4}$ in. (angle columns diagonally by about $3\frac{7}{8}$ in.). The entablature follows the tilt of the columns up to the corona, which leans outwards. While the outer surfaces of the cella's lateral walls slope inwards (though the inner faces are vertical, so that the walls have a one-sided taper), the antae lean towards the inner portico columns. Moreover, the huge entrance-doors were also curved. On the other hand, the capital profiling that formerly bulged so strongly now restrains itself, and in taut, hyperbolic curves approximates to straight lines.

As a result of credulously accepting the assertions of a Roman architectural theorist, at first an attempt was made to explain all these refinements, achieved with unbelievable precision and immense labour, as perspective or optical corrections. Today, the view has become widespread that the sculptural nature of the Greek temple has found its most manifold expression in all these curves, from which flows the temple's specific vitality, only discernible at an unconscious level. Valéry has the last word on the subject in his *Eupalinos*: 'The architect knew the mysterious power of imperceptible modulations. No one was aware, before a pile lightened with delicacy and appearing so simple, of being inspired with a kind of happiness by almost indiscernible curves, by flexions at once hardly apparent and all-powerful, and by those profound unions of the regular and the irregular that he had introduced and hidden, and made as imperious as they were indefinable.'

However, tangible things also contribute to the individual life of the temple. Firstly, there is the enrichment, now likewise raised to the classical plane. Tenseness and relaxation merge in the frugal but surely distributed decorative elements. Above all, the turbid admixture of Ionic elements characterizing the older Parthenon and the Theseum has been renounced (e.g. the Ionic profile at the foot of the wall, which in the Parthenon rises directly from the stylobate, according to the Doric custom). The one, well-considered exception is provided by a delicate bead-and-reel over the frieze; otherwise—on the anta faces, above the horizontal and below the sloping corona—the Doric cyma reigns supreme.

Greater freedom was granted to the ornamentation of the roof. Variegated palmette antefixes stood along its lower edges, and a convex sima painted with a lotus frieze in three colours bordered the pediments, at the apex of which grew the acroterium—a richly intricate growth of acanthus, crowned by a palmette.

Then there was also the effect of the colours themselves, which one must imagine not robustly gay as on archaic buildings but sensitively attuned to each other in conformity with the achievements of the great contemporary painters. The marble's glazen translucency remained dominant, steps, columns, walls, architraves, and corona faces being left unpainted. By colouring the triglyphs, regulae, and mutules blue, the rhythm of the frieze was emphasized. The thin band of the taenia and the moulding above the frieze were embellished with a gold meander on a red ground, like sumptuous woven borders. Rows of variegated palmettes framed the coffers of the ambulatory's marble ceiling, and in the middle of these coffers a delicate floral pattern stood out against a blue ground.

And now at last for the sculptural decoration! The remains of it that have come down to us are Greek sculpture's greatest legacy, and as such they have been exhaustively appreciated in many descriptions where the building that carried them has generally come off second best. Here, as an architect is writing, the order is perforce reversed.

The peristyle was ringed by a many-linked chain of ninety-two metopes, with battle as the theme: men against nature, daemons, centaurs, on the south side; Greeks against Trojans on the north, and against Amazons on the west; gods against giants on the east. The pairs of opponents have been dignified as sundered halves of a single whole, as complementary opposing forces united in their conflict by strangely intimate glances.

Round the cella, at the very top, stretched a continuous sculptured 'Ionic' frieze (assimilated to the Doric structure by means of an encircling taenia, beneath which even hang the regulae proper to a triglyph frieze). Upon it, the entire Attic people marched towards its gods in the procession of the Panathenaea (page 84). At the west end, the young nobles of the city set out on horseback; above the side walls, the illustrious procession advanced with chariots and sacrificial beasts to the east end, where the majestically simple group of the Olympian gods awaited in informal conversation the delivery of the cult robe to Athena. Closely packed like the columns, the figures were no longer strung out in narrative form as on earlier friezes, but woven together by interlocking movements and by the references of calm gestures. Hence, the frieze was more than an account of the festival, and more, too, than a glorification of the Attic people. This triple alliance of equals linking gods, men, and animals surrounded the cella as a symbol of the meaning and essence of the living world.

Fully cosmic, fully inclusive of the universe was that which crowned the whole: the pedimental groups of gods, which the architectonic setting could hardly still contain. At the west end appeared a combat between gods—but how far it had outgrown every tradition of such battle scenes! Here, Athena and Poseidon disputed the Attic region, cosmic powers contending for the earth. On the east pediment, Athena the mistress of wisdom and the mind was born from the head of Zeus.

Like a tidal wave, the excitement of the central group communicated itself to the gods reclining at the sides. The world's new day was framed by the rising and descending four-in-hands of the sun and moon. Significant of the way in which space and invisible connexions now played leading parts is the construction of the group at the centre. No longer did a figure stand there about whose dominant axis all the others arranged themselves, as at Aegina, at Olympia, and on the Theseum; instead, a void 'filled' the middle of the gable, but a void that appeared far more powerful and compact than any corporeal axis. It was the field of spiritual force between each pair of gods at the centre, and in it the tremendous clash of the west pediment and the dynamic moment of creation of the east came to pass. This, too, has its parallels in the architecture.

Many hands, indeed three generations of sculptors, worked side by side on the colossal programme. Phidias, the chief master, was able to subject them all to his will, and to unite them in the use of a new formal language of his own that seemed to absorb and reduce the previous accomplishments of Doric and Ionic art: the 'Parthenon style'.

So also with the architecture: the formal framework is Doric, yet one would hesitate to call the Parthenon a typical Doric temple. Ionic elements can, if we will, be identified in the ground-plan and the enrichment, but one gains nothing by the use of terms like 'Ionicizing'. The limits of the orders have, in fact, been passed. Ictinus created a wholly individual Attic style, in which the entire architectural heritage of the Peloponnese and Ionia was deposited and sublimated. The fact that the Greek temple here achieved perfection, that its forms are written out clearly for all eternity, allows us to see this building, despite its being so exceptional, as *the* classical temple *tout court*, beyond all bounds of style.

Plutarch rightly admired the speed with which the Parthenon was raised (*Pericles* 158 f.). The foundation-stone was laid in 447. Nine years later, during the Great Panathenaea of 438, the building could be handed over to the goddess of the city. In 432, at the outbreak of the Peloponnesian war, it stood complete with all its sculptural decoration. A host of artisans, carters, and labourers must have been employed on the job, and Plutarch tells us that it kept half Athens fully occupied.

For 2,000 years, the firmly jointed marble structure withstood almost undamaged every assault of a chequered history. During late Roman times (after a fire?), the inner colonnades were replaced. When, in the Christian era, Athena had to surrender her shining home to the Virgin, the pronaos was converted into an apse. Under the Frankish feudal lords of Athens, a bell-tower was built at the west end, and the Turks turned it into a minaret after 1458. While the Venetians were besieging the citadel around 1687, a lieutenant from Lüneburg exploded the gunpowder stored in the Parthenon by the Turkist defenders with probably the most unfortunate bull's-eye of any German gunner. The cella walls and fourteen columns along the north side collapsed. Further wounds were inflicted by Morosini's crude attempt to plunder the west pediment. Much of the sculptural decoration was carried to England round about 1800. Since 1900, work has begun on re-erecting the fallen parts, with the result that almost all the peristyle has been standing again since 1929. Preparations have recently been made for the restoration of the coffered ceiling of the west portico and the pavement of the cella.

THE PROPYLAEA   *Plates XV, 5–7, fig. 63*

Before approaching the Periclean Propylaea, in which an at first unassuming type of structure reached perfection, let us outline the origins of this type. To begin with, the propylaeum was no more than the gateway in a temenos wall, through which one entered the sacred enclosure. It soon came to be protected and stressed on both sides by a sloping roof, which rested on two projecting lateral walls, and at first the ridge lay in line with the peribolos (cf. Aegina, page 348). However, when, in the sixth century, such gate-buildings were assigned the forms of temple architecture to mark them out as divine property, and when, therefore, columns appeared between the anta faces of the side walls, these entrance fronts had perforce to receive gables, which meant setting the roof ridge at right angles to the peribolos. This gave the propylaeum the sacred form of an anta temple, though instead of a naos it contained only a cross-wall with one or several gateways.

There were unpretentious gate-buildings like this at every Greek sanctuary, and even on the Acropolis individual, specially demarcated precincts were adorned with a propylaeum of the simplest form till into classical times (confirmed for the so-called Chalcotheca, and the precincts of Zeus Polieus and Pandion, fig. 58).

When, after the expulsion of the tyrants, the citadel was handed over entirely to the gods, it became necessary to replace the threateningly tall, massive Mycenaean fortifications of the western approach (the 'nine gates'—probably nine gate-structures barring step-like one behind the other a long, winding walled alley) with a ceremoniously welcoming sacred gate-building. This propylaeum, destroyed by the Persians in 480 soon after its completion, was bigger and more magnificent than any before. Its entrance front, over 62 ft. wide, boasted four Doric columns between the antae of the side walls, and it appears to have been executed with extreme care chiefly in marble. Apart from slight traces in the rock, all that remains is the south-west corner (plan dotted in fig. 63; surviving corner black).

When, on finishing the Parthenon, the same builders began in 437 to erect a new gate-structure, all the potentialities of the traditional formula had here also to be developed as freely as possible. Mnesicles, a master unknown prior to this, is recorded as the architect.

fig. 63   With widely spreading wings on either flank, the new design spanned the entire western side of the citadel, giving it an architectonic conclusion of hitherto unimaginable grandeur. In achieving it, Mnesicles mastered the very difficult conditions of the steeply rising slope, and, with assured intuitive understanding, made them contribute to the impact of the structure. Many parts unfortunately never got beyond the planning stage, for owing to opposition from the conservative priests of the adjacent Nike and Artemis precincts, the design was curtailed. Then, when the Peloponnesian war broke out in 431, building operations had to be entirely discontinued before the Propylaea was complete. (On the ground-plan in fig. 63, the parts proposed but not executed are shown by hatching.)

XV, 7   The tall central section—the gate-building proper —stands out clearly in the original project from the rest of the broadly spreading structure. It forms, as it were, the body of the whole, while the low halls at the sides constitute its wings. In no wise does it renounce the propylaeum tradition: on either side of the transverse pierced wall are set roofed vestibules,

while both the confining side walls terminate in antae. Thus far, everything corresponds to the pre-Persian propylaeum—indeed, even the dimensional relationships and the division of the exceptional width into five interaxials, probably already matched by five gateways, seem to have been taken over from that building. However, the introduction of porticoes with six Doric columns and fully developed pediments before the antae in place of columns between them, thus giving the Propylaea's inner and outer façades the appearance of a peripteral temple, constitutes an unprecedented step. It was only made possible by the octastyle front of the Parthenon, since under no circumstances could one have allowed the latter's pre-eminence to be diminished by a gate-building.

A great deal bolder still is the use made of space, the architectural element newly discovered in creating the Parthenon cella. The sequence of 'spaces'—conceived severely and cubically in terms of corporeal form—seems positively to be the key-note of Mnesicles's gate-building. One experiences this afresh each time one walks through it. After climbing the narrow, twisting rocky path, one stands before the colonnaded front that towers up unadorned, and, despite its hallowed temple form, is clearly recognizable as a gateway. For the tall base of four steps is interrupted at the centre, where the rough rock-way leads with an even gradient into the building. On it once entered the riders and sacrificial beasts of the Panathenaic procession. To accommodate this processional way, the middle interaxial was widened by a third (middle 17 ft. $10\frac{1}{8}$ in., normal 11 ft. $10\frac{7}{8}$ in.), so that three triglyphs and metopes had to be set above it in the frieze, instead of the usual two.

If, already gripped by the spiritual power of the building, one now obeys its austere summons and climbs the four high steps, the space suddenly broadens out in every direction. Enchanted and inspired, one is standing in the anteroom of the sanctuary. All this requires description in concrete terms, however. The clear width between the side walls (59 ft. $5\frac{3}{8}$ in.) approximately corresponds to that of the Parthenon's cella, while the depth (42 ft. $6\frac{1}{4}$ in.) almost reaches that of its west room. Such measurements were and remained unparalleled for an open vestibule. Yet it is not so much the dimensions that determine the impression of space as the ingenious arrangement of the inner supports. Three very slender Ionic columns ascend on either side of the processional way, which is the true axis of the space, and they carried the coffered marble ceiling. The shallow marble architraves once spanning these columns in the direction of the way

5

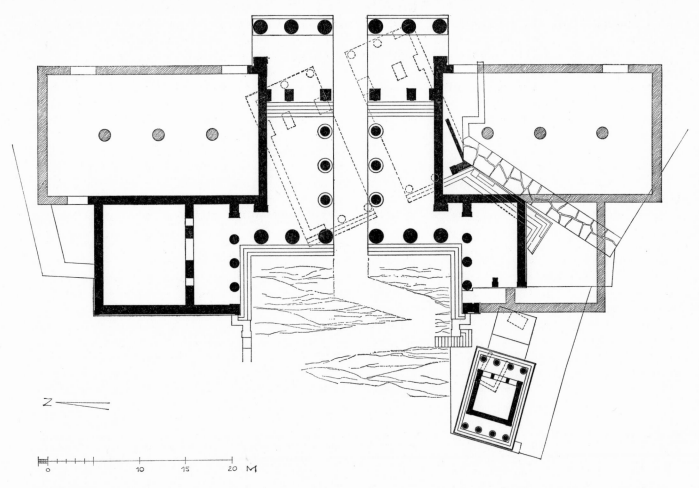

63 Athens, Acropolis. Propylaea. Plan (1 : 400). Unexecuted parts of design indicated by hatching. *Front right:* temple of Athena Nike. *Centre right:* Mycenaean citadel wall. Earlier propylaeum and archaic shrine of Athena Nike cult statue both dotted. New drawing

are divided into three thin bands or fascias, according to the eastern Ionic custom. They lay over the Doric outer architrave, at the level of the triglyph frieze, as a result of which the interior gained an extension upwards too. Right up to imperial times, the wide-stretching marble ceiling of this airy hall was celebrated as the most perfect of its kind. Its special charm was its lightness. Like a transparent canopy, it floated above the effortlessly rising columns, its star floral patterns shining down in gold from the blue coffer panels. To achieve this effect, Mnesicles used the most daring static means: into the over-delicate Ionic architraves, which had to bear immense loads of stone, were let concealed iron beams.

The gate wall closing, or rather opening, this room to the east is broken up so uncompromisingly that it acts, with its four remaining narrow pillars between the doorways, like a pendant to the Doric colonnade opposite it. The size of the openings increases rhythmically from the smaller ones at the sides (4 ft. 9⅞ in. by 11 ft. 3⅜ in.) to the huge central one for the processional way (13 ft. 6⅜ in. by 24 ft. 2½ in.). In Roman times, the probably wooden framing of the doorways was replaced by a revetment of marble.

It is thus that one is called on to set foot in the sanctuary and hence upon a higher plane. For by incorporating the slope in his construction and by setting before the gate wall five steps, the topmost of which forms the actual door-sill and is stressed with contrasting dark marble, Mnesicles imbued a condition imposed on him by the terrain with the symbolic meaning of ascent. The again hexastyle Doric portico extending to the east of the gate wall lies on a level higher by 4 ft. 8¼ in.—a fact expressed logically in its external form. Its roof level rises above that of the west hall, with a gable of its own resting over the gate wall.

The east room is not so deep as the west, and can be crossed in a few strides. It opens, however, on to a last, matchless area: the broad sanctuary of Athena. Like the west front, the east has a widened middle interaxial and contracted corner ones, so that the intercolumniations are graduated similarly to the doorways. The stylobate is set directly on the rock as a final threshold to the sanctuary. A curvature of this stylobate cut in the middle by the processional way would have been ineffectual, and so none was executed. On the other hand, the entablature, which extends uninterrupted, has a rise of $\frac{3}{4}$ in. (visible in plate 7 with the aid of a ruler), and to achieve it, the columns had to be given different heights.

Judiciously, the colonnaded façade was kept smaller than the Parthenon front by about a fifth, though it still considerably exceeds all other Attic buildings. That Ictinus was probably Mnesicles's teacher is revealed by many reminders of the Parthenon, such as the related proportions (column height of 27 ft. $11\frac{7}{8}$ in. = 5·47 lower diams. of 5 ft. $1\frac{1}{4}$ in., Parthenon 5·48 lower diams.; entablature height 1·74 lower diams., Parthenon 1·73 lower diams. The 3 : 4 ratio of column to inter-columniation is a modification of the Parthenon's 4 : 5.). So too, no doubt, does the Ionic west room of the Parthenon live on in the Propylaea's west hall, and it is permissible to visualize its four lost columns as the immediate forerunners of those inside the Propylaea. Just as the Doric columns, loosening up and stretching, have a suggestion of an Ionic trait, so inversely do the Ionic ones seem tautened and consolidated by the Attic sense of form. The excessive slimness of early Ionic columns about 12 lower diameters tall was moderated in Attica by introducing heights of from 9 to 11 lower diameters, but the difference from Doric columns remains striking enough. With a diameter reduced by a third (3 ft. 5 in.), the Propylaea's Ionic columns reach up substantially higher (33 ft. $9\frac{1}{8}$ in.). We also meet here for the first time the characteristic convexity of Doric shafts—the entasis—transferred to an Ionic one with almost imperceptible delicacy (only $\frac{1}{4}$ in. for a height of 33 ft. $9\frac{1}{8}$ in.!). The capital is probably the most perfect known to us, on account of the clear, tectonic arrangement of its parts and taut curve of its volutes.

6

In the Ionic west hall of the Propylaea, Mnesicles plainly increased the *contraposto* effects of harmonious contrasts that we met in the Parthenon to a downright symphonic variety. Thus, the longitudinal axis of the processional way flanked by Ionic columns opposes the wide shape of the space; the western colonnade confronts the gate wall broken up into pillars with a similar rhythm, to its east; and the apparent lightness of the bold ceiling construction formed a contrast to the conspicuous weight of the marble cross-beams spanning 18 ft.

Mnesicles's finest idea, however, was undoubtedly to combine the gravity and discipline of the west front with the open grace of the Ionic columns inside. Never before had the two orders been linked together so directly as here, where the Ionic architrave rested immediately on the lower Doric one, and both the inner rows of columns run towards the middle exterior columns, which thus form their weighty terminations. (In contrast, the hypothetical Ionic inner porches of the old temple of Athena, page 370, are clearly distinct structures, and in the Parthenon the western door wall actually separated the two orders.) This difference of character fully emerges in the ground-plan. Since—contrary to every tradition—only three divisions of the west hall (or two colonnades), instead of five (or four colonnades), correspond to the five interaxials of the façade, and since, therefore, the width of space announced in the façade is doubled in the aisles, where two front interaxials were bridged in one bold jump by the marble ceiling, the compactness of the façade and amplitude of the interior do not, as with the Parthenon, form a succession but, so to speak, interlock. As a result, these antitheses here intensify each other to produce an overwhelming effect.

In order to share the enthusiasm of Mnesicles's contemporaries and descendants, who never referred to this structure except in the plural ('Propylaea' instead of the singular 'Propylaeum'), we must try, with our eyes dulled by the most glaring architectural contrasts, to see these calm, clearly balanced, yet still powerful contrasts freshly.

Another feature may seem commonplace to us now, but to contemporaries it must have appeared a tremendous innovation: the wing buildings. If, however, we realize that every Greek edifice—temple or stoa—was complete in itself and led an independent life of its own, we shall understand that the combination of different types of building (propylaeum and halls) as a deliberately composed complex structure was bound to promote a revolution in architecture. According to Mnesicles's plan, the east front of the Propylaea was to be framed by two low halls, which would have closed in the entire western side of the citadel. They were never built. The south hall was evidently objected to by the priests of the Artemis precinct, which would have been curtailed by it, and the north hall would have been meaningless once the overall symmetry had been thus destroyed. It is plain that Mnesicles clung stubbornly to his grand design until the outbreak of the Peloponnesian war in 431 put a stop to the building activity: he had all the connexions for the projected halls, from door jambs to beam sockets, executed with extreme precision, although not even the foundations of the wings had been laid. From these traces, Wilhelm Dörpfeld was able, in 1885, to make out the original design.

On the authority of more recent investigations, the eastern wing buildings seem not, as previously supposed, to have been planned as open stoas with eight Doric columns, but as closed rooms with two large doors at each end. The citadel walls would thus have been accorded monumental grandeur and architectonic form, and another of those fruitful contrasts that everywhere bring the structure to life would have been effected, for the Doric east portico could then have opened up all the more deeply before the solid wall surfaces.

With even greater independence and intellectual boldness, Mnesicles subjected the western wing buildings to a general idea: that of reception. Two structures to have been completed in the form of temples with three columns in-antis appear before the impressive entrance front, laterally and at right angles to it. Smaller by a third in their proportions (lower diam. 3 ft. 6⅛ in., interaxial 8 ft. 2⅞ in., column height 19 ft. 2¼ in.) and topped with a simple hip-roof instead of pediments, they are unable to detract from the dominant effect of the middle façade. Yet so sensitively were they united with the latter that, out of the three structures, an architectonic whole was created—something previously unachieved. Thus, the three colonnaded fronts stand upon a common ⊓-shape stepped base. Moreover, the east columns of the wings are aligned with the central front's colonnade (which is why the east corner interaxials had to be made abnormally wide), so that the grand rhythm of the main façade flows unbroken into the wing colonnades. 'Anyone climbing up was received into a wide forecourt by the two wings, as though with open arms' (F. Noack). Indeed, this forecourt enclosed on three sides by columns had become 'space' in a newly discovered sense: the strictly symmetrical and interrelated wing structures bridge the open expanse of the court with connexions no less distinct for being imponderable.

Furthermore, in the four steps running round, an earlier motif lives on as well. Steps set before the Mycenaean citadel wall connected up with the older propylaeum. At the entry of the great procession, the spectators evidently sat on them, and the steps, in part quite unclimbable, that now surround the forecourt seem likewise to form a small theatre for receiving the Panathenaic procession.

Of the wings, only the northern one—the so-called Pinacotheca—was erected without changes.

Its walls were prepared for murals, like those of the Theseum's naos. Through a window at either side of the entrance door, light entered the interior, which later contained panel paintings by the most famous Greek artists.

To have laid out the south wing as planned would have meant shifting the altar of Athena Nike and demolishing the 'Pelargikon', a fragment of wall from Mycenaean times that had evidently meanwhile become sacred. It seems, however, that Pericles no longer had a sufficiently firm hold on the reins to carry through the project against the will of the narrow-minded priests of this precinct, behind whom sheltered the conservative opposition party. For, when constructed, the wing had to be trimmed both in length and breadth. The fact that Mnesicles retained his mastery even in this emergency solution cannot have consoled him for the curtailment of his design, any more than it can us. So important to him was the symmetry of the wing fronts—indispensable for the spatial effect of the forecourt—that he seized upon a daring solution: in front of his building shrunk to a width of three interaxials, he did not hesitate to set a façade one interaxial broader, so that the outer bay was left free-standing and the west anta became a pillar. Now aligned with the western column, the side wall had to be entirely dissolved, as it certainly could not have run up against a shaft. In its place rose a slender pillar, on which rested the entablature and roofing of the west side. The rear wall was brought forward to roughly the position of the door wall initially planned, with the result that nothing more remained of the wing than a modest hall leading through to the Nike precinct. This was originally to have been reached, via a stairway, through its own gate adjoining the wing structure.

Even though it may have been thought of as something provisional, the 'blind-front' points to a fundamental change of attitude: the beholder was beginning to play a part. Conceptually, the Propylaea as a whole was attuned to human beings, whom it received, conducted, and discharged into the sanctuary in a graduated ascent, but optical references were adjusted to the visitor as well. Thus, the columns of the west front were made 11 in. taller than those of the east, in order to compensate for the foreshortening apparent to anyone on the way up. The door and windows of the Pinacotheca have been given a conspicuously asymmetric arrangement, so that, on entering the forecourt, one sees them exactly between the columns. The entrance axis of the gate-building was trained on Phidias's colossal bronze statue of Athena Promachos.

Here, an incredibly vigorous mind gave its best

and, as far as we know, its only performance. A discreet perfecter and impetuous innovator, Mnesicles adapted the objective classical structure to a most diversified harmony, built up on balanced contrasts, and, at the same time, he laid the foundation-stone of a new, man-orientated architecture. The architectonic principles of the western wing buildings underlay the great open-space compositions of the Hellenistic age, and reached their most uninhibited development 2,000 years later in the colonnades of St. Peter's square. There, according to Bernini's own words, the church of the apostle as it were spreads out its arms with Baroque ardour, and embraces the world; here, the sanctuary of Athena opens in a reserved, lucid spirit with a similar but restrained gesture.

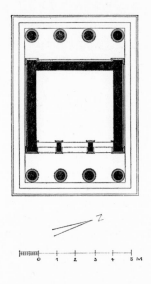
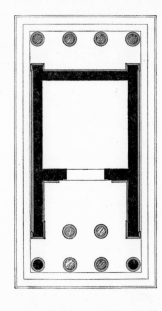

64–65 Athens, Acropolis. Temple of Athena Nike (*left*) and so-called temple on the Ilissus (*right*). Plans (1 : 200). New drawings

THE TEMPLE OF ATHENA NIKE   *Plates XIV, 30, 31, figs. 63–65*

'On the right of the Propylaea stands the temple of Nike Apteros. From here, the sea is visible, and it was here, so they say, that Aegeus threw himself down.' This much we learn from Pausanias (I, 22, 4 f.). When the travellers Spon and Wheler visited the Acropolis in 1676, the sumptuous little marble temple still rose above grim, medieval fortifications, and the marble ceiling of the Propylaea's west hall still rested on the Ionic columns, which ascended from rubble a yard deep. The front of the Propylaea was walled up, but over this bulwark still spread the Greek pediment, crowned by Venetian battlements. Above everything, a Frankish tower loomed up, defiant and forbidding. It must have been a strange sight, this mixture of the most mutually alien worlds—an appropriate setting for Faust's meeting with Helena. By the time the Acropolis, which in the course of conflicts extending over centuries had become ever more strongly fortified and more devastated, was finally cleared of troops and guns in 1834, after the founding of the new kingdom of Greece, the Propylaea had collapsed owing to a powder explosion and the Nike temple had completely disappeared.

Two classicist architects, Eduard Schaubert and Christian Hansen, whose plans and buildings moulded the features of modern Athens, exposed in 1835 the crepidoma buried under a Turkish bastion, in which most of the members were also found. The temple could therefore be erected for the second time. Nothing reveals the character of this architecture more clearly than the fact that, during such a reconstruction, each stone only fits exactly into a single place: its original one. This is even recogniz-

able in the ashlar by the extremely subtle variations of the form due to tapering and the distribution of the joints, and by the bronze clamps that, let into the marble, bonded the squared blocks. Thus, each part can only be understood from the meaning of the whole, and each carries this meaning within itself in coded but unequivocal signs.

When, in 1936–40, the Nike temple had to be taken down again and once more rebuilt, because of the settling of its foundations, there were only a few errors by the two sensitive architects that required to be put right, for all the shrewdly scientific procedure developed since their day.

The temple was not—and here we must correct Pausanias—dedicated to the wingless goddess of victory (according to later tales, the Athenians cut off her wings lest she should fly away from them), but to Athena Nike, the city's goddess as bringer of victory. Hence, its building history is bound up extremely closely with politics. There had long been an open Nike precinct. It was placed at the strategically most important point of the Mycenaean fortifications, on a bastion projecting well to the west and belonging to the gate works. In the sixth century, the goddess probably only had an altar. After her very evident help during the Persian wars, a tiny limestone chapel (about 8 by $11\frac{1}{2}$ ft., dotted in fig. 63) was erected for her wooden cult image, which held a pomegranate and helmet in its hands. After the peace negotiated by Callias with the Persians in 449, Callias's son, a nephew of Pericles's conservative opponent Cimon, moved in the public assembly that a new Nike temple be raised after the plans of the architect Callicrates, who later worked on the Parthenon. Pericles seems to have put a stop to his adversaries' project, which encroached on his own building schemes, just as quickly as he could.

When this occurred—whether before, during, or after the erection of the Propylaea in 437–431—is a problem still unsolved by scholars.

As the Mycenaean bastion was too narrow for the new structure, it was encased with neat ashlar masonry in the style of Cimon's citadel wall. Thus enlarged, this tower-like substructure—the 'Nike-pyrgos'—jutting out to the west stood in line along its north flank with the bottom step of the southern *fig. 63* Propylaea wing. Hence, it appears to take into account at least the design, if not even the construction, of the Propylaea. Nevertheless, the temple project remained a bone of contention between the parties. Pericles obviously went on delaying the start of building operations, while the embittered conservatives based their case on the sanctity of the old Nike altar, and actually forced Mnesicles to curtail his south-western Propylaea wing, which was to have cut into this altar (page 383).

In the second year of the war that almost saw the ruin of Athens, Pericles died of the plague (429), and the circle of artists gathered round him broke up. Ictinus went to Bassae. Phidias, wrongfully accused of having embezzled gold while at work on his Athena Parthenos, is said to have died in prison. About Mnesicles, finally, we know nothing: did he share Pericles's fate?

During the first breathing-space in the war, Nicias's peace of 421, the Nike temple seems at last to have been erected—supervised by the same overseers as the Erechtheum. This venture now took place wholly in the spirit of the conservatives. Callicrates's entirely outmoded design of 448 was adhered to faithfully, only the most essential changes being made.

After the intervention of Pericles, Callicrates himself appears to have executed his design somewhere else. It has been recognized, so it is believed, in a little Ionic temple on the Ilissus, which by good fortune was thoroughly measured before the Turks dismantled it in 1778 as building material for a city wall. The ground-plans of the twin temples—a similarity that extends into such detail justifies this adjective—appear together as figs. 64 and 65. In the Ilissus structure, the simple form of the anta temple (with a naos and a pronaos closed by two columns) was significantly enriched, open tetrastyle porticoes appearing at either end as a kind of peristyle confined to the fronts. The new type of building thus created —the amphiprostyle temple—enjoyed a great suc-

cess, for it entirely corresponded to the inclination of the times, walls and porticoes forming a harmonious antithesis. Instead of being enclosed by antae, the Ionic portico columns were allowed to stand free, which is what they seem in truth to have been created for. This gave small temples, too, the concordant effect of a pure colonnaded façade, and the threefold graduation of the space into portico, pronaos and naos. The fact that, here, the west end was also honoured with a colonnade confirms that this plan really had been developed for the Nike temple, which, after all, was destined to reign over the citadel's western salient as a monument visible from afar.

When, a generation later, the old design was finally carried out, the reduced south-western wing of the Propylaea now in its turn forced a compromise. The temple had to be made shorter than intended, so that its east end should have, *vis-à-vis* the Propylaea wing, the clearance essential for the physical independence of a Greek building. Its architect— was he the aged Callicrates or a pupil conversant with his style?—found a solution that in its formal clarity and consistency seems quite brilliant. In the first design (Ilissus temple), the opisthodomus had already been left out, the position of its antae being indicated by two corner pilasters, and now the pronaos was abolished as well. This meant, however, that the door wall formed the east end of the cella. By replacing this wall with two slender pillars, the architect preserved for the cella front the rhythm of an anta temple, since the antae are fully developed and the two pillars take over from the columns. At the same time, these rectangular pillars represent the disintegrated wall, and accordingly are crowned by anta capitals. The central opening formed the entrance, those at the side being closed by grilles. Even the cella had to be shortened unsparingly. Broader than it is deep (13 ft. 7 in. by 12 ft. 4⅞ in.), the tiny room is really little bigger than the earlier shrine for the cult image; and though this chapel was showered with all the gifts of exquisite architecture, no one tried to bestow on it what it could not have borne, namely grandeur and monumentality. Instead, it was given grace and daintiness—but only the Ionic style could bestow these.

Though the Athenians felt themselves to be Ionian, purely Ionic structures had previously been erected only seldom and for unusual functions (Athenian stoa at Delphi, page 337). Hence, the planning of an Ionic temple for such a prominent spot was a momentous step that brought about a 'renaissance' of the Ionic style in Attica, and consequently in the Greek world. This did not involve copying eastern building forms, but rather coining an original, Attic style that seems to have found its inspiration chiefly in the island-Ionic treasuries of Cnidus and Siphnos at Delphi. As there, a sculptured frieze runs round the whole structure, ousting the short-measured rhythm of the dentil course, above the austere architrave. (The fascias of the Nike temple, absent on the Ilissus temple, appear to be a change made by the builders.) A more severe sequence of profiles replaces the eastern three-layered anta capitals, swelling tenderly and succulently—again as at Delphi. It is above all the logic of the form that constitutes an Attic gift. Thus, the *fig. 110* bipartite Ionic column base has become the rhythmically complete trinity of a scotia between two tori, and the walls rest upon the same expressive profile. The slight inward tilt of the columns, the walls, and even the risers of the steps is also an Attic refinement.

Showing a certain resemblance to Doric proportions, the columns are remarkably squat (height of 13 ft. 3½ in. = 7·8 lower diams. of 1 ft. 8½ in.) and closely set (ratio of lower diam. to intercolumniation of 3 ft. 4½ in. about 1 : 2). One cannot but be struck by a certain old-fashioned awkwardness, as compared with, say, the Propylaea's columns. The base lacks that free impetus, the capital that taut though fluid resilience of the curves. The large volutes hang heavy and replete. The column as a whole does not yet form a harmonious unity to the same degree, but, if anything, breaks up into its parts: base, shaft, and capital. Nevertheless, 'progressive' details, such as the fuller coil of the volute or the curving 'wedge' palmette, reveal the fairly recent genesis of these members, as do the architrave fascias mentioned above.

The discrepancy between design and execution will not be hidden. Completely without restraint, the style of the times appears in the scenes of the frieze, where the battle at Plataea against Persians and disloyal Greeks is shown occurring before the gods assembled as witnesses of the agitated groups of combatants. (Four slabs, now in the British Museum, have been replaced by casts.)

Above the frieze jutted the smooth corona, undercut in a slight curve, and on it lay the convex sima, which was painted with gay floral patterns. Pediments spread over both ends, but only a few sinkings in the top of the corona now provide evidence of their sculptural groups. The acroteria—gilded Victories?—that once crowned this enchanting cabinet-piece of Attic architecture have likewise disappeared.

Athena Nike did not remain faithful to her city. With the Sicilian expedition instigated by the gifted but reckless Alcibiades, misfortune began to close in upon Athens, and so all the more lavish was the celebration of one of the last victories scored by her fleet, under the same Alcibiades (410, off Cyzicus). The Nikepyrgos was surrounded on its three outer sides with a marble parapet on which a unique victory feast took place in reliefs facing out towards those who approached, and no longer in towards the temenos of the goddess. Winged Victories prepared *31* the sacrifice for an Athena enthroned in the centre on each side (Lullies-Hirmer, *Greek Sculpture*, plates 189–191). Still more freely than on the temple frieze, Attic art was here developed to an extreme of virtuosity in the so-called 'rich style'. A new element was introduced by the effects of light and shadow. This 'rich style' came at the end of Athens's great century: in 404 the city capitulated.

THE ERECHTHEUM *Plates XVII, XVIII, 22–29, fig. 66*

The last great new building on the Acropolis was begun decades after the completion of the Parthenon and the Propylaea, during the peace of Nicias, which interrupted the struggle between Athens and Sparta from 421 to 414. It was finished after a pause from 409 to 406 imposed by the defeat in Sicily. An Ionic temple of singular appearance, it rises immediately next to the site of the old temple of Athena razed by the Persians (page 370). As in the case of the Propylaea, different structures have been united to form a *fig. 66* complex whole, and, as there, these parts lie at different levels. A rectangular block running east-west (38 ft. 1⅞ in. by 74 ft. 8 in. on the stylobate) constitutes the actual cella. Before its eastern door wall stands a portico with six slender Ionic columns (height 21 ft. 7½ in., lower diam. 2 ft. 3⅛ in.). As with the Nike temple, no pronaos was included, and the antae are therefore indicated by corner pilasters here too. This east front and the unbroken south wall of the building raise themselves on their crepidoma of three steps above the platform of the old Athena temple, whereas the north side and west front rest at a level lower by about 10½ ft. The west front had accordingly to be given an entirely distinct appearance. Here, on a high, wall-like base between lateral *22* antae, there stand four strange supports (height 18 ft. 4⅞ in., lower diam. 2 ft. 0⅜ in.), blended from an Ionic half-column (front) and a half-pillar (back).

Two more very diversely formed colonnaded porches are set against the continuous flanking walls of the cella—both, outlandishly, right at the west end of this main block instead of in its middle, so that the structure as a whole is entirely asymmetrical. The smaller, southern 'Caryatid porch' *23* rests upon the stylobate of the old temple. Here, the

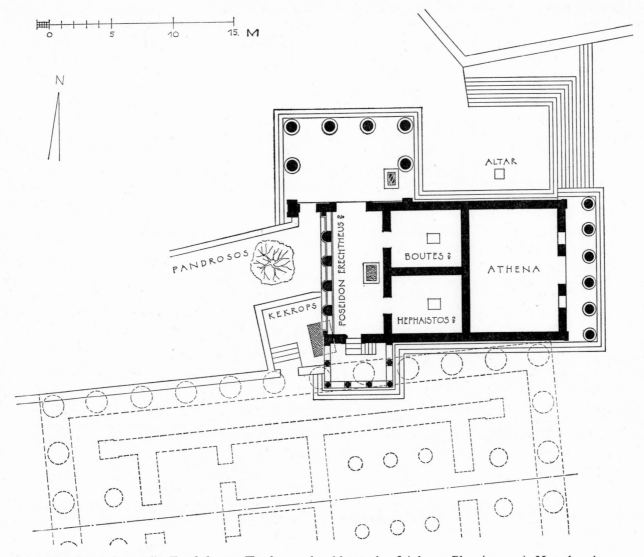

66 Athens, Acropolis. Erechtheum. To the south, old temple of Athena. Plan (1 : 300). New drawing

columns have, as it were, changed into living figures of maidens (*korai*), with four at the front and a further one at either side. Standing on a tall podium, they support the shallow entablature and flat marble roof. The ground-level of the larger north porch is 10 ft. 7⅝ in. lower. Though the grouping of its columns that shoot up slenderly (height 25 ft. 0½ in., lower diam. 2 ft. 8¼ in.) corresponds to that of the *korai* (4 by 2), neither its central axis nor its west flank match the Caryatid porch—indeed, its western side projects in a remarkably inorganic way some 10 ft. beyond the west front of the main block. Moreover, the north porch is cut off even more sharply from the central block by a lower-lying ridge-roof, with its own pediment facing north.

Is there any logic in such a confusing multiplicity of structural forms? Can an architectonic conception still underlie it? We find here, in a by no means extensive building, four differently proportioned sets of columns (*korai* included) on four different levels, and three structural units possessing three separate roofs thrust together without being clearly related.

The temple's interior is no less complicated. From the east, one has access to a naos lying at the highest level and entirely cut off from the western part of the building by a cross-wall. This, extending down to the lower level, was approached through a great ceremonial door in the rear wall of the north porch, and walls to half room-height divided it into a vestibule-like compartment on the west side running cross-wise and chambers adjoining the latter on its east side. One could also enter the west room from the Caryatid porch down a little stairway with a

29

rectangular bend, as well as through a small, un-adorned doorway at the west end.

Consequently, the Erechtheum has often enough been criticized, and there has been no lack of ingenious attempts to account for its incomprehensible irregularity as the outcome of changes and cuts in an originally more meaningful, symmetrical design. Whereas, however, the Propylaea becomes fully intelligible through a knowledge of the underlying plan, the Erechtheum—that 'living riddle', as it has been called—just wraps itself more closely in its mystery when faced with such efforts to explain it. Hence, the key would seem to lie in a sphere other than the architectonic one: that of Greek religion.

Though the Erechtheum has diverged no less far from the typical and conventional than the Propylaea, it has taken, so to speak, the opposite direction. In the Propylaea, we meet the severe, symmetrical design of an autocratic architect who has expressed an idea in a precise formal language; with the Erechtheum, every side of the building displays a different countenance. In the former, autonomous structures, fused by relations of symmetry and the tension of 'harmonious contrasts', combine as a monumentally unified architectural complex; in the latter, three blocks differentiated down to the last detail are packed together as though by chance. If, with the former, older holy places were to have been abruptly swept aside for the sake of a great project that was ultimately frustrated by the opposition of the priests and conservative party, now it was these very guardians of tradition who supported and directed the new scheme. (Nicias, the leading politician of these years, was pious to the point of superstition.) Just as, in the Propylaea's case, we had to seek out the architectonic or artistic aim behind every peculiarity, now, faced with this almost freakish building, we must always enquire into the religious background. While there the Doric gate-façades, sustained by the symmetric wing structures, have a notable outward-reaching effect and sequences of mutually enhancing spaces have been created, here holy places have with reverence been enclosed as luxuriously as possible, architecture being allotted a wholly ancillary role. One thing, however, both buildings have in common and it can be precisely described as 'Attic': the way this architecture has performed its task, whether as mistress or servant, with the same effortless and consummate skill, the same natural flexibility, thus producing there the most solemnly impressive, here the most studiously refined construction, each a perfect entity in its very distinctiveness.

The site of the Erechtheum had been the most sacred spot on the Acropolis since primitive times.

Stripped of its peristyle by the Persians and only roughly repaired, the old temple of Athena still formed the religious focus of Athens, even as it was. Here, not in the Parthenon, stood Athena's wooden cult image, wrapped in legends, which had fallen from the sky and for which the Panathenaic procession was held. The foundations of the temple rested on the Mycenaean palace of the first Attic kings—'the splendid dwelling of Erechtheus' (*Odyssey* VII, 81)—and to its north side clung sanctuaries from remote antiquity. There lay buried the mythical kings of Attica, in whom earlier, pre-Greek divinities lived on: snake-footed Kekrops, and Erechtheus whom Poseidon struck dead in anger, thereby to some extent merging him with himself. Another figure can hardly be distinguished from Erechtheus—Erichthonius, the divine child of chthonic powers later called Hephaestus and Gea. He was nursed by Athena, who entrusted him, secretly hidden in a basket, to the three daughters of Kekrops. Against her bidding, two of them looked at the snake-footed child and, seized with madness, leapt from the citadel wall. The third, Pandrosos 'the all-bedewing', received a small open sanctuary beside the tomb of her father. Erichthonius, however, dwelt on as a serpent in a near-by crevice, and watched over the city's prosperity. When this 'citadel snake' vanished during the Persian advance, the Athenians knew that they, too, would have to abandon their city.

In these myths we meet a dark undercurrent of the otherwise luminous Apollonian religion: chthonic daemons of death and fertility, who, inherited from the pre-Greek ancestors, were protected by the earth in graves and snake-inhabited clefts, as at Delphi and Epidaurus. This links up with another myth, which concerns the fight between Poseidon-Erechtheus and Athena for Attica, and was represented on the Parthenon's west pediment. Poseidon drove his trident into the rock, causing a saline spring to rise, but Athena gave the olive-tree. Thereby the goddess of mental alertness gained victory over the subterranean powers, at the same time absorbing the vanquished foe into her own ample being. Even the radiant Athena Parthenos of Phidias was accompanied by the Erechtheus serpent.

For this reason, the Erechtheum likewise united under its roof two opposing cult rooms. Its east part was intended to supplant the old Athena temple and receive the wooden cult image, and accordingly presents the normal appearance of a naos. Its west part, the true Erechtheum, embraced all the above-mentioned chthonic signs, and was therefore compounded of various traditional types of building: megaron, monumental tomb, and monopteros. Thus, this curious structure served not only to replace the old Athena temple, the four-roomed ground-plan of which it repeated, but also to combine all these holy sites architecturally in one new temple.

28 Under the pavement of the north porch, visible through an altar opening like a well, lies the mark of Poseidon's trident. Above it, an aperture has been left in the ceiling of the porch, because the site had to remain open to the sky. This explains the exceptional depth of two interaxials, the spacious, loose-knit form, and the emphatic separation of the porch from the main block. The structure was conceived as an open, 'monopteral' canopy on columns, like those erected elsewhere and over similar relics—at Olympia, say, and on Samos.

Athena's gift, the olive-tree, grew in the adjacent Pandrosos precinct, which one reached through a little door in the rear wall of the north porch, here taking the place of a special propylaeum. This, then, is why the north porch had to project so inorganically beyond the west end of the main block. In the middle of the same rear wall a far bigger door (about 8 by 16 ft.)—the most magnificent of antiquity—gave access to the Erechtheum's west room, which in the building inscriptions is called the 'prostomiaion', probably signifying the antechamber of a tomb. Beneath its floor, in a sort of crypt connected by a little underground door with the trident-mark under the north porch, lay the crevice of the Erechtheus serpent and a 'salt sea' plenished by Poseidon's spring. In the compartments adjoining on the east and divided by walls to half room-height, there stood, according to tradition, altars for Hephaestus, Butes (another primitive king, whose descendants included the hereditary priests of Athena), and Poseidon-Erechtheus.

The last of the sacred things—the grave of Kekrops—lay beneath the building's south-west 22 corner. At this spot, a gap bridged by strong marble beams was specially left for it in the foundations. To Kekrops belonged a small temenos abutting on the substructure of the old temple and the Erechtheum's west wall. Part of the tomb reached under the peculiar Caryatid porch, which revived an old form of sepulchral monument that was to culminate barely a century later in the Mausoleum at Halicarnassus. There, on the tall base of the tomb 25 chamber, a wreath of free-standing columns supported the canopy of the roof. If here, instead of columns, calmly dignified figures of girls bear the entablature upon their heads, this means that one of the most charming notions of Ionic treasury architecture at Delphi (page 334) reached perfection in the present masterpiece. Are these *korai* at the same time images of the daughters of Kekrops? Does the

capital—an echinus garlanded with an Ionic egg-and-dart below a rectangular abacus—represent the covered container of the child Erichthonius? At all events, we hear of mystical rites alluding to something of the sort (Paus. I, 27, 3). Two maidens, known as *arrephoroi*, had annually to carry mysterious receptacles upon their heads into the sanctuary of Aphrodite on the north slope of the Acropolis. The other ancient stories about Athena, Poseidon, and Erechtheus were probably likewise acted out every year in cult performances. Recently, a small rectangular theatre was detected against the north side *fig. 66* of the Erechtheum, its seating steps enclosing an altar court on two sides. A similar but very much older construction seems to have preceded it. The cult square reminds one of the telesterium at Eleusis (page 399) or the steps for spectators near the temple of Despoina at Lycosura (page 357), which were also intended for mystery plays.

If the Erechtheum, that sacred building, was from the start denied the simple, monumental grandeur of the Parthenon, its builders made up for this by adorning it with all the richness, all the supple delicacy that Ionic architectural decoration ever had to give, so that it could not but appear as a luxurious reliquary on the scale of a temple. The central block *29, 26* was crowned and embraced by a three-fascia architrave, which, only interrupted by the roof of the north porch, even ran above the long, unpierced side walls. It bore a frieze, 2 ft. 0⅜ in. high and 197 ft. long, which, enclosed between bands of carved leaves, introduced the delicious but trivial charms of handicraft into architecture. With a technique previously applied only to expensive materials like ebony and ivory on, say, the pedestals of cult images, the figures were separately worked in white marble, and then attached to their background of dark Eleusinian stone. Over a hundred figure fragments have been found, but the subject of the frieze cannot be accurately deduced from them. Though stylistically related to the reliefs on the Nike 'balustrade'—the same masterly handling of light, the same contrasting duet of line and mass—it seems less dramatically excited, and to have been created in a gentler, more lyrical style wholly in keeping with the character of the building.

Above, the normal corona was topped by a sima adorned with lions' heads, over which stood palmette antefixes (only bits of a replacement from Roman times have survived). This means that two elements hitherto excluding each other as clear-cut alternatives were mixed, and that, for the first time, the peculiarly Greek logic of form was assailed by a more decorative tendency.

Together with the clear surfaces of the saddle-roof, the entablature constituted the sole bond imposing unity on the highly dissimilar sides of the building, as the three sets of columns differed in detail and in proportions. The six columns of the east colonnade are the slenderest, not just on the Erechtheum but in all Attica (height of 21 ft. 7½ in. =9·52 lower diams. of 2 ft. 3⅛ in.). Hence the fragile delicacy of this portico. Certain refinements, such as the slight inward tilt of the columns (by only ¾ in.), were taken over from the Parthenon, but, according to Ionic custom, neither entasis nor curvature were introduced.

In conformity with their more loose-knit character, the columns of the north porch have been set further apart (here interaxial = 3·85–3·76 lower diams.; east portico 3·05). This is countered by their being less elongated (height 25 ft. 0⅜ in. or 9·35 lower diams.).

The Attic base is now fully mature, the relationship of its parts—a tight scotia between two resiliently swelling tori—being carefully adjusted. On the eastern columns, the upper torus is still channelled (as in the Nike temple), and the same profile runs round the whole structure as a wall footing. In the north porch, a band of triple-cable ornament covers the upper torus, and—the most original enrichment —a similar guilloche-carved torus is inserted above the encircling egg-and-dart of the capital, between the volutes. To us, it seems quite fabulous that all the interstices of this plaiting were once filled with variously coloured glass beads, and that the volutes of the almost springy capitals were inlaid with strips of gilt bronze. Starting out from a golden rosette at the centre, these ended in a delicate metal palmette that filled the triangle between volute and torus. Were ordinary stonemasons at work here—or goldsmiths?

Round the neck of the columns runs a band of carved anthemion pattern, which organically grips the rising shaft. An identical frieze tops the walls and anta pillars. In it, a long-established type of ornament—the alternation of stylized lotus blooms and palmettes above twisting tendrils—has been fully converted to the spirit of the 'rich style' through the 'naturalistic' adjunct of little acanthus leaves, through hollow forms casting shadows, and through a nervous sinuosity of the lines. Above, an egg-and-dart and crowning leaf-and-dart are together an 'expression' of the joint between supporting wall and supported architrave, bracing themselves against the latter's weight. All this is more than a decoration, since it is chiefly in these ornaments that the static framework of the building becomes apparent.

Not only in its adornment, which reached an often imitated climax in the rich yet unobtrusive framing of the door, was the north porch the object of its builders' greatest care. The columns again lean inwards by about ¾ in., at the same time tilting towards the middle interaxial, while their entasis is, with its increment of barely ¼ in., so slight that even a practised eye can scarcely detect it. Above this garland of columns, the coffered marble ceiling, borne by low beams, appears to float. Its spread of 18 ft. 8⅜ in. actually surpasses that of the Propylaea's.

Mention has already been made of the west end with its strange amalgam of columns and pillars, a form that found an eager following above all among theatre façades of the third century. The intercolumniations were, here, originally closed by low barriers and wooden lattices, except for the southernmost one above the tomb of Kekrops. Perhaps on religious grounds, this end space remained entirely open. (The intervening walls and windows visible today date from Roman times.)

This building's most graceful marvel, the Caryatid porch, seems to us now to have little connexion with its daemonic origin, the grave of the snake-footed mythical king. The Athenians may have seen things differently, or else preferred to raise their dark heritage into the cloudless sphere of classical form. It is believed that the six korai were created by Alcamenes and a pupil. Faithful to the traditions of Phidias, they both gave a clearly architectonic structure to the maidens standing at ease, yet so subtly composed that the vertical folds of the peplos strongly suggest the fluting of a column. Nevertheless, the laws of sculptural form were stringent enough to set aside an architectonic rule. In order that the two korai on each side should turn slightly outwards, their bent leg had to be the inner, their supporting leg the outer one. This shifting of the weight produced an appreciable slant of the whole figure outwards instead of, as is usual with columns, inwards.

The entablature resting on the heads of the korai was not to be allowed to appear oppressive. Therefore, not only was the architrave kept particularly shallow, and loosened up with an application of rosettes (left unfinished), but instead of a tall, heavy frieze, the lighter east Ionic motif of the dentil course (fig. 109) was introduced.

Of special interest are the building accounts, which have survived unusually complete. Petty items were entered with a bureaucratic pedantry that must in its turn be called 'classic', and is in significant contrast to the summary accounting of the liberal Periclean age. During the one year 408/7, over 2,600 lines of writing were engraved on marble slabs, and set up as a permanent reckoning. First, a commission in 409 drew up an inventory of the building, work on which had been suspended for years owing to the unfavourable turn taken by the war, and every unfinished stone was listed with its measurements. From this, it emerges that the structure had reached the height of its entablature, that the Caryatid porch and west end were completely finished, and that the north porch was nearly so. The columns of the east portico were still unfluted, and the walls lacked their final polish. Frieze, corona, ceilings and roof had not yet been begun. In the accounts that come next, the name, native place, work, and pay of every single artisan are recorded. All, from the architect (who here plainly acted as overseer), the gilder, and the carpenter, down to the last stonemason, received the same daily wage of one drachma. From the detailed statements, even the wooden coffered ceilings of the east and west rooms can be reconstructed: they were richly gilded, and adorned with acanthus motifs and rosettes.

One example will suffice as evidence of the care and precision of the stonemasons' technique. Groups of from four to seven masons were engaged in fluting the six portico columns, and we occasionally find a master at work with several of his sons. Each column kept a group occupied for two working months or 350 working days, which were distributed among four processes: first, the rough columns were accurately rounded (50 days), then faceted as a polygon corresponding to the flutes and fillets (90 days); next, the flutes were hollowed out with claw and chisel (100 days); lastly, the ultimate form was achieved with a finer chisel and the surfaces polished (110 days).

The frieze figures, which are always referred to descriptively instead of by their mythological names —e.g. 'Agathanor from Alopeke [received for] the two women beside the vehicle and the two mules 240 [drachmas]'—were carved by several masters, who naturally must have worked from models. Some of them were also those who collaborated on the designing and execution of the ornament. Thus, in view of the freedom accorded to every craftsman in his job, which was never carried out mechanically, one cannot value the artistic contribution of these simple workmen too highly.

Let us look across once again at the Parthenon. Can one think of two buildings that, despite such a difference, are in more harmonious agreement? There, the heroic tension, the grave and grand form of the Parthenon; here, the charming pliancy, the loose and rich, but complex form of the Erechtheum. One does not need the hint provided by the caryatids to find that this structure endorses the opinion of Vitruvius, who likens the Doric order to the vigorous beauty of the male body, and the Ionic to the graceful, richly decked female form (IV 1, 6–8).

ATHENS, THE CITY

THE 'THESEUM' (HEPHAESTEUM)   *Plates 32–35, fig. 67*

On a hill at the western edge of the agora, once the centre of the city, a Doric peripteral temple was raised between 450 and 440 for a pair of gods: Athena and lame Hephaestus, the divine smith. Both were gods of technical skill, and, according to one version of the myth, were even bound in not exactly harmonious wedlock. As Heracles and Theseus play a special part in its sculptural decoration, people were long inclined to connect the temple with these two heroes, which is why its customary name is still the 'Theseum'. However, building inscriptions and, above all, the workshops of smiths and bronze-founders discovered in its environs speak in favour of the modern attribution.

For two and a half millennia, the peripteral structure has reigned over the agora, now un-earthed again, as the best preserved temple in Greece. During the Byzantine period, it was converted without fundamental changes into a church of St. George. The disfiguring vault over the cella dates from these alterations.

Though the temple was erected at almost the same time as the Parthenon, and accordingly has much in common with it, it is entirely overshadowed by the latter. This would seem to be due not only to its modest size (the whole Theseum would almost fit into the Parthenon's cella!); for between the two there exists, both formally and inwardly, a difference in rank that makes us all the more conscious of the unique spirit of the builders on the Acropolis. The Theseum represents the 'normal' development of Attic building (in so far as one can speak of 'normal'

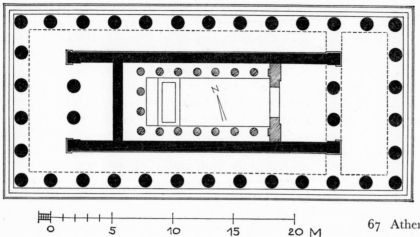

67 Athens. Hephaesteum, so-called Theseum.
Plan (1 : 300). New drawing

at all in connexion with this ever extraordinary architecture), as it proceeded without a Phidias and an Ictinus. Their stimuli were, here, only superficially received, but were still powerful enough to force a change of plan in the second phase of construction.

The marble quarries recently opened up on Mount Pentelicum provided the material, as already for the older Parthenon. In addition, imported Parian marble was used for the sculpture and a few architectural members. Strange to say, an economy was made in the bottom step, which consists of ordinary limestone, and therefore links up more with the ground than the building. This may be connected with the fact that the projected dimensions of the peristyle have obviously been established in the lowest marble step (i.e. the middle step), instead of the stylobate. The rectangle of this step is not only exactly 100 Doric ft. long, but proportioned as 4 is to 9 (47 ft. 4⅞ in. by 106 ft. 8 in.), just like the Parthenon. There is something indecisive, however, about the way this rectangle is repeated at the top by the faces of the corona, yet does not coincide at all with the main mass outlined by stylobate, columns, and entablature, so that the basic proportion is marked out quite literally in the air.

As with the Parthenon, the elevation was developed from the same basic ratio of 4 to 9, though in a manner once more lacking clarity. Thus, the temple's width at the middle step is related to the column height plus the height of the two marble steps as 9 to 4 (47 ft. 4⅞ in. : 18 ft. 8¾ in. + 2 ft. 4 in.), and the sides of this rectangle are again left in the air. More successful is the application of the 9 : 4 ratio to column height and intercolumniation (18 ft. 8¾ in. : 8 ft. 5⅝ in.).

Can it be due to chance, this remarkable identity

not only of the Theseum's basic proportion with the Parthenon's but of its triply interlocking use of them in ground-plan, elevation, and column arrangement? Could not plans and theories of the Parthenon circle, which were doubtless already being eagerly discussed before construction began, be at the bottom of it? In any case, the obscure, indeed absurd placing of the proportion rectangles supports the thesis of an imperfectly understood imitation.

Discussing the Parthenon's peristyle, we recognized as essentially new the tense combination of density (in the colonnades) and lightness (in the elevation). With the Theseum, the appearance of the Doric order was determined solely by the tendency of the period towards a looser texture. Slimmer and more widely spaced columns (height = 5·61 lower diams., Parthenon 5·48; interaxial = 2·54 lower diams., Parthenon 2·25) carried on the tradition of Aegina and the Athenian treasury at Delphi. There, too, lay the source of the comparatively tall and heavy entablature (height = 1·98 lower diams., Aegina 1·99, but Parthenon 1·73). The former severity and tectonic force of the Doric order have declined, and for this very reason the Theseum comes a long way behind its dominant neighbour in innate grandeur.

Like tendencies characterize the ground-plan, though superficially it appears normal: 6 by 13 columns, simple angle contraction, alignment of the external surfaces of the cella walls with the second and fifth end columns, naos plus pronaos and opisthodomus, west portico 1½ interaxials deep, two columns in-antis at each end. However, owing to the exceptional width of the interaxials, the porticoes and pteromata cannot help being unusually spacious. This was undoubtedly intended on aesthetic grounds, as is made plain by a notion of the architect no less

fig. 67

32

34

392

original than prophetic. He extended the east portico facing the agora to two interaxials, so that the pronaos columns stand in line with the third flanking columns. Nor is that all. By carrying the pronaos entablature over the side walls and binding it into the inner faces of the external entablature, instead of having it end normally above the antae, he made the portico—at least in the zone of the entablature—a separate, clearly defined room lying crosswise before a pronaos also rigorously deepened to two interaxials. Thus, not only did one pass through a graduated sequence of three spaces when entering the naos, but the new, classical sense of space that was so fundamentally expressed in the Parthenon naos here infused also the outer form of the temple, which, with the Parthenon, was still so compact. Previously, this had only occurred in Ionia and Magna Graecia, and it meant that a big deviation had been made from the always 'corporeal' Peloponnesian architecture.

Moreover, the east portico has been marked out even more clearly as a separate room by sculptural decoration. Externally, this part of the temple is lent weight by carved and once gaily painted metopes, which, like those of the Athenian treasury at Delphi, are devoted to the national hero Heracles and the Athenian hero Theseus. On the ten metopes of the east end, Heracles performs his arduous deeds, while on the four metopes of the adjoining pairs of interaxials at either side, Theseus overcomes the Minotaur and a rapacious mob. All the other metopes were left as plain, white marble slabs. Within, an Ionic frieze with groups of gods watching mythical battles runs across the lengthened architrave above the pronaos, and it is continued round the other three sides of the east portico interior as a smooth, blue-painted band. To it, there corresponds above the opisthodomus entrance another frieze, on which a dramatic and agitated battle between Lapiths and centaurs rages; but, like the architrave, it is confined to the width of the cella's west end from anta to anta.

Further developed, we shall meet the new, 'spatial' conception of the east portico at Sunium—in a temple by the same architect; indeed, it was even able to influence Ictinus himself and, after him, Scopas. Front porticoes, two interaxials deep, reappeared at Bassae (page 351) and Tegea, though a more delicately judicious approach to monumentality led to the abandonment of the questionable extended architrave, which, after all, did break the continuity of the ambulatory.

In the course of recent investigations, the extension of the east portico was linked up with a change of plan during construction. It is said that the present cella with relatively thick-set proportions was substituted for a longer, narrower one under the stimulus of the Parthenon project, begun in the meantime. This does not, however, clear the matter up, as an idea completely opposed to the Parthenon's has been realized in the peristyle: wideness instead of compactness. It would have to be a case of the self-willed 'Theseum architect' not wanting to let himself be drawn into the strong current of the Parthenon scheme, but only being able to demonstrate his originality vis-à-vis Phidias's overwhelmingly superior team through contradiction. Be that as it may, in the planning of the naos interior, he just could not help adopting Ictinus's compelling design as an afterthought; for the two-storied Parthenon arrangement of Doric columns running round three sides was undoubtedly introduced (with 4 by 7 columns) when the construction of the cella was already well advanced. In the much narrower space, this of course made everything constricted and mean. The architect found himself obliged to push the lateral colonnades as close as possible to the walls, so as to obtain a fairly spacious nave for the cult images of Hephaestus and Athena, which were not set up till about 420.

The naos walls were made ready to receive large murals, and coated with plaster. If the paintings thus prepared for really were executed, they must certainly have included the architecture—i.e. the columns standing close up to them—in their composition; possibly the odd amalgam of architectonic and pictorial elements that spread in late Hellenistic times arose from such paintings.

The workmanship is not inferior to that on the Parthenon, although different technical practices clearly reveal other masons. Curvature can be detected on all four sides from the crepidoma to the entablature (rise at the fronts about $1\frac{1}{8}$ in., flanks about $1\frac{3}{4}$ in.), and the columns, which tilt inwards by $1\frac{3}{4}$ in., have a very slight entasis.

Seeing that, in the slenderness of the columns and the amplitude and openness of the porticoes, Ionic formal principles have everywhere penetrated the Doric fabric, it is not surprising that Ionic architectural ornaments also prevail far more strongly than on the Parthenon. There, the cella frieze was assimilated into the structure by retaining the Doric taenia; here, Ionic mouldings flaunt themselves without restraint above and below the frieze, even spreading to the wall base.

Lively colouring must have further enhanced the open, cheerful appearance of this temple. As usual, the triglyph frieze displayed an alternation of red and blue, while the encircling sima with lion-head spouts bore rows of coloured palmettes along the eaves. The richest decoration was on the marble coffered ceiling of the ambulatory, where intricately winding meanders, Doric and Ionic cymas, stars and palmettes formed a magnificent and gaily stylized ensemble.

Remains of the pediment groups, previously believed lost, were at last discovered during recent American excavations in the agora. On the east gable, an enthroned central figure (Zeus?) seems to have been flanked on either side by standing figures, teams of horses, and, in the corners, lying figures. This corresponds to the early classical composition of the east pediment at Olympia. They have been interpreted as Heracles's elevation to Olympus.

The author of all the sculpture, which shows complete unity of conception, is thought to have been a pupil of Myron, owing to the dramatic movement and the severe, hard bodily structure of his figures. He appears to have finished his work before the execution of the Parthenon pediments, which even his freest creations, the floating Hesperides of the central acroterium, do not approach. H. Koch's words apply here, as they do to the architecture: 'Perhaps there is nothing that marks the difference in spiritual rank between the two masters more clearly than the mighty cosmic symbolism that pervades the entire Parthenon; the Theseum master hardly had an inkling of such a thing.'

THE OLYMPIEUM   *Plates XXX, 36, fig. 68*

In a spacious, rectangular walled precinct to the south-east of the Acropolis, fifteen huge Corinthian columns still tower up today. They belong to a temple of Zeus Olympius which was once surrounded by 104 such columns. A colossal structure, it was regarded as a marvel by Roman philhellenes, but now appears a lost stranger on Attic soil, and, hence, stands almost unnoticed in the shadow of the Acropolis.

Zeus had long been worshipped on this site, for his cult there went back to Deucalion's times—or, as we should say, was 'as old as Adam'. From stretches of wall beneath the present structure, the earliest temple has been restored as a peripteral edifice measuring about 98½ by 197 ft. (100 by 200 Ionic ft.). It was probably begun before the mid sixth century, perhaps under the tyrant Pisistratus, who ruled from 561. If one reflects that the king of the gods then still did not possess a temple of his own in his big, pan-Hellenic sanctuary at Olympia, one is bound to suspect that this building, which would have been considerably larger than the home of the city's goddess on the Acropolis, expressed not so much a people's piety as a prince's pride. For all the

splendour imparted to the Olympian lord was reflected back upon the earthly one.

The two sons of Pisistratus knew the giant temples of Ionia, and the tyrant Polycrates had just begun an enormous dipteros in the sanctuary of Hera on Samos (page 454). Athens should have one too. The design of the dipteros now taken in hand by the Pisistratids clearly follows the Samian model. A double row of columns was to surround the elongated cella, before either end of which *three* parallel rows, each of eight columns, would form a veritable forest (8 by 21 columns, 108 in all; stylobate 134 ft. 6⅛ in. by 353 ft. 6⅛ in.). Specifically Ionic characteristics of the ground-plan were also taken over from Samos such as a distinct enlargement of the porticoes, which entailed widening the three corner interaxials on the flanks by about 1 ft., and a rhythmic graduation of the seven end interaxials, which became increasingly narrow towards the sides. Such irregularities could hardly be combined with a Doric triglyph frieze. The building thus seems to have been designed in the Ionic style, though the remarkably large diameter of recovered column drums is inconsistent with this (7 ft. 10½ in.; cf. Samos 5 ft. 5 in. to 6 ft. 8¾ in.). Likewise, the tightness with which the columns were packed together was usual only in Doric temples. (The average interaxial measured about 18 ft. at the fronts and slightly over 17 ft. on the flanks, so that the ratio of interaxial to lower diameter is about 1 : 2·3. Moreover, one must assume the side columns to have been rather slimmer. Compare Corinth 1 : 2·31, old temple of Athena 1 : 2·48, temple of Zeus at Olympia 1 : 2·32. On Ionic temples, the columns stood further apart: Samos 1 : 4·0 to 2·5.)

Did the architects of the Olympieum—Vitruvius names four—wish to give the Ionic columns familiar Doric proportions in order to impose upon the building, which, after all, was intended to make its effect chiefly through its vast dimensions, the austere monumentality of the Doric style? Or were the severe and always unambiguous forms of Doric architecture to have risen above an Ionic ground-plan of labyrinthine impenetrability? Whatever the answer, Athens was spared this abstruse experiment of tyrants. Work had barely progressed beyond the stylobate when, in 510, Hippias was expelled. The reconstituted democracy at once put a stop to building operations. In 479, Themistocles could presume to use the column drums prepared for the temple, which was obviously regarded more as a monument of tyrannic hybris than as the sacred property of Zeus, in constructing a near-by city gate. Aristotle took the building as an example of how tyrants impose compulsory service on the people to prevent

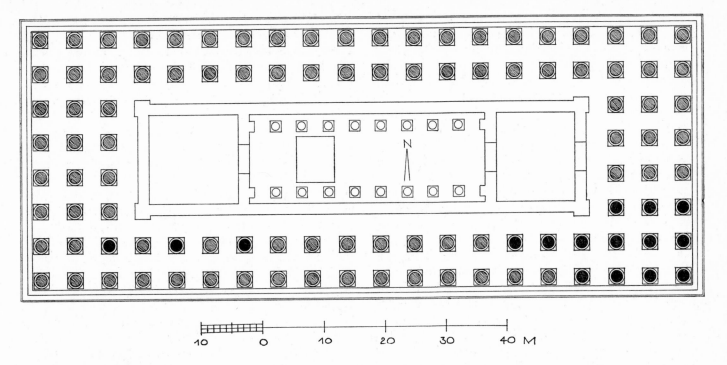

68 Athens, Olympieum. Plan (1 : 600). Parts still standing black, confirmed grey, hypothetical white. New drawing

them from thinking about liberty (*Pol.* V, 11, 4). However, the true reason for its rejection may lie still deeper: it offended against the extremely sure Attic sense of moderation. The tendency of Attic architecture was always towards perfect form, not imposing bulk or quantity.

Therefore, when the temple was begun afresh after an interval of three centuries, the stimulus again came from abroad, and the entrepreneur was again a sovereign. Round about 175 B.C., Antiochus IV of Syria had a Roman architect, Cossutius, raise a now Corinthian dipteros over the old foundations. Could Antiochus no longer find a master qualified for the task in Athens—the great school of Hellas, as Pericles once called it? The city had evidently lost its creative impulse along with its freedom. Its spiritual resources had become the common property of the Hellenistic world; and there is a touch of tragic irony in the way the powerless centre of culture and education, living on ancient glory, was now forced to accept from foreign rulers the gift of its own heritage.

A purely Attic creation, the Corinthian capital came into being as an elegantly mannered product of a craftsman, transformed by Ictinus into an architectural form at once lively and able to bear its load. It seemed designed to replace the Ionic capital which offered only two faces. Equally developed on all four sides, it even fitted in readily and easily at the angles of a peristyle, hitherto such a problem. Only one thing was not required of this bell capital encircled by notched acanthus leaves, animated by springy volutes, and crowned by an abacus with concave sides: an effect of monumentality. At Bassae, Tegea (page 356), and Nemea, as in the tholoi of Delphi, Epidaurus, and Olympia, it was always consigned to the interior, where its rich, smooth form could be freely developed. When—again on Attic soil—the Corinthian capital first appeared outside a building, the latter was a cabinet-piece half-way between architecture and handicraft: a miniature round temple put up as a base for the tripod that Lysicrates won at the Dionysia in 334.

The classical laws of form ceased to hold good in Hellenistic times. A violent urge for the imposing, for dramatic contrast and grandiose effects to be appreciated at a distance tore down all the classical barriers, especially in the newly founded kingdoms of the East. The inclination of this age was no longer for beauty, calm, and harmony, but for lavish display and huge façades that enclosed broad open spaces in striking effects of perspective. This trend towards the colossal was complemented by an exuberant decoration that relieved the weight of the massive structures. The Corinthian capital was absolutely predestined to become one of this period's favourite forms. Capable of many uses, it pandered to the need for pomp through its both lively and ornamental diversity.

Seleucus I, a cavalry officer of Alexander's who, after the latter's death, ruled over an enormous kingdom from the Aegean to the Indus, had taken the first step by building a Corinthian peripteral temple at Diocaesarea and thus freeing the foliated capital from the intimate setting of the interior, to which the classical period had confined it. His sixth successor on the Syrian throne, Antiochus IV, now developed the Corinthian order to a scale uniquely suited to the age, and, in the Olympieum, began an edifice that remained a much admired model till the end of antiquity. This Antiochus, among the most power-hungry and brilliant of potentates, had as a prince spent his formative years at Athens. As a king borne up by military success—he would have conquered Egypt, if the Romans had not opposed him—he had the audacity to consider uniting the whole of the Orient with its different religions in the common worship of Zeus Olympius. Zeus was to absorb Baal and the Yahwe of the Old Testament, and the earthly embodiment of this super-god would be he, Antiochus. A copy of Phidias's Zeus installed by him at Antioch probably bore his features, and even the Holy of Holies in the temple at Jerusalem had to put up with a Zeus statue. His coins showed the head of Zeus-Antiochus with the legend: 'King Antiochus, incarnation of god, bringer of victory'. Athens seemed to him the right place for presenting his megalomaniac notion to the educated world, and the temple that he began there for himself and his celestial counterpart had to be positively the biggest and the most magnificent. After this ruler's sudden death in 164, the temple was left unfinished for centuries. Sulla transported some columns to Rome around 85 B.C. as decoration for the temple of Jupiter Capitolinus, and their example contributed to the complete victory of the Corinthian style at Rome. In the days of Augustus, some of the shattered Syrian kingdom's petty princes, vassals of Rome and dependent on flattery, combined in order to finish the temple and dedicate it to the emperor's 'genius'. At most, they erected a few columns. The completion of the vast undertaking was reserved for Hadrian, of all the emperors the most partial to Athens. Himself a dabbler in architecture, he was possessed by an unequalled passion for building, and studied the buildings of the past with great intelligence. Around A.D. 130, he devoutly had Cossutius's project realized without changes. His capitals are faithful copies of the Hellenistic ones, distinguishable only by unintentional modifications of forms drained of their old vitality.

The thirteen columns of the south-east corner, still standing as a coherent group, date from Cossutius's time; the three isolated in the south pteroma—one of which was brought down by a hurricane in 1852—belong to the two Roman building periods. As a whole, the temple may be considered in all respects a consistent embodiment of Cossutius's design. Despite the Roman architect, who had obviously been schooled in the sound Hellenistic tradition, it displayed no specifically Roman features. Cossutius had not hesitated to adopt the ground-plan of the Pisistratid dipteros, and there is nothing surprising about this, since the Hellenistic age was by nature drawn to everything huge and extravagant. After all, it rebuilt the archaic dipteroi at Ephesus and Didyma (pages 461, 464) as well. The sole change in the old plan is characteristic enough. Instead of being graduated, the interaxials were now made approximately uniform (ends 18 ft. $0\frac{1}{2}$ in., sides 18 ft. $2\frac{1}{8}$ in.), so that all the 104 supports stood, as it were, at the crossing points of a squarely reticulated screen. (Owing to the virtual retention of the old plan's stylobate dimensions of 134 ft. $10\frac{1}{2}$ in. by 353 ft. $11\frac{5}{8}$ in., this involved reducing the formerly more closely placed side columns from 21 to 20.) The power of endless, schematic repetition, which we know all too well from modern buildings, came to the fore.

Whereas the Pisistratids had still been willing to build their temple of modern poros, now only the noblest stone, Pentelic marble, was good enough for the truly princely edifice. Its columns alone devoured an incredible quantity of marble: 15,500 tons—almost four times as much as the Parthenon's.

Yet the aura of the plainly and simply 'classical' city, and the tradition of the undoubtedly Attic builders exerted a calm influence towards clarity and pure proportioning, which guarded the structure against the tendency, spreading in the East, to overburden grandiosely with gorgeous decorations. Apart from their capitals, the columns are of the 'classical' Attic-Ionic form. The Attic base has merely been joined by a square plinth, already a feature of the archaic Artemisium at Ephesus. Relatively squat in its proportions (height of 55 ft. $4\frac{7}{8}$ in. = 8·75 lower diams. of 6 ft. $3\frac{5}{8}$ in.), the shaft with its Ionic fluting still expresses the classical sense of form, though not much later the height of the Corinthian column was given to exceeding 10 lower diameters. The capitals hark back to the best fourth-century models, and above them lay a simple architrave divided into three fascias. Frieze, dentils, and cornice have not survived, but they do not seem to have been set in place till Hadrian's time.

Two epochs were thus mingled in this temple raised by a king and an emperor before the gates of democratic Athens: the vitality that stormed earth and heaven, the stirring power and grandeur of the Hellenistic age blended with the calm, balanced 'immanent grandeur' of classical form. None the less, the Olympieum remained an alien at Athens, like all the buildings presented to the city in the post-classical period, such as the huge colonnaded courtyards of Hadrian's library and the Roman agora. Even today, it still fails to rouse an interest corresponding to its merit. A thorough investigation of the ruins has yet to be made, and so we have no certain knowledge of the structure of the cella, which, however, formed the spatial focus of the whole in more senses than one.

If Sulla had transported the whole temple to Rome, instead of a few columns, and it towered above the Eternal City on top of the Capitoline hill, it would pass for the greatest marvel of architecture apart from the Pantheon in those more appropriate surroundings, leaving Athens little the poorer.

SUNIUM, THE TEMPLE OF POSEIDON

Plates XIII, 40, 41, fig. 69

If one sails round the southernmost, precipitous cape which Attica extends into the Aegean, the north winds swoop down upon the ship with unflagging force. Here, if anywhere, it was necessary to appease with offerings the lord of the winds and waves. Hence, the cliff above the sea had probably already been given to Poseidon in Homeric times: 'But on the Attic shore, by Sunium's holy point . . .' (*Odyssey* 111, 278). During the early archaic period, a simple altar no doubt stood there, enclosed by a little temenos wall, and, in front of it, huge, double life-size statues of youths were set up for the god towards the beginning of the sixth century, the work of artists who had suddenly learnt how to achieve monumentality. They towered high above the sea for almost a century, proclaiming the sanctity of the spot.

Not until the start of the fifth century was a temple begun. Terraces were constructed all round, the temenos was marked off by straight retaining-walls meeting at right angles (as on Aegina at about the same time: page 348), a propylaeum in the guise of a small anta temple was added, and the order of artistic form was deliberately and effectively set in opposition to unruly nature.

The poros temple was still being built when the Persians laid waste the Attic sanctuaries. Its stylobate constitutes the substructure of the later marble temple, and its architectural members were included in the foundations. What we can deduce from them arrests our attention. In this Doric peripteral building were made the immediate preparations for the classical principles of design, with the result that the Periclean substitute was able to retain the scheme of the peristyle almost unchanged. Not only was the well-balanced column plan of 6 by 13 achieved, but the ground-plan was developed—for the first time in the mother-country, it would seem—out of the basic unit of an unvarying interaxial width ($7\frac{1}{2}$ Doric ft. or 8 ft. $0\frac{1}{2}$ in.), which confronted the column diameter (3 Doric ft. or 3 ft. $2\frac{5}{8}$ in.) in the predetermined ratio of 5 to 2. Even the dimensions of the stylobate (40 by $92\frac{1}{2}$ Doric ft. or 42 ft. $10\frac{1}{8}$ in. by 99 ft. 1 in.) were adjusted, its proportion approximating to the Parthenon's of 4 to 9. Unfortunately, we know nothing for certain about the form of the cella.

After the Persians had ravaged the temple, the statue of Poseidon, evidently saved, found temporary accommodation in a shrine roughly patched up from the wreckage. Then, pursuant to Pericles's resolutions in favour of rebuilding the destroyed sanctuaries, Sunium, too, shared in the new splendour of the Attic state, and, soon after 449, a temple now of marble was begun. Owing to the 'modernity' of the old structure, its ground-plan could be taken over *fig. 69* with only a slight enlargement (6 by 13 columns, stylobate 44 ft. $2\frac{1}{4}$ in. by 102 ft. $1\frac{1}{4}$ in., interaxial 2·42 lower diams. of 3 ft. 5 in., simple angle contraction by $5\frac{7}{8}$ in.). This extension made it possible, as it were, to jacket the old crepidoma with the new marble one. In the process, however, an astonishing change completely altered the appearance of the peristyle: the columns are so extremely slender *40* (their height of 5·78 lower diams. was not matched and surpassed till the fourth century, as at Delphi, Tegea, and Nemea), that one almost thinks one is looking at an Ionic structure. Other peculiarities,

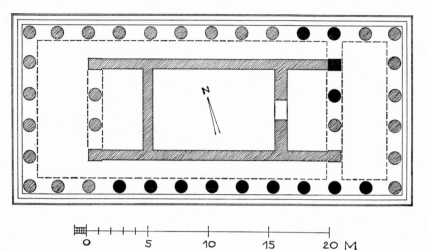

69 Sunium, temple of Poseidon. Plan
(1 : 300). New drawing

like the cella walls' pseudo-isodomic masonry (alternate low and high courses; cf. Cnidian treasury, page 334), which was no longer usual in Attica at this date, and, above all, the style of the sculpture and the vigorously sprouting palmette acroteria, do, in fact, reveal that island-Ionic craftsmen were at work. Besides, is it not obvious, in view of the Periclean building fever, that masons could no longer be found in Attica for love or money? That it was necessary to collect not just the cash but the craftsmen from the eastern allies? The architect had, of course, to be Athenian—indeed, his personal style is even thought to be that of the Theseum's creator.

For we find here the Theseum's characteristic 'spatial' principles of design carried a logical step forward. Not only was the east portico similarly extended to a depth of about two interaxials, but its spatial separation was defined even more exactly. As in the Theseum, the pronaos architrave spans the pteromata, and links up with the inner faces of the peristyle architrave, so that the space stretching crosswise before the pronaos was framed all round by an inner entablature of its own. This was already true of the Theseum. When, however, a sculptured Ionic frieze (with the usual groups of combatants representing gods and giants, Lapiths and centaurs, and the adventures of Theseus) was extended round all four sides of the portico above the inner architrave, it amounted to a covert revolution in Doric temple construction. Since the delimitation of the portico as an independent space, begun in the Theseum, had been completed, it was inevitable that an awkward discrepancy should positively cut into the building's living mass—a discrepancy between the unifying, corporeal ambulatory and the space that, subject to wholly different laws, spread out boldly within this colonnaded passageway, interrupting its

calm flow. This conflict extended even to details: on the inner faces of the same beams, an Ionic frieze backed, Janus-like, the Doric triglyph frieze of the peristyle. Interior and exterior no longer tallied.

Nor was this all. The sculptural enrichment that had previously belonged entirely to the outwards-facing body of the temple—on the Parthenon, the Ionic frieze adorns the external wall-surfaces of the cella, and, on the Theseum, it is still confined to the cella's two ends—was here changed into room decoration, and turned inwards. How lucidly the architect thought out his strange experiment may be judged from the fact that he had no reliefs carved on the peristyle metopes, which remained smooth, white marble slabs.

It is to be noted that none less than Ictinus at Bassae (page 351) fully developed the conception of space sketched out here, at the same time resolving the dilemma by a decisive innovation. He moved the inner frieze, logically combined with Ionic columns, to the real interior space of the temple, the naos, and, while preserving the deep porticoes, restored to the ambulatory its former continuity.

The Sunium architect seems to have taken a special delight in making—not always successful—experiments. In the west portico, he once more offered a new variant. Here, at the rear end, a 'reception-room' stressed like the one at the front would have made no sense, and so the cohesive entablature and frieze were absent. Nevertheless, this portico also was enlarged—to a depth of two interaxials, which means that the anta fronts were aligned with the axes of the two third columns from the end, instead of, as at the east, with their surfaces. Hence, the west portico was half a column diameter deeper than the east. This was and remained something unique in Greek temple architecture.

41

398

In the naos, the designer seems to have availed himself of the most rigorous means of enlarging his space—that of leaving out the interior columns altogether, as he had obviously first planned to do in the Theseum. Another experiment: broadly spaced fluting was intended to counteract the excessively slim proportions of the columns. Instead of the normal twenty, here the shafts have only sixteen flutes.

If here, as we have seen, a Doric temple was so steeped in Ionic influences that it lost the characteristic features of its order—tectonic force, corporeal compactness—it nevertheless gained through the thinning out of its columns, through the radical spatial breaking-up of its peristyle, a studied grace elsewhere only found in Ionic structures. It seems as if, at Sunium, Cycladic masons led by an Attic master particularly responsive to Ionic ideas faithfully gave an edifice a Doric exterior, the more to make it inwardly Ionic in character. When today those who sail past Sunium behold the white-shining filigree of the nine south columns, they could be deceived into thinking that one of Ionia's ruined temples has been resurrected there.

ELEUSIS, THE TELESTERIUM

Then she went, and to the kings who deal justice, Triptolemus and Diocles, the horse-driver and to doughty Eumolopus and Celeus, leader of the people, she showed the conduct of her rites and taught them all her mysteries, to Triptolemus and Polyxeinus also—awful mysteries which no one may in any way transgress or pry into or utter, for deep awe of the gods checks the voice. Happy is he among men upon earth who has seen these mysteries; but he who is uninitiate and has no part in them, never has lot of like good things once he is dead, down in the darkness and gloom. HOMERIC HYMN TO DEMETER

Plates 38, 39, figs. 70, 71

In the sanctuary of Demeter, a peculiar and mysterious cult (cf. page 47) brought into being a peculiar building, with which the whole Greek world had nothing to compare: the telesterium. A relatively narrow sacred precinct confined forbiddingly by strong fortified walls was almost entirely filled by the immense cuboid of a totally enclosed hypostyle hall built of dark stone over a square ground-plan (about 177 by 177 ft.). Even the Doric portico of Pentelic marble, with 12 by 2 columns, could not give it the bodily extroversion of a peripteral temple. The great, dark rectangle of walls did not reveal—it hid. Its architectonic tendency did not press outwards towards self-display, but withdrew inwards about a 'mystic' centre. One would like to think that, in the telesterium, the closed, pre-Greek megaron lived on, raised to the colossal.

Being the whole point of the building, its interior was unusually complex. Against all four walls lay flights of eight steps, like a theatre's, which together accommodated almost 4,000 standing spectators, and were only interrupted by the gangways to the six entrances. These, two of which pierced each of the three accessible sides, formed the sole openings in the outer walls. The rear side, together with the steps, was hewn from the rock of the ascending slope. A theatre hall, one could suppose, if an essential feature of a theatre—the performance on a stage—were not lacking. What was to be watched must rather have taken place in the middle, within the square of steps. Yet the central area was so cluttered up by seven rows of six columns (i.e. forty-two in all) that there could be no question of an unobstructed view. The company assembled here to participate in

399

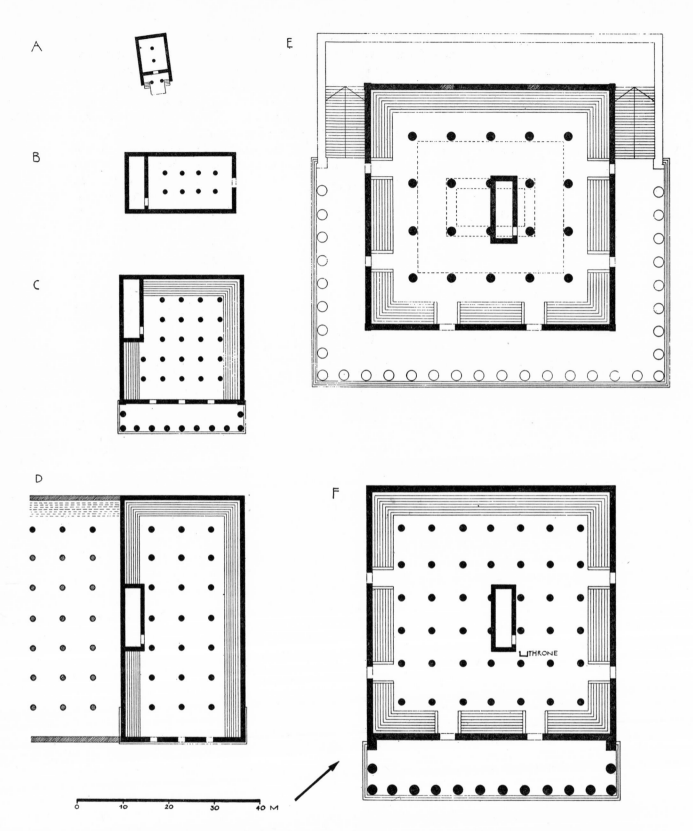

70 Eleusis. Development of telesterium. Plans (1 : 800). New drawing after J. Travlos, 1950
A: Mycenaean temple, before 1200 B.C. B: 'megaron' of Solon's time, before 560 (its adytum formed nucleus of
later buildings C to F, as 'anactoron'). C: Pisistratid telesterium, c. 525. D: telesterium of Cimon's time, c. 470
(only right half executed). E: Ictinus's design (black: confirmed, white: hypothetical), c. 440. F: executed telesterium
(fifth cent. B.C., portico second half of fourth cent. B.C., renewed in second cent. A.D.)

71 Eleusis. Anactoron and hierophant's throne in telesterium F. J. Travlos, 1950/51

the ritual proceedings more intimately than as mere onlookers.

We hear of 'erratic journeys and toilsome processions, endless troubled wanderings through darkness', during which the initiates experienced every dread of the nether world, until they finally entered 'clearings, blessed fields'. Thus, the large central area with its labyrinthine forest of columns seems to have provided space, during the long nocturnal celebration, for dramatic processions, in the course of which the myths of the sacred marriage between Demeter and Zeus, of Hades's abduction of their daughter Persephone, of the mother's search and lament, and, lastly, of the promise concerning the after-life made to the initiates who associated themselves with all this became movingly real. When, after a night full of anxiety, pierced by the dim light of torches, dawn brought the moment of deliverance, the shutters of a broad aperture in the roof (opaion) were opened—or so it is inferred from the tradition— the 'great light' suddenly broke into the hall, and, in deep silence, the priest of Demeter held up the goddess's sacred gift, the ear of corn.

The building was precisely adapted to these practices. Its mystical seclusion, the steps for spectators, and the forest of columns in the middle now becomes intelligible—yet not every question has been answered. Could this strange room have been a temple? Where did the cult images of Demeter and Persephone stand? Furthermore, there is a tradition of an 'anactoron' (palace) of the goddess in the telesterium, a kind of holy of holies that can only have stood at the centre of the hall. It was thought to have been defined by curtains between the middle columns, until, a few years ago, an important discovery not only solved this riddle, but also shed a bright light on the telesterium's development from the ancestral form of the megaron to a gigantic hypostyle hall. A narrow rectangle in the foundation, backing against the two central columns, was identified as belonging to the anactoron. Near the latter's entrance stood the canopied throne of Demeter's *fig. 71* priest, the hierophant. It was in this 'chapel', then, that the old wooden statue of Demeter was set up, and the whole building is thus shown to have been her temple. Though renewed down to the foundations in Roman times, the anactoron also constituted the fixed focus of all earlier stages of the structure,

401

which had expanded as round a germ-cell during a centuries-long process of consistent growth.

We are going to trace this process. In it the fruitful interaction of religion and architecture, as well as the peculiar logicality of Greek building, will be revealed as nowhere else.

fig. 70

In the second millennium, there stood upon the rocky slope of the then already settled acropolis of Eleusis a small temple of megaron type, unusual on account of the podium extending before its front, and flanked by little stairways (A). Were holy things displayed here as early as the Mycenaean period to a congregation assembled in the open? Were there pre-Greek mysteries? One can hardly doubt the continuity of the cult, for around 600 a bigger 'megaron' arose on the same site, but now facing north (B). At its rear end, a special chamber called an adytum was separated off, as in the Demeter megaron at Gaggera (page 421); and precisely this 'forbidden' chamber continued to exist as the anactoron till into Roman times! The south-west corner of this megaron has survived. Its stones were fitted together with endless patience in curvilinear joints as were later those of the retaining-wall at Delphi (plate 74).

Only a few local families then took part in the observances that, as the Homeric hymn to Demeter proclaims, were instituted by the goddess herself. After Eleusis had become an Attic deme, the small room was soon no longer able to contain the stream of pilgrims from Athens. Towards the end of the sixth century, the Pisistratids therefore erected a larger initiation temple (C), which now displayed all the features of the huge later building. It was a square hall (about 88½ by 88½ ft.), which, produced by doubling the old megaron breadthways, contained the anactoron in one corner at the back. The entrance wall, now provided with three portals, faced down the slope again, like the Mycenaean temple. Flights of seven steps lined the other three walls, and the central area was closely planted with —it would seem—Ionic columns (5 rows of 5 columns, except where the anactoron's wall took the place of 3 supports). While the use of Ionic columns in an interior is already an Attic trait, the construction of an ample Doric portico (with 9 or 10 columns plus another behind each angle support) before the front wall expresses even more plainly the Attic sense of monumentality and gift for creating unusual effects, for producing tensions in the varied succession of architectural forms. Painted palmette antefixes and the corner-piece of the pediment sima with an expressive ram's head have survived from the marble roof of the new structure. Both are so closely related to the corresponding parts of the old Athena temple on the Acropolis (page 370), that one would readily believe that the same builders had been at work. At the same date, the precinct was shut off like a monastery from the outside world by means of powerful fortified walls and towers. In front of the temple—for such it remained—an oval terrace buttressed by polygonal masonry was constructed, and on it the two altars of Demeter and Persephone must have stood.

The Persians set fire to this highly sacred building. When, under Cimon's ascendancy, work began towards 465 on a replacement, this was conceived in the newly awakened classical spirit. It was to have four times the area of the archaic structure, which meant creating the, till then, biggest roofed space in Greece (D). However, the truly classical idea was that of setting the anactoron, the religious focus of the whole, freely at the centre of the room. Evidently, the young Attic state undertook too much with this colossal project, for only the northern half was executed. Though the anactoron was in fact freed from the corner, it still clung modestly to the south wall of the oblong hypostyle hall (about 88½ by 170½ ft. with 3 rows of 7 columns), which again had steps along three sides. All the same, necessary preparations were made for the original scheme. Huge lumps of rock had to be broken off, and the terrace enlarged. The temenos had to be extended by means of a new fortification wall, now following straight lines, with massive round towers at the corners, in order to make room for the gigantic building.

It was left to Pericles and Ictinus, the Parthenon architect, to initiate the new structure on the grand scale prescribed by the master of Cimon's day (Coroebus?), and, in so doing, to raise the old design to a plan of inward grandeur and pellucid maturity that even the next generation hardly understood, let alone reached. Ictinus was unable to complete this building—probably his most imposing project. From marks in the rock, prepared foundations, and rock-cut steps, we can deduce his plan (E), and we visualize it with more sympathy than the building later actually constructed, which sinks back to the level of design D.

Ictinus kept to the square-based cuboid of space (169 ft. 1⅞ in. by 162 ft. 2½ in. in the clear) planned under Cimon; but he arranged all the architectural elements of the interior—entrances, steps, and columns—about the 'holy centre' of the enormous hall, thus composing, in his precisely articulated formal language, the first real centrally-planned space of antiquity. The doors now pierce in pairs all the accessible outer walls, and two more doors are to be assumed at a higher level even for the rear side

38, 39

embedded in the rocky slope. Previously set along only three sides, steps now run right round the hall.

Above all, however, Ictinus did away with his predecessors' intricate forest of columns. In project D, 7 by 7 (i.e. 49) columns were to have carried the roof. Ictinus accomplished this with 5 by 4 (i.e. 20) supports, which no longer stand beneath a passive, criss-cross network of beams (cf. fig. 71), but spread round the room in two mighty circuits. His object here was not only to make it possible, through extremely wide interaxials, to look across the previously heavily obstructed hall (with a maximum span of 33 ft. $0\frac{1}{8}$ in., even the clear breadth of the Parthenon naos is exceeded); he also aimed, by means of a significant disposition of the columns, to enhance this space to the most lucid expression of its own nature. Nevertheless, the outer, two-storied circuit of 4 by 5 columns, which, over its middle architraves, bears large galleries reached through the two doors set higher up in the back wall, has a clear enough connexion with the 'space-moulding' colonnades that ran round three sides of the Parthenon naos. Now, in conformity with the centralized plan, these rows join up as a rectangle. A second, inner circuit, likewise in two tiers, surrounds the 'holy centre' with the anactoron. Over it, the ceiling and roof are, no doubt, breached by the opaion aperture (see above). Thus, at the most solemn moment of the mysteries, bright daylight would have suddenly poured down upon this centre. Between the inner and outer circuits a wide processional passageway remains free.

Characteristic of the general tone of Periclean architecture and illustrative of the all-pervading principle of 'harmonious contrasts' is the fact that this central area is not, as would be so natural, evenly developed in both its directions, that certain tensions are imparted to it by slightly emphasized axes. Thus, the room's depth axis coincides with a row of column axes, whereas its transverse one lies in a gap. The oblong of the anactoron is parried by the rectangle of the inner column circuit set athwart it. To me, it seems that the columns cross the space either way at a different interval and in a different quantity so that, like the lively interplay of breadth and depth of space, they shall counter the stiffness of the geometrical scheme. Accordingly, one would also expect this architect to have produced a new external form for the structure in opposition to its spacious interior: a dense peristyle rising up powerfully. Remains have, in fact, been discovered of the foundations of one, which was plainly intended to enclose the block of the cella on three sides.

Steps cut in the rock ascend towards the back of the building to a rear terrace, which, set on a level with the galleries, flows organically into the ambulatory. The arrangement is such an indispensable component of Ictinus's design that it could not be separated from it, even though the foundations were not actually laid until two generations later. It seems that this part of the famous project was commenced very belatedly, and, to the irreparable injury of the whole, never finished. (N.B., there is no lack of divergent readings of the 'peristyle' foundations. According to the latest, it was decided to line the walls of the hall—enlarged to about 246 by $206\frac{1}{2}$ ft.[!]—with, now, two tiers of steps. Furthermore, a narrower and lower front portico, with two rows of eight Ionic columns, is said to be deducible for the Periclean structure from building accounts.)

Ictinus's project was ill-starred. Only in the northern half were the foundations of the internal supports constructed; to their south, telesterium D remained in existence, it being intended to demolish it at the last moment, so as not to interrupt the annual celebrations. When, under the pre-eminent architect's successors—their names, Metagenes and Xenocles, are given by Plutarch (*Per.* 13, 4)—the hall was finally completed in its full dimensions (F), the earlier, impenetrable multiplicity of columns (now 7 by 6, total 42) was reverted to, perhaps because the priests and congregation insisted on keeping their old, mystical maze. The scheme for a three-sided 'peristyle' having been abandoned, the builders confined themselves to raising a Doric portico before the east side—in total conflict with the conception of the hall, which had fully matching entrances on three sides, and hence required matching porticoes. Elucidated for us by accurate building records, the dodecastyle front portico, which was built between 330 and 310 under the Eleusinian architect Philon, none the less still reflected some features of the Ictinus design. The interaxial of 15 Doric ft. (16 ft. $1\frac{3}{4}$ in.), and, with it, the rhythm of the colonnade seem to have remained the same, though, in keeping with the style of the time, the columns were much slimmer (height of about 36 ft. 4 in. = 6 lower diams. of 6 Doric ft. or 6 ft. $5\frac{5}{8}$ in.). This interaxial is related to the lower diameter as 4 to 10, possibly as a modification of the originally intended Parthenon proportion of 4 to 9, to which columns with a lower diameter of 7 ft. $1\frac{7}{8}$ in. would lend themselves.

Now add in thought another contrast, which expresses the nature of the two components: behind the colonnade of dazzlingly bright Pentelic marble loomed dark and mysterious the plain block of the cella, built in blue-grey Eleusinian limestone. Here employed for the first time, this was soon used to achieve similar effects of contrast on the Propylaea, for the statue of Zeus at Olympia, and on the Erechtheum.

The pediment resting above the over-177-ft.-wide portico was more than 16 ft. tall at the apex of its tympanum. So hypertrophied a structure must have appeared oppressive on top of the slender columns. For the Ictinus peristyle with its frontal width of 246 ft., only a hip-roof, not a gable, can have been projected. As a shallow covering similar on all sides, it would have been very much more in harmony with the basic idea of the centrally planned structure than the ridge-roof built later.

Philon's hall remained the last enlargement of the telesterium, which, after being partly destroyed by barbarians towards A.D. 170, was later faithfully restored.

Finally, let us try to visualize Ictinus' huge hall, expressively divided by its two circuits of columns into the three rectangular zones of galleries, passageway, and 'holy centre'. How venerably touching that tiny little reliquary temple, the anactoron, would have looked in the middle of such a boldly covered expanse, even though the whole gigantic space was there to serve it. As Ictinus wanted it, the telesterium would have been the most important spatial creation in the Hellenic world. If one reflects that the domes of the Pantheon and St. Peter's, with their diameters of about 140 ft., could have been comfortably inscribed in this approximately 164-ft.-square space, one will be able to comprehend not only the scale of the Greek hypostyle hall, but also its character, which is in plain contrast to that of the domes. Ictinus's rectangular room, understood according to the laws of Euclidean geometry as, so to speak, a cuboid body turned inwards, has an objective largeness that could be made completely clear and intelligible but not 'extravagant' by order and proportion. The two domes seem to capture eternity, and they provoke in the beholder an illusion of infinite spaces through the rounded form, through perspective, and through light control, which play their calculated game with the psychological peculiarities of sight. Hence, the notion that one could place the dome of St. Peter's in the telesterium is basically absurd. If Ictinus's hall were standing it would, in its completeness, in its form developed out of intellectual relations free from the subjective and the semblant, appear to us as having a more measured, tangible mass than those boundless, soul-stirring examples of space-architecture.

The short, brilliant history of Magna Graecia or *ΜΕΓΑΛΗ 'ΕΛΛΑΣ*, as the Hellenes themselves used to call the spacious, fertile world of South Italy, was chequered, exciting, exuberant, and directed by great, often reckless men. To the predominantly Dorian colonists, it seemed to promise the fulfilment of all their dreams of power, wealth, and glory, which the niggardly motherland, grown too cramped, had denied them. These same features are displayed by the architectural history of the West in an unusually faithful reflection. The architects in the new cities strove in every way to enhance and extend the heritage of Doric forms that they had brought with them. In impatient and ever different essays, they attempted to wrest from this simple architectural framework their own ardent vitality, their own expansive ideas about space. As was bound to happen, this brought into being a new, wholly independent architecture, which had little more in common with that of the old homeland than the stock and sequence of its forms.

Two things characterize this change. In the mother-country, the ancient faith, which, filled with the dread of daemons, with mystery, and with sombre rites of expiation, had its architectonic equivalent in the closed megaron temple, was conquered by the 'Olympian religion' and its intellectually lucid approach to the gods. Accordingly, so far as we can see in retrospect, the peripteral temple had there to radiate in all directions with equal architectonic intensity the splendour of the deity whose image formed its spiritual centre. In the West, the cults of the chthonic powers retained the upper hand, Demeter and Persephone being universally worshipped as the mistresses of all Sicily. The peripteral structure, which in the sixth century lacked an opisthodomus and, hence, a balance between its east and west ends, was here derived from the old megaron. At the back of the cella, the cult statue was hidden away in a dark, inaccessible chamber called the 'adytum'. It there formed, not the centre, but the innermost goal of the construction, which was conceived as a progressional series of spaces directed from the east end to the adytum. This automatically resulted in a special emphasis of the entrance front, which, with the usual colonial taste for the imposing, could never be too grand. At the east end, we find enormous altars, flights of steps, double colonnades, greatly enlarged porticoes, and huge, magnificent doors, whereas the back, being deprived of columns in-antis, wasted away.

The second factor is the 'discovery'—as one has to call it in comparison with Greece—of space. Ample rooms, ample porticoes—that was the aim; and it tallies with the fact that in Sicily highly developed mathematics and geometry, practically applied already early on, produced a system of timbering that, around the middle of the sixth century, made it possible to cover greater spans than ever before. Rafters and ceiling beams were joined together as static triangles able to bear a load, and additionally braced. The presence of such roof trusses in very early Sicilian buildings—the second megaron at Gaggera, with a span of 27 ft. 9½ in., and the Geloan treasury at Olympia, with one of 31 ft. 9⅛ in.—has been established. In Greece, where like effects were certainly not aspired to, trussed constructions only appeared with the coming of the Hellenistic age. (The span of the Geloan treasury was never exceeded there in the sixth century, and, in the fifth, not until the nave of the Parthenon, with 36 ft. 3⅛ in.) Thus, it was practicable to fashion the temple naos without internal supports into an often huge room, which, in the case of the Olympieum at Acragas, achieved a clear width of over 42½ ft. One could also disassociate the porticoes and pteromata more and more from the cella walls, making them independent spaces into the depths of which the core of the structure withdrew almost entirely. The bodily connexion between cella and peristyle, between trunk and limbs, was thus relinquished in exchange for a new power: the effect of bounded spaciousness, long before it was even thought of in Greece itself. Possibly both these tendencies were reinforced by native Italian inclinations which, as is well known, before they reached fulfilment in history first found expression in Roman architecture.

All the same, one has to accept the remarkable fact that Greeks, transferred to a richer and more spacious foreign region, forgot their inborn sense of moderation, of *sophrosyne*, and, starting out from the same point, arrived at an architecture flatly opposed in spirit to that of their homeland. Because of the Western trading cities' boundless enthusiasm for building, most and by far the biggest Doric temples are to be found there, not in Greece. This fact should

fig. 84

not mislead us into basing our conception of Doric architecture simply on the majority of what survives; nor should we attach too much importance to the similarity of the forms. For the other side to this impetuous development towards such new, such boldly determined goals is, up to a point, the fact that the Doric order, which in Greece changed and matured in a process of steady growth directed by an inner compulsion, was here retained almost unaltered as a thing inherited once for all, and, therefore, in some degree stagnant. The comparison of Western with homeland Greek capitals has led again and again to an unwarranted early dating of Sicilian buildings, because forms still appeared there at the end of the sixth century that were already out of date in the Peloponnese half a century before. In the West, the homeland's assured sense of form very quickly disappeared altogether. We meet in the architectural decoration an ever grander, but often rank luxuriance—above all on the terracotta revetments of the cornices, covered with multi-coloured ornaments. It was often attempted here to impose order on the design by schematic, abstract means through the use of numerical connexions and geometric axes—again in contrast to the mother-country, where architects preferred to set the parts of their buildings in bodily relationships. Anyway, this produced towards the end of the sixth century ground-plans of a rational clarity and consistency that did not appear in the homeland till decades later (temple of Athena, Paestum, page 410).

At the same time, architectural schools of different character very soon developed, even in neighbouring cities. Syracuse began this, proceeding from the solid Corinthian tradition. Selinus and, as the most recently established, Acragas followed Syracuse, but shortly coined styles of their own. A special role was played by the Achaean foundations Paestum (Poseidonia) and Metapontum, less on account of the gaudy enrichment of their Doric temples with Ionic decorations, than because there, in barbarian surroundings capable of exercising a certain influence on the appearance of at least one temple, the Greeks' awareness of form remained fresh and alive. It brought forth divergent, but still corporeally dense members and forms, which possess that inner exactness and distinctness inherent in all things Greek.

We have not been able to discuss here an important link between the architecture of the motherland and that of the West, namely Corcyra, the Corinthian daughter-city on the westernmost island of Greece, which absorbed an earlier Ionian colony. Many peculiarities of Western architecture could have stemmed from this city's remarkable temple of Artemis with its ambulatory two interaxials deep and its column forms related to Western ones.

So far, we have been talking about the sixth century, the archaic period. The picture completely changes with the advent of the classical period. Around the turn of the century, a natural end was reached; the development, so to speak, got bogged down. Every variation of the ground-plan schema with double front portico and enlarged peristyle had been tried. In temple G at Selinus and in the Olympieum at Acragas, which was begun after 480 as the mightiest late embodiment of archaic aspirations, the dimensions were almost overpoweringly vast. People could not help gradually becoming aware, too, of the clumsiness of the architectural forms that had been unchanged now for nearly a century.

First, still timid attempts to bring the capitals up to date were already being made round about 500 (temple G, temple of Heracles). Then, after 480, the mother-country's classical style, which made each building as a whole into a resonant unity, had an enormous effect. At Syracuse, Himera, Paestum, Selinus, and Acragas eight peripteral temples were built in quick succession that scarcely acknowledged the hitherto prevailing local tradition. After the West's 'Salamis', the victory over Carthage at Himera in 480, this movement advanced like an awakening of the mind, a second comprehension of the native heritage. The most important model must have been the temple of Zeus at Olympia, with which two of the West's most noble buildings, the Hera temple at Paestum and the temple of Hera (E) at Selinus, are connected. Very soon, however, a new separatist and conservative tendency, similar to that of the sixth century, set in. The capital forms, which in the motherland progressively tautened during the fifth century, here retained the early classical spread almost unchanged for over fifty years (temple of Concord), and the ground-plan was again strongly penetrated by the old schematism. One example will perhaps be enough. With the new classical conception, not only the opisthodomus was adopted but also the Greek narrowing of the corner interaxials. The fact that angle contraction had previously *fig. 6* been entirely unknown in the West is a sufficient sign of the latter's insensitivity to incongruities in a building's organic structure. Obviously, the variance between triglyphs and columns, or else the widened metopes at the corner interaxials, were not felt to be at all disturbing. Yet the clearly visible contraction of these angle interaxials—for the homeland Greeks, an indispensable means of 'consolidating' the corners of a peristyle—which was now introduced, soon began to go against the grain with the Western architects and their mathematician's sense of order.

They tackled the problem by adopting the most intricate measures, and finally enforced a settlement that was, however, only apparent and optical (temple of Concord, page 441). Subdued and restrained, the Western character survived even in classical buildings. The Sicilian naos continued to be a room covered without the aid of internal columns. A new solemn and disciplined ardour was expressed in the great altars with flights of steps, which, set before the temple fronts, formed part of a composition, and in the setting, designed to be seen from a good distance, of the Acragas temples. At the same time, the growing tendency to proportion in pure numerical relationships gave these last Doric peripteral buildings of Sicily a touch of cool distinction.

In the homeland, the temple of Zeus at Olympia marked the climax and conclusion of pure Doric, because the classical architecture of Athens, overwhelmingly eclipsing all others, dictated what was built even in the Peloponnese. In the West, to which the Attic architectural hegemony did not extend, the Doric style died immaculate. What Greek poets proclaimed desirable—to expire at the zenith of one's life—was granted the flourishing cities of Magna Graecia. Towards the close of the fifth century, Selinus and Acragas were reduced to rubble, while Paestum fell into barbarian hands. Spared by the hereditary foe, Carthage, and by Rome, which was Greece's heir here as in the East, the temples have stood to the present day. Mighty Syracuse, which held out almost two centuries longer, produced nothing further in the same class, apart from fortifications and the grandiose buildings of tyrants, such as Hieron II's 650-ft.-long altar.

PAESTUM

The three temples of Paestum (Greek Poseidonia) certainly do not owe their exceptional fame simply to the fact that, when the traveller from the north has crossed the rocky barrier closing the Sorrentine peninsula and entered the changed, spacious countryside of true 'Magna Graecia', he there, for the first time, comes upon Greek temples standing erect—though what travellers, since Winckelmann and Goethe, have followed this route! It is, above all, the quality, the intense vitality of these temples that seems to impress itself upon the visitor's sensibility.

Paestum was founded by the Achaean colony Sybaris towards 600. The Achaeans, who, as heirs of the Mycenaean tradition, were able to hold their own on the north coast of the Peloponnese against the assaults of the Dorian invasion—interbreeding, of course, with sections of the Dorian and Ionian population—evidently passed on to their daughter-cities a Doric formal vocabulary enriched with Ionic elements. Two centuries of rapid, brilliant florescence were granted to these cities, before they fell into the clutches of the warlike Lucanians, who pressed down from the mountains. Later, after 273 B.C., they were annexed first to Latium, then to the expanding Roman state.

The three temples stand at the centre of the city, which lies in a broad plain that is enclosed by mountains in the east and, towards the west, slopes gently down to the sea. There being no citadel, no acropolis to dedicate to the gods, two large precincts were left open for them in the middle of the city area. (Arranged round the intersecting axes of two streets, the remains of forum, amphitheatre and houses belong to the Latin period, as do the well-preserved city walls. Nevertheless, the Greek city appears, like the old Selinus, already to have possessed a rectangular network of streets, and the Greek wall is probably to be sought along the lines of the later one, which encloses the city area as a great oblong with four gates.)

The southern temenos was dedicated to Hera. In it stand the earliest and the latest of the three temples: the so-called Basilica and the large temple of Hera II or so-called temple of Poseidon. The second precinct, about 550 yds. further north and consecrated to Athena, contains the small temple of Athena or so-called temple of Ceres (Demeter). All three peripteral structures face uniformly east. Remains of broad altars for burnt offerings found before their fronts plainly mark them out as temples. The building material, a hard but porous shell-limestone, was quarried locally.

Finds of votive offerings have securely established the identity of the temples' real mistresses, and made it necessary to correct the familiar names. We cannot here enlarge upon the important recent discoveries: smaller treasuries or naiskoi in the Hera precinct;

a little, earlier temple with rich roof terracottas beside the temple of Athena; and, above all, the uncovering of an entire sanctuary, again dedicated to Hera, outside the city at the mouth of the river Silaris. For, as exemplary embodiments of three ages of Greek architecture, the big peripteral temples fill our horizon.

THE TEMPLE OF HERA I,   *Plates I, XXV, 108–114,*
so-called BASILICA   *figs. 72, 73*

Over the still complete crepidoma (three steps; stylobate 80 ft. 5⅜ in. by 178 ft. 0⅝ in.) of the earliest Hera temple, built shortly after the middle of the sixth century, the entire peristyle with its unusual count of 9 by 18 columns stands erect. Above it runs the architrave, which in places—especially on the west and east sides—still carries the masonry that backed the lost triglyph frieze. It is true that corona and pediments are missing, and that the cella walls have been demolished down to their foundations (only the antae and three columns of the pronaos entrance survive); but this alone cannot account for the fact that, whichever direction the building is viewed from, it is not perceived as a coherent body. One is constantly made aware of the bewildering multiplicity of its columns, or else the eye is held by the insistent presence of the individual supports, whereas the neighbouring Hera temple II attracts one's gaze as something just as strongly unitary. This phenomenon must rather be rooted in the nature of the temple—in its overall plan and its separate members. The columns are, so to speak, imbued with an urge to express themselves individually. Like a drove of independent living creatures, they form an orderly file, but do not combine as a real 'order', as an organism at rest. Though they have, of course, a static function in the building, they bear their load in such an irregular, wilful way that they are no longer related at all to the entablature they have to support. In concrete terms, the shaft is not excessively thick-set (height of 21 ft. 1⅞ in. = 4·45 lower diams. of 4 ft. 9¼ in.), so that its effect is not that of massiveness and weight found in the temples at Syracuse and Corinth. All the stronger, however, is its taper (by about ⅓ lower diam.), which expresses its organic upward thrust. This shaft is characterized even more distinctly as a plastic body by a conspicuous swelling or entasis, which here appeared for the first time and more markedly than ever again. 'The surface seems to be pressed outwards and stretched to bursting point by an internal expansion made apparent and contained by the arrises of the twenty flutes' (F. Krauss).

The shaft literally bores into the shallow echinus, which spreads out widely, as though under enormous pressure. At the point where these two members meet so directly and crudely, a hollow has been cut into the end of the shaft, and in it nestles a wreath of sculptured leaves. They are distributed without regard for the flutes, thereby accentuating still further the separation of the parts. Around the bottom of the echinus there runs a shallow moulded border, which must once have been painted with delicate ornaments. At the west end, such motifs— flower patterns, guilloches, or simple astragals— have actually been worked in relief, and, moreover, differently on each capital. Here, the exquisite and dainty is combined in a fresh and natural manner with the extremely ponderous. (This graceful enrichment is probably to be regarded as an Ionic touch, whereas the foliated hollow seems to be originally Achaean. It had already appeared in the second millennium on Mycenaean columns, and was exactly repeated on early Peloponnesian capitals— e.g. at Tiryns and Tegea—and on those of the Corinthian colony Corcyra.)

Normally developed in the form of revetted wall ends, the antae too have been conceived as independent bodies. The heavy, square-sectioned pillars taper—indeed, they display the plump entasis of the columns, and are topped, as the complement of the convex column capital, by a widely flaring concave one, which supports the 6½-ft.-square abacus.

Three features of the peristyle attract attention: the seemingly endless columns (9 by 18); the nonsensical contraction of the front interaxials by no less than 9 in. in comparison with the side ones (a similar difference appears on the more or less contemporary temple C at Selinus, except that there, logically, the front interaxials open wider); and, lastly, the odd number of supports at the ends, where, in consequence, a shaft comes at the centre instead of a space.

All this stems from the curiously designed groundplan, the naos having been divided into two compartments by a row of seven columns that ran exactly down the middle. Supports were necessary for covering the room, which was 37 ft. 8 in. broad. To place them at the centre—i.e. under the roof ridge— was, no doubt, the most natural solution, and the earliest Greek temples, at Thermum, Samos, and Prinias, were planned in the same way. This could not, however, be harmonized with either an axial entrance or a cult image set up in the middle of the naos. Consequently, the tripartite division of the interior and corresponding hexastyle front established themselves as the norm in Greece as early as the seventh century.

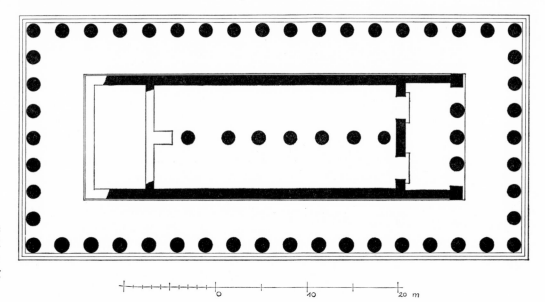

72 Paestum, temple of Hera I, so-called Basilica. Plan (1 : 400). New drawing by F. Krauss

The Achaean settlers, it is plain, doggedly pre-served this early archaic motif till well into the sixth century (cf. Apollo temple, Metapontum). Here, two entrances correspond to the two naves. So as to make room for the cult statue, the last interaxial but one of the inner supports was evidently widened by 3 ft. 3⅜ in. These columns were set in the space as sovereign bodies independent of the architectonic continuity: they have the same monumental bulk as the external ones, and carried an equally heavy architrave, on which a similar moulding in sandstone also probably rested. Their excessive weight, overwhelming in the interior space, did not trouble the builders at all, as one can see. For, owing to the subsequent raising of the floor, they appear even more squat than the external ones. Moreover, in connexion with a change of plan, the door and rear walls of the naos were pressed so close against the first and last internal columns that they overlap with them. Hence, the bodies of these columns, carefully shielded by the walls, remained notably free from injury.

The inner row of supports stretched like a back-bone through the entire building to the fronts, where it ended in the middle columns. Each nave corresponds in breadth to two end interaxials, and the same goes for the ambulatory, which is equally wide on all sides. This gives (at any rate in the original design, which, detected by F. Krauss during a recent investigation, was later modified by pushing the side walls slightly outwards and the door wall in-wards) a ground-plan schema of geometric clarity marked out, according to Ionic custom, by the wall and column axes. First, the temple's length between the angle axes was fixed at the sacred measure of 100

Ionian ells (172 ft. 8⅝ in.)—which is further evidence of the Ionic component. Then, the temple was divided lengthways into four strips—two pteromata and two naos compartments—each two interaxials wide. Eight end interaxials (i.e. nine columns) were thus obtained. The sides of the cella were brought into a simple 2 : 7 relationship, and at either end of it were partitioned off the pronaos and adytum, both two interaxials deep. Hence, with the porticoes and pteromata added, the whole temple design embodied the proportion 4 : 9, or 8 by 18 interaxials.

This logical basic plan has, however, been frustrated and disordered by the division of the long sides into only 17, not 18, interaxials (i.e. 18 col-umns). Precisely this irregularity is what makes the end interaxials so much narrower than those on the flanks (9 ft. 5 in. and 10 ft. 2 in. respectively). It has been surmised that the remarkable 9 by 18 (=2 × 9) arrangement of columns, which was, so to speak, forced upon the building, 'means' something, that sacred numbers are involved, as in the length measurement of 100 ells. With such a process of design, partly on abstract, geometric lines, and partly dictated by symbolic numbers, it is quite obvious that a clearer, more architectonic organism could not have come into being. What is more, making the ambulatory two interaxials wide in obedience to an inclination rooted in the West, and here perhaps communicated by the above-mentioned temple at Corcyra, inevitably meant dissolving the close union of cella and peristyle.

On the other hand, a feature of good Pelopon-nesian stock should not be overlooked. Unaffected by the tendency, spreading in Sicily, to over-

72, 73

409

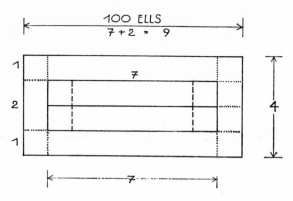

73 Paestum. Schema of design of so-called Basilica. Sketch

emphasize the east end, the cella was placed symmetrically in the middle of the peristyle, so that the ambulatory, having the same depth at either end, also has the same expressive value there. It is true that a closed adytum, usual in the West, supplanted the opisthodomus possibly provided for in the first design, and thereby ousted the crucial part, corresponding to the pronaos, of the Greek 'all-sided' temple arrangement.

With that, enough has at last been said of project and plan. It is not there, but in the formation of its individual members that the actual life of the temple flows, and so we still have to enquire into the appearance of the lost entablature and roof. The Doric taenia was here replaced by a Lesbian cyma separately worked in fine sandstone. Though it has vanished without trace, a Doric triglyph frieze certainly followed above. The surviving masonry that once backed it indicates its height: 3 ft. 3¾ in. Notches in the architrave into which the crow-bar was inserted when the heavy blocks were positioned reveal how it was divided up. There were two triglyphs and metopes for every interaxial, and they were related to each other in size approximately as 2 to 3. Above, one would expect another Ionic sandstone moulding with the corona, also lost, resting upon it. Only the terracotta revetments of the latter have survived: slabs painted with variegated ornaments and furnished with lions' heads, which here were not real spouts. Beautiful fragments have been found, too, of the terracotta sima with its intricate band of carved and painted flowers, which was pierced to let the water run off.

This completes our hasty sketch of the temple and also of the first stage in the development of building activity at Paestum. The ingenuous mixing of Doric and Ionic forms, the wilful isolation of the members, and the schematic nature of the planning are amply compensated for by an innate feeling for plasticity.

'The Basilica is not architecture in the strict sense, but an accumulation of sculptural bodies with an architectonic function. There is something physical and corporeal about the building, but it is not the image of a single living body; instead, every member has separately this quality of animation' (F. Krauss).

THE TEMPLE OF ATHENA *Plates 122, 123, figs. 74-77*

Compared with the 'primitive' Basilica, the late archaic Athena temple or so-called temple of Demeter, which lies in a separate temenos, appears graceful and well balanced. This is due less to the peripteral building's smaller dimensions—its columns are only 13 in. shorter—than to the carefully thought out, disciplined design and the refined proportions of the members, as well as to the uncommonly delicate and rich Ionic decorative forms. The savage, almost daemonic expressive power of the earlier columns has here been toned down. Although their outward form has apparently been retained, their character is altered by small but decisive changes. Instead of being a divider cut into the shaft, the ring of leaves seems to cover up the join between shaft and capital as an organic, mediating addition. The entasis is less marked, while the echinus, though still shallow and spreading, leads up to the horizontal, oppressive members of the entablature in a flowing curve. Taken as a whole, the column has become slimmer (height of 20 ft. 1 in. = 4·85 lower diams. of 4 ft. 1⅝ in.; Basilica 4·45 lower diams.). Thus, the columns now really are members of the structural body.

This body is intended to be regarded from all sides as a concordant whole. The architect knew how to make evident the well-defined mathematical order that informed his ground-plan. Here, even before it had become canonical in the motherland, the column count of 6 by 13 was achieved. What is more, the interaxial, now exactly the same at ends and sides, was for the very first time regarded as the mensural unit of the ground-plan. As with the Basilica, the starting-point was a 'sacred' length measurement of 100 Doric ft. (here 1 ft. = nearly 13 in.). Thus, the temple is a hecatompedon. The stylobate's length of 100 Doric ft. seems to have been first related to its breadth as 9 to 4, but then extended by 3⅛ in. (47 ft. 8⅜ in. by 107 ft. 10½ in.). For thereby the sides of the rectangle formed by the column axes could be proportioned as 5 to 12 (40 by 96 Doric ft.)—and this corresponds exactly to the number of the interaxials (5 by 12), which thus all come out the same size: 8 ft. 7⅜ in. or 8 Doric ft.

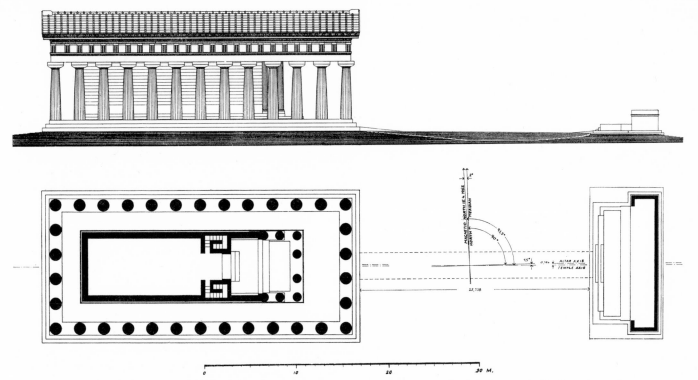

74–75 Paestum, temple and altar of Athena. South side elevation and plan (1 : 400). F. Krauss, 1960

fig. 74   Just as simple are the proportions of the elevation. The column height of 20 ft. 1 in. amounts to $2\frac{1}{3}$ interaxials, while the height of the entablature plus the sima (10 ft. $0\frac{1}{2}$ in.) equals half the column height. Like relationships also inform the frieze. The breadth of the metope is related to its height as 5 to 6 and to the triglyph's breadth as 5 to 2. In order that the third triglyph should come axially above the second column, the corner metope had to be greatly widened (fig. 6B). Angle contraction, which would, of course, have upset the systematic arrangement of the ground-plan, was not introduced.

122   A further detail probably makes a decisive contribution to the temple's serene appearance. The horizontal rectangle formed by the architrave, which still outlines the cuboid of the building most distinctly even today, is proportioned as 1 to 2·3, just like the vertical rectangle constituted by the architrave and the end columns. Here, we meet for the first time that 'interlocking' of the proportions, which, in the Parthenon, is expressed as an all-embracing, unifying principle. What we, at best, perceive as something vaguely agreeable and harmonious must have been seen more penetratingly and consciously by the more practised Greek eye, as architects for centuries devoted their highest skill to the precise adjustment of such proportions. The Pythagorean school that flourished here round about the same time may have helped to make it possible for such a flawless 'cosmos built of numbers' to be designed at Paestum rather than elsewhere.

The naos was related with like clarity to the   *123* ambulatory, which was given a depth of two interaxials at the east end, and one on the other three sides. Hence, the sides of the cella, which measured 3 by 9 interaxials, were in the simple ratio of 1 to 3, the outer faces of the flanking walls being aligned in the Doric manner with the second and fifth end columns. Then, however, in connexion with a very important change of plan, the cella walls were moved somewhat inwards on the already constructed foundations, and, according to Ionic custom, the breadth of the cella was fixed as half the temple's axial width or 20 Doric ft. This may have coincided with the designing of a unique Ionic inner porch, which had 4 by 2 slender columns 9 lower diameters tall. Two more such columns were engaged in the   *fig. 77* ends of the pronaos walls. Though this porch was plainly marked out as part of the cella by the toichobate projecting as a step, on which it stood, and by the architrave that linked up with the pronaos walls, it must none the less still have looked strange enough inside the Doric peristyle. Both the column bases of simple Samian form and the curving capitals with   *fig. 110* their big volutes are purely east-Ionic in origin.

Nor is that all, for the peristyle itself is caught up in this current. Like the relief friezes on the Ionic treasuries at Delphi (plate 68), the triglyph frieze is

411

76–77 Paestum, temple of Athena. North-west corner of temple (*left*) and view into pronaos (*right*). Restorations. F. Krauss, 1960

bordered by a Lesbian leaf-and-dart (in place of the taenia) and by a flat serpentine pattern with a plastically convex Ionic egg-and-dart above it.

fig. 76 However, in relation to the traditional form, the cornice seems completely outlandish. The Doric mutules were absent, and had to be, since the rhythm of the columns and frieze died out in the wide egg-and-dart border. Instead, the sloping soffit of the corona was adorned with sunken coffers, in which were inserted alternating stars and rosettes. Such coffering, which here appeared to be quite independent of the frieze as its sequence did not harmonize with the latter's, customarily formed the wooden ceiling of ambulatories and cellas, so that one is tempted to look upon the eaves as the projecting part of a covering laid over the entire building like a huge inclined slab. The reconstruction of the pediment shows this view to be justified. At the fronts, the horizontal corona—an astonishing exception, this—is missing and, with it, the sharply defined gable triangle of the Doric temple. Identically coffered, the edge of the saddle-roof lies, clear and elegant, above the pediment wall built of smooth ashlar. Over it, the carved sima bore an anthemion frieze, which, along the sides, was rhythmically interrupted by lion-head spouts. Not just the sima, but also the leaves ringing the capitals, the cymas, which reappear on the inner face of the triglyphs, the coffers along the eaves, and the Ionic volute capitals must all once have glowed with varied colours. In fact, we cannot, in imagination, paint this building too brightly, gaily, and elegantly. The greatest miracle, however, is that such a positively barbarous mixture of the most diverse forms was able to succeed at all and, out of it, such a graceful whole arise. The singular roof pattern could have been borrowed from the then nascent rustic architecture of the hellenized Etruscans, who had immigrated from the East, now traded with Paestum and were themselves dependent on Greek art. We do not know whether the

Ionic architectural forms, of such animation and high quality, were yielded exclusively by the local building tradition (the fact that already on the Basilica a similar moulding replaced the Doric taenia would suggest this), whether the city took in Ionian fugitives, who brought with them new ideas, or whether Ionian daughter-cities like Cumae, Messana, or Locri were the intermediaries. Anyway, it was still Greeks that built here and could venture with masterful freedom to put together elements from the most different Greek formal vocabularies as a convincing unity, which seems to have anticipated many features of Attic architecture. Yet the aristocratic refinement itself, the fastidious sense of form that gave the little temple its special bloom, also betokened an end: that of the archaic period. By then, the immanent mass, the monumentality of the Basilica had been lost.

22, 123   The building's excellent state of preservation contributes to the fact that much of its former character is still discernible. Upon the three-stepped crepidoma, the wreath of the columns stands intact, spanned all round by the still complete architrave. Rebuilt, the central part of both pediments still rests above the frieze, which is very peculiarly constructed out of beam-like blocks with their centre lying in each case over a column, so as to reduce the burden on the architrave. The triglyphs, which have all fallen away, were set in special notches. Like the triglyphs, the Ionic mouldings were carved in fine sandstone instead of shell-limestone. Although the walls and the porch columns are missing, the rectangle of the cella stands out clearly, as the naos floor was raised by about 3 ft. 4 in.

THE TEMPLE OF HERA II,   *Plates XXVI,*
so-called TEMPLE OF POSEIDON   *115–121, fig. 78*

During the classical fifth century, the spiritual revolution that, with mysterious uniformity, profoundly changed the Hellenic world from the coast of Ionia to the outermost city of the West, also affected Paestum. Indeed, it was there that the new principles of the 'severe style' were expressed in a Doric temple more purely and strongly than anywhere else in Magna Graecia.

When the ancient Hera temple with its enneastyle front and unmannerly formal language was due to be replaced by a larger, more dignified one, it was not demolished, contrary to the usual practice in Greece where holy places were more constricted and precisely localized. Instead, the new peripteral structure, with 6 by 14 columns, was put up right beside it. The temple followed in all respects the Doric 'canon' developed in the motherland, its architectural forms

being pure Doric without a single Ionic feature interspersed. This is hardly to be explained solely by referring to the local tradition, with its hybrid buildings. Regardless of the long journey, the city took part in the Olympic games, and, in 468, one of its citizens was actually victor. The architect of the new temple must, as his design and the forms reveal, have minutely studied the temple of Zeus *figs. 9–13* on the Alpheus, completed around 460. Yet certain peculiarities of the plan and, above all, the sculpturally animated character of the members show that he made what he had seen his own, that he knew how to use it with masterly independence, and that, in short, both architect and builders came from Paestum itself.

It is a piece of inestimable good fortune that this particular temple, in which Doric architecture reached a climax, is almost perfectly preserved. Crepidoma, columns, and entablature are all practically undamaged. The east pediment is *115–117* complete, the west has two gaps. As it lacks its sima, the strongly jutting cornice appears too low and light today, but one still obtains an impression here as nowhere else of how powerfully the corona and pediments hold the peristyle together as a solid body. True, the Normans pulled down the cella walls to use the stone for their churches, so that the temple is bereft of its actual nucleus. Since, however, the base of the cella, the paving of which lay about 4 ft. 7 in. above the ambulatory's, rests clearly outlined as a low block inside the peristyle, and since both fronts, with their two columns between normal Doric antae, as well as both the rows of supports for the ceiling and roof of the tripartite naos are still standing, the eye has clues to help it *118, 119* restore what is missing. On the other hand, it is specially easy here for the visitor to effect in his mind a romantic transfiguration of the ruin, beautiful but false. Instead of being carried away by the warm, golden hue of the leached stone, one should try to imagine the hard, white lime-stucco that once clarified all the forms, and the strong accents of colour in the frieze and corona: blue for the vertical features—the triglyphs, mutules, and regulae; red for the horizontal lines—the taenia and corona soffit.

The ground-plan has been almost completely assimilated to that of the temple of Zeus, the latter's considerable dimensions only surpassing those of the temple of Hera by a few yards (stylobate 79 ft. 9⅛ in. by 196 ft. 7½ in.). To fit the cella into the peristyle *fig. 78* elongated by one interaxial (6 by 14 instead of 13 columns), the same relations between the lines of the side walls and the second and fifth end columns were observed. The porticoes are not quite 1½ interaxials deep, besides which the entrance end has been

413

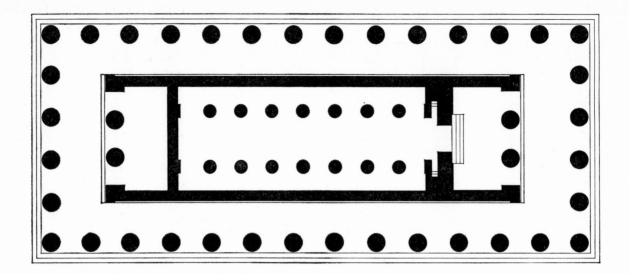

78 Paestum, temple of Hera II. Plan (1 : 400). New drawing by F. Krauss

stressed in relation to the west one by giving its portico an extra 1 ft. 6⅛ in. and extending the pronaos. In the door wall of the naos, specially thickened for this purpose, little, concealed stairways led up to the loft, as already in the Athena temple. Though the old neglect of the rear end has been overcome by balancing the pronaos with an opisthodomus likewise distyle in-antis, the cella is not quite symmetrically organized about the transverse axis of the peristyle.

118, 119
Considering the Western distaste for such obstructions of the room's width, it is astonishing that two double-storied rows of seven columns—again on the pattern of Olympia—should appear in the naos. Yet obviously the homeland's sense of plasticity prevailed here, determining that the interior, too, should be articulated with columns, and thus included in the bodily cohesion of the whole temple. The architraves of these colonnades rest upon anta-like pilasters set against the cross-walls.

The design seems to develop, not from a 'standard interaxial', as at Olympia, but, as in the case of the Athena temple, from a length-breadth relationship of 2 to 5 (72 by 180 Doric ft.), here established in the taenia above the architrave. From it, the unit interaxial of 14 ft. 8½ in. was then derived. As, however, fig. 6C angle contraction on the Greek model was introduced (simple at the ends, 'double', or spread over two interaxials, at the sides, and both involving incredibly delicate displacements in the frieze, so that the irregularities in the rhythm of frieze and columns became practically invisible), the partitioning as a whole had to be much more diversified than the numerically simple division of the Athena temple. The interaxial could not be reckoned straightforwardly in feet, and it worked out slightly larger on the flanks (14 ft. 9¼ in. as against 14 ft. 8½ in.). At the same time, a distinct enlargement of the front columns—neither usual nor justified at Paestum—was taken over from Olympia (by 2 in., Olympia almost 1), inevitably and absurdly producing a marked contraction of the front intercolumnial spaces.

The elevation measurements were not derived from the interaxial—itself a derived measurement—but from the initial rectangle of the architrave and its unit of 9 Doric ft. Thus, the column height comes to 3×9 or 27 Doric ft. (29 ft. 1⅝ in.), and so the sides of the vertical rectangles formed by the colonnades themselves are related as 3 to 8 (fronts) and 3 to 20 (flanks). For the relation between triglyph and metope, which determines the general impression, the balanced width proportion of 2 to 3 has been achieved. We will spare the reader further examples, as he can already observe from the above how two heterogeneous principles of design—that of Olympia and the native—here interpenetrate, carefully attuned yet not finally reconciled.

The important structural forms speak to us more 115 distinctly and directly. Among them, it is above all the royal figure of the column that sets its individual life, a monumentality more powerful than ever again, in the harmonious context of the whole. The incomparably heavy appearance of these columns, which to Goethe at first seemed 'oppressive, indeed terrible', is due to the shaft's thick-set build, which is only matched on the mature archaic temples at Syracuse and Corinth (height = 4·23 or 4·33 lower diams., Syracuse 3·97, Corinth 4·15) and at Paestum itself has no precedent (Basilica 4·45). Furthermore, these sturdy bodies are pressed so close together that the intervening space is only slightly broader than the shaft (lower diam. to intercolumniation 1 : 1·13 or 1 : 1·20). Goethe, however, soon felt 'on friendly terms': the movement leading upwards, the controlled flow of forces calmly balanced by the architrave, must have deeply stirred him. He who observed just as reflectively as intuitively in so doing called to mind the 'severe style of sculpture'. There and then—without qualification, for contemporaries, including Winckelmann, knew the 'Doric order' merely as one architectural system among others—the point was made: these columns are 'sculptural'. Imbued with the feeling for plasticity that, from the outset, distinguished builders at Paestum, the architect moulded his creation as something corporeal, and precisely here went even beyond his classical model. The might of the columns is tempered by finer channelling (24 instead of 20 flutes). In this connexion, it is interesting to see how

exact consistency in the application of the fluting increases the bulk of the smaller interior columns: while the lower supports have 20, the upper have only 16 flutes. The capitals correspond to those at Olympia, except that here, too, the sculptural part —the echinus—stands out more strongly. Likewise, the frieze is articulated by bolder relief, and the powerful corona juts out further (3 ft. 2⅝ in.) than on any other Doric temple. As does the entasis of the columns, a subtle curvature of all the horizontals, from the steps to the entablature, animates the structure. It was here introduced for the first and last time in the West, except at Segesta. On the other hand, the inward tilt of the columns detected at Olympia is absent. It has been replaced by a frank deformation of the angle supports, which appear to be slightly inclined through being similarly contoured in the front view to the thinner flanking columns.

Thus, there is something inwardly right about the way the building, itself a vast, harmoniously composed work of sculpture, more monumental and severe than any other Doric temple, forgoes all sculptural decoration.

METAPONTUM

Plate XXXII

At about the same time as Paestum, the city of Metapontum was resettled by Achaeans on the site of an earlier Greek colony destroyed by the native Lucanians. Situated between two marshy river-mouths in a wilderness as dreary as it is fertile, it has preserved two archaic temples, which, despite having much in common with those at Paestum, present a totally different aspect of Achaean architecture. The bigger of them, adjoining the agora of the old city, was dedicated to Apollo Lyceus, according to an archaic inscription. Its foundations, only parts of which had, until lately, been uncovered since 1828, would appear to indicate a ground-plan wholly similar to the Basilica's: a stylobate measuring about 92 by 174 ft. with 9 by 18 columns, and a symmetrical cella with a pronaos, a naos divided into two equally broad naves by a central colonnade, and an adytum. Of the superstructure, there have been found large, obviously late archaic capitals (abacus 6½ by 6½ ft., upper column diam. about 3½ ft.), oddly formed and embellished triglyphs, and richly decorated remains

of clay roof ornaments. Though the entire foundations were at last excavated in 1939, the finds still have not been adequately published, so I can here only refer to a recent but unverifiable assertion that the temple is, in fact, to be reconstructed as one of completely normal design, with 6 by 12 columns on a stylobate measuring 74 by 136 ft.

A smaller peripteral structure lies upon a low hill by the river nearly two miles north of the old city, and was probably dedicated to Hera. Five columns on the north flank and ten on the south are still upright, both rows being spanned by the lower course of the architrave. The ruin is popularly known by the fanciful name of *Tavole Paladine* (Knights' Tables), which goes back to the Middle Ages (*Mensae Imperatoris*: Commander's Tables). People may have imagined, at this fever-tainted spot, that they saw gigantic armed spectres feasting off the two architraves.

The ground-plan of the temple, the dimensions of which (52 ft. 8¼ in. by 109 ft. 9⅜ in.) only slightly

XXXII

exceed those of the Athena temple at Paestum, follows the same simple principles. Within a peristyle of 6 by 12 columns, which was developed with almost equal axial spacing at ends and sides (9 ft. 8½ in. = 9 Doric ft. of 12⅞ in.) from a standard interaxial of 9 Doric ft. (instead of Paestum's 8), there stood a symmetrically placed cella with pronaos, columnless naos, and adytum. Its axial breadth again seems to have corresponded to half the axial breadth of the peristyle. The columns, their height of 16 ft. 10¼ in. having been fixed as 1¾ interaxials, resemble those of the Athena temple too. Indeed they present the same degree of slenderness (height = 4·84 lower diams. of 3 ft. 5¾ in.) and a similarly strong entasis. The only differences are that the hollow is incised not in the end of the shaft but the bottom of the echinus, and that, instead of leaves, the flutes themselves are sunk into it. Their arrises run against two rings at the foot of the echinus. This highly eclectic attempt to combine the motherland's austere passage from shaft to capital with the old hollow, which it was not found so easy to relinquish, marks the transitional stage between the archaic and classical styles (cf. temple G at Selinus, page 430), and dates the temple to the period around 500. Above the architrave, there followed a second course, perhaps separated because, as at Paestum, an Ionic leaf-and-dart of fine-grained stone was to replace the Doric taenia.

Yet, despite all these family likenesses, the temple gives a completely different impression, for the columns, with their lower diameter related to the intercolumniation as 1 : 1·79 or 5 : 9, are much more spread out than on any other Western temple. Even in the mother-country, only very early temples that, like the Heraeum at Olympia, were closely connected with the original wooden structures displayed such wide spacing. Hence, the airy, open, light character of the two colonnades, which entirely lack the heaviness and compactness of stone construction, and which a superstitious people interpreted, by no means so absurdly, as huge pieces of furniture. However, the fact that such contrasts were possible even within the same building tradition—on the sister-temple at Paestum, the intercolumniation is hardly wider than the columns (1 : 1·1)—plainly indicates the vacillating nature, swinging from one extreme to the other, of archaic architecture in the colonies.

At Metapontum, an ancient wooden temple of Hera, seen by Pliny, actually did remain standing till into Roman times, and may well have influenced the late archaic buildings.

SYRACUSE

Syracuse is supposed to have been founded by the Corinthian Archias in 735 as the first Doric colony. By far the most powerful city in Sicily, it has bequeathed us the island's two earliest peripteral temples. Corinth, which claims the honour of being the birthplace of monumental Doric temple architecture, has preserved no evidence of these beginnings. However, anyone expecting such evidence from the daughter-city that soon outstripped its mother in wealth and power would be well advised to take care, in view of the building remains. For the two Syracusan temples have little formally, and almost nothing spiritually, in common with the Apollo temple raised only a generation later at Corinth (page 343). It would appear that the settlers did indeed bring with them the formal framework of the earliest Doric wooden structure, but produced a new grandiose and unrestrained interpretation of their heritage, at the same time as changing their style of life. They seem to have effected the conversion into stone quite independently and in their own way, with violent overstatement; indeed, it is as though the highly characteristic relationship of Western architecture to spatiality originated right here.

THE TEMPLE OF APOLLO   *Plate 151, figs. 79, 80*

The earliest temple of Apollo commanded the approach to the island of Ortygia, to which the city at first confined itself before, grown large, it had spread over an extensive area inland. On the top step at the front of the temple, the names of the builders are inscribed in ancient lettering: 'Kleom[en]es made [the temple] to Apollo, [the son] of Knidieidas, and Epikles the columns, beautiful works.' In the motherland, even an Ictinus was not allowed thus to indulge his artist's pride.

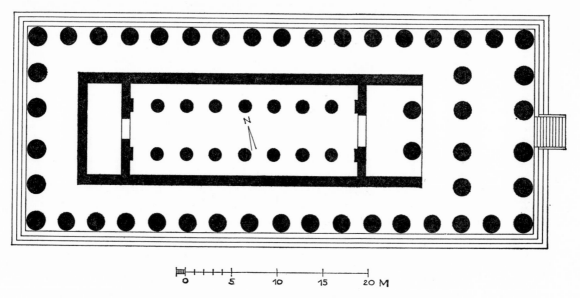

79 Syracuse, temple of Apollo. Plan (1 : 400). New drawing

fig. 79 At first glance, the ground-plan shows a certain similarity to that of the temple at Corinth. As there, an exceptionally elongated cella (38 ft. 0¾ in. by 80 ft. 8½ in.) was surrounded by a peristyle of 6 by 15 columns (without the front portico) in such a way that the west and inner east porticoes, being almost 1½ interaxials deep, took precedence over the narrower pteromata, which were slightly over 1 interaxial wide. Moreover, both temples have four-stepped crepidomas, and the stylobate dimensions approximately correspond (Syracuse 70 ft. 9¼ in. by 181 ft. 6⅝ in., Corinth 70 ft. 5⅝ in. by 176 ft. 6⅞ in.). Yet another element attests the link with home, namely two double-storied rows of small Doric columns, which, with an architrave separating the upper and lower series, here also divided the naos into a nave and aisles. The arrangement, which gave the room a severe, architectonically corporeal stamp, in itself conflicted with the Western perception of space, and hence found no following in Sicily. This exhausts the similarities, which were overlain by alien, idiosyncratic features. Thus, the cella did not display that balance of front and rear, of pronaos and opisthodomus, on which the calm, 'all-sided' effect of the Greek peripteral structure depended, for its back was closed by a plain wall, behind which lay concealed the adytum. Instead, all accents were concentrated at the front, which was not just emphasized with a distyle in-antis pronaos. The simple hexastyle east colonnade was, so to speak, doubled by having a second portico with 6 by 2 columns set before it, and, with the introduction of such magnificent 2-interaxial-deep porticoes, a pronounced frontality was substituted for the 'universality' of the Corinthian temple. Including the addition, the peristyle comprised, lengthways, 17 columns—a total never reached on any hexastyle temple in the motherland.

In the superstructure, the West's extravagant attitude of mind, always reaching out to extremes, is apparent. The link with wooden buildings still had not been completely broken. Thus, the mighty stone architraves of the peristyle were cut along their inner faces to receive a wooden beam, on which lay those of the ceiling. Stone was evidently not credited with being really able to bear loads. While it is also apparent in the temple at Corinth that the translation of the light-limbed wooden structure into the heavy, durable medium of stone led to forms of excessive weight, at Syracuse the stone seems actually to have been conceived as oppressive bulk, and laboriously shaped by a race of Titans. Never again did such burly columns, pressed together so tightly, appear in the Greek world. Their height amounts to less than four times their diameter (height 26 ft. 2⅛ in.; lower diam. 6 ft. 7½ in. at ends, 6 ft. 0⅞ in. at sides), and the intercolumniation on the flanks is *fig. 80* narrower than the column diameter. These supports, round which four men can just link hands, are so close together that one man is able, with outstretched *151* arms, to reach across the intervening space! The projecting abaci almost touch each other (breadth 9 ft. 4⅝ in., interval about 1 ft. 8 in.).

Below the abacus, the shallow echinus spreads out beneath the enormous burden of the entablature like a round bun. It is separated by a deeply incised

417

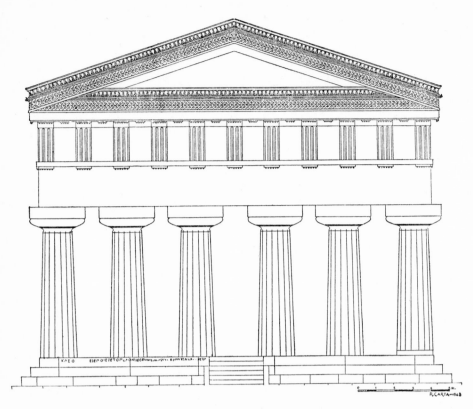

80 Syracuse, temple of Apollo. Restored east elevation (1 : 200). G. Cultrera and R. Carta, *Mon. Ant.* 41, 1951

hollow from the shaft, which, for its part, is 21 ft. 8⅝ in. tall, and consists of a single piece of stone weighing about forty tons! These monstrous columns lack the enlivening swell of entasis, their torpid weight being further stressed by uncommonly broad, shallow fluting (16 flutes instead of the usual 20). In conformity with archaic custom, the column spacing varied at the ends and sides. Here, however, the differences are so conspicuous—the flank columns were packed most densely (interaxial 10 ft. 11⅛ in.); though the front corner interaxials were already much broader (12 ft. 9½ in.), the middle one, as thoroughly befitted the temple's frontality, was ruthlessly widened to 13 ft. 7⅜ in. at the expense of its neighbours, which thereby, with 12 ft. 1⅝ in., became the narrowest at the ends—that it has been doubted whether a Doric triglyph frieze could have been combined with such a chaotic graduation. Recently, however, remains of triglyphs and positioning marks on the architrave were found. They attest that the tall, narrow stone triglyphs and likewise tall metopes were distributed with amazing unconcern, simply filling up the space without reference to the column axes. Along the flanks, five triglyphs went to about three interaxials, while, at the ends, though two triglyphs were associated with each interaxial, not one was aligned with a column. Over the supports lay a heavy, awkward architrave—one such stone

beam still links the two standing columns on the south side—its height (7 ft. 0⅝ in.) amounting to more than a quarter of the column height.

In comparison, the decorative motifs must have appeared oddly fragile. Above the architrave ran a narrow taenia enriched, triglyph-like, with three fine grooves. The regulae were let in separately, and from these insertions the abnormal triglyph distribution can be deduced. Below the corona which projected nearly 20 in. hung mutules that, alternately broad and narrow as on temple C at Selinus, are clearly recognizable as copies of the plank-shaped rafter ends. For the guttae, of another material (bronze?), were driven into narrow holes, and in them lived on the bronze nails of the old carpentered construction.

The face of the corona had a gaily painted terracotta revetment, which, together with the terracotta roof sima, formed a magnificent succession of ornaments (double guilloche, chequers, Doric leaf-pattern), of similar construction to that on the Geloan treasury (page 324 and fig. 14).

The 'primitiveness' of the Apollo temple—expressed in its clumsy proportions, the independent organic life of its members, and the unresolved contradiction between the dense, bulky peristyle and the spacious porticoes at the front—is only partly explained by the building's great age. If one bears in mind that the first stone temples of the mother-country still displayed the light proportions of wooden structures, that as early as about 600 angle contraction appeared on the Heraeum at Olympia (i.e. the triglyph frieze was fully developed), and that, apart from the old tholos at Delphi (fig. 35), incongruities like the present structure are met with neither early nor late in Greece proper, then one will see the Apollo temple, which cannot be dated earlier than 570–560 on account of its acroteria, as the splendid beginning of a separate style in architecture: that of Magna Graecia.

THE TEMPLE OF ZEUS (OLYMPIEUM)
Plate 150

150

Perhaps a decade later, between 560 and 550, the Syracusans erected a temple to Zeus Olympius with almost the same ground-plan and elevation in the broad valley of the Anapus outside the city. In the few, but critical innovations, a certain consolidation and systematization of the structural principles is apparent. The long, narrow cella with pronaos, naos, and secluded adytum was retained, as were also the peristyle of 6 by 17 columns and double portico stressing the east end. However, the six front columns were now disposed with completely even spacing, and the narrower interaxials on the flanks were at least made sufficiently like the end ones to allow a division of the triglyph frieze that harmonized with the columns (end interaxial 13 ft. $4\frac{5}{8}$ in., side 12 ft. $3\frac{5}{8}$ in.). The bulky proportions of the again monolithic columns—two stumps are still upright on the south flank—appear somewhat moderated, the column height of about 26 ft. 3 in. corresponding to 4·3 lower diameters of 6 ft. $0\frac{1}{4}$ in. Doubtless, the roof decoration and multicoloured terracotta casing of the corona tallied with those of the earlier temple.

The cult of Zeus seems to have flourished here. A section of the colonists came from around the Alpheus. Did they bring the worship of the Olympian god with them, or did some tyrant—Syracuse never lacked them—found the sanctuary for the ruler of the gods? Tradition does not say. For the Athena statue of Phidias forty gold talents sufficed, but Gelon, after his victory at Himera in 480, is said to have paid out the fabulous sum of eighty-five for the robe of the image of Zeus. It may be wondered whether this magnificent statue really remained hidden away in the inaccessible adytum, or was displayed in the naos. At all events, it did not keep the gold mantle for long, as Dionysius I took possession of it, dressing the god in a woollen garment.

THE TEMPLE OF ATHENA
Plate 152, fig. 81

On Ortygia, not far from the archaic Apollo temple, there has survived one of Magna Graecia's most mature architectural creations, built during the first decades of the early classical period.

The spot and the building itself are thus very well qualified to bring home to us the continuity of the island's 3,000 years of history. It seems that the Doric immigrants enclosed an Athena sanctuary on the site of a settlement of the ousted Siculi. Remains of walling and many roof terracottas, as splendidly and colourfully adorned as those of the Apollo temple, have been dug up here and they indicate a large archaic temple and two smaller temple-like structures, perhaps treasuries. According to Diodorus (figs. 8, 9, p. 549 and 16, 83), Agathocles—a king of the old Syracuse?—supervised the erection of the temple, putting aside the best stones for his own dwelling. Thereupon the wretched man was struck dead by lightning in the home he had built for himself.

After the brilliant victory over the Carthaginians in 480, Gelon and his brother Hieron had two wholly similar peripteral buildings with 6 by 14 columns raised: one at Himera, the site of the battle, the other here in the sanctuary of Athena. Cicero saw and praised the Athena temple.

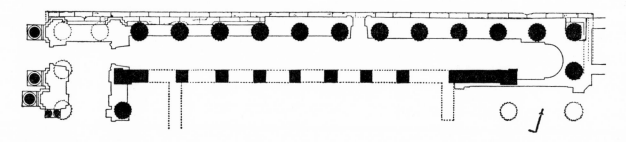

81 Syracuse, temple of Athena. North half of temple incorporated in cathedral. Plan (1 : 380). B. Pace, 1938, plan by S. Agati, 1927

In early Christian times, at the latest under the episcopate of St. Zosimus during the seventh century, the temple was converted into a basilica with a nave and two aisles. Henceforth, the walled-up peristyle constituted the basilica's outer shell and the pierced cella walls provided arcades, so that the cella became the nave, and the pteromata the aisles. Nothing can elucidate better the immensely different demands made by the Greek and the Romano-Christian eras upon interiors than the fact that this spatial compilation of cella and pteromata amounts to a big temple but only a moderately spacious church.

When the Saracens came, Allah moved into the ancient temple of Athena, but the Norman King Roger returned it to the Virgin in 1093. Ever since then, the building has been the cathedral of Syracuse. The Renaissance embellished it—the beautiful pavement was laid during the Quattrocento—and Sicilian Baroque clad it in gorgeous ceremonial robes, adding the rich façade after the terrible earthquake of 1693. Yet the Greek columns have always remained the framework of the cathedral, and, during a restoration about 1925, they were as far as possible stripped of all that had overgrown them.

Now for the temple itself. It was built, like all Sicilian temples, of the plain native limestone, which it was customary to finish with a fine coat of stucco. Yet this did not satisfy the great Gelon and his brother Hieron, who, for the sima and the outer roof tiles, had the finest marble brought from the Cyclades. Not only the marble was imported from the mother-country, however. Under these far from insular tyrants, the hitherto eccentrically withdrawn architecture of the West became receptive to the now mature achievements of classical architecture in the ancient homeland. First, the closed and therefore, in a sense, dead rear end of the cella had to be abandoned and replaced by a distyle in-antis opisthodomus. The designer went still further, however, and even did without the firmly established adytum, thus overcoming the excessive elongation of the peristyle, which, with 6 by 14 columns, now approached the classical count of 6 by 13. At the same time, the stylobate was conceived as a lucidly proportioned rectangle (72 ft. 2⅛ in. by 170 ft. 6⅛ in., ratio 2 : 5). Though the columns were

still, in the Sicilian fashion, more thick-set and closely packed than contemporary Peloponnesian ones (height of 28 ft. 6⅞ in. = 4·54 lower diams. of 6 ft. 3⅝ in.; Zeus temple at Olympia 4·7), the interaxial was approximately equal all round (13 ft. 7⅜ in. and 13 ft. 8 in.). By this means, a clear order was imposed upon the structure, especially since the encasement of the cella corresponded to the Doric canon, the outer faces of its side walls being aligned with the axes of the second and fifth end columns.

To solve the Doric 'angle conflict', previously ignored in the West, not only the corner interaxial was here for the first time narrowed, but also, to a somewhat smaller extent, the adjacent one. Because of this 'double angle contraction', the narrowing almost ceased to catch the eye. That this architect tried to resolve the conflict as a sort of mathematical problem, instead of tackling it with an intuitive sense of form, is apparent in the temple at Himera. There, above the triglyph frieze so painstakingly adjusted to the columns, he contrived to place a sima on which the spouts—lion-heads as on the Athena temple—were heedlessly distributed without any alignment with the frieze.

In its details, the temple is wholly the peer of contemporary Peloponnesian buildings. Its capitals have a taut, spreading curve, and the 20 flutes of its columns braced by a delicate entasis are drawn out sharply and cleanly. The obtrusive heaviness of all the members is accounted for by the Sicilian tradition.

It is said that an enormous gilded shield on the east pediment flashed far out towards incoming ships, as the city's landmark. The doors of the naos, artistically decorated with figured carvings in ivory and studded with gold nails, were famous. On the inside of the walls, there hung a large panel-painting of a cavalry battle and the portraits of twenty-seven Syracusan rulers. This information handed down by Cicero (*Verr.* 4, 55, 122) accords ill with the not at all convincing deduction of the excavators from drainage conduits that the whole naos lay open to the sky, as a kind of courtyard. All the same, it is conceivable that the room was lit through an aperture in the roof, like an Italian atrium. No traces of interior columns have been found.

fig. 81

Ancient Selinus formed the last outpost of the Greek cities in the direction of the western tip of Sicily, controlled by the Elymians, Phoenicians and Carthaginians. It was established about the middle of the seventh century by Syracuse's neighbour Megara Hyblaea on a low plateau projecting towards the sea between two river valleys. The colonists enlisted their 'founder', who had to decide on the site, plan, and laws of the city, from the old mother-city of Megara, near Corinth. Thus, the formal heritage of their native place must, so far as it was known to the settlers, have come from the Megarian-Corinthian sphere.

In the Megarian citadel, as Pausanias relates (I 39, 5 and 40, 6), there stood a 'megaron' of Demeter, which was founded by the mythical king Car, and is supposed to have provided the city with its name. This venerable building, not a trace of which survives, seems therefore to have had its origin in the Mycenaean tradition, like the anactoron at Eleusis (page 402). Now, opposite the city hill of Selinus, on the western slope of the river valley—like the whole city, the river was called 'Selinus' after the wild celery that grew abundantly round it—there was also a Demeter megaron, in the middle of an extensive burying-place. The goddess and her daughter Persephone, who were here invoked as 'Malophoros and Pasicratea' and held sway over growth and death, laid special claim to the whole of Sicily; their peculiarly mystical cult may have given a sombre, mysterious hue to the cults of other deities as well and, hence, to sacred architecture. In any case, we can observe this happening at Selinus, for every one of the seven peripteral temples raised by the small city is based upon the primitive form of the megaron, recognizable in the adytum common to them all.

GAGGERA,   *Plates 124, 125, figs. 82–85*
THE SANCTUARY OF DEMETER MALOPHOROS

fig. 82

The Demeter precinct, a squarish area ascending the slope and measuring about 55 by 66 yds., had a wall of carefully jointed tufa ashlar thrown round it in the *125* sixth century. One entered through a small, late-*fig. 83* fifth-century propylaeum (28 ft. 10½ in. by 28 ft. 6½ in.), both the entrance sides of which had two columns in-antis. Strange to say, the antae were not applied to the ends of the side walls, but concluded two short walls that bent round at right angles towards the columns, as on the pre-Periclean propy-

laeum of the Athenean citadel (fig. 63). In the 'wings' thus formed, stone benches set before the side walls invited those who entered to linger. Yet another reminiscence of Athens gives an idea of how far-reaching the influence of the classical Propylaea was: instead of the usual two metopes and triglyphs corresponding in the frieze to every interaxial, there were three, as, for the first time, above the Propylaea's middle interaxial space. Since the building had no actual gate-wall, both its fronts could be closed by bronze grilles, the sinkings for which have survived.

Bordering the south wall of the propylaeum, which must have been preceded by a simple archaic gate-building, there was an older precinct of a deity often associated with Demeter: Hecate, the sinister goddess of roads and great chthonic sorceress. Whoever wished and was allowed to enter the main sanctuary emerged opposite a big elongated altar for burnt offerings, behind which rose the forbiddingly closed house of Malophoros, the megaron. A plain, oblong ashlar structure (31 ft. 2¾ in. by 66 ft. 11½ in.) without columns, it had a single opening at the east end in the form of a doorway that, framed by stone beams and distinctly tapering upwards, recalls Egyptian gates. The interior was divided into three rooms: a vestibule (or pronaos) only 10 ft. 9⅞ in. deep; a dimly lit naos reached through a second door and measuring 27 ft. 9½ in. by 35 ft. 8¾ in.; and, lastly, a dark adytum barely 13 ft. deep—'the temple's most secret place, which no one may enter except the priest' (Serv. *Aen.* II, 115).

Besides columns, the megaron also lacked a Doric triglyph frieze—indeed, its only decorative element, a stone cornice along the flanks and pediment-edge, *fig. 85* is entirely foreign to the Doric formal vocabulary as we know it. A corona, but one without mutules, crowned all four walls. Its face was curiously profiled, most closely comparable, with its two fascias, astragal, and shallow cavetto, to ancient terracotta simas—and, accordingly, there was no sima here at all. Strangest of all, however, is the way the similarly moulded corona of either pediment was set above as a sharply differentiated part. At the outer angles, the raking corona—as though weightless—only just touched the horizontal one with its bottom corner, without the two members cutting or joining up. Since this raking corona also projected above the roof surface, it will have appeared as a narrow border inorganically applied to the edge of the pediment. Hence, one could believe that one was obtaining an insight into the genesis of the pediment

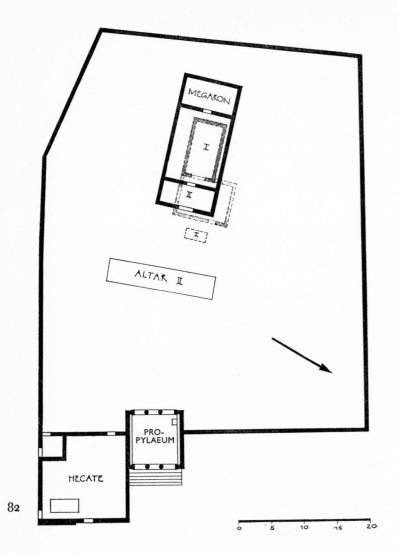

82

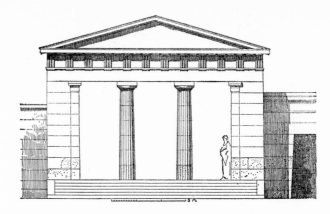

83

82–83 Selinus, sanctuary of Demeter Malophoros

83 Propylaeum, front elevation (1 : 150).
R. Koldewey and O. Puchstein, 1899

82 Plan (1 : 550). New drawing after E. Gabrici,
Mon. Ant. 32, 1927/28

form out of the 'primitive' roof—for it is as though the gable moulding had been set in a naïvely additive fashion above the encircling cornice of a hip-roof—if the building's age (on account of the developed ashlar technique, it cannot have gone up much before temple C, i.e. 550) and the very outlandishness of the decorative form did not warn against drawing such conclusions. Carthago-Phoenician influences may have taken this provincial architecture along byways that we cannot trace.

Thus, an even smaller temple from the beginning of the sixth century, the remains of which came to light under the megaron, had a cornice construction that, though certainly more primitive, was quite normally formed on the pediments (megaron 1 in the plan). Here, the coronas of plain rectangular profile, perhaps once adorned with terracotta revetments, cut into each other at the corners of the gable.

In the Hellenistic age, people ceased to be content with the mystic but hidden presence of the cult images. The old adytum was abolished, and the statues of the 'great goddesses' were set up in a vaulted apse at the end of the naos. This made manifest the relationship with the spatial layout of Christian churches that had been inherent from the start in the megaron, leading as it did towards a 'holy of holies'.

About 22 yds. north of the Demeter sanctuary lies a tiny precinct, under 19 yds. square, dedicated to Zeus Milichius, an aspect of Zeus associated with *124, be* chthonic expiation rites, and here the cult partner of Persephone-Pasicratea. Countless, in part archaic stelae, thick layers of rubble from offerings, and fountains with holy, lustral water all show how highly frequented this small sanctuary was. Not earlier than the end of the fourth century, a temple-shaped shrine was raised for the image of Zeus. Measuring only 9 ft. $8\frac{7}{8}$ in. by 17 ft. $0\frac{3}{4}$ in., it had at the front two little Doric columns that supported an entablature of Ionic profile. With this began that decorative mixing of the orders beloved by the Hellenistic age. Everything was in miniature, for each part firmly preserved its due size in relation to the whole. The steps, barely 4 in. high and broad, certainly cannot be climbed.

More important is the new, as yet unpublished discovery of a second megaron some 440 yds. further north-west. The oblong structure, measuring about 12 by 27 yds., seems to have carried a Doric triglyph frieze as well as a normally formed corona above its walls, and thus belongs to a more advanced period. Here again, before the east end, there lay a large altar about 79 ft. wide but only $16\frac{1}{2}$ ft. deep.

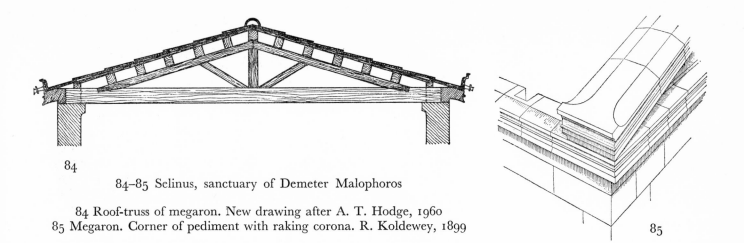

84

84–85 Selinus, sanctuary of Demeter Malophoros

84 Roof-truss of megaron. New drawing after A. T. Hodge, 1960
85 Megaron. Corner of pediment with raking corona. R. Koldewey, 1899

85

SELINUS, ACROPOLIS

Let us now turn to the city itself, which no doubt offers the most impressive example of the enthusiasm for building by which the Western Greeks were literally possessed. A good third of the inhabited surface of the citadel plateau, an area of 7½ acres, was partitioned off for the gods. There, in two separately walled-off precincts, were raised four big peripteral structures and several small temples, not to mention altars, a strange propylaeum with a T-shaped ground-plan, administrative buildings, and a wealth of votive offerings.

Two broad, intersecting axial streets, to which was attached a rectilinear network of side-roads, gave the residential area a monumental character. Since this arrangement was not, as previously believed, established by Hermocrates when the city, completely razed in 409, was rebuilt, but, according to very recent conclusions, already existed much earlier, at a time when such principles of order were still unknown in Greece itself, one must accept that the settlers knew and adopted the ancient Italian axial cross of *cardo* and *decumanus*. Selinus thus turns out to be the forerunner of the famous geometrical city layouts (see Priene, page 473) held to have been invented by Hippodamus of Miletus.

In the oldest temenos, to the north of the east-west axial street, there were first built, along with the altars indispensable for every cult, at least three archaically elongated 'megara', to house the statues of the gods: one with open porch and adytum, a second with a succession of three chambers, and a third over which the city's first peripteral structure, the mighty temple C (6 by 17 columns, stylobate 78 ft. 6½ in. by 209 ft. 0¾ in.), was raised around 550.

About a decade later, a second peripteral temple, known as 'D' (6 by 13 columns, stylobate 77 ft. 6¼ in. by 182 ft. 8⅛ in.), was erected in the same temenos, directly north of C. Which deities the precinct was dedicated to is still unknown. Heracles, Apollo, and Athena have all been considered, but a more reasonable suggestion, in view of the megaron-like cellas, is Demeter and Persephone, the 'great mistresses' of Sicily.

In the sanctuary to the south of the *decumanus*, two more, almost identical peripteral temples were built round about the middle of the fifth century, probably for Apollo and Athena: A with 6 by 14 columns and a 52-ft. 11-in. by 132-ft. 2½-in. stylobate, and O with the same ground-plan. Both were fully under the influence of the classical style but retained the selinuntine adytum, even though a distyle in-antis opisthodomus was now introduced. Because of their similarity to temple E, described below, we shall not consider them here.

TEMPLE C   *Plates XXII, 126–129, figs. 86–88*

Temple C, the biggest and oldest building in the city, comprised an elongated cella that was nothing else than a megaron grown to monumental proportions. *fig. 86* As with the Malophoros temple, the pronaos was shut off by strong walls, instead of being opened up in an arrangement of columns. The only entrance, a huge doorway at the east end, could be closed by a sliding-folding door of four heavy bronze leaves. From the tracks and bolt holes, which have survived, one can reconstruct its complicated mechanism. The pronaos was followed by a long naos, in the middle of which, it seems, a gigantic sacrificing table stood.

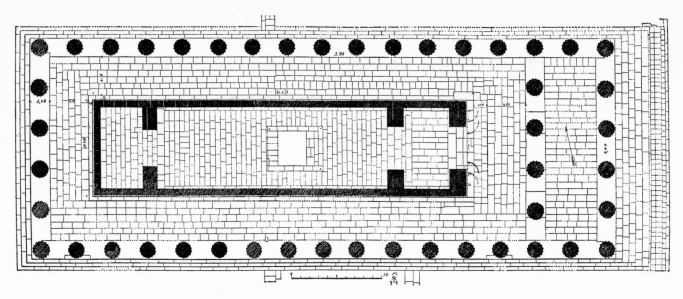

86 Selinus, acropolis. Temple C. Plan (1 : 400). R. Koldewey, 1899

At the far end of this straight series of rooms lay the dark adytum—the 'holy of holies' mysteriously concealing the god's image.

Around this cella, which, with 34 ft. 1½ in. by 136 ft. 3¾ in. (or 20 by 80 ells of 20½ in.), was proportioned as 1 to 4, and which rose above its own 21⅝-in.-wide socle-like step—the toichobate—there lay an unusually deep ambulatory. The enclosing colonnades of 6 by 15 columns stood at the same distance from the cella at the back and sides (8 ells or 13 ft. 7¾ in. + stylobate breadth of 4 ells or 6 ft. 9⅞ in.), but was extended at the front to a depth of 2 interaxials. To give this front unqualified precedence, a second portico with 6 by 2 columns was erected before it, probably inspired by the earlier Apollo temple at Syracuse (page 417). The peristyle thus became double here, and provided two 2-interaxial-deep spaces. As if this were not enough, a normal flight of 8 steps—the first of its kind in the Greek world—was laid right across the temple's width before the east colonnade. The arbitrariness of the axial spacing is positively naïve. Interaxials and intercolumniations alike already varied considerably on one and the same side (up to 9 in. and 6¾ in. respectively), and columns with 16 flutes stood beside others with 20 for no obvious reason. Between the end interaxials (average 14 ft. 5¼ in.) and flank ones (12 ft. 8 in.), however, there yawned a difference of 13 per cent! Averaging 6 ft. 3¼ in. at the ends and 5 ft. 11¼ in. along the sides, the column diameters resembled the axial spaces in their variety.

As clearly as temple C matched the Apollo temple at Syracuse in ground-plan, it contrasted with it in elevation. No longer did awkwardly bulky members determine the impression. The columns were much slimmer (height = 4·53 instead of 4·0 lower diams.) and less densely packed (flank interaxial = 2·13 instead of 1·81 lower diams.). Since, as at Syracuse, the corner interaxials were not contracted, one may wonder what solution to the 'angle conflict', which Syracuse completely ignored, was found here. The answer is that no conflict whatever arose. As the architrave was quite narrow on account of the small diameter of the columns that tapered upwards considerably, and the triglyphs were quite broad owing to the wider interaxials, the corner triglyph almost came over the column axis anyway, and the slight remaining deficit was very easily made good by widening the corner triglyph itself (by 4–6 in.). Admittedly, this involved juxtaposing triglyphs and metopes of almost equal breadth, and hence value, without the rhythmic tension of later friezes. The alternating width of the mutules thereby became all the more glaringly conspicuous. Since the mutules above the triglyphs extended across the whole breadth of the latter, those above the equally broad metopes had to be made much narrower so that there should still be an intervening space (via).

Arrogantly indifferent to rules, the builders here just went ahead, quite heedless of precision and regularity. Hence, the temple did not derive its character and effect from the harmonious balance of parts, the pure timbre of the whole, but from the untempered expression and exuberance of these parts, from a wild, still uncurbed vitality, which one cannot fully estimate and apprehend until one has added in imagination the gay, lavish terracotta revetments and crowning members that covered pediment and roof-edge. The fronts of the coronas were garnished with decorated terracotta slabs.

fig. 6

129
fig. 87

424

Above them curved a similarly multicoloured sima, which consisted of a pierced interlace of flowers and tendrils on the flanks, and bore a heavy leaf pattern over a painted anthemion frieze along the pediments. Moreover, as in the case of the Geloan treasury, it was felt necessary to include this sima above the horizontal corona under the tympanum, where such roof elements are entirely out of place.

The front—these 'frontal' temples of the West had only one: that of the entrance end—was lent special emphasis by the famous metopes sculptured in relief. These display vividly narrated incidents, such as Perseus beheading Medusa or Heracles carrying off the Cercopes. The bold attempt to indicate depth—a quadriga is shown in front view—elucidates from another side the builders' penchant for spatial effects. An unparalleled, 9-ft.-high relief in brightly painted terracotta filled the tympanum, a gorgon's head of uncanny expressive power. It would not have taken much for the whole temple, with its columnar limbs stirred by vital energy and its snarling demon's face, to have changed into an unruly creature of fable.

A later period intervened in this archaic savagery, moderating it and 'modernizing' it in accordance with its own more sensitive taste. The roof ornaments were partly replaced with more delicately adorned substitutes, and the deep scotias separating the flattened echinuses from the shafts were filled in with stucco. It was thus that the temple stood over the progressively wasting city, until, during early Christian times, a severe earthquake brought it down upon the hovels of the villagers who dwelt around it. In 1926, parts of the north colonnade were re-erected.

87 Selinus, acropolis. Temple C. Front elevation (1:200). Bend at corners of pediment incorrect. R. Koldewey, 1899

88 Selinus, acropolis. Temple C. E. Gabrici, *Mon. Ant.* 35, 1933. Gorgon's head from centre of pediment (terracotta relief)

425

Cut off from the city by a small valley that opens into the now silted harbour of Selinus, the mountainous ruins of three more large peripteral temples rise up on the edge of a gently rising plain. There has been much speculation as to why a second precinct was laid out within sight of the city temples for a trio of gods, as sanctuaries outside towns were usually dedicated to a single deity. Had the space on the plateau become too cramped? Did a populous suburb grow so rich and proud that it raised bigger temples than those on the acropolis in rivalry with the city? Whatever the answer, this small trading city's boundless enthusiasm for building cannot have been due to piety alone, without that urge to compete which is innate in every Greek. The 'competitor' was probably the much more powerful Syracuse.

fig. 89   **TEMPLE F**   *Plates 134, 135, figs. 89–91*

When one examines its basic plan, the middle and oldest temple of the group, erected towards 530, shows itself to have been the direct successor of and, indeed, the counterpart to temple C: the same excessive stretching-out of a still narrower and almost equally long naos (about 30 by 131 ft.), its east end again closed by stumpy walls and large, now two-leaved bronze doors; the same spatial sequence of pronaos, naos, and adytum. This temple, too, was a monumentalized megaron.

It is otherwise with the peristyle, which, thanks to that delight in experimenting which is characteristic of the Selinuntine builders, marks a new stage of development. True, the double colonnade and 2-interaxial-deep outer portico were retained at the front; but, at the same time, it was now sought to adjust the column count at ends and sides, previously 6 by 17, to the balanced proportion of 6 to 14, which perhaps here recorded a distant echo from architecture in the motherland, and remained the rule for a whole series of Western classical temples. Considering the excessively long cella and the extra east portico in front, it was indeed a bold venture, only to be brought off by using the oddest of means: firstly by widening the temple through an increase in the breadth of the pteromata, which, made 19 ft. 4¼ in. across in the clear, became almost as wide as the cella interior; secondly by pushing the east end of the cella so close to the inner colonnade of the front porticoes that the leaves of the door almost knocked against the columns; and thirdly by unhesitatingly

reversing a formal law, held sacrosanct throughout the Greek world, to the effect that, where the interaxials varied, the end spaces had to be the wider (here, ends 14 ft. 8 in., sides 15 ft. 1⅛ in.). There thus came into being an archaically elongated peristyle, which hardly differed in its dimensions from that of temple C (79 ft. 11½ in. by 203 ft. 0¼ in. as against 78 ft. 6½ in. by 209 ft. 0⅝ in.), with an approximately 'classical' column count. Incidentally, the but slightly earlier temple D on the acropolis, not described here, constituted a similar but differently handled experiment. There, the inner colonnade at the east end was left out, but, so to speak, represented by the cella front itself, where columns replaced the antae. Moreover, the end interaxials were again made narrower than the side ones. The 'canonical' column count of 6 by 13 thus achieved was never lowered in the West.

In elevation, too, temple F demonstrated extremist tendencies, through the exaggerated slimness of its columns and the lightness of its entablature. Though a distinct partiality for light, attenuated proportions also characterizes the Selinuntine building tradition generally in comparison with, say, the obstinately heavy temples of Syracuse, it remains true that the extravagantly slender effect of temple F's columns (height of 29 ft. 10⅝ in. = 5·1 lower diams. of 5 ft. 10½ in.) was not surpassed even by Ionicizing Attica till the erection of the Athenian treasury at Delphi. In the West, even classical temples kept to more squat proportions (temple of Concord: 4·6 lower diams.).   *figs. 90*

The bias towards spaciousness and an open texture was stressed by the wide intercolumniation, the columns being related to the intervening gaps as 2 to 5, and by the astonishingly roomy ambulatory, into the depths of which the cella inevitably almost disappeared.

One last peculiarity of this freakish temple may be connected with the broad ambulatory. The spaces between the columns were closed by stone screens 14 ft. 9⅛ in. high, in such a way that the ambulatory was entirely cut off from the world outside. If the strict megaron form already suggests, as in the case of temple C, the mystical cult of Demeter, this passageway, which seems made for secret processions, does so even more strongly. Is it impermissible to concede so many places of worship to the same goddess in a single city? Megara possessed three Demeter sanctuaries, and Paestum built three big temples for Hera. Frieze and roof structure approximated to the 'canonical' form, though the triglyphs were, admittedly, still broad enough to allow a settlement of the 'angle conflict' by widening the corner metopes. At all events, the angle interaxials were not con-

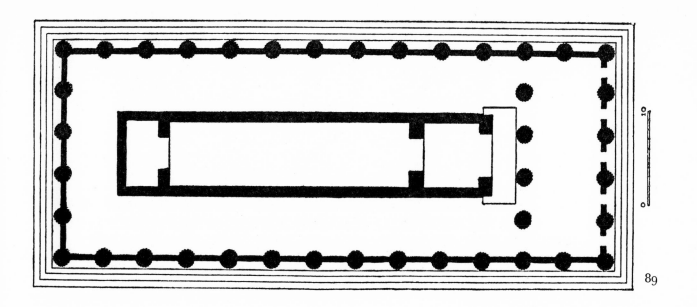

89

89–91 Selinus, temple F

89 Plan (1 : 400). J. Hulot and G. Fougères, 1910

90 East elevation. J. Hulot and G. Fougères, 1910

91 Order on flank. R. Koldewey, 1899

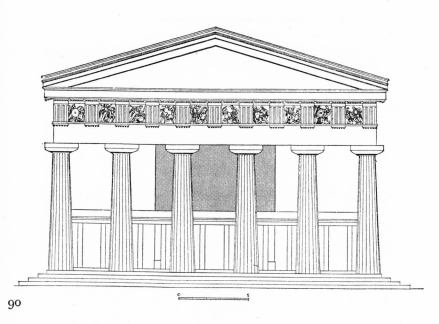

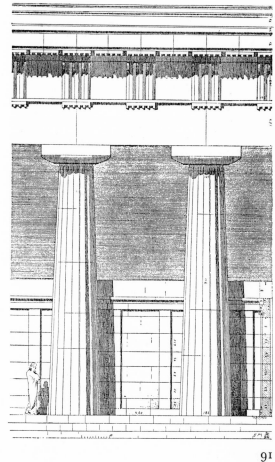

90

91

tracted. In contrast with C's, the corona mutules were all equally broad. Likewise, the wild gaiety of terracotta revetments had disappeared from along the gutters, to be replaced, so it seems, by a simple stone sima painted with delicate palmettes. The east end was distinguished, like C's, by sculptured metopes, and two slabs with gods—Athena and Dionysus?—overpowering giants have been found.

427

134, 135

The ruins of the northernmost of the three temples, once dedicated to Apollo according to an inscription found there, appear as a virtual mountain of debris even in the distance. From it projects like a tower one solitary, re-erected stump of column. Temple G stood, with its stylobate measuring 164 ft. 3¼ in. by 361 ft. 2½ in., in the same tradition as the gigantic dipteral temples of the East, the fame of which, on penetrating as far as Sicily, may have been the stimulus for its construction; and as the temple of Zeus at neighbouring Acragas, which was built to overtrump the work of the Selinuntines. Perhaps some megalomaniac tyrant at Selinus, which certainly did not lack overweening rulers, wanted to raise an eternal monument to himself. Herodotus tells (V, 48) of a tyrant called Pythagoras, against whom the Selinuntines, at the end of the sixth century, invoked the aid of an errant Spartan condottiere, who then, in his turn, seized power, holding it till he himself was slain at the altar of Zeus in the agora. Anyway, even if under a democracy, the citizens proceeded eagerly with their temple, its colossal dimensions corresponding only too well with their ambitious nature. They formed a complete contrast to the Athenians, who would have nothing to do with the Pisistratids' Olympieum, which exceeded the 'proper limits' (page 394).

It should be noted here that, thanks to its lighter proportions, the Ionic order could stand being expanded to a gigantic size, which, after all, made more clearly apparent its free, unburdened thrust upwards, much better than did the Doric, which, swollen to a state of crushing, mammoth-like heaviness and given column diameters, of from 10 to 13 ft., lost all connexion with man. Besides, according to its conception, a Doric temple ought to have been sensible and comprehensible as a sculpturally corporeal entity from every point, and such was really no longer the case with this colossus, which could only be taken in at a distance.

Nevertheless, one must admire the way the Selinuntine builders, having achieved in the course of all their previous experiments a considerable assurance and mastery, showed themselves able to cope with the problems set by such an enormous structure, unprecedented in the Doric domain. The layout is new, original, and also attractively clear. Though the elements of the design belong entirely to the native tradition, here they are combined in surprisingly novel ways, and there indecisive beginnings have been carried through to their full logical conclusions.

The building was evidently begun towards 520, directly after the completion of temple F. So protracted was the enormous undertaking that the wave of influences from the motherland, observable throughout Sicily from the early classical period (i.e. about 490) on, swept over the nascent structure, imposing on it new forms of capital, more harmoniously proportioned columns, and even alterations to the ground-plan in the spirit of the new style. Let us first consider the layout. Around a rectangular *fig. 9* cella measuring about 74 by 227 ft. which began, with its approximately 1 : 3 ratio, to overcome the tendency towards elongation, was set a peristyle of 8 by 17 columns. Its axes related it clearly to the cella, the wall axes and antae of which were aligned with the corresponding peristyle columns. Temple F received a 1½-interaxial-broad ambulatory and a 2-interaxial-deep front portico, and now the characteristically Selinuntine spaciousness of these features was increased still further, and the ambulatory made 2 interaxials wide on all sides. Owing to the colossal volumes of the temple, however, this meant that there was a clear width of about 38 ft. right round the cella to be spanned with wooden ceilings! Bear in mind that the breadth of the Parthenon's nave was exceeded here by nearly 6½ ft. Covering this ambulatory, only possible with trussed constructions, presupposed a highly developed technique in timbering.

As two end interaxials went to each pteroma and another three to the cella width, the fronts necessarily had eight columns each, and hence can in no way have been copied from the octastyle dipteral temples of Ionia. Despite its similar form, the 2-interaxial-deep ambulatory had equally little to do with those of the pseudo-dipterals popular in the East from the third century on (Sardis, page 472). The latter were produced by omitting the inner ring of columns from a dipteros, whereas this one was the outcome of progressively widening the simple ambulatory. An inner colonnade before the cella front, like those of C and F, would have obstructed with its second and seventh columns the pteromata's majestic spaces. Therefore, an arrangement already sketched out in temple D on the acropolis was chosen whereby a prostyle portico with 4 by 2 columns forming part of the cella was set before the antae, on which the architrave of this portico logically rested. By this means, an ambulatory was achieved that really did have a width of 38 ft. all the way round. One would expect two more columns between the pronaos antae, but, the ruins having so far been disentangled only here and there, these can neither be detected nor excluded. If such supports were lacking, as, in the absence of counter evidence, is generally

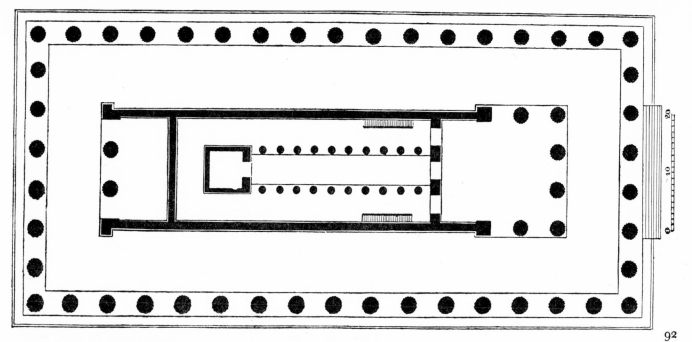

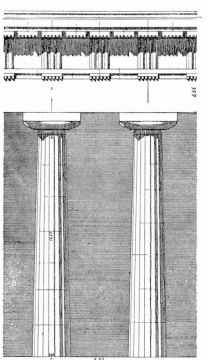

92

93

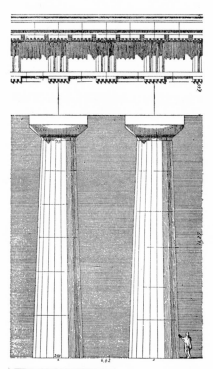

94

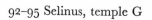

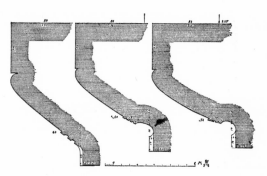

95

92–95 Selinus, temple G

92 Plan (1 : 667). J. Hulot and G. Fougères, 1910

93–94 Order of east side, *c.* 510 B.C. (*left*) and of west side, *c.* 470 B.C. (*right*, 1 : 250). R. Koldewey, 1899

95 The three types of capital (*c.* 470, *c.* 490, *c.* 510 B.C.). R. Koldewey, 1899

accepted, then the rectangle of pronaos and inner portico must have been open to the sky, for its area of about 55½ by 65 ft. was too big to roof over with an ancient wooden construction.

Entirely contrary to Sicilian custom, the naos was divided lengthways into three almost equally broad parts by two colonnades. Owing to the room's clear width of about 58 ft., these columns were indispensable for supporting the ceiling and roof beams, and positively prove that the naos was, or was to have been, roofed over. (Reconstructions with an open nave rely principally on Vitruvius's statement that temples of the celestial gods are supposed to be 'hypaethral'—i.e. open to the sky—and have octa-

429

style fronts. The Olympieum at Athens, unfinished in Vitruvius's day, is given as an example. This theorizing assertion has caused much confusion with regard to Didyma [page 463], especially in the eighteenth and nineteenth centuries.)

With a diameter of 3 ft. $9\frac{1}{4}$ in., the interior columns were about a third as thick as those of the peristyle. Broader ones would doubtless have appeared overpowering inside the naos. Consequently, these supports, ranged in two rows of 10, had to be superimposed in three tiers, so as to reach the height of the ceiling.

It is believed that, to start with, the usual Selinuntine adytum was partitioned off at the west end of the cella, but that later, in accordance with the 'modern' spirit of the fifth century, it came to be converted into a distyle in-antis opisthodomus. As a substitute for the adytum, a separate, quadrate structure was erected in the western part of the nave. The space behind its rear wall was left clear, so as to bring the aisles together in a broad, ⊓-shaped ambulatory, which, linked with the pronaos by a doorway at the east end of each aisle, closed up to form a complete circuit. It is possible that processions took place at Selinus in connexion with other gods besides Demeter, and such practices may have provided the outward motive for that enlargement of the ambulatories conspicuous in all Selinuntine temples. More important, though, is the latent cause: the Western Greeks' sense of space.

In the peristyle, the various building periods showed up clearly. The east end was still executed without angle contraction, according to archaic custom. Basically fixed as 20 Doric ft., the interaxial spacing constituted the most progressive features, for it hardly differed any longer as between front and flank (21 ft. $5\frac{1}{8}$ in. and 21 ft. $8\frac{1}{4}$ in. respectively. The difference of $3\frac{1}{8}$ in. or $1\frac{1}{2}$ per cent.—as against 13 per cent. on temple C—was of no consequence whatever, since the interaxials varied anyway by up to $9\frac{7}{8}$ in. because of inexact construction). On the later west front, contraction of the corner interaxials did appear, but at 1 ft. $1\frac{3}{8}$ in., the difference fell somewhat short of the 1 ft. $6\frac{1}{8}$ in. theoretically required. This discrepancy was made good by widening the angle metopes.

The time lag showed up much more strikingly in the columns themselves. Along the east, north, and
93, 95, right half the south side, slender, strongly tapered columns (height of 48 ft. $2\frac{3}{4}$ in. = 5 lower diams. of 9 ft. $8\frac{7}{8}$ in.) displayed archaic capitals with shallow, jutting echinuses. These have at the bottom four low, angular rings, below which comes the deeply incised hollow that was to be found between shaft and capital in almost identical form even on the earlier buildings at Selinus. On the 'transitional' capitals *fig. 95, middl*
from the west half of the south side, one can follow how a new formal tendency that was opposed to the old custom took possession of and confused people's minds. The profile has tightened into a steeper curve, *135, b*
now truly capable of bearing a load, yet at the base these capitals are nonsensically cut by an as yet undiscarded hollow. Finally, those from the west end confront us with the motherland's 'classical' form, its meaning now really understood. With an elastic bound, the echinus rises up out of the shaft, *figs. 9*
opposing its 'shoulder' to the load. The original *95, l*
hollow has vanished, and the three rings, against the lowest of which run the flutes, provide an element of transition rather than division.

With the change in style, the whole appearance of the columns inevitably altered. The place of the excessively thin columns, made about 5 lower diameters high, after the example of temple F, was taken by more thick-set shafts, which visibly took the strain of the entablature's burden of stone. With a height equal to about 4·5 lower diameters, they came near to obeying the laws of Peloponnesian buildings (Olympia 4·7 lower diams.). Similarly, there were normal Doric anta capitals flanking the entrance to the homeland-type distyle in-antis opisthodomus, which belonged to the latest building period, whereas the eastern antae were adorned with curious, Ionicizing decorative forms: volute bands, a large palmette at their centre. (They are a variety of the 'sofa' capital widely used in the West for crowning pillars, and Megara Hyblaea, with its rich admixture of Ionic ingredients, has provided a similar example. At the end of the sixth century, exiles from the mother-city were admitted into Selinus. Mention must be made of another Ionic element in temple G: a big dentil course, which seems to be evidence of an Ionic entablature over the interior columns or cella wall.) The development that we can follow in temple G took place, as it were, with a sudden jolt. Bear in mind that not only do the capitals of the first building period, set up towards 510, scarcely differ from all previous Western forms, but, with their shallow echinus, their scotia, and their rings, they resemble the earliest stone examples in the mother-country (Delphi, temple of Athena *fig. 2*
Pronaea I, about 600). The colonists thus hardly altered, in a hundred years, the shape they had inherited. With the migration, the steady sense of direction and the consistent growth of form which characterizes Greek art obviously disappeared. Here, architecture seems to have progressed not so much by steady development as by experiments, in an irregular course which led towards always new, always original, and often impressive feats, which,

however, had not nearly enough of the inevitable character of Greek design.

Like the majority of such buildings too big to measure by a human gauge, the Apollo temple was never finished. Only on a few columns was the fluting completed, the others having been abandoned at different stages: some round, some faceted, and some roughly grooved.

THE TEMPLE OF HERA (TEMPLE E) *Plates 130–134, fig. 96*

After all its deviations, all its self-willed experiments, Selinuntine building finally reached the clear heights of classical art with the southernmost and latest of this trio of peripteral temples. Temple E, begun for Hera when victory over Carthage had brought a revival of prosperity, is the peer of the West's other most mature creation, the temple of Hera II at Paestum—indeed, for all its differences, it ranks with the temple of Zeus at Olympia too. It was destroyed by the earthquake that threw down all the other buildings of Selinus, but has recently been reconstructed.

With a stylobate measuring 83 ft. $0\frac{7}{8}$ in. by 222 ft. $2\frac{7}{8}$ in., it is a little bigger than the three older peripteral temples C, D, and F, but must have looked unassuming beside the Apollo temple, which, at 164 ft. $3\frac{1}{4}$ in., was twice as broad. To retain an idea of these dimensions, bear in mind that, with

regard to size, the entire mother-country had only three temples in the same class as these four creations of a small trading city—not to mention the monstrous temple G: the Parthenon, the temple of Zeus at Olympia, and an almost unknown peripteral edifice near Corinth! With the coming of the classical change of spirit, the Selinuntines plainly lost their taste for extravagant ventures. Temple G was left unfinished, and the new Hera temple seems to have claimed all their available energy.

Though now informed in all its parts by the new principles of order from the motherland, the ground-plan does not break with the native tradition. This is evident even outwardly. To the pronaos at the east end corresponds an opisthodomus at the west, both having two columns in-antis, and the whole temple is quite symmetrically organized, with matching, 2-interaxial-deep porticoes, about a central axis. Instead of a frontal building that shows off one end, we find a temple sculptured in the round that makes an impression on all sides. At the same time, however, the adytum was faithfully retained, giving rise to the excessively long peristyle with 6 by 15 columns that also characterizes adytum- or double-temples in the motherland (Corinth, Delphi, Bassae). The cella was fitted extremely neatly into this peristyle, its anta faces being aligned with the third flank column from each corner and its side walls with the second and fifth end columns. An interaxial of 15 ft. $5\frac{3}{8}$ in. or 16 Ionic ft. of $11\frac{39}{64}$ in., the same at

fig. 96

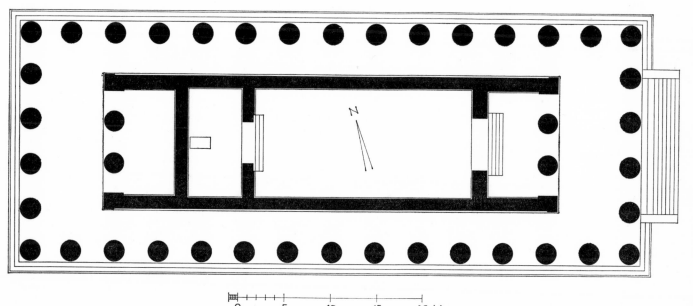

96 Selinus, temple of Hera (E). Plan (1 : 400). New drawing after R. Koldewey, 1899

431

ends and sides, is now the basic unit from which everything has been built up.

Furthermore, the architect knew how to relate the sides of the two dominant rectangles in his precisely calculated design: 3 interaxials wide and 10 interaxials plus 1 lower diameter long, the cella measuring 46 ft. 4⅝ in. by 162 ft. 0⅛ in. is proportioned as 2 to 7, while the stylobate has acquired—by addition, so to speak—a proportion of 3 to 8. Compared with the unstable and attenuated columns of temple F, the supporting members here are full of newly comprehended monumental weight, and enclose the cella in exceptionally compact rows (height of 33 ft. 3⅝ in. = 4·5 lower diams. of 7 ft. 5¾ in.; intercolumniation of 8 ft. 0½ in. almost amounts to column thickness—proportion 13 : 12). The angle contraction, which, thanks to the exact concordance of the joints, is already prepared for in the distribution of blocks in the bottom step, follows the practice of the homeland. No fear was felt over narrowing the angle axial spaces considerably (by 1⅝ in.), since this made the corners of the colonnades look denser and firmer. Through the noble details of the superstructure—tightly curving capitals, clearly articulated frieze, Doric cymas crowning antae, coronas, and cella walls—shines forth the classical model that the architect kept before his eyes: the temple of Zeus at Olympia, where Selinus customarily took part in the games, and where, since the end of the sixth century, it had maintained a treasury. Olympia was also the source of the, for the West, uncommonly discreet arrangement of sculptural decoration. As there, smooth, unadorned metopes ring the peristyle, while over the pronaos and opisthodomus entrances —closer to the deity but scarcely visible from afar— six carved slabs once graced both of the cella's now equally emphasized fronts. In each of the square fields, two figures organized about straight, unbroken bodily axes were opposed in, so to speak, architectonic compositions. These, like the characters' inward relationship which is now represented instead of

violent action, reveal the affinity with the Olympia metopes across the gulf of the regional style. Mythical encounters provide the subject-matter—Zeus and the far more majestic Hera; the savage tale of Artemis and Actaeon, whom the goddess's hounds tear to pieces—and are here accompanied by strangely calm gestures. Its connexion with Olympia also dates the temple to between 465 and 450.

If we have spoken of influences from the motherland this does not mean that the Western builders copied blindly. Rather was the stage reached, with the advent of the early classical period, at which the courses followed by the West and the Greek homeland met again, and the long-interrupted spiritual current uniting Greek with Greek once more began to flow. Remember the journeys to Sicily of Aeschylus and Plato. Moreover, it would appear that the heritage from the homeland, which the West here entered into for the second time, was only now really acquired and made their spiritual property.

In the process, the Selinuntine builders did not renounce their own tradition. Besides retaining even in this, their most perfect temple, the space sequence of pronaos, columnless naos roofed over without internal supports, and adytum beyond—the layout of a cella directed towards something hidden in its furthest depths—they actually made it still more evident through a gradation of heights. Thus, one ascended to the east portico by a flight of 10 steps (here the old frontality still asserted itself), another 6 steps took one up to the naos, and a final 3, which it was forbidden to climb, led into the adytum, where the base of Hera's statue can still be seen.

The temple of Hera remained the last big building raised at Selinus, which was dashed down to untimely destruction from the pinnacle it reached during the fifth century. In 409, the Carthaginians took the unprepared city after a nine-day siege. They razed it to the ground and butchered all its citizens, sparing only the women and children, who had taken refuge in the four large temples of the acropolis.

130, 131

132, 133

ACRAGAS (AGRIGENTO)

Between its founding round about 582 by settlers from neighbouring Gela and the latter's motherisland, Dorian Rhodes, and its destruction by the Carthaginians around 406, the Greek city of Acragas enjoyed a life-span of barely two centuries. Thereafter

resettled, but twice conquered and sacked again in the third century by Rome and Carthage, the place existed as a shadow till into late imperial times. It produced nothing further of importance, which makes its flowering in the sixth and fifth centuries seem all the more brilliant. Today, the remains of ten temples still bear witness to the extravagant enthusiasm for building with which Empedocles ominously and tauntingly reproached his fellow citizens (page 106). They were obviously blinded by this passion. Thus, hardly fifteen years after the city had been founded, control over the erection of a temple of Zeus on the acropolis—the first building in the West about which we have written information—was given to a man with an unscrupulous lust for power, who barricaded the citadel 'against thieves', and then fell with his labourers upon the unsuspecting citizens at the Thesmophoria festival. This Phalaris became a terror of a tyrant, but that did not prevent almost the same story from being repeated in 488, when Theron was entrusted with raising a temple to Athena in the citadel!

The above-mentioned temple of Zeus is supposed to lie beneath the present cathedral (though it has been searched for there in vain), while Theron's temple of Athena has been identified with the remains of a peripteral structure under the church of S. Maria dei Greci.

After the victory gained jointly by Theron and Gelon of Syracuse over Carthage at Himera in 480, the city stood at the peak of its power. The enemy's wealth and the host of captives were used to erect for Zeus Olympius the most enormous temple in Magna Graecia. Simultaneously, work began on a row of five temples set in loose succession against the broad ring of the city wall. It is a layout unique in the Hellenic world. On the south side facing the coast, *XX, XXVII* the wall follows a rocky terrace of the gently sloping city plateau. In the north, it encloses two rounded eminences: the 1,050-ft.-high acropolis hill, on which extends the modern town, and the 1,150-ft.-high 'Rock of Athena'. Already visible from afar, and overtopped by temples that once, stucco-coated, shone into the distance, this wall thus really does encircle the city like a costly diadem. Even if it was the pious notion of placing sections of the wall under the care of individual gods that gave rise to this curious arrangement, the imposing way in which Acragas thereby displayed itself may not have been unwelcome to its rulers and citizens.

THE NYMPHAEUM   *Plate 136*
AND TEMPLE OF DEMETER (C)

Let us first consider two unusual holy places of primordially simple form that date back to the founding of the city, and, like the earliest structures at Selinus, have preserved the pre-monumental elements of native Italian architecture. Both were dedicated to chthonic deities, no doubt principally Demeter and her associates.

The older, a spring-and-cavern sanctuary outside the city wall at the foot of the 'Rock of Athena', was taken over by the Greek immigrants from the expelled Siculi. In neat ashlar, they built a narrow room (40 ft. $5\frac{1}{8}$ in. by 9 ft. $10\frac{7}{8}$ in.) abutting crosswise *136* against the rocky slope, which was hollowed out for it. This chamber constituted, as it were, the pronaos to two confined natural caves, accessible through a pair of (as with the megaron at Gaggera) sharply tapering doors in the inner long wall. In Greece itself, caves aroused a feeling of reverence—often full of dread and directed towards the nether world, but also often trustfully serene and devoted to the nymphs. Here, the caves were both naos and adytum. From the one on the right welled forth a spring, the holy water of which was collected under the floor of the chamber and led into a number of basins lined up in an open court at the front. The room itself had the appearance of a cave, inasmuch as its walls leaned inwards considerably. Like that of the first megaron at Gaggera (page 421), the cornice of this structure consisted of a primitive corona without mutules. The forecourt with the basins opened outwards in an arrangement of pillars.

Ritual washing and rites of purification formed part of the Demeter cult everywhere. There was a highly venerated fountain by the sanctuary of Eleusis, and a spring wells up near the temenos at Gaggera. Demeter was not, however, a fountain deity, and so I am inclined to believe that the strange precinct was at first dedicated to a water divinity of pre-Greek origin, whom Empedocles names as mistress of the fourth element in the same breath as the mightiest gods of Olympus. 'Hear, first, the four roots of things: glittering Zeus, and life bestowing Hera, and Hades, and Nestis, who makes a mortal spring rise from her tears' (Fr. 6).

Nestis, goddess of 'tears and springs', belonged to the company of the subterranean powers, and was intimately related to mourning Demeter, who distributed the earth's fruits and death. She may gradually have merged with the latter, who, towards the beginning of the fifth century, did in fact receive a temenos set a little higher up the slope and reached by steps in the rock.

Here, a simple, megaron-like temple of Demeter (C) with naos and pronaos (43 ft. $7\frac{1}{2}$ in. by 99 ft. 1 in.) was built of beautiful isodomic masonry at the centre of a terrace cut in the rock and measuring about 27 by 105 yds. Today, it still stands to a height of 25 ft. 9 in., as the naos was converted by the Normans into a little church of S. Biagio. From the pronaos

433

97 Acragas, sanctuary of the chthonic deities. Restoration. P. Marconi, 1931. Temple L in background; before it, temple I (so-called temple of the Dioscuri), then, from left to right, naiskoi 3, 2, and 1; in foreground, two sacred precincts with round altar behind them

have survived the entrance steps, the orthostat course of the side walls, and the stone grid on which the paving slabs lay. Not a trace exists of the two columns between antae that, since the remains of a normal Doric corona have been found, one would really expect.

To the right of the temple stood two of those remarkable round altars, hollowed out inside, that we shall meet again in the second chthonic sanctuary at Acragas.

THE SANCTUARY OF THE $\qquad$ *Plate 137, fig. 97*
CHTHONIC DEITIES AND TEMPLES I AND L

During the last few decades, a spacious temenos has been uncovered on the southern edge of the city, near a gate through which the road led down to the shore. It was not the object of the peculiar buildings that crowded together in it to reveal the splendour and dignity of their deity, but to guard and conceal its secrets. Here, in fact, the subterranean powers were worshipped: Demeter who made the corn—Acragas's wealth—sprout from the soil, and Persephone who dwelled above in the light or below in the dark, according to the season—but also, as the great number of altars suggests, Persephone's gloomy consort Hades and the sorceress Hecate.

It appears that the Siculi had a nature sanctuary at the same spot before the city was founded. (I can see no need to assign the Greek buildings to the seventh century on the strength of the few votive

offerings from this period, which the natives too, of course, obtained through trading with the Greeks. The Siculi were not so peaceable as to tolerate foreigners building over their cult site. Besides, the developed ashlar technique argues against a date prior to the city's foundation.)

A big round altar, about 26 ft. across, formed the focus of the sanctuary. One climbed up over 3 large circular steps to the centre hollowed out like a well, in order to pour a libation down it. The terracotta vessels (*kernoi*) intended for such libations were discovered in the sacrificial pit (*bothros*). A great many other altars—fifteen altogether—were dispersed throughout the sanctuary, some rectangular, some round, some with a pit, some without. In addition, three megaron-like little temples of the most unassuming appearance and dimensions were grouped about the round altar in what seems a wholly arbitrary way (1: 16 ft. 2⅞ in. by 34 ft. 11⅛ in., with pronaos and naos; 2: 13 ft. 9⅜ in. by 30 ft. 2¼ in., like 1 but with adytum; 3: 30 ft. 6⅛ in. by 34 ft. 3½ in., set at right angles to 2, with open porch formed by four supports and naos). None of these naiskoi appears to have possessed a stone Doric cornice or even a triglyph frieze. Strangest of all, however, are two little walled precincts, which, since they consisted of a series of roofless compartments, are to be conceived as a mixture of temple and temenos. Despite its regular ground-plan, the first formed a small labyrinth. From the north, one entered a kind of pronaos and naos (should this middle section perhaps be restored with a roof?), turned left into a

*137
fig. 97*

434

space containing a cuboid altar, and then had to pass through a narrow chamber behind the naos, in order, finally, to reach the right-hand part, almost the entire breadth of which was filled by a large round altar with a sacrificial pit. Were the 'mystae' initiated here, as at Eleusis, on being received into the fellowship of the cult? Did secret sacrificial rites take place? The second precinct, which was more simply formed, also contained a round altar for libations.

There remains the conspicuous absence of a natural order, of the orientation of all parts towards a religious focus such as characterizes sanctuaries in the motherland which gradually grew up around a very ancient sacred core. Here, the buildings were seemingly thrown together. Though the big altar was set nearly at the centre, it did not have the slightest influence on the direction and situation of the temples and precincts. In this colonial city, things went forward with hurried, giant strides, there being no time for the calm continuity of organic growth. It was thus possible for architecture at Acragas to bound, in one century, across the enormous distance from such rustically primitive little temples to the mightiest, most colossal building ever raised in Doric territory: the Olympieum.

In the fifth century, the modest temple structures pressed close to the earth no longer sufficed for the newly comprehended dignity of the 'great goddesses'. Around 550, a Doric peripteral temple was erected at the sanctuary's southern boundary in conformity with the now fully ascendant classical principles of form (so-called temple of the Dioscuri, I, with 6 by 13 columns and stylobate measuring about 44 ft. by 101½ ft.), to be followed a few decades later by a second, larger one (temple L, same ground-plan, stylobate about 56½ ft. by 127 ft.).

Along with the foundation trenches and a few squared stones on which the cella paving lay, only scattered remains of the superstructure of the first temple (I) have been found. The picturesque north-west corner, Agrigento's well-known landmark for tourists, is entirely a product of the Sicilian archaeological commission of the years 1836–71. While the crepidoma is modern, the much patched-up columns, capitals, and triglyphs actually do belong to the temple. The cornice with its surfeit of mouldings—an Ionic beaded astragal and Doric and Lesbian cymas as it were prop up the jutting corona—and the curved, widely spreading sima with separately affixed lions' heads both date from a Hellenistic restoration of the temple, which was probably burned down during the catastrophe of 406. Its much more severely modelled original sima has since been identified.

Only a few stones from the north-east corner of the larger temple L still lie in their original positions, but enough parts have been found for us to obtain a picture of the superstructure: column drums, a smallish capital from the pronaos and opisthodomus columns (lower diam. 4 ft. 4 in.), a bigger one from the peristyle (lower diam. about 4 ft. 7 in.), as well as fragments of the architrave and corona. The echinus already presented the dry, rectilinear profile, and the corona the hard, angular cutting characteristic of the end of the fifth century. It is unnecessary to go more closely into these temples—of Demeter and Persephone?—because, in those of Concord and Juno Lacinia, we shall be discussing two wholly related structures.

TEMPLE A,   *Plates XX, 138, 139,*
SO-CALLED TEMPLE OF HERACLES   *figs. 98, 99*

The series of peripteral buildings at Acragas was initiated by a large temple with 6 by 15 columns, set on a knoll about half-way along the precipitous cliff bounding the city towards the south. (We do not know if the temple of Zeus, begun on the acropolis in 570, already had a peristyle, though its cost—200 talents—suggests it did.) When the architect commenced his new structure around 500, he had the peripteral temples of Syracuse and Selinus in mind as important examples, and was bent on surpassing them in various respects: above all in size, so that temple C at Selinus, previously the most imposing temple apart from the colossal temple G, came to be exceeded by about 6½ ft.; but also in the clarity of the arrangement. Probably for the first time in Sicily, the cella had a symmetrically balanced 'canonical' layout with pronaos and opisthodomus, *fig. 98* each having two columns in-antis. The usual adytum was lacking. All this revealed the suddenly irrupting influence of Peloponnesian architecture, which, gaining strength, visibly drew the architecture of the West into its path during the next decades. In the present temple, archaic Western and pre-classical Peloponnesian features mingled in such an individual way that the term 'transitional style' has been applied.

The naos space of the still archaically elongated cella was obviously conceived in terms of simple numerical relations (38 ft. 10⅝ in. by 97 ft. 3 in. = 36 by 90 Doric ft.; proportion 2 : 5), and could thus form the 'core' around which the design was organized. On the other hand, the breadth and length of the stylobate (82 ft. 11¼ in. by 219 ft. 11⅛ in.) were related approximately as 3 to 8, so that the inner rectangle was already attuned to the outer

435

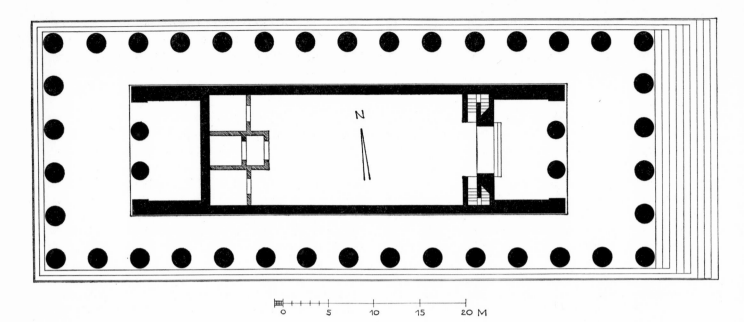

98 Acragas, temple A, so-called temple of Heracles. Plan (1 : 400). New drawing after R. Koldewey and P. Marconi

99 Acragas, temple A, so-called temple of Heracles. Order on flank with section through entablature (1 : 150). R. Koldewey, 1899

436

one, with the column count of 6 by 15 reflecting the length's predominance. According to Sicilian custom, the porticoes were made almost 2 interaxials deep—though the double front portico, hitherto usual, was abandoned—without, however, any care being taken to relate the antae to the corresponding flank columns. It was otherwise with the pteromata, since the cella walls were aligned with the second and fifth end columns—a form of alignment which was becoming the rule in the motherland also.

Yet it was only through a decisive step, which the West plainly took before the mother-country, that a real ordering of the ground-plan and a consistently even rhythm in the peristyle were achieved—namely, that of making the end and flank interaxials, hitherto always differentiated, exactly equal. Naturally, there had to be a constant column diameter corresponding to it. In the West, the standard interaxial first appeared towards 510 (see Paestum, page 414), in the motherland not until towards 480 (Sunium, page 397). At Acragas, the arcnitect met with certain difficulties in combining the uniform interaxial of 15 ft. $1\frac{1}{2}$ in. with the 3 : 8 proportion intended for the stylobate. Even the corner axial spaces had the normal width on the flanks, but at the ends a compromise was imposed. The angle interaxials had to be narrowed by about $4\frac{3}{8}$ in., and the ideal breadth measurement of the stylobate reduced by about $3\frac{7}{8}$ in. Or could the diminution of these corner interaxials, which admittedly fell far short of the 1 ft. $0\frac{5}{8}$ in. required in order really to align the triglyph frieze, possibly have been a first, timid attempt at the angle contraction previously unknown in the West?

The elevation was also derived in simple numerical proportions from the unit interaxial of 15 ft. $1\frac{1}{2}$ in. Thus, the height to the corona (45 ft. $2\frac{1}{2}$ in.) was related to it as 3 to 1, and the entablature height (12 ft. $2\frac{1}{8}$ in.) as 4 to 5. True, this hardly went beyond a playful experiment on the building of numerical series, such as must have been confided to the West by the then expanding Pythagorean school.

38, 139

The structural forms betray a critically uncertain vacillation between old and new. Comparatively slim with their height of 33 ft. $0\frac{1}{2}$ in. or 4·84 lower *fig. 99* diameters, the columns still had shafts that were separated by a hollow from the capital, the echinus of which already opposed the entablature in a resiliently steep curve (cf. capitals of temple G's *fig. 95, middle* 'transitional style'). Four rows of guttae instead of the normal three appeared under the uniformly broad mutules. Besides the peristyle entablature, a second, smaller one with its own triglyph frieze has been found, and can only have extended above the ends of the cella. Strange to say, it included a corona (now with three rows of five instead of six guttae below!), which was evidently added to satisfy a naïve penchant for completeness, although such a link with the roof had absolutely no business inside a portico. The gutter took the form of an imposing limestone sima, 2 ft. $8\frac{1}{4}$ in. high, which, despite being decorated with anthemions and lion-heads in the developed style of the mid-fifth century, imitated the steep profile, enriched by astragals and cymas, of archaic terracotta simas. It was probably substituted, half a century after the building period, for a similar moulded sima of terracotta. Though the naos—roofed over, of course—had a clear width of 38 ft. $9\frac{3}{4}$ in. (!), it contained no inner columns, to which there was plainly an aversion in the West. During Roman times, three small rooms were introduced at the rear end, the middle one obviously as an aedicula for the cult image.

Whether a Roman statue of Asclepius found on the site indicates that, at least in later times, the god of healing was adored here, whether he was rather the cult companion of Apollo, or whether the work arrived at this spot merely by chance will remain an open question. The association with Heracles on the strength of Cicero's mention of a Heracles temple by the agora is completely arbitrary.

THE OLYMPIEUM (TEMPLE B)　　　*Plates 140, 141, figs. 100, 101*

Approximately between the sanctuary of the chthonic gods and the temple of Heracles, there spreads out over a knoll sloping away towards the north and west the field of debris left by an enormous temple that Theron began for Zeus Olympius as a victory monument after the defeat of Carthage in 480. Goethe described it in 1787 with a distinct undertone of disapproval: 'The temple of Jupiter . . . lies asprawl like the mass of bones of a giant skeleton. . . . Everything with a shape to it has disappeared from this rubbish heap, except for a monstrous triglyph and a piece of a half-column of the same proportion. I measured the triglyph with outstretched arms, and could not reach across it, whereas an idea of the column's fluting can be obtained from the fact that, standing in a flute, I filled it like a small niche, touching it with both shoulders. Twenty-two men placed next to one another in a circle would just about make up the circumference of such a column. We left with the disagreeable feeling that there was absolutely no work here for the draughtsman.'

The building deserves to be showered with superlatives. It was the biggest Doric temple of all, and it is clear that it was intended to put the colossal temple G at Selinus in the shade. It was the most original, but also the most abstruse, creation of the Greek world, and in it both the West's megalomania, which here breached alike the outward and inward barriers of the Doric order, and its pronounced sense of space found their most potent expression.

Upon rectangular foundations measuring 180 ft. *fig. 100* $8\frac{1}{2}$ in. by 364 ft. $2\frac{1}{2}$ in. (ratio 1 : 2), there lay a crepidoma of 5 steps (stylobate 173 ft. $0\frac{3}{8}$ in. by 361 ft. $2\frac{5}{8}$ in.), above which rose a peristyle with 7 by 14 columns. This column count being lower than the 8 by 17 of the almost equally big temple G, all members grew in proportion to the interaxial, which was now enlarged to over 26 ft. 3 in. Hence, the columns attained the incredible diameter of 13 ft. $3\frac{1}{2}$ in., along with an admittedly hypothetical height of 59 ft. $8\frac{1}{2}$ in. or 4·5 lower diameters. However, these monstrous supports were certainly not columns in the true sense of the word, for they were only applied as half-columns to a wall enclosing the structure on every side. It is thus a question of a 'pseudo-peripteral' temple, a gigantic closed hall possessing an external circuit of engaged columns that supported a Doric entablature of correspondingly heavy proportions, with normally formed triglyph frieze and cornice. One is reminded of *figs. 89–91* temple F at Selinus, its intercolumnial spaces blocked to half their height by screens. Yet there the columns, fluted all round, remained what they were, and, by virtue of the upper openings, the ambulatory, too, exercised its proper function. Here, the half-column was intimately related to the wall even

437

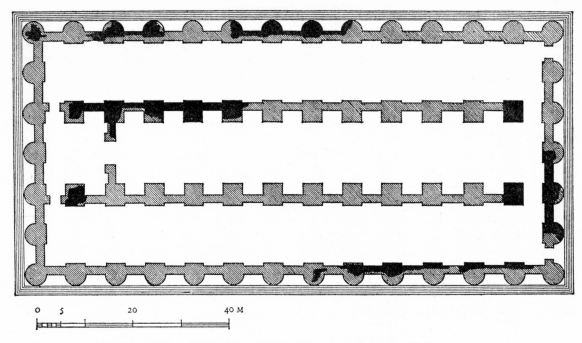

100 Acragas, Olympieum (temple B). Plan (1 : 750). A. W. Lawrence, 1957

140,
fig. 101

technically, having been built in the same way out of ashlar up to the capital! Moreover, looking at this wall from within, one saw pilasters that formed pendants to the half-columns. Obviously under the inspiration of temple F, it was attempted to simulate the effect of open intercolumniations by a device no less bold than astonishing. Powerful masses of masonry set back and topped by projecting mouldings suggested such intercolumnial screens, and on them stood huge, naked 'Atlantes', which, straining against the heavy entablature with all their strength, formed ingenious counterparts to the graceful caryatids of Delphic treasuries. Thus, the male figure conceived in the round took its place beside the Doric columns as the latter's corporeal equivalent, sharing with it the load. (The architraves had a joint directly above each Atlas, and, though additionally secured by letting iron beams into them, really did rest upon the heads and arms.) Continued behind these sculptured bodies of giants, the wall entirely withdrew into the background and shadows, in a sense dissolving. Highly successful and skilful as this solution was, one none the less observes with some disquiet how here a previously moderate inclination for façade effects—think of the popularity of overstressing the front—broke free of all restraint, and, skipping centuries, produced the first 'blind façade' as if by magic. At all events, no Greek prefiguration of such illusionistic amalgams of wall and columns are known to us.

What, however, did the interior look like, for which the open peristyle was sacrificed? Even the siting of the entrances was peculiar. They are unquestionably to be sought at the east end, since a sacrificial altar measuring 57 ft. 4⅞ in. by 178 ft. 9¾ in. extended across the full width of the temple before this front. A column blocked the central axis, and the walls in the two adjacent intercolumniations survive to such a height as to exclude doors. Hence, the doors must have been at the corners, from which one entered the 'hall' in an unsuitably furtive manner. Another entrance was recently detected in the middle of the south flank between the seventh and eighth columns. Inside, the walls of this enormous hall were articulated by pilasters 68 ft. 10¾ in. tall and 11 ft. 7 in. broad, which had Doric anta capitals and corresponded to the external columns. Two rows of piers with the same height and interval divided the space lengthwise into three nearly equally wide compartments. Except for the first at the east end and possibly the last at the west, the 'intercolumniations' were again closed by walls. These, so I am inclined to believe, here really were constructed as screens reaching only to half room height and thus made clearly evident and accessible to the eye the almost immeasurable vastness of the space.

One cannot understand this pillared hall, rising aloft in its stiff, inhuman monumentality, with the aid of Greek ideas of form. Are the nave and aisles to be regarded as cella and pteromata? A space does

141, be

101 Acragas, Olympieum (temple
B). Order on flank with section.
(1 : 250) A. W. Lawrence, 1957

0   5   10 METRES

appear to have been separated off at the end of the
nave as a kind of adytum. Yet besides failing to open
outwards like pteromata, the aisles did not even link
up right round the cella. Was the whole a gigantic
tripartite naos, then? In view of the ruin's deplorable
state of preservation and the many contradictory
attempts to reconstruct it, such questions are rather
to be answered through consideration of historical
factors. The temple was a victory monument, to
build which the Carthaginian prisoners of war slaved
away in their thousands. Did the Atlantes symbolize
the vanquished foe? At all events, as recorded by
Diodorus (13, 82), the subjects of the pediment
reliefs, which must have reached a height of about
20 ft., celebrated the glorious Greek victory. On the
east front, the Olympian gods overcame the giants,
while on the west the Greeks conquered Troy, as a
symbol of Carthage.

An attempt has been made to show that the pillared
hall was a Carthago-Phoenician type of structure
native to the southern and eastern fringes of the
Mediterranean. If it was here, so to speak, incorporated with the Greek peripteral temple, this means
that architecture, too, celebrated in its own tongue
the victory of Greece over Carthage, Zeus over
Moloch. Thus, the hybrid combination of incompatible elements, the discrepancy between inside and
outside that could scarcely be hidden by screening
forms, becomes comprehensible. Likewise, the bar-
barization of various details, such as the unusual and
stiff formation of the moulded 'bases' under the Doric
half-columns and the walling, is traceable to foreign
rather than Ionic influence. At the same time, the
Western Greeks obviously grasped eagerly at the
new possibilities offered to them by an alien world,
in order to indulge their secret passion for creating
the largest of spaces to an extent unfeasible even in
temple G. For, despite its ample porticoes and its
enormous naos, that temple was still constrained by
the severe formal laws of the Doric style.

439

Transcending human powers, this temple, too, was never finished. The roof seems, at least in part, to have been missing. It was probably intended to cover the entire hall with a saddle-roof, as the formation of the pediments suggests. This would have involved spanning the nave's clear width of about 41 ft. with wooden tiebeams (in the case of the Heracles temple 38 ft. 9¾ in. was spanned, in that of the Priene assembly hall 47 ft. 5⅝ in.).

When the Carthaginians took Acragas for the second time, the surviving citizens sought refuge in their temple of victory. Its remains stood erect long after that. The year 1401 saw the collapse of the last columns and 'giants', three of which, each bearing a tower upon its head, have formed Agrigento's municipal arms since the Middle Ages.

TEMPLE D,   *Plates XX, XXIX,*
so-called TEMPLE OF JUNO LACINIA   *146–149*

It seems the Acragantine builders exhausted on the monstrous Olympieum all the energies that they could apply to such excesses. For their next peripteral structure, the so-called temple of Juno Lacinia, erected towards 450 (the non-committal designation 'temple D' is really preferable to this demonstrably false name), was wholly under classical influence. Even as regards size, it followed the example of temples in the motherland, its stylobate, which measures 55 ft. 5¾ in. by 125 ft., being only a little bigger than that of the temple at Bassae. Thus, it looked modest beside the previous buildings of the West. Its formal predecessor, the temple of Heracles, covered more than two and a half times the area, and there would have been room for nine whole temples of its size in the Olympieum!

Henceforward, the effect of this noble architecture depended not on might and largeness, but on clarity and harmony of form. Even the situation upon the eastern prominence of the ridge bordering the city to its south appears to have been chosen with sure insight into the mutual relation of landscape and building. In Greece itself, where sanctuaries were always tied to ancient cult sites, there was never an opportunity to consider the most favourable location for a temple; but in this young city it may have been determined wholly with an eye to the effect at a distance. Today, with the warm ochre of its soft and, alas, rapidly crumbling local shell-limestone, of which all buildings at Acragas were made, the ruin is beginning in its decay to merge again with the natural rock slope. A protective coating of white stucco once clothed the porous stone.

XX,
XXIX

Before the temple's east front, right at the edge of the precipice, there lies a huge, well-preserved altar. Measuring 97 ft. 9¼ in. by 17 ft. 2¾ in., it extends in width about 16½ ft. beyond either side of the temple. A flight of 10 steps led up from the west to a platform and to the giant 'sacrificial table' measuring about 5 ft. 3 in. in height and 13 ft. by 95 ft. in area. The burnt offerings once made here (to which deity?) cast their light far into the distance across the surrounding countryside. Similar altars have been detected in front of all the temples at Acragas. A corresponding flight, likewise of 10 steps, was set against the temple's east end. Once more, the whole arrangement reveals the—by this time subdued—Sicilian desire for grandiose effects.

147

146

The temple itself attained, with its 6 by 13 columns, the balanced proportion of the motherland. Except for the crepidoma of 4 instead of 3 steps, its structure likewise conformed to the Doric 'canon', from the noble capitals, now springing up tautly, to the clear-cut frieze, the triglyphs of which were pleasingly related to the metopes as 2 to 3.

148,

The ground-plan was determined by the precise fitting of the cella into the peristyle. As the antae of the pronaos and opisthodomus corresponded to the middle of the second intercolumniation on either flank, both porticoes had a depth of exactly 1½ interaxials. The side walls were aligned with the second and fifth end columns. Thus, the size of the cella, fixed as 3 by 9 interaxials or 31 ft. by 90 ft. 5 in., was derived from the peristyle.

148

There was nothing further for the creative imagination to remodel in the structural forms, and the plan also obeyed a rigid law. Accordingly, the architect devoted all his ability to shaping the invisible and achieving pure proportions. Number, deemed sacred in Sicily since Pythagoras as the 'essence of things', had always held a special position in architecture there. The master of the Juno Lacinia temple tried to harmonize a standard interaxial theoretically equal all round, as the basic element of his building, with the simple 4 : 9 relation predetermined for the sides of the stylobate. This meant, in practice, that he had to put up with a slight disparity between the front and flank interaxials (10 ft. 2⅞ in. and 10 ft. 0¾ in.). The angle conflict was only partly settled through introducing 'single contraction' of the corner interaxials, as in the motherland, but by 3⅛ in. instead of the 13⅜ in. really required. Determinant of the columns' appearance, the relation between diameter and intercolumniation, body and intervening space, was established as 4 to 5 (4 ft. 6¾ in., 5 ft. 8⅛ in.), while the height of the order to the roof-edge equalled 3 interaxials, and that of the columns (20 ft. 10⅜ in.) 4·6 lower diameters (Olympia 4·67).

Why, though, does this arrangement, which in its proportions comes so close to that of the temple of Zeus at Olympia, lack the latter's tension and force? Perhaps because the irrational, 'sculptural' idiosyncrasies—entasis, column tilting, curvature—are missing.

There remains to be mentioned a feature that this building shared with almost all classical peripteral structures in the West, from the Athena temple at Paestum onwards: the entrance wall of the naos was thickened to such an extent that there was room within it, on either side of the door, for a little winding staircase leading up to the loft. As usual, the naos was a hall covered by a wooden ceiling without the aid of columns, and later, probably in Roman times, it received a marble floor. There is no trace of a pedestal for the cult image. Neither the written sources nor any of the finds give a hint as to which deity was worshipped here.

149

TEMPLE F,   *Plates XX, XXVII, XXVIII,*
so-called TEMPLE OF CONCORD   *142–145, fig. 102*

XX, XVII

About 750 yds. west of the Juno Lacinia temple, a twin of almost equal size was raised barely twenty-five years later on a second, low knoll at the edge of the same ridge. Once again, the accepted name—the temple of Concord—is quite arbitrary. Not only is this the city's best preserved building, but it shares with the Theseum and the so-called temple of Poseidon at Paestum the honour of being one of the three most complete temples of the Greek world. Both pediments still spread, with the corona, over the fronts. Though the west end of the cella is much restored, the walls still stand, and bear their triglyph frieze above the pronaos entrance. True, this makes the weathering and progressive decay of the soft shell-limestone, through which every detail is being effaced, all the more depressingly conspicuous.

VIII, 142

144

None less than St. Gregory of Girgenti saved the temple from destruction by turning it into a church in 597. His biographer, the monk Leontius, tells the remarkable story of this event. Injured by calumnies, the bishop turned his back on his city, and settled in the ancient temple by the south wall. He drove out the demons that had hidden there in the εἴδωλον—i.e. image or cult image—of Ἔβερ and Ῥάψ, and converted the temple into a church of the apostles Peter and Paul. (During this conversion, the side walls of the naos were pierced to form arcades, and its west wall was demolished.) Does a memory of

145

the temple's old deities perhaps live on in this legend? From which pair of gods could 'Eber' and 'Raps' derive? Are the Dioscuri, who have an attested link with Acragas, to be considered?

The preceding description of the temple of Juno Lacinia also applies to the temple of Concord, as the buildings correspond even in detail: an equal number of columns (6 by 13), an identical flight of 10 steps before the front, the same axial connexion of the cella with the peristyle (1½-interaxial-deep porticoes, 1-interaxial-broad pteromata). The little stairways, again hidden either side of the naos door in the thickened cross-wall, are here preserved up to the roof. Above the cross-walls and the cella's distyle fronts, gables on which rested the purlins were carried up to roof level. They have survived over the door wall and the west end of the opisthodomus. Low, saddle-shaped openings were made in them to connect up the loft spaces.

Apart from minimal alterations to the details, the one, but extremely important change, which reveals all the development of a generation, lies in the proportioning. The dimensional relations have here been realized with absolute precision, thanks to the extremely careful stone-cutting. Whereas, for example, the interaxials varied in size on the Juno Lacinia temple by up to 2 in., here only imperceptible errors of about ⅕ in. have crept in. Thus, the construction was ten times as accurate. The problem of combining a uniform interaxial with a firmly proportioned stylobate, still unsettled in the temple of Juno Lacinia, has now been solved. The stylobate (55 ft. 6⅜ in. by 129 ft. 3⅞ in.) is proportioned as 3 to 7, while the interaxials, fixed as 10 ft. 5⅞ in. at the ends and 10 ft. 6¼ in. at the sides, hardly differ any more. It is true, however, that an expedient of the utmost complexity caused the 'standard' interaxial actually to appear only once at the ends, namely in the middle. For in order to get the triglyphs over the column axes, given an equal distribution of triglyphs and metopes that were again related as 2 to 3, the angle interaxials had to be narrowed by 12 in. (fig. 6C). So as to prevent this contraction being too conspicuous, not only the outermost interaxials were reduced at all four corners (by 8 in.) but also the adjacent ones (by 4 in.), thus producing 'double contraction'. Because of this displacement, the second columns, too, were in danger of getting out of line with the axes of the triglyphs above them, as actually happened at Segesta, for example. To avoid this, the metopes and corner triglyphs of the first interaxials had to be widened and the metopes of the second narrowed. It was a mathematical vicious circle: to achieve apparent uniformity, a system involving three

fig. 102

*fig. 6*C

different interaxial, metope, and triglyph breadths was cunningly devised. Compare this with the Parthenon's diametrically opposed principle of angle contraction (page 374). There a feeling for sculptural form was determinant, here a formalistic misapplication of reason.

After the uncertain struggle for the valid form had ended with the perfection of a systematically balanced arrangement, after each part had been related to every other and to the whole so inevitably and significantly that one single act of interference would have disorganized everything, only a final polish, an extremely delicate adjustment could lead any further. The height at last reached was also a summit. With every additional step, the cool clarity of ratio and the abstract nature of number inevitably began to stifle the vivacity of the Doric temple— once, in temple C of the Selinuntine acropolis, so intractably wild, and later, in the temple of Hera E, consciously controlled.

Goethe, who remarked before the temple of Concord that 'its slender architecture already approaches our standard of what is beautiful and pleasant, it is related to those of Paestum as the form of a god to the figure of a giant', must have felt precisely this difference in vivacity when standing for the second time in front of the temple of Poseidon at Paestum, despite the classicist prejudice of his century. '. . . Paestum itself; it is the last and, I would almost say, the grandest image that I now carry away with

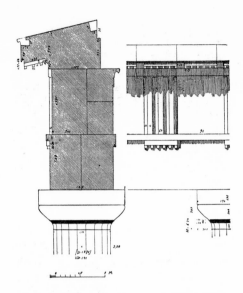

102 Acragas, temple F, so-called temple of Concord. Capital and entablature (1 : 75). R. Koldewey, 1899

me northwards. Also, the middle temple is in my opinion preferable to everything else that one sees in Sicily.'

The temple of Concord and the following temple at Segesta are the last Doric peripteral structures of Magna Graecia. This architecture thus concludes with sublimity, as if it had itself arranged its early end.

SEGESTA

Plates XXXIII, XXXVI, 154, 155, fig. 103

Lying six miles from the sea on a lonely hill at the north-west tip of Sicily, the ruins of Segesta are those not of a Greek, but of a 'barbarian' city. The Elymians, who were already established there before the Hellenic colonization, looked with admiration and mistrust at the superior towns of their Greek neighbours, and particularly at flourishing Selinus. They willingly seized all the gifts of Hellenic civilization, and expressed their gratitude by always allying themselves with the Doric cities' enemies, the Phoenicians and Carthaginians. In 416, they persuaded the Athenians to make their disastrous Sicilian expedition, by holding out false hopes of inexhaustible riches; and after the Attic army had been wiped out before Syracuse, Segesta called the hereditary foe Carthage into

the land. Selinus and Acragas were destroyed in 409 and 406, only Syracuse being able to hold its own. When, tired of Carthaginian control, Segesta wanted a century later to take sides with Syracuse, it met the same fate. In 307, the tyrant Agathocles ravaged the entire city, and derisively named its remains 'Dicaeopolis' ('City of Justice').

'The temple is strangely situated: at the top of a broad and long valley, on an isolated hill, though still surrounded by rocks, it looks across a wide stretch of countryside into the far distance, but with only a glimpse of sea. The neighbourhood reposes in melancholy fruitfulness, all cultivated and almost nowhere a dwelling. Countless butterflies fluttered over thistles in flower. . . . The wind soughed through

442

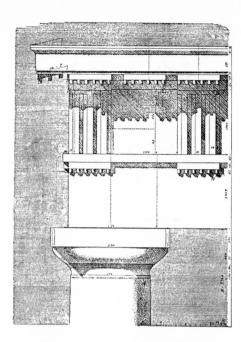

103 Segesta, temple. Capital and entablature (1 : 75). R. Koldewey, 1899

the columns, as in a wood, and birds of prey hovered screaming above the entablature' (Goethe, *Italienische Reise*).

XXIII The temple visited by Goethe stands outside the ancient city. Thanks to the wilderness around it, it has hardly been stripped let alone taken down. Two columns that had collapsed were re-erected as early as the eighteenth century. This makes it all the more 155 strange that, within the ample peristyle of 6 by 14 columns (stylobate 75 ft. 10¼ in. by 190 ft. 4⅞ in.), no remains whatever are traceable of a cella, or even of the rock bed necessary for laying the foundations. The crepidoma and columns still display all round the rough exterior that was prepared before the blocks were set in place, and from which the perfectly smooth surface of the steps and the flutes of the columns were to have emerged in the course of several ever more delicate processes. In short, the 154 building was left unfinished, probably because of the war with Selinus in 416, and one might therefore assume that a cella was indeed planned, but never executed. Temples do, in fact, exist with cellas demonstrably built after the erection of the peristyle (Aegina, Theseum), but naturally the entire founda-

tions were first laid as a whole. Hence, the only other explanation is that, unwilling to be inferior to their enemies in Selinus, the Elymians, who worshipped nature and river gods, could not dispense with the imposing exterior of a peripteral temple for their open-air cult, and therefore raised a peristyle without a cella. It is thus a shell without a kernel, a 154, 155 complete debasement, or better a voidance of the idea of the peripteral structure. No roof could correspond to the pediment at either end, and so all sockets for roof and ceiling beams are absent, too.

At the same time, it can hardly be doubted that the then still wealthy city recruited a Greek architect and builders for their sham peripteral temple. This is shown by the exceedingly careful stone-cutting and still more clearly by the fact that all the architectonic refinements of planning and detail at the fifth century's disposal were employed—though, of course, in that strangely mathematical and abstract way characteristic of the classical buildings of the West. While plainly dependent in ground-plan on the Athena temple at Syracuse and the temple close to Himera—the same column count and 2 : 5 stylobate proportion, a similar ratio of column diameter to intercolumniation (here 1 : 1·23, Syracuse 1 : 1·11, Himera 1 : 1·23)—in elevation the structure reveals all the signs of an advanced development. The fig. 103 columns are slimmer (height of 30 ft. 8⅞ in. = 4·8 lower diams. of 6 ft. 5 in.), and the capitals flatter and less spreading than on the approximately fifty-year-older structures.

Thus, double angle contraction, too, already appears here in the systematically developed manner of the temple of Concord, though without the triglyph frieze being adjusted, as there, to the displaced second columns. As might be expected from the foregoing, the stereobate of 4 steps was executed with a strict concordance of joints.

Yet how astonishing it is that here, outside the Greek world, one meets the subtlest achievement of Hellenic architecture: curvature. The stylobate has a rise of about 1⅝ in. at the ends and 3⅛ in. on the flanks, approximately equalling the curvature of the Parthenon's steps. Another, small detail gives an inkling of how carefully the peristyle, abandoned in its rough state, was to have been decorated, and recalls the state temple of the Athenian 'allies': the delicate, painted palmettes there on the corona soffit 12, below at the corners reappear here in sculptural form.

Herodotus (I, 142 ff.) did not always find it easy even in his day to distinguish between what was and what was not Ionian, and it is harder than ever for modern scholars to define this concept unambiguously, precisely because of the deepening of their knowledge. During the great population movement after the middle of the second millennium, tribes that had immigrated from the north seem to have penetrated into the then Mycenaean Peloponnese. Already feeling old-established, even autochthonous *vis-à-vis* the next wave of the 'Dorian invasion', they sought to hold their own as 'Ionians' against these 'Dorians'. In Attica, they succeeded—and, from then on, the Athenians took a certain pride in calling themselves Ionians. Multitudes of people were, however, driven from the Peloponnese, and, split up into groups according to the capacity of the little fleets, they ventured across the sea to the east. They settled the Aegean islands, and, round about the turn of the millennia, established themselves on the coast of Asia Minor and the islands offshore. At the same time, the Dorians tried to compete with them by colonizing Rhodes and Cnidus. All this certainly did not come to pass without interbreeding with the Carian population, which was permeated by Mycenaean elements. One must not picture these movements generally as one single tempestuous mass migration. Rather were they a steady infiltration similar to the later colonization of Magna Graecia. Here, also, we hear of ancestral kings and founders. On the other hand, excavations at Miletus, for example, have revealed settlements made by the Mycenaeans long before the Ionian immigration.

In the story of these colonizations, several tribal areas were distinguished. Aeolis, which comprised Lesbos and the coast opposite it as far as Troy, developed an artistic tradition of its own during the seventh and sixth centuries, but this soon petered out in a certain provincialism. Increasingly conspicuous as the true centre was Ionia, the coast north and south of the high promontory of Mycale from Ephesus to Miletus, together with the adjacent islands of Samos and Chios. Growing prosperous thanks to their maritime trade, the twelve Ionian cities at an early date—in the eighth century, it would seem—formed a league with the 'Panionium', a lonely Poseidon sanctuary at the foot of Mount Mycale, as its religious focus. The Aeolian city of

104 Top of leg of Cyprian tripod from Tiryns, before 1200 B.C. (1:2). New drawing

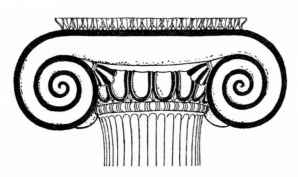

105 Ionic capital of archaic Artemisium at Ephesus, *c.* 550 B.C.

106 Aeolic capitals from Larissa (*left*) and Neandria (*right*), first half of sixth cent. B.C. F. Krischen, 1946

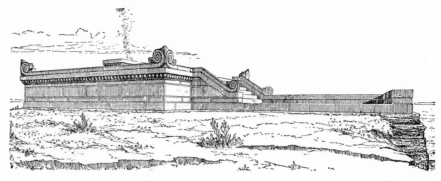

107–108 Altar at Cape Monodendri, near Miletus. A. von Gerkan, 1915
107 Corner of altar with angle volute and palmettes above Ionic ovolo (egg-
and-dart) and beaded astragal mouldings, *c.* 540 B.C.
108 Altar from north-west

Phoecae was also admitted, and only through this establishing of national solidarity were the pre-requisites of a homogeneous Ionic art created. The Cycladic isles around Delos banded together in another, no less important league, and founded a distinct, island Ionic artistic sphere, maintained above all by Naxos and Paros. We have already become acquainted with its chief works (Naxian oikos on Delos, page 364; Cnidian and Siphnian treasuries and Naxian column at Delphi, page 329 and plate 73).

In the ninth and eighth centuries, however, there was still no question of an independent Ionic art. The linear decoration of Ionic geometric vase painting is only distinguished from that of Attica and the Peloponnese by its somewhat freer structure, and one might wonder whether the ancestral difference between Ionians and Dorians in general was profound enough to be able to produce the heterogeneous character of this art. Nevertheless, despite their ground-plans related to that of temple C at Thermum (fig. 3), the earliest temples—the hecatompeda on Samos, built of rectangular posts and beams (page 448)—reveal a totally dissimilar attitude. Here, a piece of architecture was conceived less as a plastic body than as a practical, technically significant construction. The fabric of the Doric temple was, plainly from the start, laid out in an amazing congruency of structure with artistic form according to laws already prefigured in the surface art of geometric vase painting, and, needing no extra decoration, it never at any future time diverged from this mould. By contrast, the first Ionic buildings were not much more than examples of a simple framework awaiting its proper 'fulfilment'. To be sure, a characteristically Ionic feature was already evident in the clarity of the design and construction: a distinctive rationality, penetrating with logic every object it grasped. The Ionians, a versatile, extrovert, and intelligent seafaring people, would in the future bring forth extremely important technical inventions, and scientific mathematics and philosophy originated among them. This, however, is only one side of the Ionian character. The other, imagination, sprang from the fruitful encounter of these restless voyagers with the old, wise major civilizations of the East, with Babylon and Egypt. During the seventh century, a fresh wave of plant and animal motifs—palmettes, twining tendrils, spiral scrolls—invaded Ionian ceramics (orientalizing style). In the process, the oriental models underwent a change of personality, to become crisply taut in form and of intense, daemonic vitality. Subsequently, architecture, too, must have received its final cast, with the above-mentioned framework being, as it were, enveloped by new organic decorative forms, and so awakened to a life of its own. This took place according to a special formal logic, however, inasmuch as the ornament was not arbitrarily attached to empty surfaces, but blossomed forth from the temple's articulations, clarifying its structure. The early, seventh-century forms, which were undoubtedly carved and turned in perishable material—wood—have not survived. Here again we can only reason *a posteriori* from the stone forms of the sixth century. Though rounded, tapered, and fluted on the Doric

445

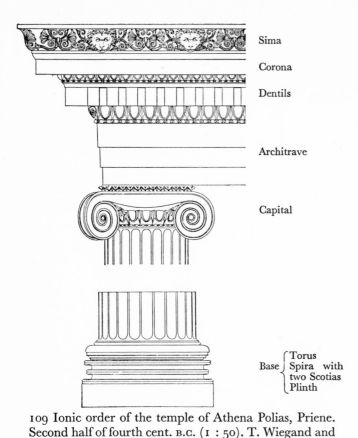

Sima

Corona

Dentils

Architrave

Capital

Base {
Torus
Spira with
two Scotias
Plinth

109 Ionic order of the temple of Athena Polias, Priene.
Second half of fourth cent. B.C. (1 : 50). T. Wiegand and
H. Schrader, 1904

model, the most important member, the column,
shot up in plant-like slenderness. It had a circular
base, the development of which from simple cylinder
to the most varied sequence of tori and scotia is
summarized here in a picture. The shaft was crowned
by a round, convex wreath of leaves and, lying
crosswise above it, a part that coiled at either end
into heavy volutes. In this, the ancient bracket cap
laid across the top of a post had been fused with the
volute motif to form a resiliently lively creation to
which memories of much earlier Mycenaean-cum-
Oriental hybrid structures of wholly different character but kindred shape may have contributed.
Moreover, in Aeolis one comes across wreath capitals
without volutes and strange capitals composed of
two volutes that spring up vertically from the shaft
with a palmette growing between them; but, particularly as they all date from the sixth century, one
can hardly claim them to be ancestral forms of the
Ionic capital. The joints, such as that between
the architrave and the projecting beam heads of the
'dentil course', were indicated by supple convex
ovolo mouldings with an egg-and-dart pattern.
These were accompanied by the bead-and-reel
astragal, which constituted the most delicate intermediary, and by the anthemion, a frieze of blooms
over tendril chains forming a vivaciously open

*figs. 110
111*

fig. 105

fig. 104

fig. 106

fig. 109

fig. 112

110–111 Attic and early Ionic column bases.
New drawings

110 Delphi, Athenian stoa, 478 B.C.; Athens, east portico
of Erechtheum, c. 415 B.C.

111 (*left to right*) Delphi, Naxian column, c. 570 B.C.;
Samos, first dipteros, c. 560 B.C.; Samos, second dipteros,
c. 500 B.C.; Ephesus, Artemisium, c. 550 B.C.

110

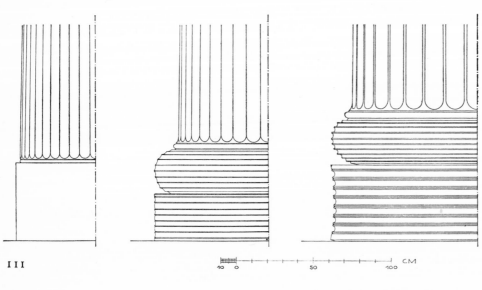

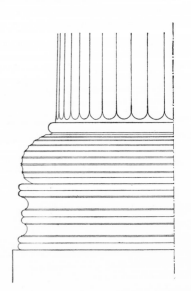

111

decorative band. Out of these elements, there developed, in the course of time, a formal language as imaginative as it is logical.

The history of Ionic architecture will be followed in its detail on the surviving monuments, since, being more varied, lavish, and rich in forms than Doric, it cannot be understood in terms of clear-cut principles. One will then perceive, taking it as a whole, a subtle inner dialectic, a highly tense interrelationship between construction and ornament, ratio and fantasy, schematism and animation, which is the peculiar charm of this architecture, but which also denies it access to classical unity. Hence, the widespread extinction of Ionia's architecture in the fifth century under the oppressive burden of Persian control and the scarcely more supportable Attic hegemony may have been more than a historical accident. Its out-and-out archaic vitality was exhausted, and it had neither the strength nor the faculties for the radical regeneration demanded by the classical spirit. Only after a break of one and a half centuries did the architect Pythius, who now imposed classical unity on the Ionic formal vocabulary under the determinant primacy of artistic ratio, bring about with his temple of Athena at Priene a renaissance of the Ionic style. He gave it such power that, in the Hellenistic age, it put the antiquated Doric order completely in the shade.

SAMOS, THE HERAEUM

The island of Samos stretches forward into the Aegean as a mountain spur only cut off by a narrow sound from Mycale which dominates the wide expanse of coast. During the upheavals caused by the Dorian invasion at the end of the second millennium, Ionian settlers driven from the Peloponnese took possession of it. Together with their powerful neighbour Miletus, the Samians extended their trade and naval supremacy, the latter being nothing else but piracy regulated by alliances, far across the Eastern seas to Egypt. At an early date, there developed a characteristically vigorous Samian art that surveyed attentively, but not subserviently, the wide range of what was familiar to it from the Orient, through Cyprus to Egypt. It enjoyed a last, refined flowering at the time of the island's greatest expansion of power under the tyrant Polycrates (538 or 532 to 522). True, Samos recovered from the disorders following the death of this prominent ruler—his body was nailed to a cross on the summit of Mycale, within sight of his wealthy island, by a Persian satrap— and, in thanks for its opportunist line during the Ionian revolt (494), it was spared the Persian vengeance; but this only made the more inevitable its experience of all the harshness of which Athens was capable. In 440, Pericles razed the walls protecting the city of his refractory 'allies'. Here too, therefore, a sturdy development was suppressed on the threshold of the classical period, though less rigorously than in the devastated cities of the Ionian coast. Samos has bequeathed us only a few, but sumptuous works from the fifth and fourth centuries. The true Samian art and architecture remains that of the archaic centuries —indeed, the island seems to have been the birthplace of Ionic architecture, occupying a position like that of Argos and Corinth in the Doric area.

The centre of this art was not the actual city of Samos, which lies still ringed by thick Hellenistic ramparts on the south-eastern side of the island, but the far-famed sanctuary of Hera about four miles to the west. Ernst Buschor's excavations there have disclosed, through a meticulous examination of the few remains which are preserved in the ground, a unique picture of the origin and organic growth of a Greek sanctuary.

Since as early as the third millennium, an extensive fortified settlement of the aboriginal inhabitants had lain in the delta of the river Imbrasus, which, though small, swelled enormously during the rainy season. The settlement continued to exist till into Mycenaean times. An earlier cult obviously preserved its continuity through the catastrophes of the migration period as well. According to a native legend, the new immigrants found in the river depression a strangely shaped plank with branches of a lygos bush twined about it. Awe-striken, they recognized it as the great goddess Hera, whose cult they had perhaps brought with them from the very ancient Hera sanctuary near Argos. This is suggested by another foundation legend, according to which it was the Argonauts who had brought the wooden image to Samos (Paus. VII, 4, 4).

447

112 Capital with portico-type anthemion from the Polycrates
temple of Hera, Samos. G. Gruben

THE ALTARS   *Figs. 113–115*

*figs. 113–
115*

As early as the beginning of the first millennium, a
plain stone altar (about 8 by 4 ft.) was raised near the
above-mentioned lygos bush on a small terrace in
the delta. It formed, so to speak, the nucleus of the
ever more imposing altars that enveloped it during
the eighth to the sixth century. The seventh, so-
called Rhoecus altar, erected about 550, remained
both for its enormous size (measuring 119 ft. 11$\frac{7}{8}$ in.
by 54 ft. 4$\frac{3}{4}$ in., it covered two hundred times the
area of altar 1!) and for the splendour of its sculptural
and other decoration the most important monument
of its kind, first eclipsed by the Hellenistic altar at
Pergamum (page 486). The simple form of the
altar for burnt offerings—a table surrounded on three
sides by windbreaks, with a platform for the priests to
stand on before the open west side—here appeared
on a colossal scale, its shielding walls covered by
carved animal friezes, multicoloured egg-and-dart
mouldings, and anthemion patterns. On the giant
'sacrificial table', the ashes of centuries accumulated
in a great cone. The table was only about 5 ft. high,
for the convenience of the priest making the sacrifice.
Therefore, the whole altar was raised on a podium
with a huge flight of steps at its west side.

THE HECATOMPEDA   *Figs. 116–120*
(TEMPLES OF HERA I AND II) AND THE SOUTH STOA

The miraculously discovered image of Hera must,
to begin with, have been installed in an open chapel
by the first altar. Remains of walls indicate that three
such naiskoi existed around the altar. Were, then,
Aphrodite and Hermes, whose cult here in the fourth
century is attested, associated with Hera from the
start? The image, which this early period was still
unable to distinguish from the goddess herself—
it was fed, clothed, bathed, and supplicated like a
being really present (*Iliad* VI, 297 ff.)—required
a house, an exceedingly large and beautiful one.
Just as the 100 sacrificial oxen of the hecatomb simply
signified abundance, the measurement of 100 ft. was
the measure of bigness. During the first half of the
eighth century, the very earliest Greek temple known   *fig. 11*
to us was built in the river depression before the old
and meanwhile enlarged altar. It had a length of 100
and a breadth of 20 ft. (21 ft. 3$\frac{7}{8}$ in. by 107 ft. 9$\frac{3}{4}$ in.).
This meant that, in relation to the tiny chapels and
the modest dwelling-houses of that age, an enormous
advance had been made, for which no technical or
formal preparatory experiments had been carried
out. The builders concentrated all their capacity for
expressing size in the length, the long, narrow space
thus being, so to speak, conceived only in one direction. For covering it posts were necessary, and here
supported the ridge-piece. This row of props
accorded ill with the cult image enthroned at the end
of the room, as in its palace, and so, under the somewhat awkward circumstances, the statue was displaced slightly to the right, as its surviving pedestal
shows. It has proved impossible either to detect or
exclude a door wall, but the cella probably opened in
its entire breadth, like the older chapels. What
remains of the walling, only 1 ft. 9$\frac{5}{8}$ in. thick and of

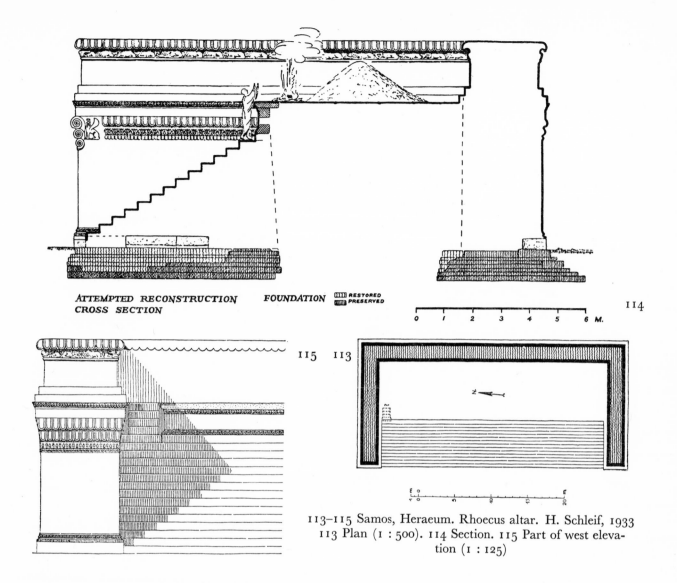

ATTEMPTED RECONSTRUCTION   FOUNDATION ▦ RESTORED
CROSS SECTION   ▨ PRESERVED

0 1 2 3 4 5 6 M.

114

115 113

113–115 Samos, Heraeum. Rhoecus altar. H. Schleif, 1933
113 Plan (1 : 500). 114 Section. 115 Part of west elevation (1 : 125)

small, carefully dressed stones, no doubt served as
the socle of mud-brick walls reinforced by posts.
Still in the eighth century, a narrow peristyle of 7 by
17(?) posts was added, surrounding the structure
like an arbour. The momentous operation that
occurred at Thermum (temple B, page 309) was here
repeated more logically, account being taken of the
orthogonal framework of beams.

117–
118
Towards 670 a catastrophic flood brought down
the first temple of Hera, over the remains of which a
new edifice with a related but more advanced
ground-plan was soon erected (6 by 18 columns, stylobate about 38 ft. 5 in. by 123 ft. 9 in., cella about
22 ft. 4 in. by 100 ft. 7 in.). Above all else, the
builders this time dared to do without the central
props in spanning the cella's width of 18 ft. The
posts, that had previously supported the ceiling
beams in combination with the mud-brick walls like
a timber frame, now emerged as visible members on

a separate low bench in front of the walls. (Here, the
later tripartite division of the space already appeared
in embryo: when the cella was widened, these
supports remained where they were.) The walls
were built to their full height, without bonding, of
small, squared limestone blocks, the surface of which,
crimped, so to speak, by vertical chisel marks,
anticipated the subsequent delicate animation of
Ionic architectural forms. Being of stone, the ends of
the side walls—the antae—could dispense with the
facing of planks found on contemporary Doric
temples, and, accordingly, the Doric anta projections
in which this revetment lived on were thereafter
absent from Ionic structures. Against the inner faces
of the antae rested the easternmost pair of interior
supports, attached to the wall by iron nails. Two
more free-standing, wooden posts must have framed
the door, the sill of which was discovered near by.
The two lateral openings may have been latticed.

449

This new design no longer proceeded from the cella but from the peristyle, the members of which were ranged all round at nearly equal intervals (7 ft. 0¼ in. or 7 ft. 1 in.). What is more, there were exactly three times as many supports on the flanks as at the ends—certainly not by chance. A crucial innovation pointing ahead to the double ring of columns of dipteroi was the double colonnade at the front. The structural members still had the extremely simple practical forms used even today by any carpenter: squared posts, which, to protect them from the dam, were set on round stone bases. Beneath them, the stone platform of the stylobate was raised only slightly above the ground. The roof, too, must have been carpentered in the simplest way, and its frame of cross-beams, purlins, and rafters can still be deduced, it is thought, from the 'constructive' organization of the ground-plan (fig. 118). Since no roof tiles have been found, the possibility of a flat mud roof must be weighed against that of a steep reed-thatch covering, hipped at the ends, as on a Samian model of a house.

There was still little sign in this trabeated structure of a deliberate moulding of the parts, of an expression of their function through artistic form. Yet it was not left entirely undecorated. On separate squared *fig. 119* stones, the heads of three warriors carrying spears have been scratched in the direct style of that period. From them, a mural frieze is to be reconstructed, not more than 1 ft. high—a scale hardly exceeding that of the related representations on vases. Probably coloured, this procession of soldiers was the primitive form of all the rich and gaily painted

friezes with which the Ionians thereafter adorned their temples and altars.

About a generation later, the sanctuary was firmly enclosed as a whole by means of a peribolos. A propylaeum orientated towards the enlarged altar received the processions approaching from the city of Samos. The south-west side, previously bounded by a river arm, now obtained an architectonic conclusion of unprecedented dimensions in the shape of a stoa—probably the first to be built by Greeks; *fig. 120* 229 ft. 5⅞ in. long and 19 ft. 4⅝ in. deep, it was undoubtedly derived from the recently realized form of the peristyle, which here achieved independent existence in the fullest sense of the expression. This building, too, before the open front of which stretched a large ceremonial square, served principally the goddess, whose votive offerings were displayed in it. However, the new type of structure also suited the enduring fondness of the Greeks for meetings and conversation, and therefore spread rapidly (Argive Heraeum, page 346).

The temple's pteroma was not only made independent, but doubled to form a two-naved structure (this also prepared the way for the dipteros), the building technique of the model being exactly repeated with a barely increased interval between the supports (7 ft. 5¾ in.). Thanks to the better state of preservation, there are here certain clues that permit a reconstruction, though one still hypothetical in its upper parts. From it, we can form a picture of the sanctuary's early buildings. It is an entirely new undertaking that confronts us here: carpentry without artistic form, a fabric of the simplest

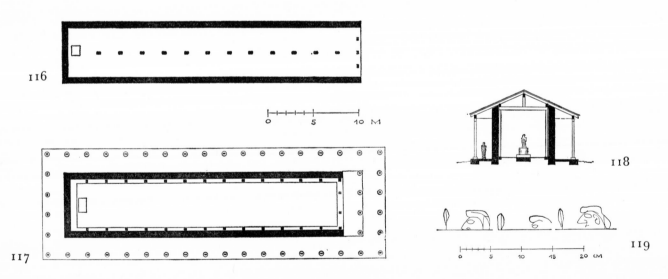

116–119 Samos. New drawings
116 Hecatompedon I. Plan. 117–118 Hecatompedon II. Restored plan and cross-section. All three on same scale (1 : 400). 119 'Warrior frieze'

450

120 Samos, south stoa. Conjectural restoration.
G. Gruben, 1957

appearance. Out of a few elements—really, only two: ashlar wall and squared beam—were put together uncommonly large buildings oddly at variance with the slightness and inexpressiveness of their members. There thus came into being an architectural framework that still awaited its casing, its 'incarnation'—very much the reverse of the Doric wooden structure, in which every form was mapped out from the start, and of necessity pressed forwards to develop inner magnitude, monumentality. The few architectural forms distinctly indicated in the wooden buildings of Samos were later either radically changed—post to column, bracket cap to volute capital—or else they went on being applied to edifices as a plainly technical element that could also be left out without disturbing the 'order', like the beam ends that subsequently became the dentils.

Further, the ground-plans of Ionia seem to cohere as ordered wholes not so much by inner ties, for which Doric architecture strove persistently, as by outward, constructional ones. Thus, the abstract connexion of the central axes already mediated between wall and column in the Samian wooden structures, whereas, in the Peloponnese, the exterior faces of the cella, which was perceived as a solid, provided the binding force. The peripteral temple as a monumental unity did not become Ionian property till the fourth century, and must be regarded as a Doric creation, whether it was re-invented afterwards on Samos at the close of the eighth century or had become known to the seafaring islanders in their old Peloponnesian homeland. One does not find 'all-sidedness' in Ionia. Instead of having symmetrical ends in the form of a pronaos and opisthodomus, hecatompedon II already displayed an overemphasized front owing to the double

colonnade there, a feature that the Eastern temples shared with those raised almost two centuries later by the Western colonies. However clearly and schematically they seem to be organized, the ground-plans in general are characterized by a fluid adaptability, a looseness that makes them fit for every task. Rather than the consistency of the eternally defined Doric temple, the Ionic chose freedom. Hence, the newly achieved peristyle of the second temple could without hindrance be converted and extended into the endlessly long stoa, which even came to dominate the temple itself. (Though they existed in Doric sanctuaries, such buildings there always avoided the limelight; cf. Argive Heraeum, page 346.) It follows that there never was an 'Ionic temple' in the sense of a fixed ground-plan pattern. These receptive mariners absorbed all foreign stimuli with a wakeful imagination, and knew how to sift and transform them into what accorded with their own nature. The dense and severe corporeity of Doric architecture, less suited to Ionia, was thus compensated for by an agitated, richly varied liveliness of the surfaces, which preferred to express itself in floral decoration; and the place of monumental force was taken by gliding, unfettered gracefulness. Now, however, we are anticipating the next step of this architecture, which again was made in the Hera sanctuary: the actual incarnation of the Ionic style.

THE RHOECUS TEMPLE   *Figs. 111, 121*
(TEMPLE OF HERA III)

Between 570 and 550, at a time when sculpture's image of man had long since found its final organic form and achieved large, often colossal stature,

451

there took place an immense rearrangement of the sanctuary, traditionally connected with the names of Rhoecus and Theodorus. These two versatile masters, who commanded the entire field of art from the hollow casting of big bronze statues and toreutics down to the carving of the most delicate images on gems, now accomplished in architecture what sculpture had already known for decades: they dared to work on a large, indeed a gigantic scale, and created the organic form of the Ionic order.

fig. 121 The new temple of Hera covered the demolished hecatompedon and the north part of the likewise sacrificed south stoa in the middle of a sanctuary enlarged many times over. It was of vast proportions. Its shallow, two-stepped substructure, which hardly rose above the ground, measured 100 by 200 Samian ells (about 172¼ by 344½ ft.), and occupied twelve and a half times as much space as the old temple. Along with the dimensions, the plan of the temple had also been amplified enormously. A double peristyle (inner ring 19 by 6, outer 21 by 8, total 104 columns) was laid round the cella, so that out of the peripteral form a dipteros arose. In the ground-plan, as far as it can be deduced from the few remains, the clear conception of the second hecatompedon appears to have been made even more precise. The whole structure was laid out over a rectangular network of axes, the columns standing from 10 to 9 ells apart at the points of intersection. There was, to be sure, a significant infringement. Behind, 5 interaxials of normal width corresponded to the gigantic naos measuring about 47 to 100 ells

(about 82 by 172 ft.), so that 10 columns stood in the outer line at the west end. However, the column arrangement at the east end, with 3 interaxials before the square pronaos (i.e. 8 columns along the front), was assimilated to the tripartite division of the pronaos space. The result was a considerable enlargement of the middle interaxials, and a diminishing gradation from centre (26 ft. 7⅞ in.) to sides (17 ft. 2¾ in.), which made the entrance end stand out conspicuously from the otherwise uniformly dense colonnading. This differentiation expresses an attitude entirely dissimilar from that apparent in Doric ground-plans, the horizontal development here taking account less of the form, the bodily cohesion of the whole, than of the function, the building's inward as well as its practical purpose, and of the appearance. Even the schematic system of axes had to adapt itself to this.

Appearance, what is pictorial, is far more strongly determinant of the character of Ionic architecture generally than is plastic substance. A delicate and graceful animation spreads over the surfaces, over the vestment behind which the body withdraws. It is thus that we are to understand the double peristyle, which, as an abundantly folded, open-textured mantle positively concealing the nucleus of the cella, infinitely enriches the liveliness of the exterior. The same disposition brought into being the new splendour of the decorative forms, which, already exemplified for a century in vase painting, in costly utensils and furniture made by craftsmen, and on single columns erected to carry votive offerings, were

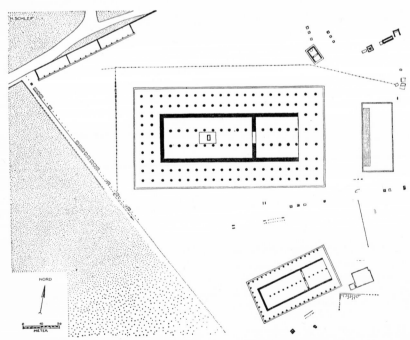

121 Samos. Sanctuary *c.* 540 B.C. *Centre:* Rhoecus temple (temple of Hera III) and altar. *Below:* so-called south building (1 : 2,000). E. Buschor and H. Schleif, 1930

here set in the largest frame of architecture with unequalled boldness and power of imagination.

It was, above all, the columns, barely held together in their vast number by the narrow band of the entablature, that determined the appearance of the Rhoecus temple. Countless bases and fragments of drums have been discovered built into the foundations of Hera's second dipteros. The shafts attained approximately three times the height of contemporary Doric ones (height of about 60 ft. = 12 lower diams. of about 5 ft.), as can be inferred by studying other early Ionic examples. Like slender tree-trunks, they shot effortlessly upwards. Though the fluting undoubtedly imitates the Doric type, it actually reverses its significance. The number of the shallow, rounded channels, which are separated by arrises and not yet by the later fillets, has been doubled (40 instead of 20), thus imparting to the surface a most delicate vibration comparable to the tight fall of the drapery folds on female statues of the period. The eye did not take in these columns, but was drawn upwards, following the thrust of their plant-like growth.

, fore-
ground

Finally, the bases are true miracles, and not just of technique. For the 2 by 10 columns in the naos, the simple primitive form of base, a cylindrical drum (cf. Naxian oikos, page 364), was employed. The peristyle bases, however, consist of two members. Above the drum (spira), now sometimes curving slightly inwards, there follows a rounded part with a convex profile (torus), both being covered by the most delicate channels, scotias, and swellings, which, moreover, follow a different sequence on every base. These profiles, the daintiness of which would be far better suited to some costly ivory utensil than to such gigantic architectural members (diam. up to 5 ft. 11 in., weight up to over 1 ton), were literally turned on a wheel! Only those who have themselves touched the silky, supple skin of these mouldings can judge how high a degree of palpable life has here been imparted to the surface of the fine-grained stone.

ig. 111

Not a trace remains of the capitals, but this very fact provides a clue: like the entablature resting upon them, they were probably made of wood. Moreover, in view of the advanced 'wood technique' of the stone bases, one must imagine the old bracket cap here carefully carved and wound up at either end into volutes, after the manner of the approximately contemporary Naxian capital at Delphi. Beneath it, there would seem to have been an intermediating torus similar to the one at the bottom, as the large number of surviving fragments can scarcely all be assigned to the bases. Though nothing of the entablature and upper structure has come down to us, the Rhoecus altar built after the completion of the temple is able to supplement our picture. The antae, too, bore capitals: three superimposed volutes, their swelling fronts defined by egg-and-darts and lively floral friezes. Convex egg-and-dart mouldings likewise projected from the building's joints—between wall and ceiling, and below and above the dentil course. Then the thing that remained most closely bound up with the technical structure of the temple—the plain cuboid of the walls—was precisely what required the strongest possible expression of life. Hence, sculptured friezes, like those that certainly appeared on the altar and the next dipteros, probably already here clothed the top or base of the walls. The appearance of the lost entablature can be inferred from later examples. It included a low wooden architrave, subdivided into three thin projecting bands or fascias (and therefore comprising three layers of beams), which was incapable of providing a counter-weight to the tall columns. Furthermore, there was no frieze corresponding to the Doric triglyphs and metopes. Directly on the supporting beams lay the jutting rafters—the dentils—which, in their turn, carried a low, concavely undercut corona. The latter ended in a drip moulding, the subsequently usual sima with its spouts thus being absent at first. A great many roof tiles of Corinthian pattern (fig. 5) survive, which proves that the temple was completed. Its upper conclusion was formed by palmette antefixes, which, with a height of only $7\frac{1}{2}$ in., will have looked excessively dainty in relation to the $65\frac{1}{2}$-ft.-tall building as a whole. Terracotta sphinxes of more than life-size sat at the corners as acroteria. Neither the slender band of the entablature nor the low rectangle of the stylobate projecting about 9 ft. 10 in. beyond the peristyle could, however, unite the forest of columns as a cuboid architectural body.

figs. 114,
115

For all its enormous size, this temple lacked, of course, the grand, simple monumentality that was the eternal language of Doric buildings. Instead, a fleeting vital force everywhere played over the surface, and all the parts were as though seized by the stirrings of real growth, this organic life being intensified in accordance with the superhuman dimensions to a magical power. 'The Labyrinth' is what contemporaries called the unprecedented structure, which was immediately imitated at Ephesus and Didyma, and they no doubt had in mind not only its size, too great to be taken in at a glance, but also its spell. And does it not transcend our power of imagination and remain beyond our understanding, this impenetrable dream-maze, this most mysterious of enchanted forests, in the middle of which stood the great goddess Hera?

453

Rhoecus's dipteros owed its origin to the contact of young Ionian art with the old civilizations of Egypt and the Orient. Miletus, together with Samos, had just founded the trading settlement of Naucratis in the Nile delta. Ionians stood in amazement before the hypostyle halls of Egypt. Already a century earlier, Ionia had learned from the Oriental empires their decorative forms and images—palmettes, volutes, entwining tendrils, lions, sphinxes, and so on—though it immediately changed them, permeating them with its own meaning. The example of Egypt gave it the courage to build on a colossal scale. Nevertheless, the idea of the dipteros, the Samian prefigurations of which have been referred to above, is something purely Ionian, for it was in the manifold loosening up and diversification of the outward form of the dipteral temple that the Ionian character found its richest expression.

fig. 122   The other new buildings of the two masters were very much overshadowed by their Hera temple. A small anta temple dedicated to Aphrodite near its north-east corner made it stand out all the more. The frame was provided by a line of stoas along the north edge of the temenos and by a row of stone posts forming an endless fence along the south-west boundary. In the south towards the sea, an odd peripteral structure, the so-called South Building, was begun, but was only finished under Polycrates. It had no front columns, and its two-nave naos would have suited the dual cult of Hermes and Aphrodite. The Rhoecus temple, Ionia's first architectural miracle, perished just after its completion, perhaps during the disturbance that helped Polycrates to come to power (538?).

The tyrant started right away on a new building, which, as regards both splendour and size, was in its turn to put the old dipteros in the shade. So as to obtain a bigger ceremonial square before the Rhoecus altar, he shifted the east end of his temple about 46 yds. westward. In Greece proper, the dimensions of the edifice (172 ft. 1 in. or 100 ells by 356 ft. $4\frac{3}{4}$ in. in the column axes, and about 181 by 368 ft. in the stylobate) remained unsurpassed. The cella of the old temple was repeated in the ground-plan, though with 2 by 11 instead of 2 by 10 naos columns, and the same goes for the layout of the double peristyle with narrower interaxials at the rear end (9 columns) and broader ones in front of the aisled pronaos (8 columns; middle interaxial 26 ft. $11\frac{5}{8}$ in., the others outwards to the corners 27 ft. $10\frac{5}{8}$ in., 23 ft. $1\frac{1}{8}$ in., 21 ft. 7 in.). After the example of the Artemisium (fig. 123), built in the meantime, a third colonnade was added at either end, the dipteros thus being extended there to a 'tripteros'. The standard interaxial at the sides was 15 ft. 5 in., though, in contrast with the Doric angle contraction, the pairs flanking the east portico were enlarged to 16 ft. $2\frac{1}{8}$ in. Similar differences were displayed by the columns themselves, their diameters ranging from 6 ft. $8\frac{3}{4}$ in. (front) to 5 ft. 5 in. (inner flank colonnades) while their height remained constant (about 60 ft. 8 in.). Thus, the degree of slenderness varied between about 9 and $11\frac{1}{4}$ lower diameters. This unconstrained adjustment of interaxial and column, the two determinant elements of the elevation, to the require-

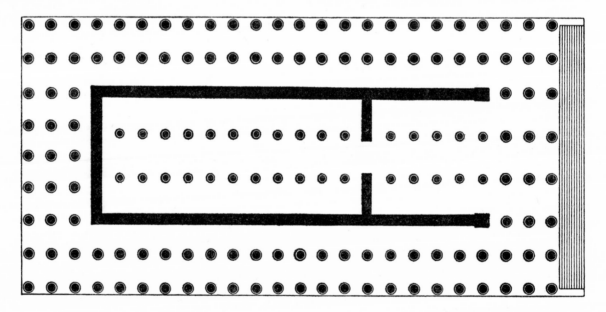

122 Samos, dipteros of Polycrates (temple of Hera IV). Plan (1 : 750). *Festschrift für Weickert,* 1955

ments, the functions of the ground-plan is a further expression of that Ionian indifference to the corporeal unity of the building. The strangely fluctuant ground-plan had only an outward order, bound up with the construction of the entablature and imposed on it by the strictly maintained axial connexion of the colonnades. Lively diversity, free variation—these are what mattered to the builders. The bases retain the old division into spira and torus, but have developed sharper accents. High, angular fillets and deeply incised, shadowy scotias alternate, richly contrasting, in a new, animated formal language now appropriate to the building's size. Moreover, this very interchange of fillet and scotia was here carried over to the shafts in place of the earlier gliding rhythm of the fluting. It endowed them with its own tense surface, and thereafter remained obligatory. (Later, 24 flutes became the rule, instead of the 36 that were better suited to the great girth of the Samian columns.) Around the upper end of the shaft, its neck, lay a band of carved ornament comprising scrolls of tendrils with palmettes and lotus flowers sprouting up from them. Again, none is like another. The columns of the outer ring, which, however, was actually executed only at the east end and along the eastern part of the flanks towards the beginning of the fifth century, were of local marble and topped by normally shaped marble volute capitals. Over the echinus, a round part covered by twenty-six plastically bulging 'leaves', rests the oblong voluted member. Rectangular only in horizontal section, it is otherwise everywhere soft and curving, and one can now hardly recognize in it its constructional ancestor, the bracket cap. Its swelling middle section, bordered by fine convex mouldings, rolls up at either end into heavy spirals. The outer faces of the volutes (i.e. the narrow ends of the voluted member or cushion) are once more, like the neck, overspread by delicate tendrils and stylized flowers. In this organically plumpish structure, the tectonic foundation now only appears beneath a veil, the static function is translated into another, no less intense language. Instead of 'supporting' we find 'growing', and the load is made evident by the sinewy, supple elasticity of the botanical form. Of course, the further such creations are removed from external similarity to nature, the more densely they are filled with primal life.

To be sure, the animated appearance of the Ionic capital brings with it a formal defect that was never satisfactorily remedied: the broad front view of the volutes is not balanced by the secondary view of the narrow cushion-side. At the corners of the peristyle this conflict inevitably comes out into the open, with the slim cushion-side of each front-facing corner capital encountering disharmoniously the lateral volute capitals turned at right angles to it. Probably, the corners of the archaic Artemisium at Ephesus actually were arranged like this, but, on the temple of Hera, the thenceforth obligatory solution had already been found. The two outer faces of the corner capitals, meeting at right angles, both took the form of volute-sides, and merged in a narrow diagonal volute at the very corner. Accordingly, cushions appeared on the two inner faces, but they clashed most unhappily in halved, mutilated volutes at the less conspicuous inner angle. This ticklish problem did not find a balanced solution even on the formally most accomplished Attic buildings, the Nike temple and Erechtheum.

The columns of the inner ring and cella were provided with unvoluted capitals, which avoided this 'frontality' because it would here have been out of place and unable to make its impact. On an echinus exactly like that of the volute capitals, but worked as a separate member, there lay a simple square abacus. This appears to be a distinct type of capital, which, in archaic times, always ran side by side with the more popular volute one. Ancestral forms of such 'wreath capitals' have been found in Aeolian territory. One comes upon another variety in the capitals of the Delphic caryatids and the Clazomenian treasury (fig. 29). It may have been this very type that provided the inspiration for the Corinthian capital, which, not least because it could be viewed all round, had the power to supplant almost entirely the volute capital which was bound only to a frontal view.

Like so many works of tyrants, the colossal building was never finished. Polycrates only lived to see the construction of the cella with its poros columns. The walls, likewise of poros, were later enlivened by friezes in relief showing varied mythical scenes. A small, late-archaic frieze, about 4 ft. high, seems to have run round inside the pronaos, and a second, larger one (height 9 ft.?), dating from the beginning of the fifth century, probably crowned the external wall surfaces. To round off this frieze, gigantic winged monsters (sphinxes?) crouched near the mighty anta capitals built up from three voluted cushions. During the last decades of the sixth century, the columns of the two inner front rows were erected, and, at the beginning of the fifth, the outer colonnade finally went up, now entirely of marble. The one column still standing, to slightly over half its original height (present height 36 ft. 9¾ in., lower diam. 6 ft. 2¾ in.), belongs to a fourth-century building period. Like all the front columns, it was left unfluted. In this manner, the building activity dragged on until the end of the fourth century.

Though the inner ring of columns does, then, seem at last to have been joined up round the cella, the outer one never was constructed along the western part of the flanks and at the west end. From the socket in an anta block for securing the wooden architrave, as well as from the information handed down, it is to be concluded that both pronaos and naos were covered over. The peristyle can, at best, have only had a temporary roof, since no remains of tiles are detectable. Thus, the temple was left standing as an enormous provisional structure. After its own fashion, the later imperial age sought to procure it a measure of stately splendour by adding before the east end a theatrical flight of steps flanked by fountains—too late, however. For Hera had already removed from her gigantic tumbledown home at about the time of Christ, when a small Ionic-cum-Doric peripteral edifice—the temple of Hera V— was raised directly in front of the great altar. Finally, the fact that a basilica was erected in Byzantine times, 1,500 years after the discovery of the image, on the spot where the lygos was found shows that, even then, the maidenly and maternal Hera was not forgotten. Though we do not know the church's dedication, who could have absorbed the old goddess more profoundly than the Virgin and Mother of God?

EPHESUS

THE ARTEMISIUM   *Plates 159–161, figs. 123–128*

159

figs. 126–128

A hundred years ago, the site of the most famous of all Ionic temples, one of the seven wonders of the ancient world, was still under the plough. Anyone who today stands before the excavation area, marshy and overgrown by reeds, out of which a stone juts here and there, will scarcely credit that, from such pitiful remains, an image of the Artemis temple and its archaic forerunners can be obtained, like that presented in the drawings of Fritz Krischen.

When, at the beginning of the first millennium, a band of Ionian emigrants settled in the broad, mountain-framed bay at the mouth of the Cayster, which has since been entirely converted into land by alluvial deposits, they took possession not only of the region but of the very ancient sanctuary of a native nature goddess, whom they recognized and worshipped as Artemis, the mistress of the animals. Nevertheless, the earliest religious establishment, which plainly only came into being at the outset of the sixth century, was still of the simplest form. A rectangular substructure (13 ft. $11\frac{3}{4}$ in. by 9 ft. $0\frac{5}{8}$ in.) appears to have supported the first altar. Before its east side and linked to it by spur-like platforms (little flights of steps?) was set a somewhat bigger socle made of carefully finished slabs and measuring 14 ft. $2\frac{7}{8}$ in. by 9 ft. $4\frac{5}{8}$ in. It would seem that upon it stood the cult image of Artemis, perhaps already protected by a naiskos opening westwards towards the altar. The un-Greek west-facing instead of east-facing alignment, repeated in the case of two other Artemis temples of Asia Minor (Sardis and Magnesia), probably went back to an old native custom.

What now followed was a very rapid process of growth, similar to the one observable in connexion with the seven Samian altars. Both socles were enlarged, surrounded with an open rectangle of walling, and lastly combined as a single base (21 ft. $1\frac{1}{2}$ in. by 36 ft. $7\frac{7}{8}$ in.), which, it would appear, already then carried a small temple. As the next step, temple base and enclosure were again extended. The outer wall now embraced an area of 48 by about 92 ft., and gained a monumental, temple-like appearance through being given antae at the west end and, hence, probably an arrangement of columns there. That the enclosure was not roofed over is shown by its considerable breadth as well as by its nucleus, which must have been an independent building. In this open 'sekos', which outwardly looked like a temple but was, at bottom, a monumentally enriched peribolos, a new type of east Ionic structure was defined. This inexhaustible architecture had produced a fresh variety, and, in it, once more demonstrated its liking for fine appearance, which it was by no means necessary to combine with a corporeally unified frame. Thus, all was ready for a further and, indeed, enormous stride.

The new conception of the dipteros, realized by Rhoecus and Theodorus on Samos (page 452), was now combined with the open sekos. Already before the middle of the sixth century, work began on a gigantic temple surrounded by a double and, at the front, even a triple peristyle. Henceforth, not a naos, but the old, now considerably enlarged sekos constituted the nucleus, at the centre of which the holy statue of Artemis remained in its hereditary place immediately over the old base. A pronaos with 2 by

fig. 12

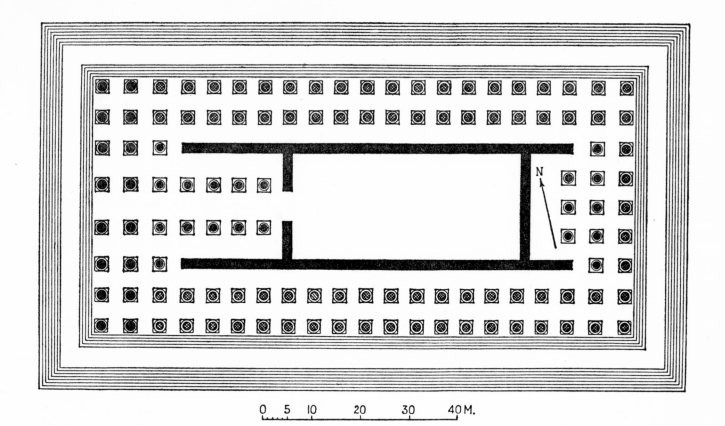

0 5 10   20   30   40 M.

123 Ephesus, later Artemisium. Restored plan (1 : 750). The archaic dipteros had the same plan but without the high crepidoma. W. B. Dinsmoor, 1950

4 columns supporting its ceiling extended in front of the sekos. (The often advocated restoration of a roofed cella would offend against the continuity, always apparent, of an architectural form prescribed by religion. Besides, no traces of internal columns are detectable, two late archaic volute capitals that were taken into consideration having proved too small.) Along with Chersiphron and his son Metagenes—two architects who came, oddly enough, from Crete—the city called in Theodorus, whose experience on the Samian dipteros had made him an expert at laying the foundations of such buildings in marshy subsoils. However, the master will not have confined himself to giving advice. The ground-plan (fig. 123 without the step construction, which belongs to the later Artemisium) largely corresponded to the Samian one, a widening of the seven front interaxial spaces towards the centre (corner interaxials about 20 ft. 1 in., middle about 28 ft. 8 in.), and the emphasis of the entrance thereby achieved, being opposed at the back by a closer spacing (8 interaxials, i.e. 9 columns). Except for these flanking the porticoes, which were 19 ft. 8¼ in. deep, the 21 side columns all had an interval

of 10 ells or 17 ft. 1½ in. Here too, therefore, we find the same functional flexibility of the ground-plan, in which contracted corner interaxials at the front were placed next to expanded ones on the flanks without scruples about form. (The restoration of the ground-plan is disputed, above all as regards the rear. Only three column sites are known for certain, and it is difficult to reconcile them with the external dimensions of 220 by 425 ft. and total of 127 columns recorded by Pliny [*N.H.* 36, 97 f.]. The first of the two more recent solutions—that of F. Krischen—sees it necessary to marshal four colonnades at the back and ignore the more-or-less securely determined position of the rear wall, in order to reach the figure 127. The second—that of W. B. Dinsmoor [fig. 123]—does show the normal dipteral arrangement at the back, but has to correct the traditional total to 117 and assume an opistho-domus, the existence of which elsewhere in east Ionia during archaic times has not been established. Perhaps one should not take too seriously what Pliny states about columns, which, in the case of Samos, is only very roughly true [150 columns instead of the 134 of the Rhoecus temple and 155 of its successor].

457

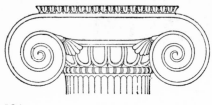

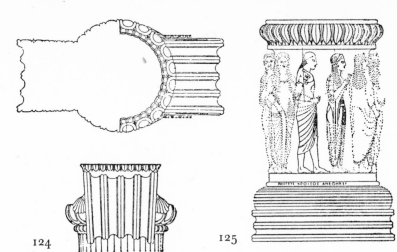

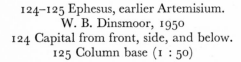

124–125 Ephesus, earlier Artemisium.
W. B. Dinsmoor, 1950
124 Capital from front, side, and below.
125 Column base (1 : 50)

124

125

If one makes Dinsmoor's opisthodomus into a closed adytum by replacing the three columns between the antae with a continuous rear wall, a ground-plan acceptable from the standpoint of historical development is obtained, and the sekos's back wall, which falls outside the axial system of the columns, becomes more intelligible.)

Its Samian model was completely surpassed by the Artemisium not only in size (stylobate about 180 ft. 9 in. by 377 ft. 9 in.) but in splendour, too. The Ionic decorative forms had achieved a more precisely articulated language of the richest expressive power and beauty, to which the noble building material made its contribution. Throughout, the edifice was constructed of a white marble with a bluish tinge, quarried only seven and a half miles inland. The *figs. 111,* column bases were raised from the still flattish *125* crepidoma of two steps by a square plinth (7 ft. 8½ in. by 7 ft. 8½ in.). There followed a spira with an impressively articulated profile made up of two deep scotias bordered by astragals. On the convex torus above, a lively and unforced diversity reigned, S-curved or gently drooping rows of leaves being found alongside the delicate 'Samian' channelling. (The misplaced upper part in fig. 125 is such a leafed torus.) Pliny mentions 36 sculptured columns, and considerable remains have in fact been found of archaic reliefs that surrounded the foot of the columns. Krischen has convincingly allocated them to the three colonnades at the entrance end and to the supports on either side of the antae (28 columns). In addition, remains have survived of similarly carved but square-shaped members. These are to be assigned to the pronaos, where the lower part of the columns thus resembled the rectangular antae, which were adorned with large bulls in a similar manner (8 columns, total 36). The dense, very shallow fall of the fluting imparted a delicate,

undulant life to the slender, soaring shafts, which must have been approximately 12 lower diameters tall (height about 59 ft., lower diam. from 4 ft. 11½ in. to 5 ft. 7¾ in.). Even here no uniformity was tolerated, for shafts with 40 or 44 flutes separated by fine arrises appeared near others with 48 alternately broad and narrow ones. Round the necks of the front columns, there ran an anthemion band, as *fig. 11* on the Polycrates temple.

In the elongated volute capitals, once gaily *figs. 1* painted, the organic life of the columns bursts forth *124* without restraint. The succulent forms swell and bulge tightly, the volutes wind up with perceptible elasticity. Their cushion-sides are characterized more than clearly as natural structures by four deep, astragal-edged scotias ending in a leaf-and-dart. Comparing them with the Naxian capital at Delphi (plate 73), which is twenty to thirty years older, one finds not only that the latter's austere, wiry wooden forms have now come to full bloom, but that, here, a fusion has begun of the parts that, there, seem to lie unrelated upon one another. Thus, the cushion nestles against the round echinus, while big palmette fans sprout from the volute-corners and spread softly over the girdle of leaves. A very thin abacus ornamented with an egg-and-dart or leaf-and-dart forms the organic transition to the architrave. The fact that this unification was striven for, so to speak, from the skin inwards demonstrates the basic difference from Doric columns, the similarly separated parts of which were progressively welded together by a centrifugal flow of inner forces. So far as is known, the first Greek architraves of marble rested *fig. 1* on the Artemisium's columns, yet they spanned the largest intervals ever achieved. The technical daring of the builders, who were capable of imposing the approximately 25-ton central architrave at a height of about 65 ft. by means of simple pulleys and

458

126 Ephesus, earlier Artemisium. Colonnades at west end from south. Restoration. F. Krischen, 1938

derricks, was so superhuman that a pious legend could grow up later telling of how Artemis herself had one night raised these marble beams into position. Fragments survive of a big Ionic ovolo (height 11 in.) that, with its plump egg-and-dart pattern, ran between architrave and dentil course, no certain remains of which exist. The smooth corona, only 13¼ in. high, lay above another such moulding over the dentils. As a splendid conclusion, it bore a slightly bowed marble sima (height 34 in.), on which a relief of mythical battles wreathed the enormous building at its very top with an endless procession of warriors, horses, and chariots. Whether or not the fronts had pediments, which representations on coins show to have been present on the subsequent dipteros, can no longer be determined.

127 Ephesus, later Artemisium. South-west corner. Restoration. F. Krischen, 1938

fig. 125 Herodotus's statement that Croesus, the wealthy king of Lydia, made a present of columns for the temple is confirmed by the monarch's dedicatory inscription at the foot of a column. Croesus lost his crown in 546 to Cyrus, the founder of the Persian empire, which means that building operations must have begun during the decade before the middle of the century. The latest fragments of the sima reliefs prove that the structure was complete about 460. (Pliny gives a building period of 120 years, which is therefore to be connected with the later edifice.) Hence, it follows, and altogether unexpectedly considering the few remains in the marshy excavation area, that the old Artemisium is the one securely dated and, in its upper structure, almost entirely known early Ionic building. And what a building! The mystical forest of columns where Artemis reigned, surrounded by a temenos, which, its size determined by the length of a bowshot, was thickly planted with trees and harboured the wild animals of the goddess. A universe of ornament, a cosmos of abundantly varied forms, each of which

460

128 Ephesus, later Artemisium. West end with view into pronaos and sekos. Restoration. F. Krischen, 1938

was perfected with loving tenderness, however far removed from human eye, and irrespective of the colossal bulk of the temple, which covered one and a half times as much ground as Cologne cathedral. For contemporaries, the Artemisium must have been a veritable miracle, possessed of boundless fame. Hence, it could come to pass that, in 356, a madman set fire to the building, the interior architraves, ceiling coffers, and roof framework of which were of cedar-wood, so as to immortalize his own name by destroying what was most celebrated of all. It is a name familiar even today: Herostratus. The same night saw the birth, so it is said, of Alexander the Great, who called a new age into existence and, above all, brought the East a tremendous revival. When, on his expedition against the Persians,

Alexander made a sacrifice in the Artemisium and offered to complete the reconstruction that had been begun, he received a response as haughty as it was flattering: 'It does not befit a god to build the house of a goddess' (Strabo XIV, 641).

It befitted the Ephesians themselves; and the new temple had to be exactly the equal of the old, so great was the latter's renown. Naturally, a copy of the architectural forms that were their organically changing property was, for Greeks, quite out of the question. However, the essentials, which meant the *figs. 123,* dimensions and the proportions, position, and *127* arrangement of all the temple's parts, had to be faithfully repeated. A new column thus stood con- *fig. 128* centrically over every old one, wall rose above wall, and the cult image remained in its place at the centre

461

of the great sekos. The length, breadth, and, of course, also height of the old structure were precisely retained. On the other hand, in the highly confused and, at times, contradictory ancient accounts, there is mention of an enlargement (Strabo XIV, 640), which can in fact be detected in the remains of the new building, and reveals the changed formal sense of late classical times. The dipteros was raised 8 ft. $9\frac{1}{2}$ in. above the low earlier stylobate on a huge crepidoma of 13 steps, thereby gaining no longer the magical power of the old earth-bound forest of columns but monumental force. Now sharply demarcated and held together by the angular succession of steps, the architectural body confronted nature as something other, as a monumentally fashioned entity. Stepped base and platform are ancient items in the Orient's stock of forms. There they were used symbolically to elevate the god's abode, but here Greeks re-interpreted them as something in itself 'sublime', over which the colonnaded temple rose on high in both a literal and a mystical sense. The new architectural idea of the lofty substructure found its highest expression in Ionia's second marvel, the contemporary Mausoleum of Halicarnassus, and its final development in the altar at Pergamum (page 486). It could be that the temple podium, the Romano-Italic embodiment of this notion, stemmed from the same roots, and was brought by the Etruscans when they immigrated from Asia Minor.

Under the influence of Attic classical architecture, the whole structure was tightened up. The columns became more corporeal and thus more thick-set (height of, according to Pliny, 60 Ionic ft. or 57 ft. $10\frac{7}{8}$ in. = 9·6 lower diams. of 6 ft. $0\frac{1}{2}$ in.), the shafts displayed 24 deep flutes separated by fillets. Aiming at shadow effects, the precisely carved decorative elements—volute capitals, cymas, and so on—abandoned soft, succulent 'naturalness' for a clearly accented formal language of balanced tensions. The heavier entablature did lay a certain burden on the columns, although the building still preserved a characteristically Ionic lightness, since, in accordance with the early Ionic system, there was no Attic frieze. Thus, the entablature opposed the movement of the freely ascending columns more as a boundary and conclusion than as a counter-weight in the full sense. Representations on coins show that the broad fronts bore appropriately huge pediments. Above the three middle axial spaces appear, on the coins, three portal-like openings, which, being so unusual, probably not only served to reduce the load on the architraves but had some religious significance as well. One thinks of ritual manifestations of gods.

The make-up of the old column bases—plinth, spira with two scotias, and torus—was retained, becoming, by virtue of this example, the classically Ionic form; and so, too, was the sculptural decoration at the foot of the shafts. It is said that Scopas carved one of these approximately life-size reliefs. The surviving base in the British Museum follows rather the lyrical style of Praxiteles, who is supposed to have created the sculptural adornment of the unexcavated altar before the temple. Hermes and Death, the youthful winged brother of Sleep, lead a departing soul—is it Eurydice or Alcestis?—into the nether world. Exalted to a restrained expression of spiritual life, Ionia's true gift to classical art, that gliding, free-and-easy animation of surfaces, has here been restored by a great, probably native master.

The building must have been completed after the middle of the third century. Details, however, remained unfinished. Thus, a capital has been found in its rough state with the lines of the apparently so spontaneously curved volutes exactly incised. Similarly, all parts were brought into rigorously thought-out mathematical relationship and balanced against each other. It was doubtless not least upon the contrast between this all-pervading rationality and the freely developed, organic profusion of forms that the peculiar charm of Ionia's late classical buildings depended. In the case of the Artemisium, another opposition had also to be accepted, namely that resulting from a classically conceived structure rising over a faithfully preserved but undisciplined archaic ground-plan, rather as did the temple of Apollo at Delphi. None the less, this does not seem to have diminished the temple's fame, which spread across the entire Hellenic world.

In 263, a Gothic horde set fire to the building, which had already been plundered. It was patched up, and remained in that state till the destruction of the heathen temple was completed in Christian times. Then, to Antipater's epigram, which, after enumerating the other wonders of the world, concludes: 'Yet when I finally beheld Artemis's temple rising into the clouds, the other faded away. I said: Has the eye of Helios ever seen the like, apart from high Olympus?', a Byzantine commentator could add: 'Now, by the grace of Christ and John the Divine, it is the most devastated and desolate of all.' During the new era, the Ephesians built a no less marvellous edifice: the gigantic, cruciform domed church, 427 ft. long, over the tomb of St. John.

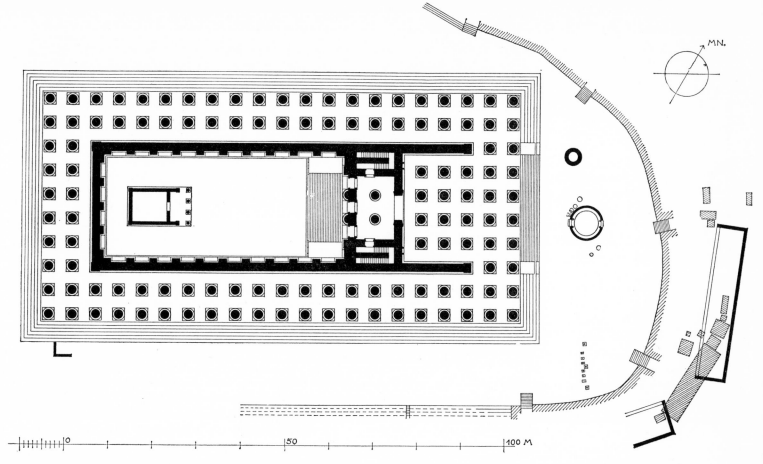

160

129 Didyma, near Miletus, temple of Apollo (Didymaeum). Plan. Before its front: round altar, fountain, and archaic retaining-wall. H. Knackfuss, *Didyma* I, 3, 1940

DIDYMA

THE TEMPLE OF APOLLO (DIDYMAEUM)

Plates 164–169, figs. 129–135

What Delphi meant to the motherland and its Western colonies, the great oracle sanctuary of Apollo Didymaeus signified to Ionians. Its protector was the powerful and wealthy trading city of Miletus, from which a processional way led up to it. Even today, the vast ruins of the dipteros, begun around 300 B.C., testify to the fact that this oracle site was on a par with the two other big Ionic sanctuaries of Samos and Ephesus. On the well-preserved marble crepidoma, there still stand erect tall sections of the walls and the only three columns along the whole Ionian coast that have been spared destruction by human hand, fire, or earthquake. Here again, let it be said in advance, we are dealing with an open sekos, its walls surrounded by a double peristyle.

Not much is known about the growth of the sanctuary, precisely because of the all-concealing crepidoma's good state of preservation. As elsewhere, the Ionian intruders appropriated an older holy place. In the shallow coomb on the edge of a spit running into the Aegean, there rose a spring, in the water of which lay prophetic power, as at Delphi. At the same time, Apollo's sacred bush, the laurel, was honoured there. Natural tokens like this spring and bush could only be architectonically contained under the open sky by a 'sekos'; and the foundations of such a sekos, a court of temple-like external form (see Ephesus, page 456), actually have been found within the later, enlarged temple court. In it, the features of the subsequent arrangement were already sketched out. An oblong of walls measuring 65 ft. 3⅜ in. wide and from 131 ft. 3 in. to 147 ft. 8 in. long and unbroken on its west side surrounded a small naiskos (13 ft. 9⅜ in. by about 27 ft. 11 in.), in which stood the celebrated bronze statue of Apollo by the Sikyonian master Canachus. While nothing is known about this court's eastern conclusion, where one would expect a door wall and a deep, aisled

463

pronaos, regular cuttings for the foundations give a clue as to the form of its interior. The space that this court comprised was articulated by heavy pilasters, which probably supported on their capitals an entablature jutting out from the wall. Such an articulation of the walls in an advanced stone structure was far removed from the passive projections and recesses of Mesopotamian mud-brick walls, even though these may have had an influence. Its significance for the future was far stronger, as the pilaster form pointed ahead to the—significantly—mostly Ionian or Corinthian articulation of walls by half-columns, which endowed the enclosed spaces of later classical times with their amplitude sustained by inner spans. Whether a double peristyle ran round this sekos, whether, that is, a dipteros already existed on the same spot in the sixth century, as seems probable, cannot be ascertained from the foundations covered by the later building. Nevertheless, important fragments of marble columns, architraves, and roof tiles have been found. To judge by them, the elevation completely resembled those of the two archaic dipteroi of Samos and Ephesus. Inside (the *fig. 111* pronaos?), there appear to have stood poros columns with a lower diameter of about 4 ft. 3 in. and bases of the Ephesian form (spira with two scotias, channelled torus or one adorned by a Lesbian leaf-and-dart). The columns at the fronts were thicker and of marble. As at Ephesus, reliefs encircled the foot of the shafts, and from them have survived two precious female heads. They stand out from the background of the filletless flutes, which even extend through the relief area (Berlin-Charlottenburg, Museum). Out of the narrow, almond-shaped eyes, the mysteriously smiling mouth, and the gentle animation of the whole face, the charm of Ionian art would seem to speak more directly than from the architectural ornament that, none the less, clearly springs from the same roots.

The big capitals with their plump and resilient coiling volutes (fragments in the Pergamum Museum, Berlin) carried an exceedingly low architrave, 3 ft. 0¼ in. high, on which something most unexpected happens. Savage creatures of fable here cavort across the supporting beams that, on Doric buildings, always expressed their static function by spanning the columns sturdily and nakedly. The angles were decorated by Gorgons in high relief. Lions accompanied them, and the supporting frame of the building was probably thus concealed by an endless succession of animals from the wilds. The three fascias appeared only fragmentarily as a background to the reliefs. There can be no doubt about it: this very framework was intended to be disguised, the severe fabric of vertical and horizontal parts

bound together by static forces was to be covered over with every vital form of imaginative Ionian art and roused to daemonic life; architecture's two polar expressions, supporting and burdening, were to be translated allegorically into a language of organic growth. Only in the genesis of the Ionic column did these almost incompatible elements achieve a real fusion. The frieze affixed externally to the architrave or walls could not hide the conflict between construction and vital form. This architrave frieze was probably no exception (nothing has survived of other east Ionic architraves), and it thus becomes comprehensible that exuberant mythical scenes once spread across the architrave of an archaic Doric temple of an odd kind in the Aeolian city of Assos. The provincial builders imprudently jumbled up Doric and Ionic models.

Axially in front of the archaic Didymaeum stood a strange altar consisting of a circular wall with folding gates around a simple cone of ash. Whether the well near this altar, and assumed to have been covered by a canopy raised on four columns, replaced the old sacred spring is uncertain. So far, it has not been possible to locate the spring in the sekos, where, according to the ancient accounts, it is to be sought. Temple and altar both faced east, but with a considerable and still unexplained deviation of thirty degrees to the north. In order to make room for the edifice, the slope of the hollow ascending eastwards had to be dug away and retained by a wall, which, about 11½ ft. high, follows a curving course. The big Ionic ovolo that crowns this wall belongs to the period around 540, and therefore gives a clue as to when building began.

After the disastrous naval battle outside the harbour of Miletus in 494, with which the Ionian revolt against the Persians collapsed, both city and sanctuary were destroyed, and the Apollo statue was carried off to Ecbatana. Evidence of renewed building activity during the first half of the fifth century is provided by volute capitals and two beautiful anta capitals of early Ionic form (three voluted cushions superimposed), which allow us to deduce a small anta building with walls 2 ft. 9⅛ in. thick (naiskos or altar?). Inscriptions and other records pass over the fifth and fourth centuries in silence. The oracle seems to have just managed to keep going until, with Alexander's procession of conquests, a new day dawned for the East. In 331, Apollo gave the young ruler—it goes without saying —a favourable response. Towards the close of the century, work appears to have begun on a new dipteros. Seleucus I brought back the old cult image from Ecbatana around 300, and gave financial assistance for the reconstruction.

130 Didyma, near Miletus, temple of Apollo (Didymaeum). Restoration of east end. H. Knackfuss, *Didyma* I, 1940

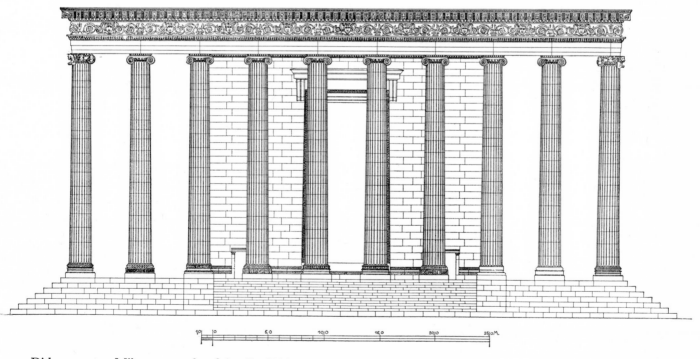

131 Didyma, near Miletus, temple of Apollo (Didymaeum). Completed front elevation (1 : 333). H. Knackfuss, *Didyma* I, 1940

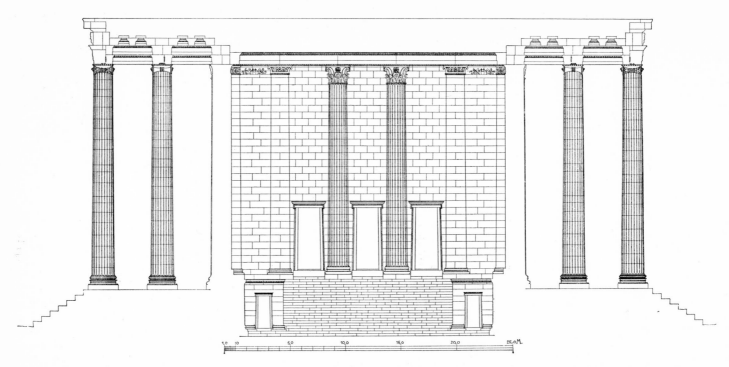

132 Didyma, near Miletus, temple of Apollo (Didymaeum). Cross-section showing north-east end of adytum with great flight of steps and entrance to hall containing two columns (1 : 333). H. Knackfuss, *Didyma* I, 1940

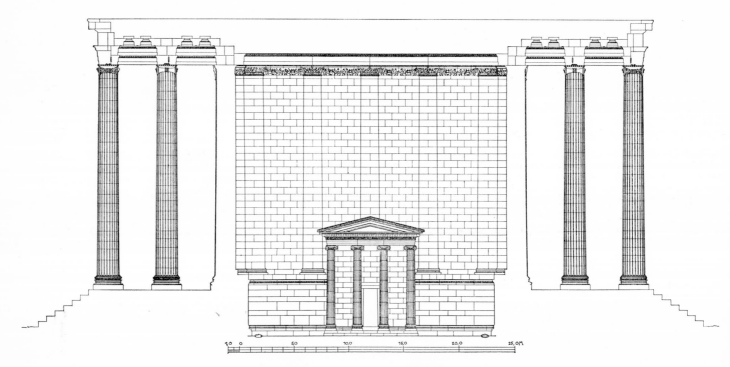

133 Didyma, near Miletus, temple of Apollo (Didymaeum). Cross-section showing south-west end of adytum with naiskos (1 : 333). H. Knackfuss, *Didyma* I, 1940

The new plan of the dipteros, which was designed by one of the leading masters on the Artemisium, Paeonius of Ephesus, and by the native architect Daphnis, remained wholly in the late classical tradition. It was differentiated from the early Ionic 'forest of columns', with its fairy-tale splendour, by a clearly evident corporeal structure, by a deliberately fashioned spatial sequence full of tensions, and by the superior assurance of the proportioning. With the new era, the dipteros changed radically, despite having an almost identical plan. However, it became apparent during the ensuing centuries that the Hellenistic age, which could not spend too much on secular buildings and on laying out enormous squares, was no longer interested in the construction of a temple like this. The expensive undertaking—calculated from surviving accounts, the cost of a column was almost 40,000 drachmas or nearly £10,000, which already comes to over £1,000,000 for the structure's 120 columns—dragged on for nearly 500 years. Not until the second century A.D. did the walls reach their full height. Caligula (A.D. 37–41), who wanted to take the god's place himself, tried in vain to complete the temple. The generous emperor Hadrian (A.D. 117–138) assumed the office of prophetes, certainly not without helping the building along. Its front entablature dated from the second century A.D., but the outer ring of columns was never finished on the flanks and at the back.

134 Didyma, near Miletus, temple of Apollo (Didymaeum). Corinthian capital of half-column against north-east wall of adytum. W. B. Dinsmoor, 1950

If the Artemisium (page 461) was a late classical structure over an archaic ground-plan, the Didymaeum was a late classical design that subsequently passed through all the stages of Hellenistic and 'baroque' execution. This design proceeded outwards from a centre. Round the small, tetrastyle prostyle naiskos, in which stood the archaic bronze statue of the god, were raised the walls of the open sekos, fronted to the east by a differentiated group of spaces consisting of a high, narrow hall and a pronaos with many columns. From the outside, this spatial complex looked like a cella, and was encased by a double peristyle of uniform density. Two constituent features in particular determined the

135 Didyma, near Miletus, temple of Apollo (Didymaeum). Pilaster capital, frieze, and entablature of adytum. H. Knackfuss, *Didyma* I, 1940

467

temple's appearance. Firstly, the high crepidoma (7 steps, height 10 ft. 4 in.; a flight of 14 steps at the east end), which was taken over from the Artemisium, gave the body of the building unity and also a new monumental grandeur by strongly emphasizing the rectangular surface on which it stood. Just how consistently this conception was expressed is shown by the form of the sekos, which, being tied to the spring and the laurel bush, could not be freed from the old, low level. As those of the archaic structure, the enclosing walls are articulated by pilasters, but now they ascend from a high plinth corresponding to the crepidoma, instead of from the ground. The second element was developed by Pythius in his temple at Priene (page 476), which served as a model. Organized from the start according to a system of axes rooted in its construction, the Ionic temple's ground-plan was now, after the example of Attica, underpinned by a standard interaxial, to which the measurements of the elevation were also firmly related. In this way, the old schema, with its fluid interaxial widths, first really found itself, the building as a whole gaining a cool, rational balance and unity. The Didymaeum's interaxial of 17 ft. $4\frac{5}{8}$ in. or 18 Attic ft. amounts to one and a half times that of Priene (12 Attic ft.). Walls and columns were arranged in a huge rectangular network of lines 9 Attic ft. (i.e. half an interaxial) apart. Planning proceeded outwards from the cella oblong, which was defined in the external plinth of the walls as 11 by 33 units (ratio 1 : 3; 95 ft. 8 in. by 286 ft. 10 in.). Everything else followed with mathematical inevitability. The first circuit of colonnades laid round the cella comprised 8 by 19 columns, each standing at the centre of a square of the grid. These squares were themselves made tangible and evident by the quadrate plinths under the columns. Logically, the second, outer circuit consisted of 16 by 21 columns. The stylobate, which measures 167 ft. 9 in. by 358 ft. 9 in., almost reached the size of the Artemisium's.

Along with the uniformity, it was above all the strikingly dense columniation that contributed to the structure's characteristic compactness, quite exceptional for a dipteros. In relation to the column, the internal (lower diam. of 6 ft. $6\frac{3}{8}$ in. related to intercolumniation of 10 ft. $10\frac{1}{4}$ in. as 1 : 1·66) was narrower than on comparable Attic buildings (about 1 : 2) and on the Athena temple at Priene (1 : 1·74). Though the towering slenderness of the columns (height of 64 ft. $7\frac{5}{8}$ in. = approx. 10 lower diams.) and lightness of the entablature (height 10 ft. $9\frac{1}{8}$ in. or $\frac{1}{6}$ of column height, without the frieze added later) remained, the dipteros closed up corporeally, in complete opposition to the original idea of the 'forest of columns', and thereby gained a firm, monumental

appearance. This use of the achievements of Attic classical architecture went so far that crepidoma, walls, and entablature were, for the first time on an Ionian temple, given a curvature, and, what is more, in the Parthenon's proportions. As a result of the narrow axial spacing, the cella's width of about 95 ft. corresponded to 5 interaxials instead of the usual 3. The columns, their interval unchanged, penetrated into the double-aisled, 3-interaxial-deep pronaos, which thereby became an emphatically transversal 'hypostyle hall of twelve columns', since its architraves ran crosswise like those of the porticoes.

Here, we touch on a new theme: that of the spaces. There is no other building in which the varied, tension-loaded spatial sequences of classical times encountered the ample and imposing Hellenistic layouts so successfully. The grandiose spirit of a new era sustained the spatial plan, which was, at the same time, based on the subtle laws of form that Ictinus and Scopas had defined at Bassae and Tegea (pages 351 and 354). Three spaces were set in contrasting relations, with the extensive, longitudinally disposed sekos, articulated by pilasters, on the one hand, and the covered, transverse pronaos, full of columns, on the other. Between them, as an intermediary, was placed a smaller hall entirely enclosed by walls. In it, the lengthwise and crosswise movements interpenetrated, the former stressed by the great doors, the latter by the shape of the space and by the transverse architrave over the hall's two Corinthian columns. Differentiated by their several ground-levels but held together by the uniform height of their entablatures and ceilings, these three spaces all had their own special religious function. The gigantic sekos, identified by inscriptions as an *figs.* 1 *133* 'adytum', was only accessible to the priests. A small independent temple containing the statue of Apollo stood before its rear wall. All around, the sacred laurel sprang verdantly from the unpaved ground. Yet this adytum was more than a corner of nature ringed by walls. Like the half-columns at Tegea, the mighty pilasters resting on their high continuous plinth held the over 70-ft.-wide space together as a whole articulated through the effect of their symmetrical opposition. Upon their unique capitals *fig.* 1 clasped by voluted bands—a new, Hellenistic version, loosened up by attractive tendril ornaments, of an archaic type of capital that spread as far as Sicily (page 430)—they carried a jutting entablature crowned by coloured mouldings. Above, the open sky extended as a ceiling. This most enormous of all the 'halls' of antiquity (71 ft. 3 in. by 175 ft. 11 in.; more than 82 ft. high), which the whole temple at Tegea would not have filled, was given an eastern conclusion of unequalled architectonic power. A

167
fig. 132

gs. 132,
134

fig. 54

flight of 24 steps, 50 ft. wide and framed by heavy, cuboid side-pieces, ascends to the height of the plinths. On either flank of the steps, the encircling array of pilasters ends in two more strongly projecting half-pillars. The eye is swept along by the even succession to this break, and there, above the steps, as an amazing and dramatic contrast, twin Corinthian half-columns grow upwards between the engaged pillars. Being its most animated limitary features, they give aim and direction to this space otherwise bounded solely by cuboid members and plane surfaces. Between and at either side of them, the partition-wall is broken by three doorways that lead through into the transverse hall linking adytum to pronaos.

The marble ceiling of this otherwise undecorated hall enclosed by smooth walls (46 ft. $0\frac{3}{4}$ in. by 28 ft. $8\frac{1}{8}$ in.) was supported by only two columns, which expressed physically the room's dominant dimension: its height of about $65\frac{1}{2}$ ft. Like the external half-columns, these supports had Corinthian capitals, their springy corner spirals and their acanthus leaves arranged in a lively rhythm being in the tradition of the Epidaurus capital. This choice form was, as at Bassae, only used to provide a special accent at the spot that, with everything leading up to it, constituted the temple's architectonic focus. The pair of columns in the plain, calm space set the scene for the crucial event: in the room's east wall a 'sacred doorway', so enormously big that there would have been room under the lintel for one of the Parthenon's columns plus its entablature, opens on to the pronaos (18 ft. $5\frac{5}{8}$ in. by about 46 ft.). Rising 4 ft. $9\frac{1}{2}$ in. above the pronaos floor, its threshold cannot be crossed by human beings. It was from here that Apollo spoke through his prophetes to the crowd assembled in the pronaos, and here, during his festivals, the most important religious ceremonies must have taken place. The jambs of this 'manifestation door', 46 ft. long and weighing 70 tons, were prepared from single blocks of stone—the biggest ever to be loaded, transported, and set in position during antiquity. Behind the walls, at either side of the hall containing two columns, are concealed staircases that led up to the flat terrace of the roof. They are called 'labyrinths' in the inscriptions, and their marble ceilings were adorned with big 'labyrinthine' meanders. These staircases must also have served the cult, the pageantry of which may have extended to the roof.

Those who were permitted to enter the god's huge court, the adytum, did so by a hidden, mysterious route. At either inner corner of the pronaos, there is a small, unpretentious doorway (3 ft. $8\frac{1}{8}$ in. by 7 ft. $4\frac{5}{8}$ in.). Through one or the other, these few penetrated into a narrow, barrel-vaulted passage, or rather tunnel, sloping down sharply under the staircase to the adytum at a lower level. They first reached a tomb-like chamber, with its delicate coffered ceiling, its Doric pilaster capitals that concluded the passage, and its lintel provided with taenia and regulae—all deliberate allusions to the Propylaea. If the outer door of this chamber concealed in one of the great side-pieces of the adytum steps now opened, they at last suddenly emerged through the 'propylaeum' from the sinister gloom into what was most luminous and spacious of all: Apollo's celestial hall.

167

Everywhere, the designers used not just the subtle inner oppositions of a purely architectonic character that the classical period had developed, but charms and contrasts of a more potent kind. They introduced psychological surprises, exploited the impact of optical successions and foreshortening (e.g. the great flight of steps in the adytum), and harnessed the majestic power of superhuman proportions (e.g. the high plinth), their effect accentuated through contrast with small architectural elements on a human scale (e.g. the slender-limbed body, richly and delicately ornamented, of the naiskos in the colossal pilastered court; or the little entrance doorway on either side of the gigantic 'epiphany door'). Indeed, such was the designers' skill at creating architectonic illusions that, through their disposition of the broad, apparently heavily loaded pilasters and the architrave that, projecting all round, must have seemed to bear a non-existent ceiling, they made the sky itself the cover of the 'hall'. What is completely unique about this building is the way in which these Hellenistic achievements combined with the outward appearance and inward order of classical architecture, in which the new illusionist effects did not yet dissolve the universe of classical forms but united with it in an infinitely rich and powerful symphony.

We still have to consider the ornamentation, which, as in the case of Ionic buildings generally, was the chief determinant of the external appearance, and here has its own particular history too. Being the shrine for the cult image, the naiskos, which came somewhere between the Nike temple and Erechtheum in size (27 ft. $0\frac{3}{8}$ in. by 46 ft. $8\frac{1}{8}$ in.), was adorned with special luxury, and displayed what was probably the richest ensemble of early Hellenistic architectural decoration. In view of this, it is striking that the walls were kept free of all ornament. They presented only a finely moulded footing with the Attic trinity of torus, scotia, and torus, such as appears, many times enlarged, on the walls of the cella. Delicate acanthus twirls spread over the

figs. 129,
133

169, below

projecting anta capitals. This plainness of the walls contrasted with the splendour of the ceiling and roof-edge. The coffers and the undersides (soffits) of the marble beams were gaily painted. Above the architrave, a new member was introduced on the model of the tholos at Epidaurus: a wave-profiled moulding, which, adorned by an anthemion frieze like the famous one on the Erechtheum, was set between an Ionic ovolo and a Lesbian cyma, their sharp, tectonically tense forms wholly divested of the old exuberant floral life. Where plant shapes did appear, as in the acanthus tendrils along the sima, they consisted of confidently stylized imitations of nature that were applied loosely and decoratively to their background instead of, as once, being made to sprout forth from the joints. In the second century B.C., the frieze crowning the adytum walls was created with an even more pronounced decorative sense characteristic of the Hellenistic age. Heraldically disposed griffins or winged lions rested a paw on Apollo's harp, and this motif spread to the curious pilaster capitals as well. The ground was now cut into the wall as a slight concavity. By this means, unexpected and, hence, interesting effects of light and shade were achieved, though at the expense of the relief's simple bodily substance. We have already mentioned the Corinthian columns, which probably number among the building's earliest parts. The twelve early Hellenistic capitals of the pronaos are also still securely in the classical tradition. Their clearly articulated tectonic structure is related to Pythius's creations at Priene, as are the somewhat later capitals from the inner ring of columns, more coarsely worked with deeper, shadow-casting convex forms.

With the construction of the front columns, a change in the ornament began, and, on this building, it had the effect of a degeneration, since it disturbed the underlying classical corporeality. The bases, elsewhere without exception of the normal Ephesian form, suddenly presented the most *recherché* variations —no longer with the joyous naïvety of early Ionic temples, but in an eclectic fashion. Near examples of the Attic shape and near cylindrical forms covered with anthemion patterns stand octagonal 'spiras' made up of panels carved in relief. Their soft, almost floating representations—floral interlace, fantastic creatures of the sea—live so exclusively through their contact with light that the firm, weight-bearing substance of the base seems to have been dissolved. The strangest of 'baroque' proliferations appeared on the capitals. At their corners, griffins' bodies sprang forth instead of diagonal volutes, and beside them protruded the heads of bulls. To the inner volutes even busts of Zeus and Apollo were applied (probably Leto and Artemis on the flanks), with fervently staring eyes, passionately contorted features, and streaming, deeply drilled hair. All this means, of course, that the capital had lost its significance as a tectonic member. A similar assemblage of heads looked down theatrically from the coffers of the portico and pteroma ceilings. This type of grandiose decoration also spread over the frieze added in imperial times to the original design (of which one can form a picture from the naiskos entablature), and even encroached on the fronts of the dentils. Deeply undercut *rinceaux* that were solely calculated to throw shadows grew luxuriantly round Medusa heads. Yet these, their expression distorted by sorrow, are moving. They are the last descendants of the avenging and protecting daemons that hovered snarling over the pediments of archaic temples. Phidias gave them an enigmatic human countenance, and now the affliction and discord of an age contented only outwardly bursts forth from them. This extravagant style of decoration is, as experts confirm, to be connected with the neighbouring school of Aphrodisias, and this last building period of the Apollo temple, which, like the Samian dipteros, remained unfinished, is datable to after the middle of the second century A.D.

SARDIS

THE TEMPLE OF ARTEMIS

Plates XXXI, 162, 163, fig. 136

The Ionians began their revolt against their Persian rulers in 499 with a provocative march on Sardis, the ancient capital of the Lydian kingdom situated in the valley of the Hermus, a three-day journey overland from Ephesus. As they could not capture the impregnable citadel ringed by three walls—'You have taken the acropolis of Sardis' was a figure of speech for 'You have done the impossible'—a soldier set fire to one of the reed-thatched huts. The flames engulfed the whole city, and also destroyed an

470

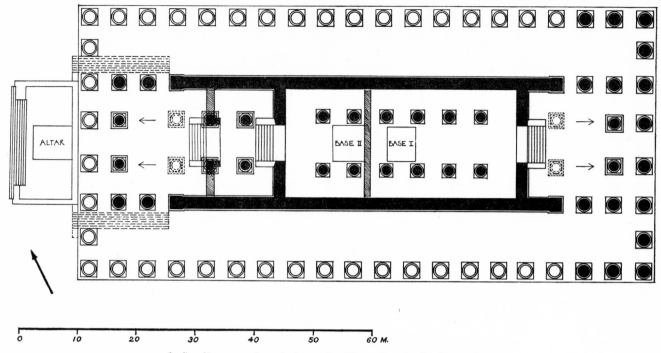

136 Sardis, temple of Artemis. Plan (1 : 625). New drawing

old sanctuary dating from Croesus's times and dedicated to the nature goddess, Cybele, whom the Greeks identified with their Artemis. Darius II, the incensed king of the Persians, was subsequently able to take this unintentional sacrilege as a precedent for razing Greek holy places to the ground.

The massive ruins of a temple of Artemis still tower below the acropolis, and, as is fairly logical, this temple has, until recently, been looked on as the successor to the old temple of Cybele. However, new excavations have revealed that, during the fifth century, this spot was still covered by a raging torrent. The sanctuary of Cybele must be sought elsewhere.

The temple was at the edge of a romantic river valley beneath the bizarre, precipitous hill of the citadel. Two columns of the east portico still stand erect to their full height of 58 ft. 2 in. and thirteen more in part. The temple walls are clearly visible, their moulded footing preserved in many places. Thus, standing out large in a magnificent landscape, the ruins number among the most impressive monuments of Asia Minor.

At the west end of the temple lies a somewhat older altar, about 68 ft. 10¾ in. by 36 ft., probably erected at the turn of the fifth and fourth centuries and surrounded by votive sites from Persian times. This seems to be the altar of Artemis mentioned by Xenophon (*Anab.* 1, 66), in front of which, in 402,

the younger Cyros, an occasional resident in Sardis, settled his differences with disloyal Orontes. As in other Greek sanctuaries, the altar seems to have been, for approximately a century, the only place of worship dedicated to the goddess. Then, after the hellenization of the East by Alexander, work started on a temple of immense size, facing the altar in the west, as were the Artemisia of Ephesus and Magnesia. The design shows a strange complexity. In its outer appearance and size it resembles the three great Ionic dipteroi, with 8 columns at the end and 20 along the flanks (stylobate 137 ft. 4 in. by 311 ft. 5 in.). The end passageways were 3, the pteromata 2 interaxials deep (cf. Samos, fig. 122). The cella, with its square pronaos over 55 ft. 9¼ in. deep and sporting 4 columns, and with its opisthodomus only 19 ft. 8¼ in. in depth, looks like the late-classical temple of Priene (page 476). The noticeable, progressive enlargement of the end axial spaces (corner interaxial 17 ft. 5 in.; then 17 ft. 10½ in., 21 ft. 9¾ in. and, centre, 23 ft. 2¾ in.) has obviously been adopted from the Artemisium at Ephesus. The interaxials along the flanks, 16 ft. 4½ in., are narrower. As in the Didymaeum, the design seems to have developed from the rectangle of the cella (75 ft. 5½ in. by 221 ft. 8 in.; ratio 1 : 3), which is distinguished by the simple and clear relationship of its measurements derived from a unit of 20 Attic ft. (19 ft. 4¼ in.).

fig. 136

471

Thus far, the temple adhered faithfully to the traditional dipteros schema. What is surprising is that it had no inner colonnades on the flanks. Was it wished to spare the expense of erecting the 2 by 18 inner columns, which, because of the close spacing of the outer ones, would have hardly shown? Is the Greek technical term 'pseudo-dipteros', meaning false- or seeming-dipteros, to be understood in this way? Consider the technical difficulty faced instead: that of covering the pteromata with a ceiling 28 ft. 6½ in. wide in the clear. Imagine the overpowering effect of perspective produced by these passages almost 100 yds. long and 11 yds. deep, their spaciousness contrasting excitingly with the massive compactness of the outer colonnades. Without doubt, the new form was based on a conscious artistic plan, whereby the radically changed conception of space, which with its calculable power over the beholder's eye had been tried out so imposingly in the Didymaeum's interior, was here applied also to the outward form of the dipteros. It is a thoroughly Hellenistic notion, and one that finally resolved the archaic idea of the dipteros, which had already been converted at Didyma from a magically labyrinthine forest of columns into monumental unity in the classical sense.

Vitruvius writes (3, 3, 8) of the architect Hermogenes as the inventor of this new form. Towards the beginning of the second century he planned his main achievement, the Artemisium of Magnesia, as a pseudo-dipteros with an encircling peristyle which was enlarged to a width of 2 interaxials by omitting the inner ring of columns. As, however, the temple of Sardis was started about a century before the time of Hermogenes, must not Vitruvius be wrong, although he gained his knowledge from manuscripts penned by Hermogenes himself? A closer look at the strange design reveals form tendencies completely opposed to the late-classical principles which strove towards unity and harmony: the increased space of the gallery is somewhat curtailed by the insertion into the porticoes on both sides of prostyle porches comprising 4 by 2 columns. As the customary pair of columns in-antis has been omitted, these porches surround a half-open hall 59 ft. 1 in. by 44 ft. 5¾ in. in size. How to cover such spaces was not learnt until the wide-span roof constructions on the Hellenistic town-halls (Priene and Miletus). Thus, behind the dense peristyle, which only preserved an outward appearance of unity for the dipteral-temple (so it *was* a seeming-dipteros, after all), was hidden an entire spatial programme as discordant as it was impressive. Here, surprise and conflict began to captivate the beholder: the contrast between heavy mass of columns and endless avenue of space in the pteromata; the dynamic tension between these long porticoes and the square halls at the ends. These are traits of changing times, of the Hellenistic era (page 481). Opposite the striking, thick-set columns at the east end (the height of 58 ft. 4 in. equals 8·9 lower diams. of 6 ft. 6¾ in.), of which one (plate XXXI, right column) carries an imperial Roman capital, the other (plate XXXI, left column) a Hellenistic capital of the second century, originally intended for a column slimmer by 4 in., stand the more slender Hellenistic columns (lower diam. 6 ft. 2⅜ in.) of the interior porches. The latters' central columns, however, stand out clearly because of their different shape: standing on socles 7 ft. 1⅜ in. high and intended for relief decoration, they tower, more slender and finely built (their height of 51 ft. 0½ in. equals 10 lower diams. of 5 ft. 1⅜ in.), over their neighbours, and are crowned by particularly richly carved capitals. This decoration intended for a visible front reveals, and architectural signs prove, that these columns, dated at about 300, did not originally stand in this position.

How, though, is the riddle posed by the plan, which conflicts with the Hellenistic conception, and by the confusion of early and advanced Hellenistic as well as imperialistic architecture to be solved? An examination of the foundations brought the answer. The complex building is not the result of a single plan, but of three different building periods. Towards the end of the fourth century the naos with its large cella was erected in front of the old altar. The cult statue of Artemis stood in the centre of this edifice. The magnificent columns, whose sculptured socles were adopted from the Artemisium of Ephesus, stood at that time in-antis, where their frontal effect could be fully appreciated. The space between the west end and the altar was occupied by 7 steps which were later covered when the peristyle was added. Towards the middle of the third century at the latest, the cult acquired the double ante-temple which was covered with a marble roof (fig. 136, black).

In 190 Sardis came into the possession of Eumenes II (197–159), a highly cultured monarch and a broad-minded building contractor to boot, who converted his castle in Pergamum (page 485) into the most impressive architectural monument of his time. He began to enlarge the temple in the spirit of the second century by surrounding it with the pseudo-dipteral peristyle which enclosed such large spaces. At about the same time, Hermogenes was using this style in such exemplary fashion at Magnesia. Here, however, the simple, rational form of Magnesia was enlarged upon by interrupting the encircling porticoes with the contrasting, columned halls at both ends. To achieve this the columns in-antis had to be removed and re-erected in the prostyle porches (fig. 136, dark shading). The building remained unfinished, however, after the last king of Pergamum, in 133, willed his kingdom to the new world power of Rome, whose rule, in the first instance, rather took the form of legalized plunder.

Not until imperial times did the East experience a new flowering. After his wife Faustina's death in A.D. 141, Antoninus Pius had built a temple in the forum at Rome in honour of the empress who, in accordance with the customs of the age, was raised to the status of goddess. He now undertook to finish this gigantic work in Sardis with the intention of having his wife worshipped as the equal of Artemis. To this end the cella was divided by a wall across the centre and what was now the west hall, which continued to serve the cult of Artemis, was enlarged by pushing the west entrance out by 2 interaxials. Thus,

the original, square pronaos was reduced to the slighter depth of the opisthodomus, thereby forming a symmetrical double-temple (fig. 136, shaded), almost an exact copy of a large pseudo-dipteral temple built by Hadrian in Rome for Venus and Roma. The colossal head of Faustina's cult statue and some fragments of a second statue of Antoninus were found in the new east cella, which was accessible through a large entrance leading from what was previously the opisthodomus.

Even this last attempt at finishing the temple was unsuccessful. The building never progressed further than the east front of the imperialistic section. Its portico—in part bearing small, older capitals—was now more thick-set (lower diam. 6 ft. 6¾ in.; height 8·9 lower diams.), but, nevertheless, looking like a huge theatrical imitation of a building, facing the acropolis, it appears to have satisfied the need for imposing appearances felt so acutely in those times.

PRIENE

Plates 156–158, figs. 109, 137–142

The high mountain-ridge of Mycale forms the northern boundary of the wide plain at the mouth of the Meander. Opposite, in the south-east, towers the jagged massif of Mount Latmus. Where now the river's glittering ribbon winds towards the sea through endless cotton-fields, a large bay once bit deep into the land, and on its shore lay flourishing Greek cities: powerful Miletus, Heraclea, Myus, and Priene. The river, which, because of its sinuosities, gave its name to the most important Greek band-ornament, the geometrically stylized 'meander', brought blessing and bane to these places. Like the Nile, it fertilized the fields with its yearly floods, formed new land, left behind it fever-swamps, and blocked the vital harbours of the maritime cities. Though it still had room in Herodotus's day for 200 triremes, the harbour of Myus became so marshy during Roman times that the citizens moved to Miletus. The ruins of Heraclea today lie at the edge of a large inland lake about twenty-two miles from the coast. Ancient Priene, which had belonged to the Ionian league since the seventh century, scraped a modest living after the disastrous Ionian revolt. Around the middle of the fourth century, the silting was evidently so far advanced that the city was refounded at another spot under the protection

of Athens. Not even the site is known of the old Priene, which lies buried somewhere in the alluvium.

The new city was laid out on the slope of Mount Mycale at the foot of a steep cliff, which was contained by the wall as an acropolis but bore no sanctuaries. Priene still maintained its link with the sea, thanks to a harbour several miles away. Though able to preserve some measure of independence within the big states of the Hellenistic age, the little city never played a prominent role in history. This only adds to its importance as the one completely excavated Greek city, a Greek Pompeii. Anybody who has wandered through its streets, public squares, and sanctuaries will not forget this image of a polis in its compactness and perfection. After all, the polis was no more nor less than the place where Greeks lived their lives, and the Greek, whom Aristotle defined not as a thinking or speaking but as a 'political' being, remained tied to his polis for better or worse. Inside its wall, which simply follows the terrain, the new Priene did not develop arbitrarily like medieval towns with their lanes conforming to the slope; instead, a precisely rectangular network of streets was imposed under the greatest difficulties on the steep ground. Hippodamus of Miletus, who took a special interest in the systematization of such

156, fig. 137

473

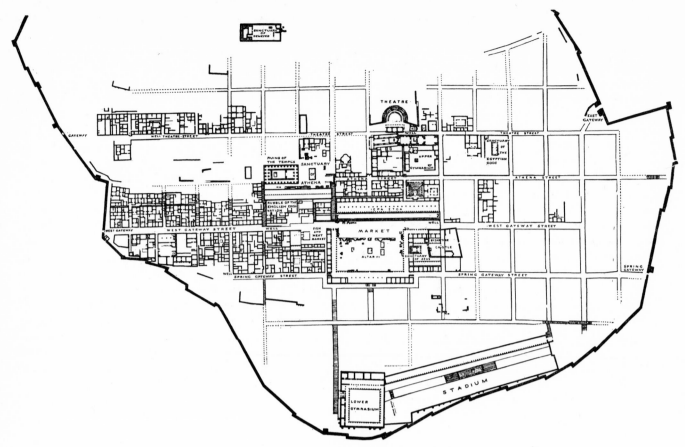

137 Priene, plan of city (1 : 4,000). T. Wiegand and H. Schrader, *Priene*, 1904

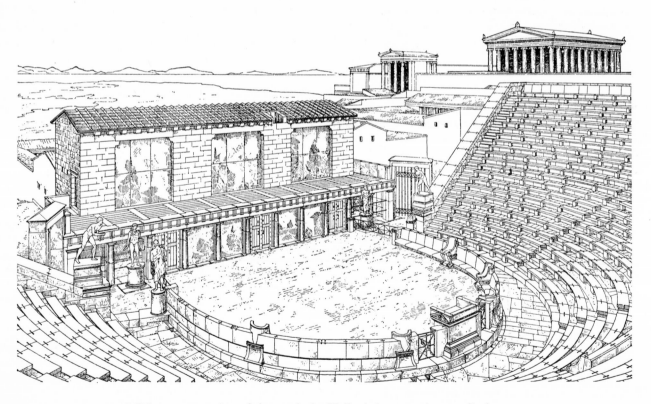

138 Priene, restoration of theatre in its Hellenistic state. A. von Gerkan, 1921

city plans and wrote on the subject, was considered to have been their 'inventor' by later authors. They were certainly wrong, as is shown by similarly conceived plans dating from archaic times in the Western colonies (Selinus, page 423). The characteristically Greek ability to give form and order was here applied also to the most extensive creation, a structure serving specific ends. Over and beyond its practical organization, the city itself became a fashioned organism—indeed, a work of art. As the political focus (not the commercial one, let it be noted, since a separate market-place was included), the agora constitutes the centre. Running east-west, the principal street leads from the western gate over this agora once surrounded by stoas, though not, significantly, across its middle as an optical axis but along its north side. The centre belonged rather to the gods, for there stood an altar of Hermes. A Zeus sanctuary, the magnificent council hall, and the prytaneum all border closely on the agora. Parallel to the principal one run five more streets, at equal intervals but very different levels, and they are crossed by fifteen steep, narrow side-roads that climb the slope partly as steps. In this way, the whole inhabited area was divided up into equal housing blocks (insulae) measuring 160 by 120 Ionic ft. (154 ft. 10 in. by 115 ft. 11 in.), each of which normally provided space for from four to six directly contiguous dwellings. The rooms of these often two-storied houses were grouped round an open court like a miniature copy of the city. There were no gardens or parks: town and countryside were incompatibles. A stadium and a gymnasium backed on the surrounding wall at the southern edge of the city. At the very top, the shell of a small theatre *158* nestles in the slope. It was already laid out to cover two insulae when the city was founded, accommodated about 5,000 citizens, and also served for council meetings until the construction of the bouleuterion. Transversely in front of the circular orchestra stood the two-storied 'scene' with its three doors, and in front of this the low 'proscenium', a row of 12 pillars, masked by Doric half-columns. Large, painted scenery panels could be fixed into the grooves *fig. 138* along their sides. The 'proscenium' was connected with the 'scene' by marble beams supporting a roof of boards, so that some scenes could also be played on the higher stage formed in this way. In the second century, with the rise of popular comedy, the action took place mainly on this upper stage. Accordingly, the seats of honour for priests and councillors, for whom the bottom row had previously been reserved, were moved up to the fifth row. Priene's intimate little theatre, built with the greatest care, is not only one of the best preserved in the Greek world, but also one of the best investigated.

THE TEMPLE OF ATHENA POLIAS   *Plates 156, 157, figs. 109, 139–142*

Above the public square and the streets stands forth another of Priene's centres: the religious one. This is the sanctuary of the city goddess, Athena Polias,

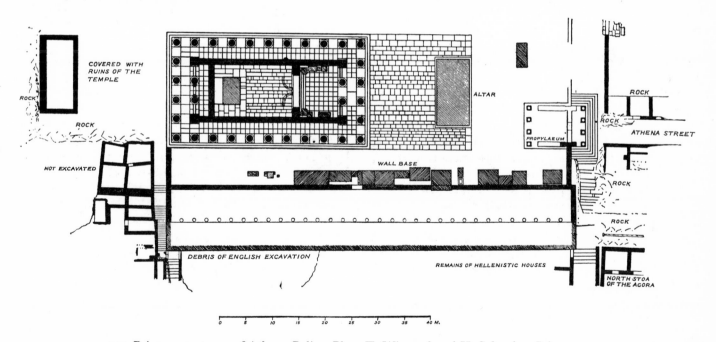

139 Priene, sanctuary of Athena Polias. Plan. T. Wiegand and H. Schrader, *Priene*, 1904

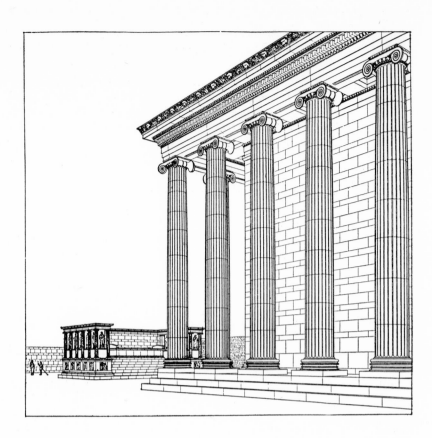

140 Priene, temple of Athena Polias and altar from the north-west. M. Schede, 1934

157, below

fig. 139

situated on a high ridge to the north-west of the agora. Extended by means of retaining-walls, the terrace was, as the goddess's temenos, kept strictly separate from the residential area. One entered from the east through a small propylaeum fronted on either side by porticoes with 4 Ionic columns. A large peripteral temple with 6 by 11 columns (stylobate 64 ft. 1 in. by 121 ft. 10 in.) occupied the western half of the precinct. Today, only the 3-step crepidoma and a few blocks of the wall base remain in position, surrounded by fragments of the columns, walls, and entablature. Yet this is the sole peripteral temple from classical times known down to its last detail that Ionia has bequeathed us. Important architectural parts are to be found at the British Museum and at the Pergamum Museum in Berlin, where a sample pair of its columns and their entablature has been restored.

That is not, however, the only reason for its outstanding consequence in architectural history. This temple belonging to a small Ionian city without special rank or renown was already regarded in antiquity as *the* classical Ionic temple. The effect of its example, clearly discernible in the later buildings of the East, can be traced right down to the theory of architecture propounded by the Roman Vitruvius and to his dogmas concerning proportion. Through this intermediary, it even remained authoritative for

the Renaissance and Classicism. Priene could afford to employ Pythius, the most distinguished architect of the day who shortly before had designed the tomb of Mausolus at Halicarnassus and thereby become world famous. Considering architecture to be the queen of the arts, the master demanded that the architect should, as a kind of universal genius, be fully conversant with all the subordinate arts, and appears, accordingly, to have worked on the Mausoleum as a sculptor. Following the custom of antiquity, he also knew how to wield the pen, and published books about his two principal achievements, from which Vitruvius obtained his knowledge (I, 1, 12 and VII, praef. 12). Pythius's share at Priene would seem to have gone even beyond designing Athena's abode, for the layout of the city reveals the same masterly ability to impose order as does the ground-plan of the temple.

Order, the most lucidly rational mathematical relations—such is the essence of the design; and so much so that the temple succeeded in making an 'impression of displeasing aridity' on a connoisseur of Ionic architecture. There may be something in this. If, however, one considers the antecedent circumstances and the aim of this design, one will find the much more favourable judgement of contemporaries not entirely unfounded. So far as can be learnt from the monuments, no 'classic' of Ionic architecture was produced in Ionia itself until the

476

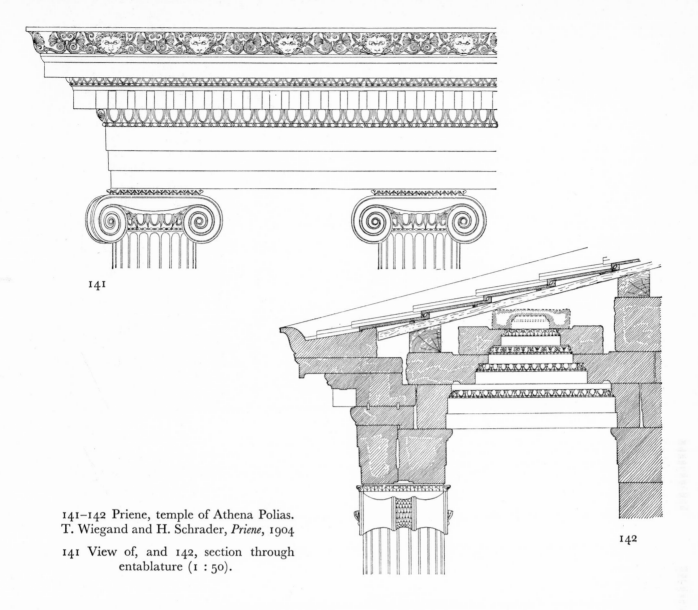

141–142 Priene, temple of Athena Polias.
T. Wiegand and H. Schrader, *Priene*, 1904

141 View of, and 142, section through
entablature (1 : 50).

141

142

erection of the Mausoleum. This curious deficiency was probably not just occasioned by the political oppression of the cities of Asia Minor. It was due even more to the archaic nature of Ionic architecture and its adornment, to the conflict between a rational construction and vivacious floral ornament. The monumental unity of a well-balanced appearance was denied to this architecture. What Ionians could not effect was achieved in Athens: a conversion of the swelling decorative members into tectonically firm structures. The volute channels became taut concave forms, the plump borders of the 'eggs' became sharp-edged shells contrasting strongly with the ovoid middle parts that they clasped (plate 6). Nevertheless, the Attic Ionic order remained, as a graceful and pliant contrast to the severity of the Doric

temple, confined to small-scale operations and informal, non-monumental tasks. The organizing of an Ionic peripteral ground-plan and creation of an Ionic temple of outward and inward magnitude in the classical spirit were not matters to which Athens applied itself.

When Pythius undertook during the last decades of the classical period, between 350 and 330, the construction of a monumental peripteral temple, he broke new ground. It is his special merit and his strength that, though knowing how to seize on the suggestions of Attica, he in no wise imitated the Attic order with its frieze introduced instead of the dentil course. He endeavoured to create a classical Ionic style deliberately linked up with Ionia's great archaic achievements. In his polemical zeal and his

477

pride in the heritage and property of his homeland, he could allow himself to reject the Doric order altogether, 'because faulty and dissonant proportions (*symmetriae*) occurred in it' (Vitruvius IV, 3, 1; with reference to the Doric angle conflict). This exclusion was, at the same time, a statement of his programme: what mattered to him was a pure harmonizing of parts in a numerically determined system of proportions. Thus, he entirely conformed to the academic, late classical trend towards clearly balanced dimensional relationships. By raising the national element inherent in Ionic buildings from the outset to the status of ruling principle, he endowed the temple with its new unity. Now, it will be conceded that this exaltation of 'ratio' (the Latin word means at once reason or judgement and proportion) suited the Ionic very much better than the corporeal Doric structure, which all too quickly froze into lifelessness under its cool breath. The light, lissom members of the Ionic order and its wealth of vivacious forms constituted too powerful a counterpoise to the hardness and inflexibility of the late classical conception, as is made convincingly apparent by a comparison with the temple of Zeus at Nemea (page 357). It was not to the danger of inanimate stiffness but of an exuberant 'baroque' proliferation of its ornament that the Ionic style was exposed (Didyma, page 469).

The ground-plan of the Athena temple is inscribed in an accurate network of squares measuring 6 by 6 Attic ft. of about 11½ in. (lines 5 ft. 9½ in. apart). Each column plinth and every interval between the plinths exactly filled one of these squares, so that the axial spacing came to 12 Attic ft. (11 ft. 6⅞ in.) all round. With its 6 by 11 columns or 5 by 10 interaxials, the peristyle was laid out in the ratio 1 : 2, its axial dimensions thus amounting to 60 by 120 Attic ft. or 57 ft. 10½ in. by 115 ft. 9 in. Walls and antae were, in each case, axially aligned with the second column from the corner, and so fitted precisely into the network of squares. The passageways were everywhere one intercolumniation across—not just on the flanks but also at the ends, which had hitherto always been deeper. Hence, the cella measured 3 by 8 interaxials or 36 by 96 Attic ft. in its wall and anta axes. Since the walls were 4 Attic ft. thick, the cella's external dimensions came to 40 by 100 Attic ft. (38 ft. 10¼ in. by 96 ft. 8½ in.; ratio 2 : 5), and this nucleus was thus, like Ionia's earliest temple on Samos, a hecatompedon. The length of the naos amounted to half that of the cella: 50 Attic ft., with a clear breadth of 32 Attic ft. The uniform depth of the passageways already meant that the early Ionic emphasis of the entrance end had been abandoned. Accordingly, the cella, too, now received symmetrical fronts on the Doric model with two columns between the antae. This was the first demonstrable appearance of the opisthodomus in East Greece. There is nothing surprising, therefore, in the fact that, following the Doric practice, the antae were made to stand out from the walls like pillars. Both opisthodomus and anta projections found disciples (Sardis, Magnesia, etc.). On the other hand, the giant early Ionic temples lived on in the big, almost square pronaos measuring 30 by 32 Attic ft., which the opisthodomus, only 16 Attic ft. deep, could not hold in balance. However, owing to a changed perception of space, Pythius entirely abandoned interior columns, covering pronaos and naos like wide halls with a wooden coffered ceiling.

Simple dimensional relationships of this kind are, of course, to be expected in the elevation as well. The important proportion of column diameter (4⅜ Attic ft. = 4 ft. 4⅛ in.) to intercolumniation (7⅝ Attic ft. = 7 ft. 4⅛ in.) is 4 : 7. For the column height, which could not be directly determined, only two measurements come into consideration on the strength of a reconstruction of the southern anta, which was thickly covered with inscriptions: 37 ft. 3¾ in. and 41 ft. 6⅛ in. (The pseudo-isodomic walls were constructed of two tall courses alternating with one low. Hence, the securely restored part can only be heightened by one or more such tripartite groups, each of which had a height exactly corresponding to the lower column diameter: 4 ft. 2¾ in.) If they were 41 ft. 6⅛ in. tall, however, the columns not only achieved the slenderness of the Didymaeum's supports (height = 9·9 lower diams.) but had a height of exactly 43 Attic ft.; and, as the entablature was 7 Attic ft. tall, the temple's height came, perforce, to 50 Attic ft. This ought to dispose of all doubt. The entablature itself, which kept the early Ionic sequence of architrave (with three fascias), dentils, corona, and sima, was similarly articulated in rhythmic mathematical relations. With its crowning ovolo, the architrave had the same height as the cornice (3½ Attic ft.). There developed a chain of proportions, which, thickening, loosening up, and coming to an end—in ¼ Attic ft., 11 (architrave) : 3 (ovolo) : 6 (dentils) : 3 (corona) : 5 (sima)—signifies far more than a lifeless dalliance with numbers. Every receptive eye will surely discern its inner harmony before the example restored at the Berlin Museum. The dentils and the egg-and-darts above and below them are distributed independently of one another, each thus following its own horizontal rhythm, which is related only to the interaxial. With its lion-heads twined about by acanthus tendrils and palmettes, the sima surprisingly opposes its triple rhythm to the interaxial. This apparent arbitrariness, which seems to hark back to archaic—and therefore

fig. 1.

naïve—dissonances of a similar kind, introduced an irrational element into the general regularity, a delicate chromatic cadence into the building's grand and pure chord. Both this, so to speak, patriotic archaizing and the extremely refined proportioning, which was only achieved with the aid of a carefully thought-out mathematical construction, can even be observed in the seemingly freest and most animated decorative members, the volute capitals. Their models, the capitals of the archaic Artemisium, with which they have in common widely separated volutes, have here been translated into another stylistic idiom: that of the classical period. The taut, corporeal structure is, in its turn, sustained by a numerical framework, from which the beautiful creation derives its unity. At least two types came into being (capitals at the British Museum and at the Pergamum Museum in Berlin), obviously taking account of their particular function in the building. The outer capitals are developed more frontally, more elongated, and adapted to the order's simple proportions measured in feet, whereas the four inner ones seek through highly subtle modifications to achieve a distinct 'all-sidedness', which is, of course, denied the volute capital by its very nature. Thus, not only are the fronts of the volutes more strongly inclined (as was already the case on archaic capitals in the East), but the volutes themselves at the same time swing slightly towards the diagonal, doubtless following the example of the inner capitals at Bassae.

g. 142 Indicative of the constructionist approach of Ionian architects is the make-up of the marble ceiling over the porticoes and pteromata. Its cross-beams actually rested on the architrave, and, what is more, in each case above a column. The square between the cross-beams (about $8\frac{1}{4}$ by $8\frac{1}{4}$ ft.) was covered by a single coffer about $3\frac{1}{4}$ ft. high, built up out of two projecting layers, richly profiled with multicoloured mouldings, and a crowning-piece. Here, therefore, construction and articulation coincided, whereas, in Attica, the rows of small coffers sunk into the marble covering slabs were given a subordinate role for the sake of the unity of the ceiling plane. The anta capitals likewise allude ingeniously to the archaic form with three volute cushions, which the sequence of Lesbian cyma, anthemion, and Ionic ovolo develops (something similar had already appeared on the Rhoecus altar, page 448). Nevertheless, the tautly plump, primitive vigorous volutes at the sides have been replaced by delicate acanthus tendrils curling up into spirals.

Everywhere, then, the primitiveness of the architectural decoration, which once used to endow the whole with its vivacity, was now held in check and subordinated to the newly grasped tectonic significance of the building. This ornament here radiated not a reduced, but a restrained, reserved vitality of a different and, one might perhaps say, spiritualized nature. The form—so lively, so vibrantly animated—became the garb of something inward, of those musically adjusted 'symmetries' that made the entire structure, firmly and corporeally put together from distinct parts, ring out in a chime of crystal clarity and cool, pure, almost unearthly beauty.

Since Pythagoras, who left his native Samos because of the tyranny of Polycrates, had proclaimed 'number', by which he meant law expressible in terms of mathematics, to be the essence of things and found his doctrine confirmed by the simple vibratory relationships of harmonic tones, Greek philosophy and artistic theory had never relinquished these ideas. Probably in no other late classical building was the increasingly conscious classical ideal of reducing the beautiful to laws realized so successfully.

The Athena temple embodied an aesthetic programme. An extremely well-trained master, as assured in his sense of form as he was intellectually gifted, here attempted to tie in a fresh way the sundered bonds of the Ionic building tradition. He knew how to select: the early Ionic sequence of forms, Attic principles of design and refinement, Peloponnesian corporeity—all these were at his disposal. He also knew how to renounce: so that the purity of its proportions should be the sole determinant, the temple bore no sculptural decoration whatever, and this despite the fact that Pythius had been active on the Mausoleum as a sculptor. With a rational consistency never before achieved, he developed his design on the basis of its aesthetic effects. He was thus an out-and-out eclectic, a masterly academist, and therefore, as should not be overlooked, a child of his times; but he was more as well. A sovereign artist of ascendant creative power, he towered beside Scopas above the other fourth-century architects, who increasingly spent themselves in routine labours. His work was a complete success. The temple of Athena brought about a renaissance in Ionia, the new Artemisium, Didyma, Sardis, and a temple at Teos all being indebted to its example. Moreover, the most distinguished Hellenistic architect, Hermogenes, who was probably born at Priene, would have to be regarded as Pythius's pupil if the time interval between them were not too great. In his chief work, the temple of Artemis at Magnesia, Hermogenes widened the porticoes and pteromata to 2 interaxials. Thereby, he gave them a new spatial looseness, which, though hidden behind the pretentious façade of his pseudo-dipteros, still kept to Pythius's strict system of axes and arrangement of proportions.

He who was then the greatest among men, Alexander, seems to have recognized greatness when he came to Priene in 334. The Athena temple had evidently progressed only as far as the topmost courses of the cella walls. Alexander made a present of the means, which the small city was unable to provide, and had his votive inscription carved on the southern anta:

ΒΑΣΙΛΕΥΣΑΛΕΞΑΝΔΡΟΣ
ΑΝΕΘΗΚΕΤΟΝΝΑΟΝ
ΑΘΗΝΑΙΗΙΠΟΛΙΑΔΙ

None the less, the temple's west portico remained unfinished, and there was no cult statue or altar till round about the middle of the second century, when a Hellenistic prince, Orophernes of Cappadocia, handed over to the sanctuary a large hoard of money for safe-keeping, and helped it out with another donation. At that date, it seems, the altar was erected and the image of Athena set up. The former stood magnificently surrounded by colonnades on a high podium in the manner of the altar at Pergamum, while the latter took the form of a copy, reduced by a third, of Phidias's Athena Parthenos. Orophernes hid some coins bearing his portrait in the statue's pedestal as a kind of donation record. The treasure brought the city a disastrous war. Then, before a hundred years passed, the coins with the portrait occasioned the final destruction of this unique building, the members of which, though brought down by earthquakes, had hitherto piled up so neatly that it would have been easy to re-erect them. Stone-thieves found the unlucky coins. On hearing of this 'treasure', the peasants of the neighbourhood flocked together and smashed to pieces the irreplaceable remains of the first and last temple in East Greece to be flawlessly moulded by the classical period's noble sense of form.

fig. 140

PERGAMUM

AN EXAMPLE OF HELLENISTIC ARCHITECTURE

In turning to Pergamum, the seat of a Hellenistic dynasty situated well inland on the edge of the Caicus plain, we finally leave the world bound by religion, a world that was centred reverently on the most ancient holy places, its spiritual focus the gods who were present everywhere and at all times. To be sure, the new, Hellenistic age was not wanting in cults; but, on the one hand, the rootless religiosity now produced superstitious, mystical outgrowths, while on the other, myth became the plaything of pampered, cultured intellects, entered the sphere of education, and formed the subject of well-read erudition or philosophical speculation: myth turned into mythology. Discord and inner strife characterize the last three centuries of ancient Greek civilization, which, however one considers them, present two incompatible aspects, deep passion and ironic rationality, heroic fervour and vain idyll, realism and fantasy all finding a place in the same ruptured soul. Torn from the old, nourishing faith, from the Greek cosmos of world and spirit, the individual underwent a painful extension. It is reflected in the strained features of Hellenistic portraits, where Greek art for the first time made what is purely personal its theme.

Sovereigns and sovereignties arose out of nothing when, after Alexander's death in 323 B.C., his officers disputed his gigantic empire. The empire disintegrated into states, which replaced the old mould of life, the polis; but the difference would hardly be worth mentioning if the state had not been personified exclusively by the ruler instead of by the community of its citizens. Lysimachus, one of Alexander's heirs, deposited the enormous sum of 9,000 talents on the citadel hill of Pergamum, which was then already fortified and, thanks to its steepness, impregnable. He installed as governor a Macedonian officer called Philetaerus, who, at the earliest opportunity, set himself up as an independent ruler (283–263), and founded a dynasty of powerful kings. His nephew, Attalus I (241–197), considered himself the champion of the Greeks, after having defeated the savage Gallic hordes. Attalus's energetic son, Eumenes II (197–159), repelled the Gauls again, and extended his realm across the whole of Asia Minor. This highly cultivated and ambitious king did not rest content with his political successes. He wished to make his capital into a new Athens, the intellectual centre of the Greek world. Poets and scholars flocked together at his court. In the first century B.C., the Pergamene library already included 200,000 scrolls, which was only made possible by the invention of parchment (i.e. *pergamena charta*). The rulers of Alexandria forbade the export of Egyptian papyrus through jealousy, in order to maintain the primacy of *their* famous library. Eumenes also fashioned the acropolis, with obvious allusions to Athens, into an architectural complex that remained unsurpassed in grandeur till the construction of the imperial forums at Rome.

THE ACROPOLIS   *Figs. 143, 144*

If one takes a look at the plan of the acropolis, one will first of all feel the absence of a consistent arrangement like that, say, of Priene. This is not just due to the fact that building operations occurred at several periods, and that the confined, arching ridge was harder to utilize. More important is the dominant presence of a different ordering principle that no longer produced the unassuming structure, founded on harmonious regularity, of the little classical city, but a new, optical order related to man. Through its action, each of the big enclosures was afforded a highly impressive, eye-enthralling development, and the separate precincts were bound together by view-lines and enticing perspectives. It must be mentioned that the practical system of roads intersecting at right angles did continue to be used in the laying out of Hellenistic cities, but it henceforth had only to serve as a groundwork for the striking perspectives, for the majestic streets bordered by stoas and running towards magnificent gates, that now determined a city's appearance. If, as here, an orthogonal plan met with difficulties, it was abandoned as something of no consequence, provided that the optical order could be preserved. The outward cohesion of the buildings on the acropolis was established by a street that, climbing the hill from the south, crosses an agora once enclosed by stoas, reaches the actual acropolis plateau through

figs. 143, 144

481

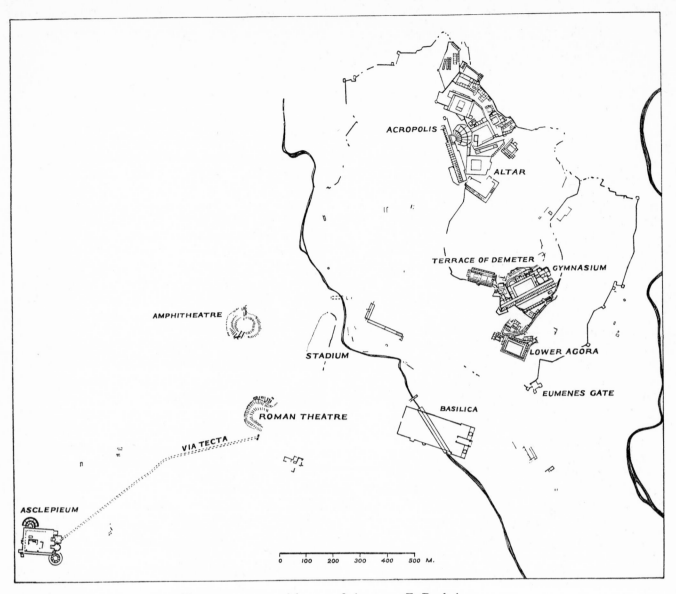

143 Pergamum, general layout of city area. E. Boehringer, 1950

174, below

174, above,
175

a fortified gate, and then follows the ridge in a wide curve. On its right, towards the east, stood the remarkably modest palaces of the Attalids, each grouped about a colonnaded court, together with barracks and storehouses. On its left, over a far greater area, extend the sanctuaries, in which the might and lustre of the young kingdom displayed themselves imposingly. These holy places embodied a political idea or, alternatively, the heroic image of the ruler was realized in the sanctuaries; yet this very process still remained Hellenic. Power was valid only as the support of something spiritual that neither could nor would express itself in stately palace layouts or public buildings. Hence, the pre-eminent status of Pergamene art.

Four big enclosures, all more or less rectangular in plan, fan out along the western edge of the plateau, while at the same time ascending as steps, one above the other, from south to north: the agora, the huge terrace of the Altar of Zeus, the sanctuary of Athena, and the 'Trajaneum', which, it is surmised, covers a Hellenistic temenos. They all open to the west, and give a clear view across the wide valley, which is dominated by the citadel. The layout thus reproduces on a large scale the shape of a theatre, and a theatre does in fact form its centre, embedded like a gigantic shell in the western slope of the acropolis. Before its semicircle, there extends at a lower level a narrow terrace about 270 yds. long and once bordered by stoas: the chord of the whole monumental arc.

XXI,

482

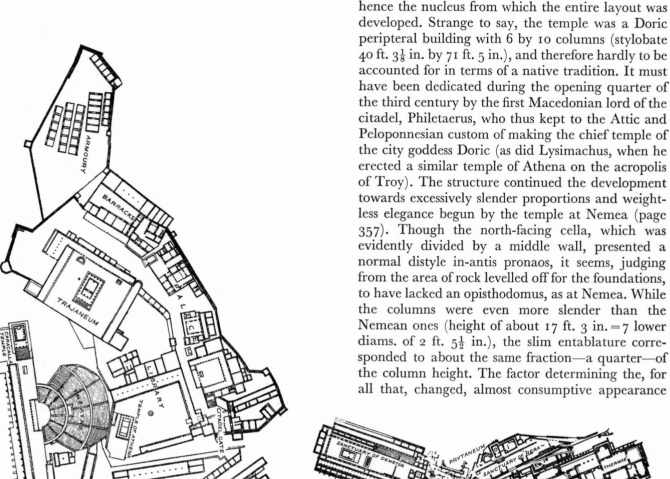

The sanctuary of Athena is the oldest part, and hence the nucleus from which the entire layout was developed. Strange to say, the temple was a Doric peripteral building with 6 by 10 columns (stylobate 40 ft. 3⅛ in. by 71 ft. 5 in.), and therefore hardly to be accounted for in terms of a native tradition. It must have been dedicated during the opening quarter of the third century by the first Macedonian lord of the citadel, Philetaerus, who thus kept to the Attic and Peloponnesian custom of making the chief temple of the city goddess Doric (as did Lysimachus, when he erected a similar temple of Athena on the acropolis of Troy). The structure continued the development towards excessively slender proportions and weightless elegance begun by the temple at Nemea (page 357). Though the north-facing cella, which was evidently divided by a middle wall, presented a normal distyle in-antis pronaos, it seems, judging from the area of rock levelled off for the foundations, to have lacked an opisthodomus, as at Nemea. While the columns were even more slender than the Nemean ones (height of about 17 ft. 3 in. = 7 lower diams. of 2 ft. 5½ in.), the slim entablature corresponded to about the same fraction—a quarter—of the column height. The factor determining the, for all that, changed, almost consumptive appearance

figs. 146,
147

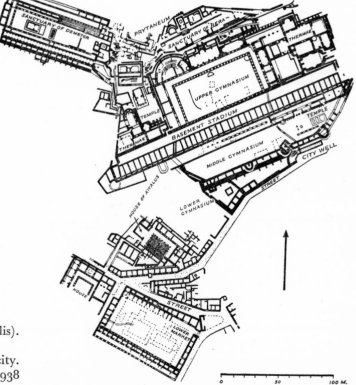

144 (*Above*) Pergamum, plan of upper city (acropolis). Same scale as fig. 145
145 (*Right*) Pergamum, plan of middle and lower city. Both W. Zschietzschmann, *Realenzyklopädie* XIX, 1938

483

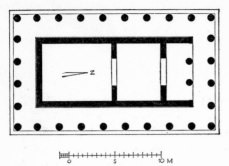

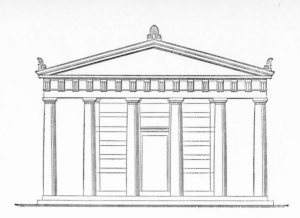

146–147 Pergamum, temple of Athena Polias Nikephoros.

146 Plan (1 : 400). New drawing
147 North front elevation (1 : 200). R. Bohn, *Die Altertümer von Pergamon* II, 1885

of the order was the entirely unwonted incongruity between the columns and the exaggeratedly wide intercolumniations of 8 ft. (2 ft. 5½ in. : 5 ft. 3¾ in. = 1 : 2·16; Nemea 1 : 1·29). Three metopes and triglyphs, instead of two, accorded in the frieze with each very broad interaxial. What, in the case of the Propylaea, served to stress the entrance interaxial as a conspicuous exception, here became a meaningless rule, and so it henceforward remained. Thus, the strong, simple rhythm of the Doric entablature was abolished, and the old corporeality of the Doric fabric eaten away in an irresistible process of disaggregation. The temple—and particularly the Doric temple—which, in spite of everything, as a form of building with a cuboid nucleus, was and continued to be a structural body, hardly interested this period any more. In all its architectural splendour, the whole acropolis only boasted two other, unimportant temples: a small, second-century Doric prostyle structure, dedicated to Hermes or Dionysus, beside the agora (4 columns at the west end, 22 ft. 2⅛ in. by 33 ft. 2⅞ in.), and the barely larger Ionic one (see below) on the theatre terrace. Furthermore, is it not significant that Eumenes II, who surrounded the city's principal temple, dedicated by his ancestor, with expensive and showy buildings, did not consider it worth the trouble to have this temple's still unfinished columns fluted?

Here we have a regression bearing within it the seeds of an advance. One form grew weak and died away: the peripteral temple; another thrust itself forward and conquered the future: the space-creating stoa. A primordial idea of Greek architecture passed into disuse: that of the autarchy, the majestic loneliness of the temple, its formal self-sufficiency; another idea, with its roots extending back to Attic classical architecture, disclosed undreamed-of possibilities: that of architectonically fashioning clear spaces on a huge scale by means of long lines of stoas and the perspective effect of endlessly repeated colonnades. The new stoas were thus no longer independent, self-contained structures, but archi-

tectonic means. Every element of the Greek formal vocabulary had to adapt itself to the new tendencies. The limits of the orders lost their validity, Doric and Ionic being mixed at will according to the requirements of the picturesque and decorative end in view. For the relationship between this architecture and painting is unmistakable. These façades for spaces, these rhythmically graduated boundaries of squares had to be seen from a good way off, if they were to make their chiefly visual effect; and there very soon developed a highly competent, illusionist architectural painting, which dashed off effortlessly with the brush playful or ostentatious façades, first for stage scenery and later for mural decorations as well. Sculptural detail thereupon ceased to evolve, rigor mortis setting in, unless it came to terms with the new decorative bent by putting forth the most exuberant growths, as did, for example, the Corinthian capital and all acanthus motifs. Thus, in this Janus-like period, aridity and decorative profusion could merge completely on the same building. This final stage, characterized here, did not fully emerge with all its powers of deception until the Roman imperial age, as, for example, in the gateway to the agora of Miletus, which has been reconstructed at the Berlin Museum. Advancing and bending round at right angles, its colonnades no longer enclose a space that can really be entered. Its nervous and shifting forms, which recall stage-scenery, dissolve the substance of the stone, and open up a different kind of architectural realm that lives in the fluctuating play of light.

The three pre-Christian centuries of Hellenistic culture brought all the transitions from the old corporeity to, on the one hand, the picturesque world of mere appearances and, on the other, a technically based architecture aiming at the encasement of great interior spaces, which reached its climax in Roman vaulted and domed constructions. This being so, it is noteworthy that architecture, which, till classical times, had followed the energetically advancing stylistic movements only slowly on

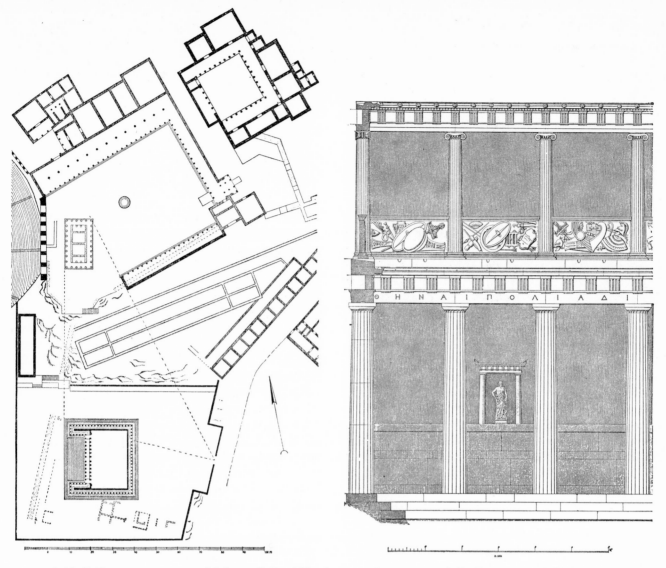

148 (*Left*) Pergamum, court of Athena Polias Nikephoros and enclosure of the Zeus altar. H. Kähler, 1949
149 (*Right*) Pergamum, north stoa of court of Athena Polias Nikephoros. Part elevation.
R. Bohn, *Die Altertümer von Pergamon* II, 1885

account of its inert conservatism, now, once deprived of its footing, declined and lost its vitality more quickly than did sculpture. Turning back towards the classical ideals, sculpture retained its bodily substance for longer. This event did not now take place as a process of growth by stages. Rather it was an inward struggle, a dialectical action between the poles of spatiality and corporeality, an eventful revolt, submission and interpenetration of the two forces space and form, which endowed all Hellenistic creations with their conspicuous inner tension. This conflict was even apparent in the buildings at Athens that kept closest to classical standards: the Olympieum (page 394) and the great stoas presented to the city by Eumenes II and Attalus II.

THE COURT OF ATHENA POLIAS
NIKEPHOROS

*Plate 174 above,
figs. 148, 149*

The two-storied stoas with which Eumenes II *fig. 149* enclosed the Athena precinct on its east and north sides after his victory over the Seleucids and Gauls were still functional buildings put together out of structural parts in the old sense, even if displaying a strange, eclectic mixture of styles. Each ground floor consisted of widely spaced Doric columns carrying an extremely low architrave, over which now four triglyphs corresponded to every interaxial. The upper story was formed by Ionic columns between which slabs carved in relief were inserted as a parapet. Above extended a Doric frieze with five (!) triglyphs

485

per interaxial and an Ionic cornice. The deeper, double-naved north stoa added as a third element inner columns with leaf-girt capitals that were academically copied from an unusual archaic type (Massalian treasury, fig. 29). One entered Athena's court from the street of the acropolis through a tetrastyle propylaeum of kindred form. Behind the north stoa lay hidden the rooms of the celebrated library, in which not only was the literary heritage from the past amassed, but works of art, partly in reproduction, were displayed as in a gallery. Apart from the similar collection at Alexandria, it was the first museum ever to exist. In this way, the spiritual mission of Pergamum's rulers as guardians of Greek culture was itself placed under the tutelage of the goddess Athena, but, at the same time, the whole layout showed itself to be a political monument: the slabs of the stoas' parapets bore representations in relief of weapons taken from the vanquished foe. This was a clear allusion to the Greek custom of raising a victory monument (*tropaion*) out of captured enemy weapons at the site of a successful battle and in sanctuaries. The stoas, indeed the entire sanctuary, was such a *tropaion* on an enormous scale. Accordingly, at the centre of the square, there stood neither an altar nor a temple, but the victory monument with which Attalus I had celebrated his defeat of the barbarian hordes: that famous group of conquered and dying Gauls, to which copies still bear testimony.

The whole paved square, soon completed through the erection of another stoa along its south side, had very little reference to the older Athena temple standing close to the open western edge of the terrace. Not even the temple's alignment was turned to account. Temenos and temple alike took their places rather in the more comprehensive order of the enclosures ranged about the theatre. The Athena sanctuary was most closely connected with the colossal altar of Zeus, begun, also by Eumenes, towards 180 B.C. on an adjacent terrace at a lower level.

THE GREAT ALTAR OF ZEUS   *Plates 175, 176,*
figs. 144, 148, 150

The almost square altar terrace (about $75\frac{1}{2}$ by *fig. 14* 84 yds.) has its axis roughly across the line between the court of Athena and the upper agora. Its divergent eastern limit follows the oblique course of the street, from which one entered the enclosure through a propylaeum now completely destroyed (unless it was only planned). The great altar occupied approximately the centre. It faced west towards the open countryside, in such a way that its first step was exactly aligned with the west flank of the old Athena temple across a distance of almost $76\frac{1}{2}$ yds. The intimate link between the two buildings, thus indicated, also gained expression in their dedications. Along with Zeus, the altar was consecrated to Athena, the bringer of victory, while Zeus, so it seems, was installed in the temple as Athena's cult companion. Nevertheless, despite the studied reference, the magnificent altar was a strongly individual monument, and, in this respect, remained wholly independent of the temple, being four times as big as the latter and immeasurably superior in rank and splendour. Moreover, the well-read Pergamenes could here appeal to the tradition regarding altars of Zeus. All over Greece, there stood solitary altars of the sky god on hilltops, and even the altar of Zeus at Olympia did not lie before the front of the temple, which was only erected much later. The shape as well owed a debt to ancient, highly *figs. 11* sacred examples. Like that of the great altar of Hera *115* on Samos (page 448), the actual altar table was raised on a huge base, to which a flight of steps about $65\frac{1}{2}$ ft. wide led up from the west. Indeed, there seems to have been a deliberate reference to the altar of

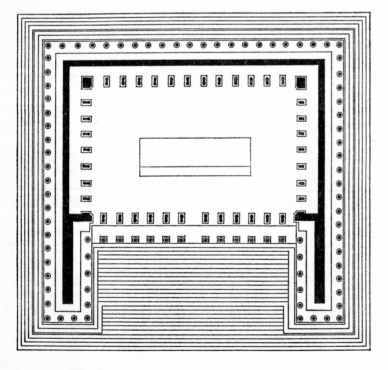

150 Pergamum, altar of Zeus. Plan (1 : 400).
A. W. Lawrence, 1957

486

Hera, the latter's breadth (120 ft.) being repeated at Pergamum (119 ft. 6¾ in.) and depth approximately doubled (Samos 54 ft. 4¾ in., Pergamum 112 ft. 1¾ in.). A doubling of the number of steps from 14 to 28 corresponded to this.

Yet the new building still presented a fundamentally changed appearance. Even in its architectonic configuration, everything already ran to extremes. In the case of the Samian altar, the mighty cuboid of the substructure was conceived entirely as wall, and, accordingly, had anta capitals crowning the fronts of the wings; but here it became a broadly spreading podium, raised in its turn over 4 steps. The power of these basic lines alone did not suffice, for the podium was itself built up in two stages. On a low, delicately profiled base rested a second, higher one with strongly projecting foot and head mouldings that enclosed the famous battle of the gods and giants. In this manner, the horizontal was stressed by every means. In place of the simple wind-breaks of the Samian altar, this heavy mass required—so one would expect—a superstructure of corresponding vertical counter-weights. A superstructure did in fact follow; but the massiveness was answered, not by a carefully adjusted opposing force, but surprisingly, by a contrary principle: lightness, spatial looseness, cool elegance. The low, heavy early Ionic wind-break was reinterpreted as an architectural fabric of the most diversified form. The solid shields were opened up into spatial structures, and became double-sided 'porticoes'. Their nucleus, or rather background, was provided by a wall that enclosed the altar base on three sides in a ⊓, and, at the front, ran out along the two wings flanking the steps. On either side (i.e. front and back)—and this was a completely new notion—they were ringed by Ionic columns. Even the fourth side of the altar, the west front above the mighty flight of steps, was at once opened and shut by such a double colonnade, but without the wall inside. All Greek architectural ideas were here inextricably mixed together in a complex creation of extraordinary impact. The cuboid block of the altar turned into a peripteral edifice wreathed by 90 columns; and yet it did not, as the three closed sides with their endless colonnades (22 columns on the east, 21 on the south and north) were opposed by the powerful discordant note of the west front, which was ripped wide open. There, the steps engaged forcefully with the building, proving it to be a spatial structure. Seen from the front, the two projecting porticoes repeated the gesture of welcome sketched by the wing buildings of the Propylaea, but now it was given a swelling ardency by the flight of steps.

Having climbed these steps and passed through the west portico, one stood in an altar court that was again surrounded by Ionic porticoes. (The fact that, owing to the death of Eumenes II in 159 B.C., the inner columns were only executed along the open west side can be disregarded here, since we are concerned with the idea of the building—with its design, that is.) Was this a repetition of the outside reflected inwards—the shell mould of the structural body, so to speak? Hardly, for the substructure was, of course, missing, and the columns had a different form. Would one have been standing in a peristyle court like those of the royal palaces from the same period? This enclosure had neither the practical import nor, since the eye roamed freely into the distance through the west colonnades, the seclusion of such a peristyle. May we liken the court to the squares bordered all round by stoas that this age produced? This would be nearest the mark formally but furthest from it spiritually. What, then, was the meaning of this court?

At its centre, the actual altar stood as a separate part—an arrangement that was both strange and new, since the early Ionic examples embodied the altar as a whole, the steps leading straight up to its enormous sacrificial table. Here, it was different. What we have grown used to calling the altar of Pergamum was not an altar at all, but just the architectonic frame of an altar. The court in question formed firstly the space for the altar, but more besides: it was the altar's realm, raised and exalted above the profane world, cut off from its surroundings, open only towards the broad horizon of the mountains in the west and to the sky overhead. The rows of columns all round it constituted the real limits of the space, and, for that reason, were more strongly accentuated than the external ones. On each plinth, two three-quarter columns were joined with a pier set between them. Beyond these supports began an imaginary world. Just as one looked into the distance towards the west, so a different, mythical distance presented itself on the other three sides. There, a frieze in relief recounted, as it ran round, the life of Heracles's son Telephus from his birth to the founding of the Pergamene royal house, to the institution of the Athena cult, and, finally, to the death of the dynasty's progenitor. This courtly epic in images not only, as a kind of Aeneid of the Attalids, established the Hellenic and semi-divine origin of the rulers, but, beyond that, led into previously unentered realms of a spiritual, lyrical order. Through multiple graduations of figures that diminished in perspective, and through the inclusion of wide, idyllic landscapes, the shallow relief arrived at a picturesque effect of depth such as sculpture had, until then, neither been able nor wanted to achieve. Moreover, it is plain that the columnal architecture

487

of the court simply made ready for the frieze's pictorial space, which flowed away to infinity. The earlier relation between building and sculpture had been reversed. Once, the temple's life was realized in its plastic adornment. Now, the structural members framed the imaginary spaces of the sculptured scenes as the frontiers of reality.

176 Let us return to the exterior, and devote our attention to the great frieze of the giants, which ran round the podium below the outer porticoes. With its height of 7 ft. 5¾ in. and length of about 130 yds., it is the most extensive work in relief to have been produced during the whole of antiquity, apart from the figurative decoration on the Parthenon. This battle fought by the Olympian gods of light against the unruly powers of the earth is in the starkest contrast to the delicate and intimate Telephus frieze. Small importance will be attached to the admittedly clear reference to the Attalids' victories over the Gauls in view of the monstrously terrible event enacted here. Often as the gigantomachy had been treated in archaic and classical times, no period had produced such an expressively tense mêlée of powerful bodies bursting their architectonic frame, reaching out beyond the mouldings, plunging on to the steps, and, worked in the round, freeing themselves from their background. It is the last impassioned rally of a sculptural corporeity under assault, and, at the same time, the last great image of the essence of antiquity, an image that confronts on an equal footing the ensemble, so different in character, of the Parthenon. If one looks back at the 12 noble pairs of combatants on the Parthenon metopes, which, in their very conflict, their tragic conjunction, exemplify the cosmic unity wherein they rest, one becomes aware of the distance covered between then and now. This is no longer a world belonging to the gods, however plainly the artists have still specified the deities by means of mythological attributes and incidental references.

In the defiant desperation, in the painful death of the vanquished, in the cruelly nonchalant advance of the victors, the titanic struggle of a soul divided and embroiled with itself has erupted as myth. This tormented spirit was obliged to create, no doubt as an evasion, an idyllic and playful imaginary realm, which took form right here in the same building, beyond the steps, as a scenic and epic interior accompanying the sculptural and dramatic exterior. In the frieze of the giants, there is a conscious renunciation of all picturesque effects, of that graduation of the figures into depth, and of spaces defined by natural scenery. The two friezes could be used for an academic demonstration of the ability to produce either corporeal or scenic results by a masterly chisel technique. As one would expect, the gigantomachy also bore a different relation to the architecture. In the court, the porticoes framed representations which flow into depth. Here, podium and porticoes provided the background for the tremendous, physically present battle. The architecture again played a subservient role, and this may explain the slightness of the porticoes. (With a lower diameter of 1 ft. 1¾ in., the columns were only 8 ft. 9⅛ in. tall! The whole entablature had a height of 1 ft. 9⅝ in.) Were one only to judge it from architectonic viewpoints, this diminutive superstructure would appear most deplorably out of harmony with the colossal dimensions of the whole. In fact, the outer porticoes had lost their practical significance. After a continuous pedestal, on which a later set of statues representing defeated Gauls were to be displayed, had been placed before their rear walls (probably in connexion with a change of plan) there remained only a gap of about 20 in. between pedestal and columns: an ambulatory without room in which to stroll. The portico itself had been literally abased to an ornamental element, a fact that may be a further sign of the break with the classical autarchy of architecture. Like its sculpture, this building was related to the beholder externally as well. Thus, the frieze's principal group including Zeus, Athena, and Heracles did not occupy the middle, which belonged to it by right. Instead, it was shifted towards the north-east corner, exactly in the axis of the entrance to the altar enclosure, so that it immediately caught the eye of those who came in.

After the death of Eumenes II, his brother, Attalus II (159–138 B.C.), concluded the gigantic undertaking in only a makeshift fashion. The inner colonnades remained unfinished, and the ornamental detail of the sima with its lion-heads was left in the rough state. Along with this supreme self-representation, this sublime interaction of the conflicting poles —substance and space—in the unity of a work of art, the age had laid aside its spiritual trust. Attalus III, the great builder's melancholy nephew, recognized the new masters of the world, and bequeathed his kingdom to the Romans in 133 B.C. Pergamum became the seat of the proconsul of the province of Asia. Immediately included among the wonders of the world, the huge altar survived well into Christian times. Not until the eighth century A.D. was 'Satan's seat', as St. John calls it, demolished, to provide material for a defensive wall to keep out the Muslims. In 1878, Humann discovered the slabs of the frieze built into this wall, and thus made possible a reconstruction of the altar with original fragments at the Pergamum Museum, Berlin, which is one of the West's most important artistic possessions.

The northernmost and highest temenos of the acropolis was devoted to the cult of the emperors Hadrian and Trajan, and would not require our attention here but for the fact that an important late Hellenistic principle of arrangement is apparent in its Roman layout. As in the Athena precinct, the terrace raised on big, arched substructures was formed into a 'square' (about $74\frac{1}{2}$ by $63\frac{1}{2}$ yds.) by enclosing it on three sides with stoas. The fourth, open side gave an unobstructed view far out across the Pergamene countryside. However, exactly in the symmetrical axis of this clear space—and here we come to what is new—rose the temple: a Corinthian peripteral structure with 6 by 9 columns set on a podium instead of a crepidoma. Apart from the imposing effect that strictly observed symmetry always entails, this layout reveals a sophisticated attempt to make evident the corporeity of the temple, the extension in space of its four sides, after a visual faculty over-stimulated by optical and scenic means had lost its innate, natural sensitivity, its inward tactual feeling for the simple external form of an architectural body.

Now it was surrounded with a negative, with a kind of shell mould that was capable to some extent of reflecting the sides of the building invisible to the spectator, so that the depth of its flanks and also the lie of its back became apprehensible in their relation to the symmetrical stoas. Nothing can throw a sharper light on the complete change of vision, of its turn away from the plastic and self-evident to the merely apparent. (So, too, the design, which till into the fourth century had always been based on a solid model, and, apart from this, had only made use of plans and elevations drawn to scale, had since the third century also been developed from perspective drawings, properly shaded.) The once self-sufficient structural body became part of an optically conceived overall arrangement. First consistently developed during the second and first centuries through the framing with stoas of the famous temple of Artemis built by Hermogenes at Magnesia, this principle was enthusiastically taken up by Roman architecture, but very soon the stateliness that was one of its constituents became dominant. In the case of, for example, the forums at Rome, the temple was inserted in the rear line of stoas, from which its front stood out as a bodiless façade.

At Pergamum, the great heritage was clung to tenaciously, and so it is possible that we here still meet, in a layout from Hadrian's times (second century A.D.), the pure expression of a Hellenistic architectural idea.

The hollow curve of the citadel's western slope, along the top of which the sanctuaries spread in an arch, must have positively invited the construction of a theatre. Polygonal retaining-walls are the only remains of a still comparatively modest auditorium from the early days of the dynasty. The big, surviving theatre forms, as we have seen, the focus of the extensive recast of the royal citadel by Eumenes II, who may have had in mind the parallel at Athens: a Dionysus temenos below the sanctuary of Athena. In grandeur, the new complex knew no equal. Its basis was a terrace, about 247 yds. long and from 17 to 19 yds. wide, bordered on either side by stoas. One entered it from the upper agora to its south through an arched gateway. At the northern end of this notable architectural prospect, there rose, above a flight of 25 steps (height about 14 ft. 9 in.), an Ionic temple with a tetrastyle portico, probably dedicated to Dionysus. The extremely accurately built marble edifice (stylobate 38 ft. $8\frac{5}{8}$ in. by 66 ft. 4 in.) still showed all the signs of Attic refinement, the outsides of the walls inclining slightly inwards and the steps above the base having a distinct curvature (rise about $1\frac{3}{4}$ in.). After a fire, the temple was repaired by Caracalla at the beginning of the third century.

On the level of the terrace and half overlapping it lies the round 'dancing place': the orchestra. The semicircular stepped seats (eighty rows, maximum difference in level about 118 ft.) ascend the hill from the eastern edge in three ranges separated by broad horizontal passages (diazomata). Narrow stairways (2 ft. $5\frac{1}{8}$ in. broad) allowing access divide these zones into seven or six wedges. There is room for over 10,000 spectators in the huge shell, which covers more than 5,000 sq. yds.

In the second century, the primordial part of the Greek theatre, the round orchestra, had long since lost its significance as the dancing place of the Dionysian chorus. The play was performed on a raised stage, but here, at Pergamum, its structure would have cut across the accentuated optical axis of the theatre terrace; and, after all, it was precisely the perspective of the long, straight line of columns, at the end of which the Dionysus temple rose up to catch the eye, that everything was calculated to enhance. This problem was solved by designing a wooden 'scene' structure with its supporting posts set in specially prepared sockets. After 'seasons' limited to the major religious festivals, the Dionysia and the Nikephoria, the 'scene' could on each occasion be dismantled. Not until the growing enthusiasm for watching plays caused the theatre to remain constantly active was a marble stage erected, and this evidently occurred when Pergamum had already ceased to be the capital of a kingdom (i.e. after 133 B.C.). Finally, a bigger, ostentatious structure was substituted during imperial times.

The later stage buildings have also disappeared. Owing to the collapse of every other structure, the strong basic forms of the terrace and auditorium to-day determine the appearance of the acropolis hill more forcibly than they did once. They testify to a new, monumental conquest of landscape, to a peculiarly Hellenistic relatedness of architecture to nature. In this sensitive relation to the countryside, which, having gained an insight into its laws, man now knew how to enhance artificially, one can recall the monumental contrast of the idyllic landscapes in the Telephus frieze. With this begins what as 'landscape figuration' is more taken for granted than understood by modern architects. Indeed, the entire acropolis hill is, in a certain sense, a landscape monument, and a far subtler, more effectively harmonized one than the first, lunatic plan of this kind, which, so it is said, an architect of Alexander's had the presumption to conceive: an image of the great Macedonian with a whole city in one hand and a river thundering down from the other was to have been fashioned out of Mount Athos.

THE TERRACE OF DEMETER   *Plates 172, 173, figs. 145, 151, 152*

fig. 145

The people had no share in the cults and buildings with which their rulers surrounded themselves in the citadel. Under Eumenes II, the last dwelling-houses of the ridge, which was still thickly settled at the time of Philetaerus, were demolished so as to make room for the great altar. The residential city spread out at the foot of the new royal acropolis in a repeatedly enlarged ring of fortifications.

There, too, lay the holy places loved and revered by the people. The foremost among them was the sanctuary devoted to the mystic cult of Demeter and Persephone with its comforting promise concerning the hereafter, and it came under the special patronage of the queen consort.

172, below

In honour of their mother Bora, Philetaerus and his brother, Eumenes I, dedicated the first temple to the fruit-giving goddesses of the lower regions in the sanctuary which obviously already existed outside the city of that time. Like all buildings from the early period, the plain megaron (about 21 by 41½ ft.) with two Ionic columns in-antis was built of the local trachyte. Its one peculiarity was a marble frieze

figs. 151, 152

extending above the wall architrave and decorated with bulls' skulls between which hung festoons. This ornamental motif (bucrania) enjoyed great popularity during the Hellenistic age. Before the temple, which faced east, stood an altar (about 23 ft. by 7½ ft.) with strange 'horns' wound up into volutes at either side.

On its north edge, towards the slope of the citadel ridge, the terrace was bordered by a low stoa, about 142 ft. long, its eastern end in line with the altar. The temple's forecourt of the same length and about 65½ ft. wide was intended for mystery plays. Along its side nearer the acropolis ran stepped seats that provided room for 800 initiates (mystae). Towards the end of the third century, the sanctuary of Demeter was taken charge of by Apollonia, the wife of Attalus I. A homely, middle-class girl from Aeolian Cyzicus, she was loved alike by sovereign and people. This queen had her votive inscription carved on the otherwise smooth, unadorned frieze of the small distyle propylaeum through which one entered the terrace of Demeter. Noteworthy is the hybrid form of its columns: above a Doric shaft without a base (the 20 flutes were roughly prepared at the foot, but left unfinished), the capital comprised a girdle of leaves crowned by a low, square abacus. It has been surmised that Apollonia brought this archaic type of capital, which soon spread across the whole Orient and even reached Rome, from her Aeolian homeland. By means of two 279-ft.-long stoas, which, provided with similar columns, bounded the terrace lengthwise and also continued round its western end, the queen gave the temenos the imposing appearance that this age considered desirable. The northern stoa, on the acropolis side, rose high above the theatre steps and the older stoa, while the southern one, nearer the valley, gained a basement running its entire length like a passage by using the fall of the ground. Whether it was used for religious purposes or simply for storage can no longer be determined. (Similar large-scale basements existed beneath the western theatre stoa—for storing the wooden components of the stage?—and in the city's huge gymnasium, where a 'basement stadium' about 220 yds. long was constructed. They foreshadowed the mysterious, splendidly decorated underground galleries known as 'cryptoporticus' that play an important role in the layout of Roman palaces.) It is interesting to see how here an old, mystical precinct aiming at cloistral seclusion gradually altered in accordance with Hellenistic ideas, and achieved an effort of solemn stateliness. Connexions with the Demeter sanctuary at Eleusis were not lacking: beyond the propylaeum, there was a sacrificial pit and a holy fountain that, during imperial times under Antoninus

173, b

172, a

figs. 152

173,

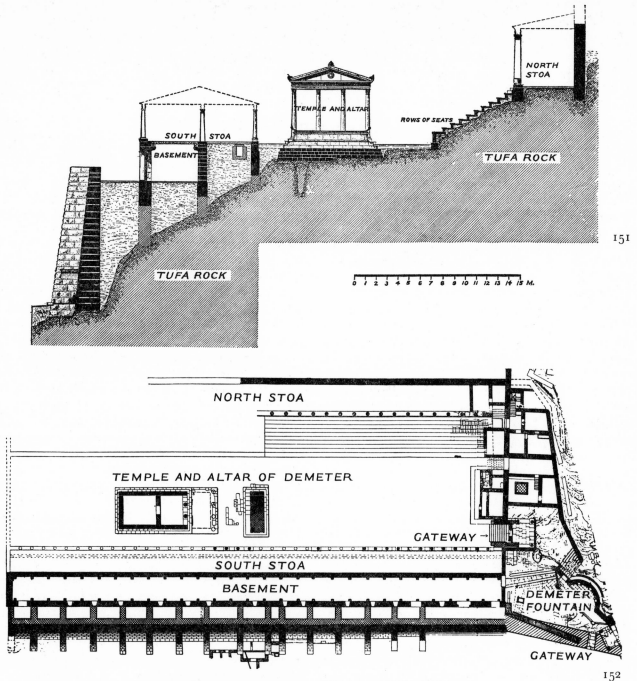

151

152

151–152 Pergamum, sanctuary of Demeter. W. Dörpfeld, 1910
151 (*Above*) Cross-section showing south stoa, temple, seating steps, and north stoa. 152 Plan

Pius, had to submit to being given a more magnificent form, with a semicircular recess in which the water rushed down in three powerful jets. At the same time, the temple was adapted to the world empire's need for splendour: a marble portico was set before it, and the marble architecture of the stoas was richly adorned.

THE SANCTUARY OF ASCLEPIUS *Plate 170, figs. 143, 153, 154*

A certain Archias, a citizen of Pergamum who had been miraculously cured by Asclepius at Epidaurus, felt a call to establish the cult of the healing god in his native place. Information about the appearance of

491

the, in any case, modest rural sanctuary that he founded at the beginning of the fourth century beside a spring roughly one and a half miles south-west of the acropolis will come from the current excavations. The god, who appeared to those with faith in him while they slept in rooms set apart for that purpose, immediately demonstrated his power, and the water from the spring its remedial action. During the century that followed, the sanctuary had a great vogue among a people increasingly inclined to believe in miracles, and it expanded rapidly. At the time of Eumenes II, the sleeping room and an Ionic temple erected on a low ridge near the holy spring were surrounded with stoas in the then customary manner. Some columns that were re-used in stoas dating from imperial times have been assigned to these buildings, only the foundations of which still remain on the site. Their capitals have a peculiar form. The cup-shaped echinus of double curvature with a delicately profiled abacus above it constitutes a new variety, assimilated to the Doric capital, of the early Ionic leaf-girt capital, which has already been repeatedly mentioned. In 156 B.C., the sanctuary was plundered and perhaps also destroyed by Prusias II, an enemy of the Attalids. Although it seems to have recovered from this blow, it was subsequently, at least for a time, so neglected that the dead could even be buried in the temenos—an unheard-of sacrilege.

170
The Asclepieum enjoyed its real heyday during the Roman imperial age. Under Antoninus Pius (A.D. figs. 153, 154 138–161), the enclosure was magnificently developed thanks to private endowments. Stoas on a grand scale now encompassed the square, which had been enlarged to about 111½ by 153 yds. on three of its sides. At its centre, the sleeping rooms, the spring, which had meanwhile been given a stone surround, and three small temples—Apollo and Hygieia were worshipped along with Asclepius—remained in their old positions. To this extent, the layout still conformed, as a square limited spatially by straight rows of columns, to Hellenistic custom, but the ostentation of the new structures already went far beyond it. The sanctuary turned into a luxurious watering-place, where pampered patients from all over the world (they included the Roman emperor Caracalla) sought healing and amusement. A secularized architecture had to satisfy all the requirements of a highly developed civilization—just to what point may be illustrated by an example. The most elegant Corinthian capitals to have been found anywhere in the Asclepieum come from the well-appointed marble latrine adjoining the basement of the south stoa.

fig. 154 (13)
A theatre could not be left out. It was now hidden away behind the north stoa, fitting into the general plan as a dependent part. Characteristic is its auditorium, which, provided with twenty-nine marble seating rows (room for 3,500 spectators) and forming an exact semicircle in rigid symmetry, was closed at the top by an ornamental Ionic gallery on a diminutive scale. Above the stage, which, following the Roman custom, was once more set in the plane of the orchestra as a platform (pulpitum) about 3 ft. 4 in. high, there rose a gleaming marble façade composed of advancing and receding columels with many small pediments of varying form in three superimposed stories. It awakened to a distinctively immaterial life in the play of light and shadow.

The eastern, principal side of the court otherwise bounded by stoas had a similarly scenic configuration. In its middle axis, a curious cult recess opened, and on either side of this projected, with four Corinthian columns and a pediment, a temple-like façade, each being raised above a flight of 13 steps. They were, so to speak, amputated Greek temple-fronts, to which no structural body of like nature corresponded. Behind the classicizing mask of the old sacred form lay concealed something that was wholly different, decidedly new, and thoroughly Roman: moulded space. Passing through the northern columned façade of the 'propylaeum', one fig. 1 entered a square colonnaded court, into which debouched the sacred way linking the Asclepieum with the city. Not just the court—which, on its own, would not be so remarkable—but the street itself had been planned spatially. Its first section was flanked by vaulted stoas, and then, suddenly, it changed into the opposite form: a cross-vaulted arcade, which led for a distance of nearly 900 yds. (at one stage, beneath the massive stonework of a theatre dating from imperial times) to the precincts of the city.

The second, southern 'temple façade' actually did extend before a temple (the fact that the fronts of the fig. 1 temple and the propylaeum were treated equivalently for the sake of optical symmetry already sets one thinking)—but what a strange temple it was! From the portico, one entered a rectangular hall, passed through the great doorway in its rear wall, and stood amazed in a round room with a diameter of 78 ft. 3 in., over which curved a vast, semicircular dome. No longer was the space broken up by means of structural members but through extensions and the use of hollow forms. Thus, seven alternately curving and angular niches meshed with the massive, nearly 10-ft.-thick walls. They contained the statues of the gods, which were now likewise bound into the spatial sphere of the walls: Asclepius on the axis, opposite the entrance, and, all around

153–154 Pergamum, Asclepieum. Sketch-plan and detailed plan. E. Boehringer, 1959

1 Sacred way and entrance gate; 2 Forecourt; 3 Propylaeum; 4 Ceremonial square; 5 Cult recess; 6 Temple of Asclepius; 7 Cistern; 8 Peristyle house; 9 'Pump-room'; 10 Cult recess; 11 Imperial hall; 12 North stoa; 13 Theatre; 14 West stoa; 15 West exit; 16 West room; 17 South-west hall; 18 Small latrine; 19 Big latrine; 20 South stoa, basement; 21 Underground passage; 22 Hellenistic draw-well; 23 Roman bathing fountain; 24 Rock spur steps, and rock cleft; 25 Hellenistic temple; 26 Hellenistic temple; 27 Incubation complex, Hellenistic sleeping room; 28 Incubation complex, late-Hellenistic extension; 29 Rock fountain; 30 Hellenistic south stoa; 31 Hellenistic east stoa

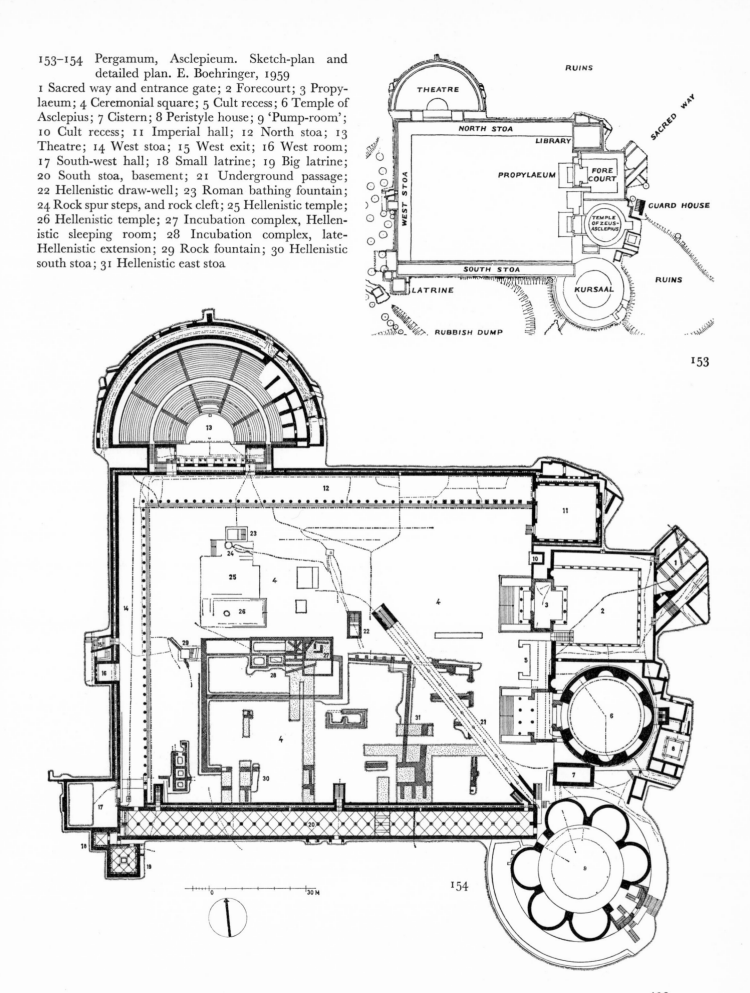

153

154

him, his divine attendants, who were understood as elements of his being. A last, disembodied reminiscence of the Greek architecture of orders survived in the gorgeous revetments. Flat pilasters and variously coloured facings of marble were applied to the walls as articulatory decoration, like a coating of jewels, but they no longer had anything to do with the construction of the building's solid masonry, which they rather concealed. The construction, on its side, represented nothing more than an integument for space, despite its huge masses of stonework, and, accordingly, the temple's external appearance was only a meagre positive of its interior. Above a simple cylinder, the dome stood out shallow and formless, in contrast to the peerlessly moulded domes of the Renaissance. There was good reason for hiding this amorphous pile behind a columned façade.

Yet, in this very building, we sense the earnestness of Rome's mission. We have crossed a deeper gap than that between the classical and the Hellenistic. The concepts applicable to the Greek corporeal and articulated structure—and, above all, the negative ones—fail in the face of the new grandeur. This is more than beauteous pretence, than screening and façade. To comprehend, we must undergo for ourselves the spiritual crisis separating Hellas from Rome. Such a space, in the middle of which stood not columns, nor cult image, nor altar but man—experiencing and observing—was capable of stirring the soul both powerfully and intimately. Light entered through a single round opening in the top of the dome, lost its sharpness in the multicoloured mosaics of the enormous hollow hemisphere, was variously caught by the seven niches, and pervaded the domed space as an element newly understood.

It was not just outwardly that the Imperium Romanum united the ancient world. By deciding unequivocally in favour of the primacy of space and by revetting its colossal space-enveloping walls with the Greek forms that a classicist reformation reinterpreted as incorporeal and light-catching (but no less effective for that) articulatory enrichment, Roman building restored to an inwardly divided architecture its lost unity, but in a sense exactly contrary to the Greek one. The prerequisite to this, the vaulted structure, had been developed in the secular sphere, particularly on the great Roman bathing establishments, out of Hellenistic rudiments. When, having grown to the fullest technical maturity, it was passed on to sacred architecture, this occurred at a time of religious change. Antiquity's most notable spatial creation, the Pantheon, was dedicated to the seven deities of the planets. The dome, with the light penetrating vertically downwards, is an image of the all, the magnificent central space reflects the more philosophically than religiously conceived oneness of the earthly and heavenly order of the universe.

Founded by the Roman consul Rufinus about A.D. 140, the temple of Asclepius was a repetition on a reduced scale of the Pantheon, which had been erected about twenty years earlier (diam. of dome: Pantheon 142 ft. 8½ in., Pergamum 78 ft. 3 in.). Its substructure, carefully built of dowelled blocks without mortar, indicates how long the native craftsmen clung to their old methods. Another round edifice was raised beside the temple at a later date. It was a two-storied, unvaulted 'pump-room' for *fig. 1* therapeutic bathing that opened up loosely into big apses, and a comparison of ground-plans is enough to show how nicely the temple's central space was calculated to achieve an effect of unity and calm, light-suffused omnipotence. Aelius Aristides, a writer of that time who spent thirteen whole years seeking a cure at the Asclepieum, observes in this connexion: 'The power of Asclepius is great and manifold—indeed, it is even truly universal, so that a human lifetime is not long enough to get to know it. It is in this . . . conviction that the temple of Zeus-Asclepius has been founded here.' Zeus-Asclepius! The name indicates a speculative monotheism that was now scarcely veiled. It designates the all-embracing, the one-and-only, the miracle-working saviour whom this age surfeited with cults and sects awaited. No longer was it Asclepius who had the power to heal these sick. Was a new epoch already under preparation in the highest development of Roman spatial art? It is precisely the dome with which, in forms ever new, Christian architecture created a transcendent image of heaven and divine omnipotence: how un-bridgeably far from the self-sufficient cosmos of the Greek temple.

BIBLIOGRAPHY

Only works directly concerned with architecture are mentioned. They may be roughly classified in two groups, the first composed of standard works and treatises well suited to the layman and the second comprising works of specialist research and articles that have appeared in the course of the last thirteen years. A bibliography covering the subject up to the year 1949 has been compiled by W. B. Dinsmoor and published in the third edition of his *Architecture of Ancient Greece*. Occasional reference has been made to this bibliography for which purpose the abbreviation 'Dinsmoor' has been used.

ABBREVIATIONS USED OF THE TITLES OF SPECIALIZED PERIODICALS

Abh. Berl. Akad.	Abhandlungen der Deutschen (Preussischen) Akademie der Wissenschaften zu Berlin. Phil.-hist. Klasse
AJA.	American Journal of Archaeology
AM.	Mitteilungen des Deutschen Archäologischen Instituts. Athenische Abteilung
Arch. Class.	Archeologia Classica
BCH.	Bulletin de Correspondance Hellénique
BSA.	Annual of the British School at Athens
ΕΦ.ΑΡΧ.	*᾽Εφημερὶς ᾽Αρχαιολογική*
JdI.	Jahrbuch des Deutschen Archäologischen Instituts
JHS.	Journal of Hellenic Studies
Ist.Mitt.	Istanbuler Mitteilungen
MdI.	Mitteilungen des Deutschen Archäologischen Instituts
Mem.Amer. Acad.Rome	Memoirs of the American Academy in Rome
Mon.Ant.	Monumenti Antichi pubblicati per Cura della Accademia Nazionale dei Lincei
Notiz.Scavi	Notizie degli Scavi di Antichità
ΠΡΑΚΤ.	*Πρακτικά τῆς ἐν ᾽Αθήναις ᾽Αρχαιολογικῆς ῾Εταιρείας*
RE	Paulys Realencyclopädie der classischen Altertumswissenschaft. Neue Bearbeitung
Rend.Pontif. Accad. Romana	Atti della Pontificia Accademia Romana di Archeologia. Rendiconti
Rev.Arch.	Revue Archéologique

I. INTRODUCTION

GENERAL SURVEYS AND MANUALS

F. Noack, *Die Baukunst des Altertums*. 1910

D. Robertson, *Handbook of Greek and Roman Architecture*. 1943

W. B. Dinsmoor, *The Architecture of Ancient Greece*. 1950 (for other titles cf. Dinsmoor pp. 344 and 348 ff.)

W. H. Plommer, *Ancient and Classical Architecture*. 1956

A. W. Lawrence, *Greek Architecture*. 1957

THE DORIC TEMPLE

General:

F. Krauss, *Paestum, die griechischen Tempel*. 2nd edition. 1943

H. Koch, *Der griechisch-dorische Tempel*. 1951

G. Rodenwaldt, *Griechische Tempel*. 2nd edition. 1951

Specialized:

Dinsmoor p. 349 f.

A. von Gerkan in: JdI. 63/64, 1948/49, 1 ff.

M. L. Bowen in: BSA. 45, 1950, 113 ff.

II. THE GREEK MOTHER-COUNTRY

OLYMPIA

General:

Olympia. Die Ergebnisse der . . . Ausgrabungen 1890–1897
Berichte über die Ausgrabungen in Olympia, Bd. I–V. 1937 ff.
Olympische Forschungen, Bd. I–VII. 1945 ff.
G. Rodenwaldt, *Olympia*. 1936

Specialized:

Dinsmoor pp. 366 f.

H. Riemann in: JdI. 61/62, 1946/47, 30 ff.

F. Krauss, *Die Säulen des Zeustempels in Olympia*. In: *Robert Boehringer, eine Freundesgabe*, 365 ff. 1957

—— in: *Neue Ausgrabungen im Nahen Osten, Mittelmeerraum und in Deutschland*, 28 ff. 1957

'*I. Κοντὴς, Τὸ ἱερὸν τῆς 'Ολυμπίας κατὰ τον Δ. π. χ. αἰῶνα*. 1958
E. Kunze in: *Neue deutsche Ausgrabungen im Mittelmeergebiet und im vorderen Orient*, 263 ff. 1959
Olympia in der Antike. Ausstellungskatalog Essen. 1960

DELPHI

General:

Fouilles de Delphes II: Topographie et Architecture. 1915 ff.
P. de la Coste-Messelière, *Au Musée de Delphes*. 1936
—— *Delphi*. 1943

Specialized:

Dinsmoor pp. 368 f.
P. de la Coste-Messelière in BCH. 68/69, 1944/45, 5 ff., and 77, 1953, 346 ff.
K. Schefold in: *Museum Helveticum* 3/4, 1946/47, 87 ff.
G. Roux in: BCH. 76, 1952, 442 ff.
A. Orlandos in: BCH. 84, 1960, 148 ff.

CORINTH

General:

Corinth: Results of Excavations . . . 1932 ff.

Specialized:

Dinsmoor p. 365
M. C. Roebuck in: *Hesperia* 24, 1955, 153 ff.
H. S. Robinson in: *Hesperia* 29, 1960, 225 ff.

ISTHMIA

General:

O. Broneer in: *Archaeology* 8, 1955, 56 ff.

Specialized:

O. Broneer in: *Hesperia* 22, 1953, 182 ff.; 24, 1955, 110 ff.; 27, 1958, 1 ff. and 28, 1959, 298 ff.
W. B. Dinsmoor in: *Hesperia* 29, 1960, 304 ff.

THE HERAEUM OF ARGOS

General:

Ch. Waldstein, *The Argive Heraeum I and II*. 1902–1905

Specialized:

Dinsmoor p. 364
P. Amandry in: *Hesperia* 21, 1952, 222 ff. (cf. also 165 ff.)

AEGINA

General:

A. Furtwängler, *Aegina, das Heiligtum der Aphaia*. 1906
G. Welter, *Aigina*. 1938

Specialized:

Dinsmoor p. 364

BASSAE

General:

C. R. Cockerell, *The Temples of Jupiter Panhellenius at Aegina and of Apollo Epicurius at Bassae near Phigaleia in Arcadia*. 1860

Specialized:

Dinsmoor p. 364
W. Hahland in: JdI. 63/64, 1948/49, 14 ff.
G. Roux in: BCH. 77, 1953, 124 ff.
H. Riemann in: *Festschrift für F. Zucker*, 299 ff. 1954
W. B. Dinsmoor in: AJA. 60, 1956, 401 ff.
F. Krauss, *Beobachtungen am Apollotempel von Bassae*; in: *Neue Ausgrabungen im Nahen Osten, Mittelmeerraum und in Deutschland*, 14 ff. 1959
N. Γιαλούρις in: *Τὸ ''Εργον τῆς 'Αρχαιολογικῆς 'Εταιρείας κατὰ τὸ* 1959, 106 ff. 1960
F. Eckstein in: *Θεωρία, Festschrift für W. H. Schuchhardt*, 55 ff. 1960

TEGEA

General:

C. Dugas, *Le Sanctuaire d'Aléa Athéna à Tégée au IVe siècle*. 1924

NEMEA

Specialized:

Dinsmoor p. 366
A. Frickenhaus in: AM. 36, 1911, 27 ff.

EPIDAURUS

General:

A. Defrasse and H. Lechat, *Epidaure*. 1895
P. Kavvadias, *Fouilles d'Epidaure*. 1893

Specialized:

Dinsmoor p. 365
F. Robert, *Thymélé*. 1939
R. Martin in: BCH. 70, 1946, 352 ff.
J. Bousquet in: Rev. Arch. 41, 1953, 41 ff.
Ch. Picard in: Rev. Arch. 1959 II, 118 f.
J. Papadimitriu in: *ΠΡΑΚΤ*. 1948, 90 ff.; 1949, 91 ff.; 1950, 194 ff.; 1951, 204 ff.; and BCH. 1949, 361 ff.
A. von Gerkan and W. Müller-Wiener, *Das Theater von Epidauros*. 1961

DELOS

General:

Exploration archéologique de Délos. 1909 ff.
N. Κοντολέων, 'Οδηγὸς τῆς Δήλον. 1950

Specialized:

Dinsmoor p. 372
R. Vallois, *L'Architecture hellénique à Délos*. 1944
R. Vallois, *Les constructions antiques de Délos*. 1953
H. Gallet de Santerre, *Délos primitive et archaïque*. 1958
Ch. Picard in: Rev. Arch. 1959, II, 113 ff.

ATHENS: THE ACROPOLIS

General:

O. Walter, *Athen, Akropolis Führer.* 1929
G. Rodenwaldt, *Die Akropolis.* 1930
C. Picard, *L'Acropole d'Athènes . . .* 1930
G. Stevens, *Restorations of Classical Buildings.* 1958
E. Buschor, *Winke für Akropolispilger.* 1960

Specialized:

Dinsmoor p. 357
G. Stevens in: *Hesperia* 15, 1946, 1 ff., 73 ff. and 24, 1955, 267 ff.
O. Broneer in: AJA. 52, 1948, 111 ff.
G. Becatti, *Problemi Fidiaci.* 1951
'I. Τραυλός, Πολεοδομικὴ ἐξέλιξις τῶν 'Αθηνῶν. 1960
W. H. Plommer in: JHS. 80, 1960, 127 ff.

ATHENS: THE PROPYLAEA

General:

R. Bohn, *Die Propyläen der Akropolis zu Athen.* 1882
   (For further titles cf. above under: Acropolis)

Specialized:

Dinsmoor p. 359
A. Bundgaard, *Mnesikles.* 1957
A. Hodge, *The Woodwork of Greek Roofs.* 1960

ATHENS: THE PARTHENON

General:

A. Michaelis, *Der Parthenon.* 1870
M. Collignon, *Le Parthenon . . .* 2nd edition. 1926
   (For further titles cf. above under: Acropolis)

Specialized:

Dinsmoor p. 358 f.
C. Weickert in: Abh. Berl. Akad. 1950, 3 ff.
Κ. Συριόπουλος, "Ο Στερεοβάτης τοῦ Παρθενῶνος. 1951
G. Stevens in: *Hesperia* 24, 1955, 240 ff. and 30, 1961, 1 ff.

ATHENS: THE TEMPLE OF ATHENA NIKE

General:

L. Ross, E. Schaubert and C. Hansen, *Der Tempel der Nike Apteros.* 1839

Specialized:

Dinsmoor p. 359
H. Schleif in: JdI. 48, 1933, 177 ff.
G. Stevens in: *Hesperia* 15, 1946, 73 ff.
A. Orlandos in: BCH. 71/72, 1947/48, 1 ff.
B. Schweitzer in: *Festschrift für W. Schubart*, 1950, 116 ff.
A. Bundgaard, *Mnesikles* p. 117 ff. 1957

ATHENS: ERECHTHEUM

General:

J. M. Paton, *The Erechtheum.* 1927
C. Picard, *L'Acropole d'Athènes . . .*, vol. II. 1930

W. Dörpfeld and H. Schleif, *Erechtheion.* 1942
H. Koch, *Von jonischer Baukunst.* 1956

Specialized:

Dinsmoor p. 360
B. H. Hill in: AJA. 14, 1910, 291 ff.
G. P. Stevens in: *Hesperia* 15, 1946, 93 ff.
Ν· Κοντολέων, Τὸ 'Ερεχθεῖον. 1949

ATHENS: 'THESEUM' (HEPHAESTEUM)

General:

H. Koch, *Der griechisch-dorische Tempel.* 1951

Specialized:

Dinsmoor pp. 360 f.
B. H. Hill in: *Hesperia*, Suppl. 8, 1949, 190 ff.
H. A. Thompson in: *Hesperia* 18, 1949, 230 ff.
G. Stevens in: *Hesperia* 19, 1950, 143 ff. and 165 ff.
W. H. Plommer in: BSA. 45, 1950, 67 ff.
H. Koch, *Studien zum Theseustempel*, Abh. d. Sächs. Akademie d. Wissenschaften. 1955

ATHENS: OLYMPIEUM

General:

G. Rodenwaldt, *Griechische Tempel.* 1941

Specialized:

G. Welter in: AM. 47, 1922, 61 ff. and 48, 1923, 182 ff.

SUNIUM

General:

G. Rodenwaldt, *Griechische Tempel.* 2nd edition. 1951

Specialized:

Dinsmoor p. 363
W. H. Plommer in: BSA. 45, 1950, 78 ff., and 55, 1960, 218 ff.

ELEUSIS

General:

F. Noack, *Eleusis . . .* 1927
G. Mylonas, *Eleusis and the Eleusinian Mysteries.* 1961

Specialized:

Dinsmoor p. 363
K. Kourouniotis in: Arch. f. Religionswissenschaft 32, 1935, 52 ff.
L. Shoe in: *Hesperia*, Suppl. 8, 1949, 342 ff.
I. Travlos in: *Hesperia* 18, 1949, 138 ff.; ΕΦ.ΑΡΧ. 1950/51, 1 ff.; "Εργον, 1955, 8 f.; also 1956, 13 ff.; also 1960, 13 ff.
K. Jeppesen, *Paradigmata* 103 ff. 1960

III. MAGNA GRAECIA

General:

R. Koldewey and O. Puchstein, *Die griechischen Tempel in Unteritalien und Sizilien.* 1899 (in subsequent entries abbreviated to Koldewey-Puchstein)

B. Pace, *Arte e Civiltà della Sicilia antica.* 3 vols. 1935–1946

E. Langlotz in: *Antike und Abendland* 2, 1946, 114 ff.

Specialized:

Dinsmoor p. 381

P. Griffo, *Elementi ionici nell'architettura arcaica.* 1949

A. Hodge, *The Woodwork of Greek Roofs.* 1960

PAESTUM

General:

F. Krauss, *Paestum, die griechischen Tempel.* 2nd edition. 1943

Specialized:

Dinsmoor p. 383

C. Gottlieb in: AJA. 47, 1953, 95 ff.

H. Riemann, *Poseidonia,* in: RE XXII, 1, 1230 ff. 1953

H. Kayser, *Paestum, die Nomoi* . . . 1958

F. Krauss in: MdI. 1, 1948, 11 ff.

—— in: *Festschrift für C. Weickert,* 1955, 99 ff.

—— *Die Tempel von Paestum.* Gesamtpublikation. 1959 ff.

METAPONTUM

General:

Koldewey-Puchstein pp. 35 ff.

M. Lacava, *Metaponto.* 1891

Guida d'Italia. Touring Club Italiano, vol. 21, 75 ff. 1956

Specialized:

Dinsmoor p. 383

E. Galli, *Metaponto* . . . in: Atti e Mem. Soc. Magna Grecia, 1926/27

M. Mayer, *Metapontum,* in: RE XV, 2, 1326 ff. 1932

P. Sestieri in: Notizie. Scavi 65, 1940, 51 ff.

G. Schmiedt and R. Chevallier, *Caulonia e Metaponto.* 1959

SYRACUSE

General:

Koldewey-Puchstein pp. 56 ff.

Specialized:

Dinsmoor p. 384

M. Guarducci in: Arch. Class. 1, 1949, 4 ff.

G. Cultrera in: Mon. Ant. 41, 1951, 812 ff.

SELINUS

General:

Koldewey-Puchstein pp. 77 ff.

G. Hulot-I. Fougères, *Selinonte* . . . 1910

Specialized:

Dinsmoor p. 384

Ziegler, *Selinus,* in: RE II A 2, 1266 ff. 1923

E. Gabrici in: Mon. Ant. 32, 33, 35 and 43

G. Ballet in: BCH. 82, 1958, 16 ff.

ACRAGAS (AGRIGENTO)

General:

Koldewey-Puchstein pp. 138 ff.

P. Marconi, *Agrigento arcaica.* 1931

—— *Agrigento.* 1929

—— *Agrigento* (guide). 1958

P. Griffo, *Agrigento* (guide). 1955

Specialized:

Dinsmoor pp. 381 f.

P. Griffo, *Ultimi scavi* . . . *in Agrigento.* 1946

—— *Sulla collocazione dei Telamoni nel Tempio di Giove Olimpico in Agrigento.* 1952

—— in: Atti Accad. Agrig. 1947 and 1951

S. Ferri in: Rend. Pontif. Accad. Romana 22, 1946, 61 ff.

SEGESTA

Koldewey-Puchstein pp. 132 ff.

IV. IONIA

General:

F. Krischen, *Die griechische Stadt.* 1938

—— in: *Antike u. Abendland* II, 1946, 77 ff.

—— *Weltwunder der Baukunst.* 1956

H. Koch, *Von jonischer Baukunst.* 1956

Specialized:

Dinsmoor p. 350

R. Martin in: BCH. 68/69, 1944/45, 340 ff.

A. von Gerkan in: JdI. 61/62, 1946/47

H. Drerup in: MdI. 5, 1952, 7 ff.

J. Boardman in: *The Antiquaries Journal* 39, 1959, 197 ff.

SAMOS

General:

E. Buschor, *Frühe Bauten,* in: AM. 55, 1930, 1 ff.

Specialized:

Dinsmoor p. 373

E. Buschor in: *Festschrift für A. Rumpf,* 32 ff. 1950

D. Ohly in: AM. 68, 1953, 25 ff.

O. Reuther, *Der Heratempel von Samos.* 1957

O. Ziegenaus in: AM. 72, 1957, 65 ff. and 87 ff.

G. Gruben in: AM. 72, 1957, 52 ff.

A. von Gerkan in: *Charites, Festschrift für E. Langlotz,* 1957, 12 ff.

E. Buschor in: AM. 68, 1953, 1 ff.; AM. 72, 1957, 1 ff.
and 77
—— in: *Neue deutsche Ausgrabungen im Mittelmeergebiet und im Vorderen Orient.* 1959

EPHESUS

General:

J. Keil, *Ephesos* (guide), 3rd edition. 1955
F. Krischen, *Weltwunder der Baukunst.* 1956

Specialized:

Dinsmoor p. 375
W. R. Lethaby, *Greek Buildings . . .* 1908
F. Krischen, *Die griechische Stadt.* 1938
P. Jacobsthal in: JHS. 71, 1951, 85 ff.
E. Robinson in: JHS. 71, 1951, 156 ff.

DIDYMA

General:

H. Knackfuss, *Didyma, I. Die Baubeschreibung.* 3 vols. 1942

Specialized:

Dinsmoor pp. 375 f.
A. Rehm in: Abh. Münch. NF. 22, 1944
A. Rehm, *Didyma, II. Die Inschriften.* 13 ff., 321 ff. 1958
F. Krauss in: Ist. Mitt. 11. 1961
G. Gruben in: MdI, 78, 1963 (In preparation)

SARDIS

General:

H. Butler, *Sardis.* 1922 ff.

Specialized:

Dinsmoor p. 378
G. Hanfmann and C. Detweiler in: *Archaeology* 12 1959, 53 ff.
G. Gruben in: AM. 76, 1961, 155 H

PRIENE

General:

Th. Wiegand and H. Schrader, *Priene . . .* 1904
A. von Gerkan, *Das Theater von Priene.* 1921
M. Schede, *Die Ruinen von Priene* (guide). 1934

Specialized:

Dinsmoor p. 378, cf. also pp. 221 ff.
G. P. Stevens in: Mem. Amer. Acad. Rome, 9, 1931, 136 ff., and 24, 1956, 33 ff.
H. Drerup in: JdI. 69, 1954, 1 ff.
A. von Gerkan in: AM. 23, 1918, 165 ff.; Ist. Mitt. 9/10, 1959/60, 97 ff.
G. Kleiner, *Priene,* in: RE XXIV. 1960
H. Riemann, *Pytheos,* in: RE XXIV. 1960

V. PERGAMUM

General:

Die Altertümer von Pergamon. 1885 ff.
H. Kähler, *Pergamon.* 1949
O. Deubner, *Das Asklepieion von Pergamon.* 1938
A. Schober, *Die Kunst von Pergamon.* 1951

Specialized:

Dinsmoor p. 378

ALTAR OF ZEUS

H. Kähler, *Der grosse Fries von Pergamon.* 1948
K. Schefold in: *Universitas* 5, 1950, 795 ff.
E. Rohde, *Der Altar von Pergamon.* 1960

SANCTUARY OF DEMETER

W. Dörpfeld in: AM. 35, 1910, 355 ff., and AM. 37, 1912, 235 ff.

THE THEATRE

W. Dörpfeld in: AM. 32, 1907, 215 ff.
A. von Gerkan, *Das Theater in Priene,* 101 f. 1921

SANCTUARY OF ASCLEPIUS

Th. Wiegand, *Zweiter Bericht über die Ausgrabungen in Pergamon.* 1932
H. Hanson in: *Bericht über den VI. Internationalen Kongress für Archäologie,* Berlin 1939, pp. 473 ff., and in: *Die Jubiläumstagung der Koldewey-Gesellschaft in Stuttgart,* 18 ff. 1951
E. Boehringer in: *Neue deutsche Ausgrabungen im Mittelmeergebiet . . .* 121 ff., in partic. 154 ff. 1959 (with bibliography)

Abacus (pl. *Abaci*): slab forming the crowning member of a capital.

Acanthus: plant of which the jagged leaf was copied in a conventionalized form as decoration from the mid-fifth century onwards (figs. 49, 54, 134).

Acroterium (pl. *Acroteria*): one of the sculptured figures or ornaments placed at the lower angles and the apex of a pediment (figs. 4, 57).

Adytum (pl. *Adyta*): innermost room in certain temples to which only priests had access.

Agora: square or market-place that was the centre of public life in every Greek city.

Angle capital, Ionic: see page 455.

Angle conflict, Doric: see fig. 6 and page 314.

Anta (pl. *Antae*): pilaster-like end of a wall. On Doric temples, the antae involve a thickening of the wall and, on both Doric and Ionic, they have special anta capitals (plate 112, fig. 10).

Anta temple: temple having antae at one or both ends, usually with two columns between these antae, but no peristyle. Such columns are said to be in-antis.

Antefix: one of the ornaments (usually palmettes) placed along the eaves as shield-like terminations of the lowest cover-tiles and along the roof-ridge on top of the ridge tiles.

Anthemion (pl. *Anthemia*): continuous pattern of alternating palmettes and lotus flowers above tendril 'chains'.

Architrave: squared beam of stone or wood; the lowest member of the entablature (fig. 4).

Arris: sharp edge formed by the angular contact of two plane or curved surfaces, as in the fluting of the Doric column.

Astragal: small convex moulding of semicircular section. Sometimes enriched with a painted or carved bead-and-reel pattern (plate 67, fig. 27).

Base: in general, that on which anything stands (e.g. the pedestal of a statue); in particular, the lowest, moulded member of an Ionic or Corinthian column.
Attic base: sequence of torus, scotia, and torus (fig. 110).
Ephesian base: cylindrical spira articulated by two deep scotias with, above it, a large torus (fig. 125).
Samian base: cylindrical spira and large torus.

Bed-moulding: moulding or group of mouldings directly below a projecting member such as a corona.

Bothros (pl. *Bothroi*): sacrificial pit for libations to the nether gods.

Capital: uppermost member of a column.
Doric: see plate 33, below; fig. 4.
Ionic: see plate 6, fig. 105.
Corinthian: see figs. 49, 54.
Aeolic: see fig. 106.
'Leaf-girt': see fig. 29.

Caryatid: statue of a girl used in place of a column (plate 25, fig. 25).

Cauliculus (pl. *Cauliculi*): one of the fluted stalks from which spring the acanthus leaves surrounding the volutes of the Corinthian capital (fig. 49).

Cavea (pl. *Caveae*): shell-shaped auditorium of a Greek theatre (plate 100, fig. 138).

Cavetto: concave moulding used chiefly on cornices and more or less quarter-round in section.

Cella (pl. *Cellae*): body of a temple, as distinct from its porticoes and other external parts (sometimes applied to the naos alone, though not here). In a peripteral temple, it usually consists of a pronaos (vestibule), naos (principal room), and opisthodomus (equivalent to pronaos at rear) (fig. 13).

Clamp: metal connector, secured with molten lead, let into horizontally adjacent blocks to bind them together.

Coffers: sunk, usually square panels between the intercrossing beams of a ceiling; usual in the case of wooden and marble ceilings (plate 97, fig. 142).

Cornice: crowning part of the entablature (horizontal cornice) or of the pediment (raking cornice). Its composition varies, but its possible elements are sima, corona, mutules with guttae, and bed-moulding.

Corona: projecting member with a vertical face, forming part of the cornice.
Raking corona: that above the tympanum (fig. 4).
Doric: with *Mutules*, i.e. flattish rectangular, slabs, and *Viae*, i.e. the spaces between the mutules, on its soffit. From the mutules project *Guttae*, i.e. cylindrical 'pegs', usually in three rows of six (plates 12, 129, fig. 4).

Crepidoma: platform of a temple, usually composed of three steps (fig. 4).

Curvature: slight rounding towards centre of steps and beams.

Cyma: wave moulding of double curvature.

Cyma recta: concave above and convex below.

Cyma reversa or *Lesbian cyma:* convex above and concave below. Normally enriched with the leaf-and-dart (or heart-and-dart) pattern (plate 68). See *Ovolo* and *Hawksbeak.*

Dipteros (pl. *Dipteroi*): temple with a double peristyle and at least eight columns at the front (figs. 121, 122).

Pseudo-dipteros: temple having the same plan and front-view as a dipteros but without the inner peristyle, so that the ambulatory is 2 interaxials deep on all sides (fig. 136).

Dowel: usually rectangular peg of wood or metal for attaching a block to the one above.

Echinus: round, convex member of the Doric capital (fig. 4) and corresponding member below the volutes of an Ionic capital (fig. 105).

Ell: see *Foot.*

Entablature: upper part of an order of architecture including architrave, frieze, and horizontal cornice.

Entasis: slight swelling of the shaft of a column (plate 110).

Euthynteria: horizontally levelled-off and protruding top course of a foundation (fig. 4).

Fascia: one of the bands projecting stepwise into which Ionic and Corinthian architraves are subdivided.

Fillet: narrow flat band, including that between the flutes of columns other than Doric.

Fleuron: flower-shaped ornament at the middle of each side of the abacus of the Corinthian capital, or each face of the bell between the volutes (fig. 54).

Flutes: vertical channels in the shaft of a column (plates 6, 13).

Foot: most common working measure of antiquity, together with the ell, which is one and a half times as long as the corresponding foot. In Doric territory the most widespread was the Doric foot, equal to $12\frac{7}{8}$ British inches. In Ionic territory the early Ionic or Samian foot of $13\frac{3}{4}$ inches and Samian ell of $20\frac{5}{8}$ inches prevailed at first, but, from the fifth century, an Ionic foot of from $11\frac{37}{64}$ to $11\frac{39}{64}$ inches, which was also used in Attica, from the sixth century onwards, alongside the Doric foot.

Frieze:

Doric: succession of triglyphs and metopes running round above the architrave, the metopes sometimes enriched with reliefs (plate 12, fig. 4).

Ionic: horizontal band enriched with sculptured figures or other carved decoration and running along the walls on early Ionic structures, but above the architrave on the Ionic treasuries at Delphi (plate 68) and on Attic Ionic buildings, in imitation of the Doric frieze.

Guilloche: continuous pattern composed of curving bands that interlace in such a way as to leave round spaces (plate 169, below).

Guttae: see *Corona.*

Hawksbeak: Doric moulding of multiple curvature related to the cyma recta and enriched with a succession of painted, tongue-like leaves.

Hypaethral: 'open to the sky'. Used particularly of a temple with an uncovered central room.

Interaxial: interval or distance between adjacent columns from axis to axis.

Intercolumniation: space or distance between adjacent columns.

Meander: continuous fret or key pattern (plate 97, above: along base of sima).

Megaron (pl. *Megara*): principal or men's hall in a Mycenaean palace or house. Also used of temples with a simple, house-like ground-plan and no portico.

Metope: see *Frieze.*

Monopteros (pl. *Monopteroi*): canopy-like columned building without a cella.

Mutule: see *Corona.*

Naiskos (pl. *Naiskoi*): small temple without peristyle.

Naos: see *Cella.*

Opisthodomus: see *Cella.*

Orthostats: large slabs set on edge and generally serving as the lowest course of the walls of a Doric temple (figs, 10, 11).

Ovolo: convex moulding. The Ionic ovolo is enriched with the egg-and-dart (or egg-and-tongue) pattern, usually in relief (plate 68, figs. 107, 108).

Palmette: ornament comprising a fan-shaped arrangement of leaves or petals.

Pediment: triangular part of a building at the end of a ridge-roof above an entablature. It comprises the tympanum and the raking cornice.

Peribolos (pl. *Periboloi*): wall enclosing a sanctuary or precinct; the precinct itself.

Peripteral: having a single external peristyle.

Peristyle: range of columns all round a building or a court; such a court itself.

Pilaster: rectangular pillar engaged in (i.e. partly built into) a wall (figs. 132, 133, 135).

Plinth: square block sometimes placed under the base of a column (fig. 109); the projecting lowest part of a wall.

Portico: roofed and colonnaded space at the front or back of a temple, or serving as a porch before any entrance to a building.

Pronaos: see *Cella.*

Proportion: relationship, expressible in numerical terms, between two or more dimensions. For example, dimensions of 2 ft. and 5 ft. are related in the proportion 2 : 5, as are dimensions of 6 ft. and 15 ft.

Propylaeum (pl. *Propylaea*): entrance gate building (figs. 82, 83).

Prostyle: having columns in front; used of an anta temple with a portico at the front only (fig. 2). *Amphiprostyle:* having porticoes at front and back but no pteromata (figs. 64, 65).

Pseudo-dipteros: see *Dipteros.*

Pteroma (pl. *Pteromata*): passage between the lateral wall of a temple's cella and the temple's flank colonnade.

Regula: see *Taenia.*

Rinceaux: pattern of leafy branches forming curves and S-scrolls.

Rosette: round floral ornament (plate 97, above).

Scene: building forming the architectural background of the stage in a Greek theatre (page 362) fig. 55. *Proscenium:* low portico set before the 'scene', its roof also providing a stage.

Scotia: concave moulding used chiefly on column bases and generally more or less semicircular in section (fig. 125).

Sekos: enclosure for the statue of a deity; in particular, a court-like space taking the place of a roofed naos (see pages 456 and 463).

Shaft: main body of a column below its capital but excluding any base.

Sima: terracotta or marble gutter of a building. Usually decorated with an anthemion pattern; then, later, with acanthus ornaments (plate 97). Along the flanks, it is provided with water-spouts, generally in the form of lions' heads.

Socle: slightly projecting footing of a wall or pedestal; a plinth.

Spira: lower, cylindrical part of Asiatic (i.e. Ephesian and Samian) column bases (see *Base*).

Stereobate: substructure of a temple.

Stoa: building with its roof supported by one or more colonnades parallel to the rear wall; an independent portico.

Stylobate: platform for columns; the top step of the crepidoma (fig. 4).

Taenia: projecting band crowning the Doric architrave; below it lie narrow strips (Regulae) corresponding in width and position to the triglyphs, and from each of them six cylindrical 'pegs' (Guttae) extend downwards.

Temenos (pl. *Temene*): sacred enclosure.

Tholos (pl. *Tholoi*): Greek circular building.

Toichobate: platform for walls.

Torus (pl. *Tori*): convex moulding larger than the astragal and used principally in the bases of columns (see *Base*).

Triglyph: see *Frieze* (plate 129, fig. 4).

Tympanum: triangular surface framed by the raking and horizontal cornices.

Via: see *Corona.*

Volute: painted or carved ornament taking the form of a spiral scroll and providing the distinctive feature of the Ionic capital (figs. 107, 108).

N.B. Colour plates are given in Roman *and monochrome plates in* Arabic *numerals. The textual references to architectural matters are given under place-names and not under names of deities.*

9058

0824   X